Information Age Economy

Information Age Economy

F. Rose
The Economics, Concept, and Design
of Information Intermediaries
1999, ISBN 3-7908-1168-8

S. Weber
Information Technology in Supplier Network
2001, ISBN 3-7908-1395-8

K. Geihs, W. König and F. von Westarp (Eds.)
Networks
2002, ISBN 3-7908-1449-0

F. von Westarp
Modeling Software Markets
2003, ISBN 3-7908-0009-0

D. Kundisch
New Strategies for Financial Services Firms
2003, ISBN 3-7908-0066-X

T. Weitzel
Economics of Standards
in Information Networks
2004, ISBN 3-7908-0076-7

J. Dibbern
The Sourcing of Application
Software Services
2004, ISBN 3-7908-0217-4

F. Steiner
Formation and Early Growth
of Business Webs
2005, ISBN 3-7908-1552-7

Valerie Feldmann

Leveraging Mobile Media

Cross-Media Strategy
and Innovation Policy
for Mobile Media Communication

With 17 Figures
and 13 Tables

Physica-Verlag
A Springer Company

Dr. Valerie Feldmann
McKinsey & Company
55 East 52 Street, 21 Floor
New York, NY 10055
USA
E-mail: valerie_feldmann@mckinsey.com

ISBN 3-7908-1575-6   Physica-Verlag Heidelberg New York

Library of Congress Control Number: 2005920593

Physica-Verlag is a part of Springer Science+Business Media

springeronline.com

© Physica-Verlag Heidelberg 2005
Printed in Germany

Softcover Design: Erich Kirchner
Production: Helmut Petri
Printing: Strauss Offsetdruck

SPIN 11375616   88/3153 – 5 4 3 2 1 0 – Printed on acid-free paper

Preface

Mobile communications emerges as new distribution channel for media content and services. This development raises the question how media companies can use this new channel for their existing content and create cross-media and cross-network audience flows; how they can take the social use of mobile communications into account for the development of innovative mobile content and services; and how the regulatory framework should be designed to foster innovation and strengthen user innovation networks.

Three research stages have influenced the development of my thoughts and arguments on leveraging mobile media: my time as visiting doctoral fellow at the Columbia Institute for Tele-Information (CITI), Columbia Business School, New York; as a telecom policy consultant for the Strategy and Policy Unit (SPU) of the International Telecommunication Union (ITU) in Geneva; and as visiting scholar at the Free University Berlin. During these times, many mentors, colleagues and students have inspired and challenged my thinking and my hypotheses. The contents of this book have greatly benefited from their valuable contributions.

I would like to express my sincere gratitude and thanks to my academic teachers and mentors: Prof. Dr. Axel Zerdick, Prof. Dr. Eli Noam, Prof. Dr. Jo Groebel, Prof. Dr. Dres. h.c. Arnold Picot, Prof. Dr. Miriam Meckel and many other professors who took the time to discuss and challenge me in seminars, at conferences, and in joint research projects; to my colleagues at Columbia University, Prof. Dr. Jim Alleman, Bob Atkinson, Kenneth Carter, Rueben Abraham, Dr. Tracy Cohen, Laura Forlano; to my colleagues at ITU, Dr. Tim Kelly, Bob Shaw, Lara Srivastava, Dr. Tad Reynolds, Yoshi Takada, Vanessa Gray, Claudia Sarrocco; to my colleagues in Berlin, Prof. Dr. Wolfgang Muehl-Benninghaus, Norbert Herrmann, Jan Krone, Dorothea Leffek-Hubatschek, Andreas Scholz, Li Zeng, all members of the PhD colloquium; and to my students at the Free University Berlin who have taught me more than they may think.

I have received generous scholarships and grants from the German National Academic Foundation, the Fulbright Commission, and the Alcatel Foundation and met great people in these organizations who provided valuable guidance and advice: Dr. Jochen Schamp, Dr. Roland Hain, Prof. Dr. Detlef Leenen, and, last but not least, my long and dear mentor and friend Prof. Dr. Hermann Real.

The sudden and unexpected death of my PhD advisor Axel Zerdick shortly before the defense of the thesis is a great personal loss. His critical attitude, al-

ways questioning common (academic) beliefs, designing unorthodox arguments without any fear to be disputed; his strong support, challenging me inter-
nally and greatly supporting me externally with confidence and trust; and his
open, curious, and warm personality have strongly influenced me. He is and will
remain to be greatly missed. I cannot express in words my gratitude to the fan-
tastic faculty of the media and communication studies department of the Free
University Berlin for the support they provided in times of grief and despair,
above all to Prof. Dr. Gernot Wersig who took over the role as my advisor and to
Prof. Dr. Jo Groebel for the immediate willingness to render a second opinion to
my thesis, to my PhD committee members Prof. Dr. Lutz Erbring, Prof. Dr. Win-
fried Goepfert, Dr. Michael Meissner, and to Dorothea Leffek-Hubatschek and
Charlotte Jenkel from the examination office.

Many dear friends have provided invaluable support and were continuous
sources of motivation, encouragement, ideas, and welcome distraction when
needed: Rueben Abraham, Angie Broer, Anne Buddenbaum, Bianca Dormuth,
Iris Graf, Melanie Guese, Dr. Michael Koch, Mischa Koedderitzsch, Dr. Katrin
Muehlfeld, Dr. Vinay Nair, Nina Schneider, Daniel Stengel, Warnar van Eeden,
and Sabrina Zeplin.

My most sincere and warmest thanks go to my wonderful family, Gabriele,
Berthold, and Nadine Feldmann, who have supported me in so many ways at all
times and across countries and continents. To them I dedicate this work.

Valerie Feldmann

Table of contents

Introduction

What if wires had just been invented? Mobile wireless data communication users could finally deliver large amounts of data at very high speeds across the globe without technical limitations of bandwidth and congestion and without economic limitations due to high international interconnection fees. Mobile wireless voice communication users would be astonished due to the voice quality of fixed-line telephone calls that would additionally not be interrupted by cellular network quality of service difficulties. What could the future role of established wireless services be as a result of the new challenges arising through wires? This **reverse invention test** serves as a good illustration of the fact that each old technology has advantages in the face of emerging technologies, but that its role and strategic positions can change. The same applies to areas where traditional media and its role are changing as a result of the advent of newly emerging media. In fact, the diversification of media channels under the influence of digitization not only attribute new roles to traditional media but also fosters innovative forms of recombination of old and new channels through cross-media strategies.

In this context, mobile communications emerges as a **new digital distribution platform for media content** due to the migration to next generation networks[1] and their capabilities for broadband data communications. As such, mobile communications offers opportunities for media development because of an increased overlap between interpersonal and group communications with mass media communications.[2] Next generation wireless networks combine features of mobile communications, Internet access, and mobile computing. The evolving infrastructure and equipment may serve as a technological platform for a broad array of media content and services including mobile voice, data, audio and video applications. Yet, as MARVIN (1989) observes, "new media" is a historically relative term. In this context, the analysis of mobile communications as a new distribution platform for the media needs to critically ask in which ways

---

1   Mobile cellular is differentiating network 'generations'. First generation networks are analogue and second generation networks are digital networks under different standards. Third generation cellular networks that allow for digital voice and data are specified under the ITU's IMT-2000 project, see http://www.imt-2000.org/portal/index.asp. 4G is sometimes referred to as integrated wireless/wireline broadband provision, see Steinbock (2001), p. 179; Dornan (March 4, 2002); Lehner (2003), pp. 79. For a comprehensive description of the mobile telephone system see Tanenbaum (2002), pp. 152-169; Lehner (2003), pp. 23-111. For a discussion of different mobile communications standards see Funk (2002a).

2   See for example Schneider (1997), p. 102; Doyle (2002); McQuail (1999); Zerdick et al. (2000).

mobile media reexamines and challenges or defends patterns anchored in older media that have provided a stable currency of social exchange.[3] Given the early stage in the development of mobile data services, **cross-media strategy and innovation policy choices** can shape the trajectories for the evolution of mobile media content and services and mobile media markets.

1
Motivation of the book

Mobile content and services are starting to become an **emerging asset in media markets**. In the music industry, for instance, mobile ringtones generated revenues in 2003 that will be five times as high as online music sales.[4] In the UK music market, mobile ringtone revenues are expected to overtake even revenues from the music single market in 2003.[5] Mobile gaming participants are expected to overtake the number of game console users due to its high growth rates.[6] Moreover, the potential customer base for mobile media is a lot larger than, for instance, potential online media customers. Worldwide, 665 million people have Internet access, but 1.3 billion own a mobile phone.[7] In Germany, 28.3 million online[8] users are facing 59.2 million mobile subscribers[9] in 2002.

The growing importance of mobile communications is also reflected in its relation to fixed-line telephony: in 2002, the number of mobile cellular subscribers worldwide has overtaken the number of fixed telephone lines.[10] Mobile voice communications as well as mobile messaging services have experienced **unprecedented diffusion and growth** and they are integrated into social practices of everyday life across macro-economic factors of nations such as GDP per capita as well as across socio-demographic factors among users such as age, education, or income levels. Yet, mobile data communications has not experienced similar growth rates. With the exception of the Asia-Pacific region that has the most advanced mobile data markets, consumer adoption of mobile data services has been slow.

Media companies to date have been very cautious with investments into content and service development for mobile data communications markets due to the high uncertainty of demand. As a matter of fact, **initial excitement about mobile media services** such as mobile audio and video applications has come from mobile operators. Their motivation is obvious: high investments in licenses and network building are facing diminishing returns from voice communications, measured in the industry performance metric average revenue per user (ARPU).

---

3   See Marvin (1988), p. 4.
4   In Europe, mobile ringtones generated revenues of EUR 293 million in 2002 and are expected to grow to EUR 353 million in 2003, see Clark (October 10, 2003).
5   See Jobson (2003).
6   See N.N. (2003a).
7   See Standage (2003).
8   See van Eimeren, Gerhard, and Frees (2003), p. 339.
9   See RegTP (2003), p. 3.
10 See ITU (2003b). At the end of 2002 there are 1.2 billion fixed telephone lines and 1.3 billion mobile communication subscribers worldwide.

Additionally, revenues could be cannibalized from competing technologies such as wireless LAN and digital terrestrial broadcast. Mobile operators hope to overcome the revenue trap they are facing with innovative mobile media offers based on the reasoning that mobile customers are used to paying for mobile communications services. Yet, these arguments may not lead to the right set of questions when it comes to the provision of mass media content via mobile cellular networks.

For media companies, **mobile media is indeed old news**. Print media such as newspapers or magazines are mobile, the same holds true for media in vehicles such as the car radio, or portable storage media, e.g. the walkman. The emerging new user contexts for media consumption based on mobile cellular transmission have, however, resulted in a misconception about the value of mobile communications. Mobility is not the prime reason for the use of mobile communications; rather it is the **directness to reach a person instead of a location** and the related degrees of personalization that offer essential benefits of mobile communications for the provision of mobile media.

Media companies have started to **extend their cross-media strategies** by implementing SMS and MMS based messaging services, or WAP and PDA channel content. Yet, further and more profound analysis in the context of the media economics research tradition[11] is needed on the incentives and strategies for the provision of mobile content and services. Next to this positive media economics approach, a normative media economics approach on the policy dimensions of mobile media provision is just as essential.[12] Media development under the influence of mobile communications can still emerge into content, format, and processes that are "unknown unknowns"[13], developments nobody even anticipates. In the light of this background, there is a need for heuristics that develop insights for the discussion of potential trajectories. Therefore, a systematic media economics approach is suggested that regards media development under the influence of mobile communications under the perspective of two potential levers: it analyzes (1) the development of cross-media strategies and (2) innovation policies for mobile media within a framework that considers media economics incentives, characteristics of the mobile communications system, and its social appropriation.

---

11 See for example Picard (1989); Schenk and Donnerstag (1989); Altmeppen (1996); Sjurts (1996); Latzer (1997); Albarran and Chan-Olmsted (1998); Alexander, Owers, and Carveth (1998); Ludwig (1998); Goldhammer and Zerdick (1999); Knoche and Siegert (1999); Meckel (1999); Schumann and Hess (1999b); Compaine and Gomery (2000); Karmasin and Winter (2000b); Schumann and Hess (2000); Zerdick et al. (2000); Kiefer (2001); Siegert (2001); Doyle (2002); Hass (2002); Mueller-Kalthoff (2002b); Picard (2002); Zerdick et al. (2004).
12 For the distinction of positive and normative media economics see Kiefer (2001), p. 41.
13 Compaine (2000b), p. 475.

2
The notion of mobile media

The notion of mobile media can produce manifold associations. Therefore, it is essential to provide a definition in which ways the following analysis will refer to mobile media. According to DENNIS & ASH (2001) it is important to have a common language for both the nature and the scope of a new medium to understand the links between the technological platform, content and business strategies of new media, and to quickly develop taxonomies involving programming forms from a content perspective as well as revenue streams from a business perspective.[14] Currently, mobile media lack that common language. We will distinguish a wide and a narrow definition of mobile media (I-2.2). The first essential differentiation is made for the mobility dimensions as well as the entities that are mobile (I-2.1).

2.1
Mobility dimensions of information, devices, and people

Although directness and personalization have been identified as essential characteristics in mobile communications, mobility is an important distinguishing criteria for the delimitations of mobile media. One crucial question for the discussion of mobile media concerns the entities that are moving and the dimensions of mobility. The first differentiation determines which part of the media offer and consumption process is mobile: the information, the device, or the user.[15] Mobility dimensions can be distinguished into the categories stationary wireless, nomadic wireless, mobile transportable, and mobile portable (see Table I-1).

Table I-1: Mobility dimensions and moving entities

	Stationary wireless	Nomadic wireless	Mobile transportable	Mobile portable
Moving information	++	++	++	++
Moving device	--	+	+	++
Moving person	--	-	+	++

Legend: ++ applies; -- does not apply

Stationary wireless: **Stationary wireless** refers to a usage context in which information is transmitted wirelessly, but both device and user are stationary.

14 See Dennis and Ash (2001), p. 26.
15 This differentiation goes back to Zerdick (2002). The delimitation expands and further develops Reichwald & Fremuth's delimitation who stress the mobility of information as the essential characteristic of the mobile economy, see Reichwald, Meier, and Fremuth (2002), p. 7.

Nomadic wireless: **Nomadic wireless** is defined as wireless access in which the location of the end-user termination may be in different places, but it must be stationary while in use.[16] The analogy to nomads can be made due to nomads' separation from the resource while they are moving, even though the lack of resource is also the reason why nomads are moving. This does not necessarily have to be reflected by users of stationary wireless connectivity who are moving between hot spots.

Mobile transportable: **Mobile transportable** refers to devices that are connected to transportable objects from ground transportation, navigation, and aviation. Examples comprise the car radio, subway TV, or movie screens in planes. Users are not moving but they are transported as well.

Mobile portable: **Mobile portable** refers to devices carried by a (moving) person, e.g. a walkman. In the case of mobile cellular, users can move ubiquitously without being disconnected from information and communication technologies (ICT) access, because mobile cellular provides ubiquitous coverage, contrary to nomadic wireless access systems.

Taking a closer look at the moving entities it becomes obvious that mobile communications does not make users more mobile per se; however, device portability is a precondition for users' connectedness to the information and communication infrastructure while users are moving. Therefore, in the grid of moving entities the **mobility of people** is the essential criteria combined with the option to use mobile portable media devices.

From a historical perspective, LING & HADDON (2001) differentiate the relationship between mobility and communications into three phases. In the period before the telegraph, communications could only be delivered **by being mobile**. When messages were carried by men or animals, distance was a major barrier to communicative interaction and transporting a message was a very expensive task.[17] The telegraph freed communications from the constraints of geography and permitted for the first time the effective separation of communication from transportation; **messages could travel faster than the messenger.**[18] However, a limitation in this second phase is that a person who wants to send a message needs access to a sending device at a fixed location and needs to know the physical location of the person who is receiving the message. The third phase **removes this condition on fixed locations.** A person is free to choose where to initiate communication and is independent of the location of the receiver;[19] infor-

16 The ITU-T recommendation on the vocabulary for wireless defines *nomadic* wireless access as wireless access in which the location of the end-user termination may be in different places, but it must be stationary while in use; it defines *mobile* wireless as wireless access in which the location of the end-user termination is mobile, see ITU (2001b). For the remainder of the book the distinction between mobile and nomadic will be based on this terminology.
17 See de Sola Pool (1990), p. 34.
18 See Carey (1992), p. 203; McLuhan (2001), p. 89. However, de Sola Pool points out that the relationship between communication and transportation is two-sided. People save themselves trips by using means of electronic communication, but they also develop relationships by communicating which lead them in turn to travel so as to come together, see de Sola Pool (1990), p. 16.

mation and communication access becomes ubiquitous. This ubiquity of tele-communications activities also bears potential to extend mobile media applications and services.

2.2
Definition of mobile media

The definition of mobile media uses a bundle of elements from channel-specifics of the media to the understanding of media as communication spaces that enable exchanges between agents.[20] To date, 'mobile' is a term that is used quite differently in various definitions which analyze the influence of mobile communications. For example, the notion of the mobile Internet is widely used although it is not clearly defined.[21] 'Mobile Internet' can refer to the convergence of mobile communications technologies with the (IP-based) Internet and information and data communication services such as e-mail.[22] On the other hand, existing definitions of mobile business, mobile commerce, or mobile applications rather stress the location flexibility and instant connectivity of the user through mobile cellular networks as well as the execution of any kind of electronic transaction via a mobile personal device;[23] only some additionally demand the device to be IP-enabled.[24]

The **notion of mobile media** can also refer to a wide radius of different media, including books, newspapers and magazines, music CDs and DVDs, car radios, or portable game console. For the purpose of this book a differentiation into a wide and a narrow definition of mobile media is suggested. It will take into account five dimensions of mobile media. Following ZERDICK & ZOCHE's (1997) approach to a definition of multimedia,[25] the notion of mobile media refers to a combination of

– networks, hard- and software (technology dimension)
– connectivity (mobility dimension),

---

19 See Ling and Haddon (2001), p. 2.
20 As such, it combines two recent media definitions in the context of multiple utilization of content and cross-media strategies. For the discussion of the dis- and re-integration of media products under the influence of digitization Hass uses a channel-specific view on the medium as a means of representation for information in order to differentiate between signal (medium) and message (information), see Hass (2002), pp. 17. Caspar, on the other hand, selects a broader, channel independent definition for the discussion of cross-channel media brand strategies. It recurs on the definition of the media as communication spaces that enable the exchange between agents. A medium in this view consists of a channel system, a syntax a semantic space, roles, and protocols, see Caspar (2002a). For a synopsis of further media definitions see Siegert (2000), pp. 17; Kiefer (2001), pp. 14.
21 This effects the data on mobile Internet use. In data on use of the Japanese mobile Internet, for example, mobile e-mail that delivers the majority of content services is registered as mobile Internet use whereas surfing to a mobile Internet site via a URL is rarely used in Japan, see Funk (2001b), p. 35. The European equivalent, SMS-based content services, is not registered as mobile Internet use although it is counted as mobile data use. Therefore, a general confusion of terminology also contributes to misinterpretations of data and statistics.
22 See ITU (2002b), p. 2; Sabat (2002), p. 508; Sadeh (2002), p. 129.
23 See Wirtz and Mathieu (2001), p. 2; Reichwald, Meier, and Fremuth (2002), p. 8; Schmid and Stano-evska-Slabeva (2002).
24 See Clarke (2001), p. 133; Sadeh (2002), p. 5.
25 See Breiter et al. (1997), p. 5.

- integration (content dimension),
- interactivity (interactive dimension), and
- content production (organizational dimension).

Technology dimension: The technology dimension is a central element in the definition, because the delimitation between mobile media in its wide and its narrow form is predominantly based on the differentiation of devices and the transmission medium (see Figure I-1). The parameters that are used to distinguish mobile devices are 'physical',[26] 'electronic', IP-enabled',[27] and 'telephony-enabled' (see also the taxonomy of mobile devices in B-1.1). The exclusion of mobile devices that will not be subject to further analysis is closely related to their mobility dimensions (see I-2.1). Thus, both dimensions will be jointly discussed.

The first distinction towards a narrow definition of mobile media in the context of technological deployment differentiates **physical media** and **electronic media** stored on or transmitted via an electronic device. We will exclude physical media such as newspapers, magazines, or books, and focus on electronic media. The next differentiation concerns the mobility dimension of the device. We will focus on **mobile portable devices** and hence exclude stationary wireless devices such as a DVB-T enabled TV sets as well as mobile transportable media such as car radios. Further, we will distinguish if the mobile portable device is **IP-enabled and telephony enabled respectively.** Mobile portable devices that are not IP-enabled are, for instance, portable gaming consoles; handheld computers such as PDAs that have Internet access capabilities are among IP-enabled devices that are (mostly) not telephony-enabled.[28] Any mobile portable or wearable device that has mobile cellular telephony capabilities and is an Internet appliance will be included in the narrow definition of mobile media.

Since next generation mobile devices aim at integrating hardware components such as WiFi cards or DVB-T antennas (see B-1.23), three wireless transmission modes are considered relevant for mobile media provision: transmission via **mobile cellular, nomadic wireless, and mobile (digital terrestrial) broadcast networks**. The development efforts of next generation networks are working towards integrating these wireless networks.[29]

---

26 Wersig uses the term 'physical' media that is delimited from energetic media, see Wersig (2000), p. 25. It is a similar proposition to Hass' notions of self-decoding and decoding-supported media. Prime media ('human media') such as speech and secondary media (print media) are classified as self-decoding media. Tertiary media such as broadcast media or CD-Rom's and quarternary media that support interactivity can only be used with technological equipment that supports the decoding, see Hass (2002), p. 3. A distinction into carrier media such as print media, VCRs, or CDs and transmission media, e.g., cable or broadcast networks is not as useful, because 'new media' such as the Internet are hybrid media that combine the characteristics of both forms.
27 For a taxonomy of Internet appliances see Eisner Gillett et al. (2000).
28 Notebooks that are used for VoIP are not considered to be telephony enabled.
29 See for example the ITU-T standardization efforts at http://www.itu.int/ITU-T/worksem/ngn/index.html

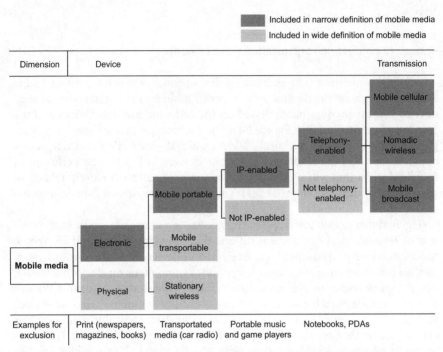

Figure I-1: Device and transmission delimitations for a narrow definition of mobile media

Content dimension: Since the media transmission via mobile cellular networks is an essential element in the context of this book that analyzes media development under the influence of mobile communications, new media content that will be specifically produced for mobile devices and mobile cellular transmission is suggested to be called **cell media**.[30] Cell media is **small format content** designed according to the characteristics of the mobile communications system. Media content that has been produced for another medium and will be multiply utilized for online media as well as for mobile media purposes will be referred to as **repurposed content**. Online media used via laptops in hot spots that are characterized by nomadic wireless connectivity, e.g. via a wireless LAN, will in some cases be referred to as **nomadic media**. The important distinction here is that online media does not have to be repurposed at all, since it is only the user context that is changing and not the content itself.

Interactive dimension: Mobile media not only refers to media content but also to mobile services that are related to a media organization or a media content offer. Mobile services include all types of **mobile messaging services** such as text-based SMS or picture-, audio-, and video-based MMS. Next to these pushed mobile media services, **pulled mobile service applications** can comprise mobile

---

30 The notion of cell media goes back to a discussion with Eli Noam on 'Cell TV', see Noam (2000).

browsing, streaming, and downloading. Location-based services are integrated in the service category when they are related to a media offer. Interactive services can also concern the synchronous and asynchronous communication modes of mobile users among themselves when they integrate mobile media. Mobile media content that is delivered to a mobile device can, for instance, allow the user of a service to forward (pieces of) the content to other mobile users and add a personal message. This form of **user-contextualized mobile content** is included via the interactive dimension in the mobile media definition as well.

Organizational dimension: The media organizations that will be considered for mobile media content and service provision in the narrow mobile media definition comprise media organizations from the print, broadcasting, recorded music, film and Internet industries. This selection is based on the mass media institution definition of MCQUAIL (2000) who describes publication and wide dissemination of information and culture as key activity of media institutions and integrates print, film, broadcasting, recorded music and new electronic media into his definition.[31] The explicit differentiation between a media content offer and a media organization will become essential for the discussion of media brand management and cross-media strategies as forms of media brand extensions.[32]

As a result, mobile media as used in the context of this book refers to media content and services produced or repurposed by mass media institutions for the consumption on mobile portable devices and transmitted via mobile cellular networks or next generation networks that may integrate more wireless networks.

3
Objectives and structure of the book

This book uses a heuristic approach for the systematic media economics analysis of mobile communications influence on media strategy and policy development. As such it reverts to both the **phenomenological- hermeneutic and the analytical tradition of science theory**.[33] The comprehensive theoretical framework for the media economics analysis consists of elements from information economics, innovation diffusion theory, the cultural studies approach, media sociology, competitive strategy, and media and telecommunication policy.[34]

Among the methods that are used are **classifications and typologies**[35] that aim at systematizing problems connected with mobile media and contributing

---

31 See McQuail (2000), pp. 14.
32 Siegert characterizes the distinction between media offers and media organizations as essential for the analysis of media brand strategies, see Siegert (2001), p. 19.
33 A method is phenomenological when it tries to apply a holistic understanding of our living surroundings and uses the interpretations of everyday life for scientific analysis, see Seiffert (1996b), p. 41. Hermeneutics is a method that aims at grasping and explaining these living situations, see Seiffert (1996b), p. 57. The term analysis refers to its basic meaning of 'dissolving into elements', see Seiffert (1996a), p. 17. Carey argues that the hermeneutic intent is nowhere more needed than in theoretical discussions of the mass media, see Carey (1992), p. 69.

to generate new insights in the matter. The provision of predictions on the future use of mobile media is not among the objectives of this book, following the argument that the importance of predictions in the social sciences only refers to a heuristic function, i.e. the formation of hypotheses.[36] This book analyzes media companies' extension of cross-media strategies under the influence of mobile communications and the developments of an innovation policy design. In the context of these two potential levers of mobile media, the structure of the book (see Fig. I-2) is derived from the following **guiding research questions:**
1) What incentives do media companies have to invest and engage in mobile media content and services?
2) What are the relevant elements and characteristics of the mobile communication system? How is mobile communications appropriated into social interaction and everyday life?
3) What strategic options for the extension of cross-media strategies can be developed in light of the technological evolution of wireless networks and the social use of mobile communications?
4) How should media and telecommunications policies and regulatory frameworks be designed to foster innovation in mobile data communications in general and mobile media development in particular?

Chapter A asks for the incentives, barriers, and drivers of media development under the influence of mobile communications. Media companies' incentives for engagement in mobile media markets are analyzed from a supply-side point of view on revenue forms and revenue models, multiple utilization of content, and network economics, and from a demand-side point of view on personalization and interaction options. Barriers to innovation diffusion are discussed against a historical background of media and ICT innovations; the introduction of the influence of social use on innovation diffusion serves as a bridge to suggest user innovation networks as a potential driver for mobile media diffusion.

Chapter B describes the central elements of the mobile communication system, mobile devices and wireless networks, and asks what kind of usage reasons this communication systems offers. A taxonomy of mobile devices is followed by a more detailed discussion of the functions of the mobile phone. The comparison of wireless networks takes next generation cellular networks, wireless local

---

34 The theoretical framework acknowledges a holistic approach to media economics that integrates economic, political, social, technological, and institutional elements. Media economics is a still emerging area of research that consists of a number of approaches, but lacks a broader concept, see Kiefer (2001), pp. 35. Therefore, the theoretical framework cannot be subsumed under a media economic paradigm in the sense of Kuhn. The term paradigm, in his definition, stands for the entire constellation of beliefs, values, and techniques shared by the members of a given community that for a certain time provide model problems and solutions, see Kuhn (1996), pp. x; 175.
35 For a differentiation of typologies and classifications see for example McKelvey (1982); Bailey (1994); Doty and Glick (1994).
36 Seiffert suggests that predictions in progressive inductions are only made to control hypotheses, not for the sake of predicting something. He argues that even Popper's differentiation of two types of predictions in the social sciences - prophecies and technological predictions – are either tautological or provide practical functions, but don't offer scientific value, see Seiffert (1996a), pp. 196; Popper (2000a), pp. 487.

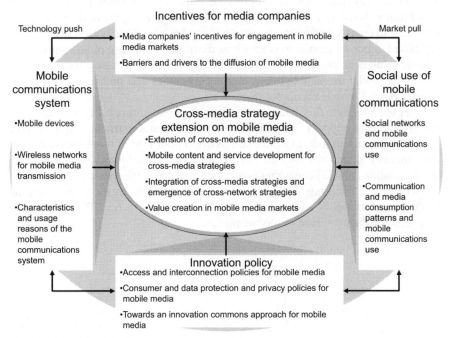

Figure I-2: Structure of the book

area networks and digital broadcast networks as well as their integration into account. Mobility characteristics with regard to space, time, and the personal communication sphere are analyzed next to the usage reasons and the context of mobile communications use.

The question how this communication system is appropriated into everyday life – i.e., the social use of mobile communications - is subject of analysis in **chapter C**. It asks for the role of mobile communications in social networks and for communication usage patterns of mobile voice and SMS communications. Mobile identity and mobile community concepts in social networks are discussed. Among the relevant communication patterns the focus lies on impulsive mobile communications use of habituated media use patterns, changing politics of power and control, and the emerging phenomena of micro-coordination, collective action, and user-driven innovation in mobile communications use.

Based on the analysis of the potential technology push of the mobile communication system and the potential market pull derived from its social use, **chapter D** analyzes the strategic options for media companies to extend their cross-media strategies onto mobile communications platforms. Cross-media strategy extensions are defined and classified. The following discussion of mobile content and service development systematizes (1) the functional developments mobile media adds to cross-media strategies, (2) format and substance of mobile media offers, as well as (3) the options for bundling strategies. Further on, the way mobile media offers are integrated in existing cross-media strategies and extended to cross-network strategies across a variety of distribution networks is discussed. Since co-opetition emerges as dominant structure of relationship in mobile value nets, another area of interest are the changes in negotiation power in mobile media markets between media companies and mobile operators for the delivery of mobile media services.

Chapter E depicts the challenges for public policy and regulation to create a framework that supports innovation in mobile media markets. Three central questions are discussed: (1) from a competition policy point of view essential issues are open access to platforms, portals, and content and interconnection pricing for mobile data; (2) consumer protection and privacy issues are central from a user-perspective; and (3) elements that constitute innovation commons in ICTs - spectrum policy and mobile intellectual property rights (IPR) policy - are analyzed for the provision of mobile media.

A
Incentives, barriers, and drivers for media development under the influence of mobile communications

Media content for mobile wireless communication is a new and emerging option for the expansion and development of cross-media strategies across digital distribution platforms. To date, media companies have been cautious with their engagements and investments in mobile media content due to high uncertainties regarding customer demand, technology evolution, and regulatory developments. Yet, mobile communications may offer interesting options for media companies as it develops into an emerging new distribution channel for media content. With respect to potential opportunities as well as risks of a mobile media market entry, media companies need to evaluate the incentives, potential barriers and potential drivers of their mobile media engagement.[1]

Therefore, this chapter asks for **incentives for media companies** to enter mobile media markets such as revenue models, strategies for multiple utilizations of content, personalization and interaction options for mobile customers, and the potential for exploitation of network economics (A-1) in order to increase the speed of diffusion. Further, it assesses **barriers to innovation diffusion** through taking a historic view of media and ICTs innovations; and potential drivers for mobile media diffusion such as **user-innovation networks as emerging paradigm** in research on the diffusion of innovations (A-2).

1
Media companies' incentives for engagement in mobile media markets

In mobile media markets, the extension and creation of new revenue forms is an essential rationale for cross-media diversification. Digital information goods[2] transmitted via mobile cellular networks and Internet access via mobile cellular will reinforce developments in media economics that have been initiated by digitization and the Internet:

---

1   Media companies' market entry into mobile media markets raise incentive issues as their new offers raise uncertainty about value and the distribution of risks for both sellers and buyers. Imperfect information and related problems are the essence of incentive questions in economic thought of New Institutional Economics. In this school of thought, conflicting objectives and decentralized information are the basis for the analysis of market behavior and resource allocation efficiency, see for example Laffont and Martimort (2002).

2   Examples for digital information goods are text, images, sounds, video, and software that can be distributed in digital form. Digital information goods are characterized by high first copy costs and low incremental costs, see Varian (2000b), p. 137.

1) the same channel offers two-way synchronous and asynchronous communication capabilities and can carry all known media forms such as print, sound,
   still and moving images both in combinations and at the same time;
2) new ICTs emphasize point-to-point media rather than center-peripheral or
   point-to-multipoint media and can give rise to many new configurations of
   individual and group communication; and
3) digital media have higher interactive capabilities whereby interaction can
   mean greater individual choice from a menu of options or a genuine process
   of exchange and conversation between participants in the network.[3]

The capabilities of digital media combined with new capabilities of mobile communications allow for new and innovative sources of revenue that primarily
drives incentives for media companies to enter mobile media markets (A-1.1).
An expansion of revenues can be accomplished via the generation of new sources of revenue respectively via improved exploitation of existing revenue sources.
From a **supply-side point of view** the development of strategies for multiple utilizations of content can contribute to an increase in direct revenues (A-1.2).
From a **demand-side point of view** enhanced personalization and interaction
options for media audiences may lead to an increase in both direct and/or indirect revenues (A-1.3). Overall, network economics that apply to mobile media
markets can **leverage the scale, scope, and speed of engagement** in mobile media
markets (A-1.4). As the mobile voice market reaches saturation mobile communications industry growth is increasingly contingent on the development of new
mobile data services and revenues.[4] Therefore, incentives for media companies'
engagement in mobile media markets are likely to be supported from mobile
carriers as well (see D-4.12).

1.1
Systematic overview of revenue forms and revenue models in mobile media markets

Mobile media revenues can exploit existing and develop new revenue forms (A-
1.11) and can lead to re-combinations of different revenue forms into revenue
models (A-1.12). In the identification of potential revenue models that are usually composed of more than one revenue form, mobile media models may show
different characteristics from traditional media revenue models, for example
due to an underproportional importance of mobile advertising revenues and an
overproportional share of paid content.

---

3   See McQuail (1999), p. 15; Schneider (1997), p. 95. Media changes contribute to the development
    of new lead categories for the media such as individualization, pluralization, and hybridization,
    see Schneider (1997), p. 105. Schrape argues that, in general, media changes are evolutionary, see
    Schrape (2004), pp. 219. Dennis/Ash emphasize that the technological platform evolves into the
    distinctive characteristic of new media, see Dennis and Ash (2001). Picard stresses the changes in
    business models for online content services, see Picard (2000).
4   In 2001, the mobile data market in Western Europe had 139 million mobile data users out of which
    78 percent are SMS only users; the 2001 mobile data revenue was EUR 10 billion, predominantly
    SMS-based revenues, see Kurth (2002b).

1.1.1
Typology of mobile revenue forms

Mobile revenue forms can, for the most part, be subsumed under the general typology of revenue forms in media and communications markets. ZERDICK ET AL.
(2000) have established a framework that can be extended onto a typology of
revenue forms in mobile media markets.[5] The main systematic distinction is
made between direct and indirect revenue forms. **Direct (mobile) revenue forms**
are obtained straight from the user. **Indirect (mobile) revenue forms** stem from
third parties that have an interest in the consumer who is making use of media
and communication services. Based on this main distinction, the systematization identifies **five basic types of mobile media and communications revenue
forms:**
1) direct usage-related revenues;
2) direct usage-unrelated revenues that are either one-off;
3) direct usage-unrelated revenues that reoccur regularly;
4) indirect revenues from media companies' corporate clients;
5) indirect revenues from mobile operators.

For an application of this systematization on mobile revenue forms see Figure A-1.

Ad 1: The first mobile revenue type, **usage-related revenue forms,** depicts usage
parameters relating to mobile media consumption. They can be based on the duration, the quantity, or the quality of the service. Media companies generate direct usage-related revenue forms from providing users with paid mobile media
content. A large proportion, however, also derives from mobile messaging services that are related to the media brand such as the mobile dating site function
of a women's magazine. Increasingly, usage-related revenues in mobile communications are based on the value (quality) they provide to mobile customers. **Value-added services via SMS** are already very common delivery means and pricing
scheme for mobile media offers. Value added text messaging describes the use of
SMS to provide a content service or product to the consumer, often incurring a
premium charge related to the content. For example, revenues from downloading ring-tones or other content to customize the handset fall in this revenue
form.[6] But also **SMS audience participation revenues,** e.g. for vote-in concepts
in radio or TV shows, can be regarded as a media content-related service that

---

5   See Zerdick et al. (2000), p. 27. Zerdick et al.'s differentiation offers a better systematic for mobile
     revenues than differentiations proposed elsewhere, - e.g. than the categories person-to-person
     communication services, advertising, commissions on transactions, business solutions, informa-
     tion services, and surfing and entertainment as suggested in Maitland, Bauer, and Westerveld
     (2002), p. 496 - because the sources of revenue for a media company are clearly identifiable. In a
     category such as information surfing, on the other hand, revenues for media companies could
     stem from customers as well as mobile operators.
6   Xing Inc., Japan's biggest supplier of ringtones, sold some $100 million worth of ringtones in 2002,
     see Kunii (March 3, 2003).

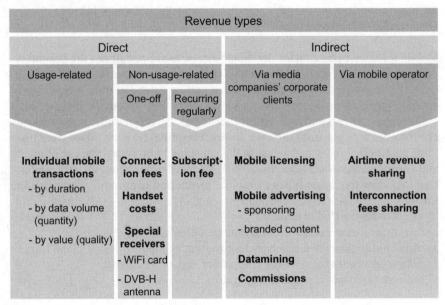

Figure A-1: Typology of mobile revenue forms
Source: adapted from Zerdick et al. (2000), p. 27

generates a new usage-related source of income. The Netherlands' top-rated music TV channel TMF receives 400,000 SMS each month and earns between EUR 0.05 and EUR 0.10 per incoming SMS with traffic at peak viewing times at up to 15,000 messages per hour.[7] However, it is the mobile operators and not the content providers who receive a large share of messaging-related direct revenues such as value-added SMS.[8]

Usage-related revenues in mobile media markets can also relate to transactions that are **valid for a certain period of time**, e.g. when users purchase the right to listen to a favorite song via a mobile device for the period of one month (duration) or when they purchase the right to use a mobile database service of a particular city (quantity). These specifications are usually controlled via digital rights management (DRM) systems (see E-3.22).

Ad 2: The second mobile revenue form, **one-off non-usage related payments**, include connection fees, e.g. to initialize a mobile service, and may in the next couple of years also include prices for handset components such as WiFi-cards or DVB-T antennas (see B-1.1; B-2.31) which may become required for certain mobile services, but do not have original (content) value in themselves.

---

7   See Obstfeld (September 25, 2002),p. 2.
8   The alternative for media companies in Germany, for example, is to use 0190-numbers in order to capture more revenue. However, the bad reputation of these numbers and the threat of negative spill-over effects for the media brand does not render this a viable solution.

Ad 3: **Recurring regularly non-usage related revenue forms** such as subscriptions are a very common model for Japanese mobile media offers; the i-mode content subscription model is not as successful in Europe yet.[9] **Subscription payments** play a major role in refinancing traditional media and communication services and are a basic revenue form in, e.g., print and pay TV markets.[10] For mobile services it is yet to be seen if subscriptions will remain the dominant revenue source.[11] Subscriptions offer option value to use mobile content. More research on user behavior concerning mobile data is needed that will shed more light on the desirability for this option value (see also B-3.11; D-2.4).

Ad 4: **Indirect mobile revenue forms** through media companies' corporate clients can be distinguished into licensing, advertising, datamining, and commissions revenues. Licensing revenues in mobile media, e.g. from syndication, are particularly interesting for popular entertainment content (see A-1.22). Music companies in particular charge licensing fees for ringtone creation from new mobile content providers which also brings the potential for conflict. EMI Music, for instance, has filed a lawsuit against the website Yourmobile.com claiming that it unlawfully allows users to download excerpts from more than 300 copyrighted songs.[12]

The **mobile advertising market** is still very immature, but advertisers may be interested in supporting mobile media services in exchange for users' short but potentially intensive mobile attention. Mobile advertising revenues, however, do not necessarily have to be a revenue source for media companies. Mobile operators are actively expanding their capabilities for mobile advertising, for instance to raise advertising support for their mobile portal space. NTT DoCoMo and the advertising agency Dentsu have formed a joint venture already in 2000 in order to service mobile advertising needs from the consumer goods industries (see D-4.21). One strategic asset of mobile operators over media companies is mobile operator's **Home Location Register** (HLR) that contains essential information on mobile users' identity and location.

Mobile datamining is another revenue form that will be more interesting to mobile operators due to their customer information resources. Media companies may improve their datamining techniques with **mobile community management models** (see C-1.31). Users sign up by choice and reveal personal data in exchange for mobile messaging or mobile content services or for coupons that can be used for purchases in retail markets. Thereby, mobile communities offer new sources of information on habits and preferences of media audiences that can open opportunities for more targeted advertising campaigns for advertising

---

9   Six months after its launch, i-mode Germany only attracted 142,000 customers, see NFO Infratest and IIE (2003), p. 109.
10 In traditional media models, license fees for public (commercial) broadcasters can also be a form of regularly recurring non-usage related payment. Since mobile devices may be capable to broadcast TV content via DVB-T, considerations in Germany are expressed to extend that license fee onto mobile devices, see Ott (September 14, 2002).
11 See Feldmann (2002a).
12 See N.N. (August 18, 2000).

clients, also in traditional and online media. In Japan there is also a trend to use the mobile phone as a market research tool. Mobile quiz games are used to test the effect of TV and other advertisements. 'Ashai' and 'Nikkei News' have started to offer daily quiz games through which users can accumulate points and can win prizes. These two content providers see potential in their large subscriber bases to recruit survey participants and, thus, generate new sources of datamining income.[13]

However, mobile customers have to give permission and opt into these datamining and advertising forms as a beneficial consequence of their privacy and data protection rights (see E-2). Location-based service offers in mobile communications will likely generate a lot of data about users and their daily routines. Therefore, legislation on privacy will (have to) protect the consumer and is likely to restrict mobile datamining techniques.

Commissions as a share of transaction revenue initiated from mobile media portals may not prove to become an essential revenue form for media companies in mobile markets. In online media business models, e-commerce commissions, for example through the sale of merchandising articles online, and commission revenues through affiliate e-commerce partnerships have become a new source of revenue for online media.[14] Mobile commerce, however, is developing slowly,[15] among other reasons due to a lack of consumer trust in mobile payment and transaction security systems on mobile devices that are easily lost or stolen; the limited adoption of mobile commerce does not indicate that commissions will play a leading role for business models in mobile data markets.

Ad 5: New sources of mobile revenue for media companies may stem from **indirect revenues via mobile operators**. Mobile operators largely capture usage-related airtime and data traffic revenues in circuit-switched (duration) and packet-switched (quantity) billing models as well as interconnection fees (quality) for terminating mobile media services into their networks. Media companies are already trying to leverage bargaining power towards participating in these revenue forms (see D-4.21). **Airtime revenue sharing** refers to the participation of content providers in mobile carriers' airtime revenue generated through mobile content use.[16] These revenue sharing models are highly disputed and may not constitute a large share of media companies' potential revenue, because mobile operators are emphasizing their role in the mobile customer relationship and these are currently not willing to share traffic fees. Nonetheless, these revenue forms are worth considering as a potential new revenue source for media companies and may expand as media companies are increasing their bargaining power towards mobile operators. One essential question, for example, is who

---

13 See Funk (2001a). In general, datamining refers to the processing of user transactions into knowledge of data. On the Internet, media companies use different forms of information generation from billing to user registrations in order to qualify for content use or e-mail alerts, see Zerdick et al. (2000), p. 168.
14 See Zerdick et al. (2000), p. 166.
15 See Hirsh (2002); NFO Infratest and IIE (2003), pp. 325.
16 See Buhse (2002), p. 174.

promotes the mobile media offer. Traditional media such as television channels can develop into a **powerful tool for cross-promoting the use of mobile media**. For example, a mobile game such as 'Who Wants to be a Millionaire' that encourages mobile users to send text messages, or online media that allow users to send SMS from their websites should result in a content provider share of the extra revenue that is generated.[17] The Catalan public broadcasting channel Televisio de Catalunya (CCRTV) attracts with its interactive daily cross-word game show 'No Tinc Paraula – Lost for Words' 7,000 SMS per day on average with monthly profits around EUR 40,000.[18] However, the extent to which content providers are currently participating in airtime revenues does not reflect the content attractiveness.

Mobile operators use the determination of **mobile data termination charges** as one essential lever to increase their revenue base for mobile data.[19] For mobile voice communication, mobile operators have developed a complex system of compensations for the termination of calls from mobile and fixed networks.[20] These interconnection agreements will have to be newly negotiated for mobile data communications. They may – depending on their extent – distort revenue shares in mobile data markets. It may have distributional effects for both media companies as well as mobile customers when mobile operators demand high mobile data termination charges; therefore, one emerging question concerns media companies' participation in mobile data termination charges that are originated through their mobile media offers. Media brands that manage to attract a lot of mobile data communications usage could, hence, participate in this indirect, usage-related revenue form as a new mobile revenue form.

Revenue sharing models of mobile indirect revenue may also become beneficial for innovation in mobile media markets. FUNK (2001) argues that a participation of content providers in the packet charges from the traffic they generate for mobile operators would set **incentives for the development of new mobile content services** and support positive feedback effects.[21]

Mobile revenue forms can be bundled into mobile revenue models. These models are characterized by the weight they attribute to the dominant revenue forms and are subject to the following discussion.

---

17   See N.N. (2001c).
18   See Obstfeld (September 25, 2002), p. 3.
19   Termination charges constitute a large portion of mobile operators overall revenues.
20   Main approaches to interconnection charges between mobile operators include 'sender keep all' models (bill and keep) and revenue sharing models. The former approach signifies that no charges are paid between interconnecting operators for termination of each other's traffic, the latter involves a payment and is used in mobile voice communications markets, see Intven (2000), p. 3-24. Corresponding models can be found in Internet backbone markets; here, interconnection charges between ISPs and operators of Internet backbone telecommunications networks are differentiated into peering and settlement models.
21   See Funk (2001b), p. 42.

1.1.2
Mobile revenue models

Mobile revenue models can be composed of different mobile revenue forms. The deployment of a single revenue form is comparatively rare in the media industry. Instead, revenue forms are combined and weighted according to the media type.[22] The weight that mobile revenue forms will receive in mobile revenue models may not correspond to revenue models in other media industries. Broadcasting revenue models, for example, rely heavily – often exclusively – on advertising revenues. Even in print revenue models with subscription fees for newspapers and magazines, advertising revenues play the most essential role. Internet revenue models are still struggling with establishing sustainability; paid content models, for instance, are only slowly gaining ground in the Internet.[23] Nonetheless, they become of greater interest due to a growing trend in unbundling and individualizing digital media offers for pushed and on demand media services. In mobile media markets, **paid content models and the generation of new revenue sources** such as airtime revenue sharing are of media companies' particular interest.[24] Here, paid content models are playing an essential role already, even though on a small scale, due to the direct usage-related revenue focus of mobile messaging services.

In TIMMERS' (1998) classification of business models for electronic markets the description of the revenue source is one of three central elements.[25] Therefore, business models in the Internet are often named depending on the **dominant revenue form**, e.g., advertising, paid content, infomediary, or subscription models.[26] For mobile operators, three models for the provision of mobile media have been identified to date: a platform provider, content aggregator, and infomediary model.[27] From the perspective of media companies, however, three different revenue models have more potential relevance for the provision of mobile media:

1) **subscription models,**
2) **advertising models,**
3) and **paid content models.**

22	See Zerdick et al. (2000), pp. 29.
23	See Breunig (2003).
24	See Englert (2002), p. 218.
25	See Timmers (1998), p.4.
26	Doyle identifies three possible streams of income to online media providers: advertising, e-commerce, and user fees, see Doyle (2002), p. 153. Online media business models, however, have encountered challenges with both advertising models and paid content models, see Bughin et al. (2001); in an analysis of business models for online content services, Picard discusses the models videotext, paid Internet, free web, Internet/ web ad push, portals and personal portals, and digital portals. He concludes that users only accept the free web model and the advertising supported (personal) portal model, see Picard (2000), pp.63. More generic suggestions on online business models include the aggregation model, broker model, agent model, and infrastructure model. Their common denominator is the focus on customer relation and customer-centered brands, scale effects, and integration into business webs, see Killius and Mueller-Oerlinghausen (1999), p. 152.
27	See Steiner (2002), pp. 80.

Their names are chosen with respect to the dominant revenue from; they will be considered, because they either relate to the most common traditional revenue models such as subscription and advertising models or because they have promising prospects for new media such as paid content models.

Ad 1: To date, **subscription models for mobile media** are dominant in 2G and 2.5G networks, both for SMS- or MMS-delivered media services or for access to certain mobile content in mobile operators' portals. Subscription fees are an essential source of earnings for media in offline markets; in the online world, very few media companies – apart from professional information providers - have committed to subscription models such as 'The Wall Street Journal'[28] or 'The South China Morning Post'. Subscription services for mobile media services are applied to most of DoCoMo's i-mode contents and services in Japan. European mobile operators who have licensed i-mode for their customers, however, have difficulties in replicating that user acceptance; it is not clear if the lack of acceptance is correlated with the subscription model.

Subscription to mobile media services also includes the fact that mobile customers have to pay for **usage-based fees** that mobile operators charge. This may be an argument that hinders consumers from adopting mobile subscription services, because an unknown additional usage-based amount will have to be paid. ODLYZKO (2001) suggests that in rapidly growing communications markets it is in the service providers' interest to encourage usage via the implementation of flat-rate pricing. He argues that user's willingness to pay for simple pricing plans is higher and that in usage-sensitive billing even tiny charges based on utilization decrease usage over-proportionally.[29] However, flat-rate pricing, which is based on a monthly fee regardless of how many bits are sent or received, may prove difficult as a model for mobile data provision to recover the cost that arise for mobile media provision (see B-2.11).

Mobile subscription models are additionally characterized by **sharing agreements** between the players of the mobile value net that are involved in delivering the service (see D-4.11). It implies collecting payment from the user and redistributing it across the different parties.[30] Revenue sharing contracts need to determine who collects the payment, who is responsible for the credit risk, and how other parties involved are compensated. For example, NTT DoCoMo has introduced a revenue sharing model with a group of preferred content providers that leaves billing services with the i-mode service. DoCoMo takes nine percent of the subscription price as compensation fee in Japan and fourteen percent in Europe. Only few content providers are participating in airtime-based fees, although they are driving traffic into the networks; mobile game providers such as Digital Bridges, for example, are generating close to 100,000 minutes of airtime

---

28   See Steinbock (2000).
29   See Odlyzko (2001a).
30   See Sadeh (2002), p. 47.

per month for mobile operators in Europe in 2002 with only one popular game, the 'Wireless pet'.[31]

Ad 2: **Advertising models** that are dominant in most media markets are not likely to be successful in mobile media markets, because ads may easily be perceived as spam. The unsolicited commercial mail tolerance of mobile users (see E-2.22) is significantly lower in mobile communications compared to PC e-mail services due to the disappointed expectation on receiving a personal message and an annoying interruption in any other foreground activity.

Therefore, mobile advertising models are not likely to challenge traditional media models in the way online advertising models do. Classified advertising and its migration to the Internet, for instance, has a compelling logic due to network effects.[32] Mobile communications, on the other hand, may rather support than substitute offline and online advertisements, e.g. via short codes in magazine ads that link to more information, ordering of sample contents and the like.

New forms of advertising have been created for the Internet that hold interesting potential for mobile advertising: mobile sponsoring as well as mobile branded content. **Sponsoring** is a popular advertising model for both traditional and online media.[33] Exclusive sponsorships can be arranged for popular formats or content community models. For mobile media, streaming media may become an option for sponsoring since streaming video is a format in which users show greater tolerance towards advertisement that may be shown before the webcast.[34] **Branded content** is advertiser produced professional media content. Following the insight that content instead of advertising attracts attention, advertisers produce and finance more and more content themselves that goes beyond advertising.[35] In the mobile sphere, branded content such as mobile games may even compete with media offers and dis-intermediate media companies in their customer relationship.

Ad 3: **Paid content models for mobile media services** offer an alternative with potential for context-specific user needs that can unlock willingness to pay for mobile media services. In paid content models users pay a fee for the disposition of media content.[36] Pure paid content models are unusual in media industries, where indirect financing or a combination of different revenue sources prevails.[37] However, direct charge of users in return for access to media offers is an

---

31   See Sadeh (2002), p 48.
32   See Evans and Wurster (2000), p. 42; Liebowitz (2002), pp. 132. Classified ads are very well received in online environments, because users are reducing their search costs with the help of search machines and may even get more detailed information through hyperlinks to pictures, videos, or animations. In 1964, McLuhan identifies classified ads as the bedrock of the press and suggests that the press will fold when alternative sources of easy access to such diverse daily information should be found, see McLuhan (2001), p. 207.
33   See Zerdick et al. (2000), p. 165; soap operas used to acquire their name because they were sponsored by Procter & Gamble and other consumer-goods companies.
34   See Bughin et al. (2001), p. 63.
35   See Zerdick et al. (2000), p. 196.
36   See Mueller-Kalthoff (2002a), p. 31.
37   See Dreier (2002), p. 54; Zerdick et al. (2000), pp. 25.

attractive option for the media supplier, because, a.o., it reduces dependencies on the cyclicality of advertising income. Paid content models can be based on personalized media offers, e.g. the provision of additional thematic, niche or specialist content and services. Internet searches in archives and databases are often connected to small payments; instant connectivity to an archival inventory gives reason to charge small amounts for each article.[38] Television channels are starting to charge for online streaming videos.[39] Overall, the scale of revenue is not satisfactory yet. However, mobile communications and mobile media offers may enlarge the potential for paid content. Users expect to pay monthly mobile phone bills or to purchase pre-paid cards in order to use their mobile phones.[40] This habituation pattern raises hopes that the general willingness to pay can be extended to mobile media offers.

Paid content models for mobile media raise interesting questions on the pricing of content (see D-2.33). The choice of the appropriate pricing model for mobile media is characterized by (1) the costs that occur to provide mobile media services ubiquitously and always on demand (see B-2.11) and (2) the consumer perception of the service value. In media markets, value-based pricing is determined by the customers' perceived value of the good. For mobile media it enables a price differentiation based on customer segments and needs; it is more customer-friendly than usage-sensitive pricing that created confusion because data volume of mobile applications is hard to estimate.[41] When the price for content disposition is related to the value the content offers in the perception of the customer, features that may drive customer value include quality, exclusivity, service value, and brand.[42] Brand is an essential value because media content is an experience good.[43] The willingness to invest in such a good increases when a user trusts a certain brand.[44] Even though mobile media may be considered to be an **inferior good**[45] with regard to traditional media sources there may be contexts in which consumers are willing to pay for mobile media services, because mobile media availability is the relatively superior option to no access to the content at all.

---

38 See Lin and Jeffres (2001), p. 569.
39 See Sewczyk (2002), p. 116.
40 In the early days of the telephone some establishments such as banks and drugstores offered free telephone use to their customers. However, by the end of the 19th century, the perception to pay for telephone services in public pay phones was well established, see Aronson (1981), p. 32.
41 See Smith, Bailey, and Brynjolfsson (2000), p. 124; Odlyzko (2001a).
42 See Mueller-Kalthoff (2002a), p. 31. Smith, Bailey, and Brynjolfsson (2000) show that even in electronic markets with strong price competition consumers are willing to pay a premium to purchase from a brand they trust, see Smith, Bailey, and Brynjolfsson (2000), pp. 103.
43 See Shapiro and Varian (1999), p. 5; Kiefer (2001), pp. 139.
44 See Feldmann (2001a); Dreier (2002), p. 54.
45 Chyi has discussed the idea of the inferior good characteristic for online media and consumers' unwillingness to pay for it, see Chyi (2004).

1.2
Strategies for multiple utilizations of content

Multiple utilization of content is one possible leverage for media companies to raise revenue potentials from existing media content and establish **multiple revenue streams**. The precondition is the production of platform-neutral content that enables repurposing of content according to the syntax specifications of different distribution platforms. **Content management systems** support the efficient exploitation of content production and the subsequent modularization.[46] For example, a text can be used for the printed version of a newspaper, it can be modified into an online article and into mobile offers such as WAP versions or SMS news services. Content then becomes disaggregated and re-bundled according to the characteristics of the medium. However, high costs related to making content available for mobile devices are still an obstacle to the creation of synergy effects. For mobile media offers this has been particularly challenging, because new program languages and complex application and service specifications are necessary to convert digital media such as HTML-content into a mobile phone compatible format.[47] WAP content, for example, poses these content management challenges. Oftentimes, mobile media creation not only requires an application service provider (ASP) as intermediary for the mobile application design, but it also puts into question if such an offer will be economically viable and will **contribute to the overall profitability of a media company** in the long term.

The development of multiple utilization of content also contradicts the often quoted concept of media convergence. The proliferation of channels and the increasingly ubiquitous nature of computing and communications rather contributes to **media divergence**.[48] Even on the device level, the plethora of specific devices does not suggest convergence, either,[49] albeit digitization enforces technological convergence to some extent (see B-1.23). Yet, consumers' demand for context specificity of content as well as parallel media usage[50] at the intersection of various media access modes, devices, and contents rather suggest an increase in media divergence.

Against this background, it may become an increasingly interesting option for media companies to either version media content for mobile platforms themselves or to license parts of their media content for mobile content use to third parties.

---

46 See Siegert (2000), p. 191; Sjurts (2002b); Hass (2004); Hess (2004).
47 On markup languages and micro-browsers for mobile devices see Lehner (2003), pp. 191.
48 See Jenkins (2001).
49 See Goldhammer (2005).
50 See Cole (2004).

1.2.1
Versioning strategies

Versioning strategies that offer different depth of content can exploit heterogeneous user needs and offer **price discrimination opportunities.** In general, versioning means offering an information product in different versions for different market segments.[51] While the firm offers a product line, the user chooses the version of the product most appropriate. Profits depend on the total value that is created and the fraction, that a firm is able to extract through the differentiated versions and prices. For example, financial information products lend themselves to differentiation depending on the degree of professionalism of the user. Institutional customers of Reuters have different needs than a person who is trading in her free time.

The integration of mobile communications as a new distribution platform for media content creates further versioning opportunities. Mobile content is likely to have a **different content scope** than digital media which is consumed on bigger screens and in other usage contexts. Newspaper articles, for example, may only display a headline; mobile audio and video may be restricted to clips. The variety of different possible levels of mobile content scope is extendable though, e.g., a newspaper headline could end with a telephone number that allows for listening to an audio piece. The design of these media offers that become adapted to the demands of mobile platforms can relate to different versioning dimensions.

Versioning strategies for mobile content can be discussed with regard to product line, price, and quality. From the point of view of the product line, SHAPIRO & VARIAN (1999) identify eleven **dimensions of the information product:** delay, user interface, convenience, image resolution, speed of operation, flexibility of use, capability, features and functions, comprehensiveness, annoyance, and support.[52] Delay respectively acceleration, convenience, flexibility of use, capability, and features and functions are among the most relevant versioning dimensions for mobile media (see Table A-1).

Acceleration of content releases is a time-related product dimension that can be used as a **tool for announcements, trailers, and promotions.** The mobile market entry that precedes the timing of the core product's market entry adds a new dimension to the emphasis on delay that has characterized media markets windowing strategies, i.e. staggered distribution through successive channels.[53]

For example, movie launch strategies are experimenting with releasing games previous to the movie as in the case of 'Matrix Reloaded'. Mobile games may become the next component in this strategy.

---

51 See Shapiro and Varian (1999), p.54; Zerdick et al. (2000), p.185.
52 See Shapiro and Varian (1999), pp. 55.
53 Windowing is an essential media economic feature in many media industries. For example, in the movie industry a film is transmitted in distinct channels of distribution such as cinema, video, pay-TV, and television that serve different consumer needs. In the publishing industry, books are issued first in hardcover and then in paperback, see Owen and Wildman (1992); Zerdick et al. (2000), p.185; Dreier (2004).

Table A-1: Product dimensions susceptible to versioning for mobile media

Relevant dimensions of the information product	Likely mobile media content	Examples
Acceleration	Mobile news flashes	MyMovies: mobile film content specialist who delivers Top 10 cinema box office charts (reviews and previews), behind the scenes features and celebrity interviews[a]
	Mobile previews and reviews of entertainment content	
Convenience	Headline news with options for further information depth	Reuters: delivers mobile news and financial data (breaking news stories, news archives, companies and market news, investor data feeds) to 3 UK customers[b] CNNlive delivers mobile top ten headlines from the international edition with the option to click and read the story and see pictures to KPN Dutch customers[c]
Flexibility of use	Digital media that can be used on more than one device	Lara Croft's latest Tomb Raider adventures can be played online or on mobile Java-enabled phones[d]
Features and functions	Interactive features and functions via messaging or gaming	Televisio de Catalunya: public broadcaster offers its channels program "No tinc paraula – Lost for words" as SMS cross-word game[e]

Source: adapted from Shapiro and Varian (1999), p. 62 and company information

a.   See N.N. (March 3, 2003a).
b.   See N.N. (January 29, 2003).
c.   See N.N. (September 9, 2003).
d.   See N.N. (August 20, 2003).
e.   See Obstfeld (September 25, 2002).

Different market segments and different prices can also be determined via discounting high-end products and can generate value-subtracted versions.[54] Mobile content can, e.g., discount video services into image services at different price levels. Ubiquitous access to information and entertainment content in a reduced form such as pulled headline news or pushed alerts that allow easy access to further information on demand contribute to the mobile product dimension convenience. **Voice activation** of content can add new capabilities; interactive messaging or gaming elements can add new features of media content and serve new functions for its users. The discussion of versioning strategies already indicates that mobile media may become a structural and functional extension of existing cross-media strategies (see D-3).

---

54   See Shapiro and Varian (1999), pp. 61.

1.2.2
Licensing strategies

Licensing of content modules becomes an increasingly interesting option for digital media.[55] Licensing is the **commercial and communicative use of a recognized name** that a third party has created. The licensing contract is the agreement through which the licensor transfers the right to exploit a given product or process to another firm, the licensee, for a certain period of time and under certain conditions.[56] The objective of licensing is to create **new sources of revenue** for assets that have not been fully exploited. Licensing can also be used as a strategy to enhance demand by creating a second source of supply.[57] Licensing in the media industry can be a means to emotionally position products, brands, or firms in order to create a unique selling proposition and increase attention and advertising revenues. The property rights to popular content can be used (1) horizontally in different media markets, e.g. the launch of a magazine as complement to a TV program format, (2) vertically which is called merchandising[58] when, e.g., characters are licensed to manufacturers in different industries, and (3) internationally when they are sold into different national markets.[59] Licensing and the revenue sharing between the license holder and the other members of the agreement depend largely on the contracts that are designed with regard to bargaining power and expectations. However, the license contract only gives the right to use the licensed good, not the property right itself.

Given consumers' adoption of mobile ringtones, screensavers, and wallpapers and the willingness to spend disposable income on these content elements as lifestyle accessories, licensing of popular media brands for mobile content and services is becoming an immediate source of income from digital media. Syndication models have offered new business opportunities for online media in the Internet. **Licensing of characters and other popular media** suggest new utilization opportunities in mobile communications. For example, the US Motion Picture and Television Archive and the Vivendi Universal Net USA company Moviso have closed an exclusive worldwide licensing deal concerning celebrity photos and graphics for mobile phones screens, e.g. from Marylin Monroe or James Dean. Moviso delivers the catalogue of mobile media to its clients around the world: carriers, operators, device manufacturers, entertainment and media companies, and retailers.[60]

---

55   See de Sola Pool (1990), p. 76; Dreier (2004).
56   Licensing contracts can be exclusive or non-exclusive, they can specify output or price restrictions as well payment conditions such as fixed fees versus royalty payments.
57   See Fosfuri (2003).
58   Whereas merchandising in the media industry relates to extra-medial activities, licensing relates to inter-medial use of content property rights. For example, a the right-holder of a movie can sell licenses to market the movie content in books, soundtracks, or a TV series, see Boell (1996), p. 235.
59   See Boell (1996), p.22.
60   See N.N. (May 2, 2002).

Licensing forms can be differentiated according to **property types,** such as designer licensing, character licensing, music licensing, movie licensing, TV licensing, and more.[61] Media companies as license providers contract with mobile operators or with established and innovative players in the mobile media market; character, movie, and music licensing are of particular interest for mobile media (see Table A-2).

Table A-2: Selected examples for mobile licensing options in the media and entertainment industry

License provider	License taker	Licensing product
Character licensing		
Disney		Screensavers and ring-tones in Asia-Pacific, Europe (2.5 million mobile Disney customers); in the US contracts with AT&T and Sprint on Disney ringtones, pictures, and mobile games for appr. EUR 4/month[a]
Comedy Central	In-Fusio	'South Park' license agreement for the creation of mobile games including the right to offer them in 27 countries in Western and Eastern Europe, China, and Japan[b]
Bandai	Sina	Bandai delivers mobile cartoon content such as Power Rangers or Hello Kitty to the Chinese portal Sina and its subscription based SMS services.[c]
Cartoon Network	Digital Bridges	J2ME games based on Cartoon Network characters such as Scooby doo, The Flintstones, and Yogi Bear[d]
MJ Entertainment	Digital Bridges	Java games from popular arcade games such as King of Fighters, Samurai Showdown[e]
Warner Bros.		Looney Tunes characters for e-cards and wallpapers are available with 16 mobile operators in Italy exclusively via newsletter marketer Buongiorno[f]
Motion Picture and Television Archive	Moviso	Exclusive worldwide licensing deal for celebrity photos and graphics on mobile phones, including Marilyn Monroe, James Dean, Elvis Presley, a.o.[g]
Movie licensing		
Charlie's Angels	T-Mobile	German customers can get screensavers, ringtones, wallpapers, and video-trailers for EUR 1,29-1,99 as well as a Java-based mobile game for EUR 2,99 in which users can take the role of one of the three angels[h]
Men in Black II	Digital Bridges	MIB themed mobile games ringtones, icons, other downloadable graphics[i]
Digital Bridges	O2	O2 subscribers can play two MIB SMS games; they start the game by sending the text 'scum' to a short number[j]

▼

---

61   See Boell (1996), p. 24.

Table A-2: Selected examples for mobile licensing options in the media and entertainment industry (continued)

License provider	License taker	Licensing product
James Bond 'Die another day'	Vodafone	Two-year sponsorship agreement with Vodafone Sweden that includes exclusive rights to all mobile content connected with the movie 'Die Another Day' as well as the other 19 Bond movies produced since 1962[k]
Lord of the Rings	T-Mobile	SMS services: multiplayer game, LoR quiz, LoR news and LoR logos exclusively for T-Mobile customers
Music licensing		
Universal Music		Vivendi cellular customers in France can select snippets from songs by Universal Music artists for $2.50/month[l]
Universal Music		T-Mobile customers can download the latest local and international polyphonic ring-tones, logos, send song greetings and are planned to be able to access videoclips[m]
Warner Music		Sprint customers get streaming music clip subscription service and animated ring-tone service[n]
BMG	RioPort	Distribution license for an online music service including right to transfer songs to portable devices (initial agreement on 22,000 tracks from BMG)[o]

a.   See N.N. (2002).
b.   See N.N. (May 1, 2003).
c.   See N.N. (May 30, 2003)
d.   See N.N. (July 25, 2002).
e.   See N.N. (July 16, 2002).
f.   See N.N. (2003c).
g.   See N.N. (May 2, 2002).
h.   See N.N. (June 23, 2003).
i.   See N.N. (May 23, 2002).
j.   See N.N. (August 15, 2002).
k.   See N.N. (November 18, 2002).
l.   See N.N. (July 15, 2002).
m.   See N.N. (March 7, 2003).
n.   See N.N. (January 8, 2003).
o.   See Mariano (January 28, 2002).

Character licensing is a popular licensing form for mobile content that can support existing contents and formats, build new audiences, and make a media brand (element) ubiquitously available. Licensed content is in many cases used for the personalization of handsets. For example, Disney has licensed its popular characters as well as film music to providers of screensavers and ring-tones. Disney-i is represented in many Asian markets and has been launched in the US due to its commercial success in the Asia-Pacific.[62] Generally, the potential for character licensing lies in the popularity of leading figures of mass-media produc-

---

62   See Feldmann (2005a); Maitland (2005).

tions. The incentive to purchase mobile media items related to these figures can lie in identification potential or the reminder of a special media event.[63]

Music licensing for mobile ring-tones is another vibrant area of creating new revenue sources for versioned content. Mobile licenses are currently not included in licensing or merchandising agreements and have to be newly negotiated. For example, the consumer brand Pepsi has paid additional music licensing fees for a mobile marketing campaign to the singer (and Pepsi advertising contract partner) Britney Spears in order to offer free ring-tones to Pepsi customers.[64] The **movie industry** is also contracting with different players in the mobile communications market such as handset manufacturers or mobile operators. The blockbuster 'Matrix Reloaded', for example, has released mobile previews on Samsung handsets. Samsung, on the other hand, is using the license in order to demonstrate the quality of their color screens.[65]

Increasingly, licensing strategies are used as a means of financing for big media ventures such as major film projects.[66] Licensing contracts are awarded before the production of the media product starts. Mobile operators as well as handset manufacturers are hence turning into interesting partners for media companies for **pre-production licensing agreements** as well as licensing contracts to support marketing and sales activities.

Versioning and licensing offer a number of supply-side incentives for media companies to enter mobile media markets. In order to create new sources of customer satisfaction personalization and interaction options can contribute to demand-driven incentives.

1.3
Personalization and interaction options for mobile media

The personal nature of miniaturized mobile devices (see B-1.21) allows media companies to expand content personalization that may tie media audiences closer to their media brands (A-1.31). The deepening of the customer relationship in the audience market can then be translated into monetary rewards from advertising clients. Moreover, mobile communications offers new channels for increased interaction between the media brand – hereby, the media brand can be a media organization such as a radio station as well as specific media content such as a soap opera – and the individual audience member (A-1.32).

---

63   See Boell (1996), p. 235.
64   See Chaillee (2003).
65   This is part of a more extended product placement agreement between Samsung, AOL Time Warner and Warner Bros including the production of a Samsung 'Matrix' phone, see Williams (February 25, 2003).
66   See Dreier (2004).

1.3.1
Mass customization and personalization of professionally produced content

Mobile media provision on personal, wearable devices demands to put even greater emphasis on the personalization of media content than for other digital information appliances because of the **importance of personal relevance** on small screens and in different (inconvenient) usage contexts. Mass customization[67] of online media has been a means to personalize media offers on the Internet. **Mass customization processes** are built on modularization of content. When content production is organized in modules, the packaging of these modules can be varied. This principle of mass customization also allows media companies to push more specified content to more targeted user segments.[68] Limitations of mobile device screen sizes and mobile user attention spans suggest expanding **personalization efforts for media content** that is pulled from or pushed to mobile devices. Since people rarely share a mobile phone, content and service provision can be specifically tailored to the needs of the individual.[69] Professional information publishing provides an example of a media sector whose customer base is generally interested in tailored provision of news.

In this process, **selection criteria** become more important to determine personally relevant customized media offers. One means to support users in determining personal relevance may become the use of **collaborative filters**. Such filter software creates a web-based recommendation system that relates a user's preferences to the preferences of other users. Since search engines are difficult to handle on small mobile device screens, other forms of searching and selecting relevant content may therefore be more suited to the mobile communication sphere. Personalization can be seen as a **specific user investment** since users often have to make the effort to reveal their preferences and selection criteria.[70] Personalization of digital media content can result in an improved experience of media consumption where the user has specific tastes and interests and where the user values the choice of taking control, exercising personal choice and self-scheduling.[71] With regard to the provision of mobile media, the trade-off for the attention that is taken from another (foreground-) activity and dedicated to the mobile device demands personal relevance of mobile content.

Taking a critical point of view, increased personalization of media content takes into question what mass media contributes to the **greater cohesion of society**.[72] Individual control over content and selection changes the everyday mass media experience.[73] For mobile media, it can be argued that it represents

---

67   Mass customization makes possible the delivery of custom-designed products to the masses at low prices. See for example Pine (1993); Smith, Bailey, and Brynjolfsson (2000), p. 124.
68   For example, a user can choose to order the (usually free) e-mail newsletters of a variety of newspapers and magazines that will only deliver their technology news. New intermediaries such as news crawler have established their business models around this feature of more selected (deepening, from one source) and more diversified (broadening, from several sources) media content.
69   See Martinez (2000).
70   See Hess (2004).
71   See Palmer and Eriksen (1999); Doyle (2002), p. 149.
72   See McQuail (1999), p. 13; Chaffee and Metzger (2001).

an additional complementary component in media use that is not likely to sub-stitute for other, potentially broader media use. Therefore, personalization of mobile media is, from a users' perspective, a rational decision that supports their effectiveness and efficiency; from a media company's perspective it is a strategic decision to use personalization offers as an incentive for users to inte-grate mobile media in their daily routines and build multiple touch points with the media brand throughout the day.

1.3.2
Interaction options for mobile media

Next to personalization, interaction with and via (mobile) media communica-tions is seen as an option to provide media audiences with more choices and to strengthen the customer relationship between the media and its audiences.[74] The interactive use of the media, however, is an often misinterpreted concept. Implicitly, it is usually assumed that interaction is a desirable activity. Yet, media consumption presents a strong case for **rational passivity** that should not be un-derestimated from relying on the editorial competences of media organizations in selection processes to relaxation. Nonetheless, mobile media can offer new options for interactive choice. **Mobile gaming** applications, for instance, are raising great expectations for interactive mobile content. According to a study on mobile users gaming behavior, already six percent of the world's 1.3 billion mo-bile subscribers are playing games on their handset and may **overtake the number of game console users** extrapolating current high growth rates.[75]

Interactive interpersonal communication is still among the prime reasons for using mobile phones; it can also be established between a media organization and an individual audience member. SMS services extend traditional **audience participation** in broadcast programs via call-in's or e-mails (see D-2.21). For ex-ample, while passively consuming a TV program the audience member can choose to integrate elements of interaction using the mobile phone without hav-ing to physically move – this could also be done with a cordless phone - or with-out having to switch on another device such as a PC. Two-way communication can include **on demand ordering of content** that is delivered to either the mobile device or another digital information appliance such as the PC or the digital TV set.

Forwarding functions may become a third option for interaction with other mobile users. Users who attach a personal message to the forwarded content thereby **contextualize professionally produced content**. Forwarding content on the Internet such as newspaper articles that can be commented on or weblogs,

---

73   However, for the Internet it has been argued that the effects of individualization on social relations can also be integrative. Integration in the Internet is based on overcoming spatial and time con-figurations. For example, specialized discussion forums on the Internet can support the exchange of opinions independent of the location of the participants, see Krotz (1999), p. 361.
74   For a critical view on the myth of interactivity see Feldmann and Zerdick (2004), pp.26.
75   The Mobinet study of 5,600 mobile users in 15 countries is conducted by A.T. Kearney and the Judge Institute of Management, Cambridge University, see N.N. (2003a).

online diaries in which users share their thoughts and evaluations with other interested parties, may become options for mobile user interaction as well (see C-2.43).

The digitization of media supports yet another trend: users increasingly bundle digital media content themselves. Digital music is an example where users gain **control over the recombination of content**; on the one hand in contrast to the product-related music store CD compilation, and on the other hand, in contrast to the temporal disposition of the radio.[76] Mobile devices may be used to share these user-contextualized bundles of digital media content. It may only involve **pointing other users to the links** where the content can be found rather than transmitting any digital media.[77] Wireless resources are relatively scarce, costly, and valuable compared to cheap computational cycles.[78] Therefore, sharing information goods via mobile cellular will be based on different motivations and will be subject to different economics than online sharing activities. It may also lead to the conclusion that messaging and interpersonal communication will remain the most important interactive element in mobile voice and data communications.

As a result, an increased customer orientation that provides more personal relevance and more choices to media audiences and that increases value to advertisers can contribute to media companies' decision to offer mobile media content. Due to the fact that mobile media is a network good, network economics can serve as a catalyst for its diffusion.

1.4
Network economics of mobile media

Mobile communications, analogous to the fixed-line telephone, is subject to network economics and their characteristics such as **positive externalities** and the speed of growth beyond the reach of critical mass.[79] The interconnection among mobile networks and between mobile and fixed networks and the development of standards - e.g., to enable inter-operator messaging services - expand these network effects beyond the network of a single mobile operator. For the provision of mobile media, there is some potential that network economics will contribute to the speed of diffusion and to the extension of both **direct leverages to increase revenue** - through strategies of multiple content utilization - and indirect leverages to increase revenue via stronger ties between the media brand and its customers.

On the Internet, network economics have shown some importance for the provision of online media under the initial formation of business webs between

---

76   See Fox (2002), p. 6.
77   See Feldmann (2005b).
78   See McKnight, Anius, and Uzuner (2002), p. 2.
79   Communications technologies such as the (mobile) telephone, e-mail, or Internet access all exhibit network externalities and direct network effects. In the case of direct network effects, the value of the network service rises with the number of users, see Zerdick et al. (2000), p. 154.

media, telecommunications and IT industries.[80] However, network effects have also been overestimated for the development of online businesses. One essential reason is the common misunderstanding that network effects come about just because business is conducted on a network such as the Internet.[81] Yet, the media is essentially a network good and **mobile media diffusion is influenced by the corresponding effects.** Therefore, the ways in which network economics contribute to value creation (A-1.41) and customer lock-ins (A-1.42) in mobile media markets are an essential incentive for the design of media companies' mobile objectives, strategies, and actions.

1.4.1
Creating values and setting standards in mobile media markets

Value creation in mobile media markets depends on the number of participants that are essential to unfold network effects and benefits of critical mass. **Network effects** create significant competitive advantage for popular systems and their users.[82] Consequently, in mobile voice communication the initial objective of mobile operators was to enlarge their customer bases, e.g. through strong subsidizations of handsets. Mobile media offers that build on a community of members and their social networks for user-initiated distribution (see C-1.3) need **demand side economies of scale** as a source of positive feedback loops; a 'virtuous cycle' that induces more users to get connected to a growing network, and in turn bringing about more direct and indirect network effects. However, supply side economies of scale are also an important feature in the production of mobile media content. Maximizing the available market for the firm's output is an obvious - and with regard to critical mass necessary - objective for digital media creators.[83]

Critical mass is defined as the minimal number of adopters of an innovation for the further rate of adoption to be self-sustaining.[84] Once a critical mass is achieved, a product takes over the market. Positive feedback effects can cause the explosive growth even after a long lead-time for technologies that are subject to strong network effects.[85] For example, the basic technology for the fax machine was patented in 1843, but faxes remained a niche product until the mid-1980s. Similarly, the first e-mail was sent in 1969, but took off only after Internet traffic started growing in the late 1980s and even faster after the Internet evolved

---

80   See Zerdick et al. (2000), p. 154.
81   See Liebowitz (2002), p. 4; Feldmann and Zerdick (2004), p. 20. It is commonly thought that most companies operating on the Internet are subject to network effects, presumably because the Internet itself is a network. However, research on e-commerce has shown that customers of many online retailers are interested in the same general factors that are essential in physical stores, among others brand, price, and return policy, see Liebowitz (2002), p. 22.
82   See Katz and Shapiro (1985); Katz and Shapiro (1986).
83   See Yoffie (1997), pp. 21; Zerdick et al. (2000), p. 156; Doyle (2002), p. 144. Demand-side economies of scale contribute to the development of temporary monopolies. Oligopolistic market structures only come into being based on the limits of the supply-side economies of scales, see Zerdick et al. (2000), p. 156.
84   See Mahler and Rogers (1999), p. 720.
85   See Yoffie (1997), pp. 25; Shapiro and Varian (1999), p. 13.

into a mass medium in the late 1990s.[86] Mobile media adoption may also be subject to a **longer lead-time**. Yet, when it manages to reach critical mass, the rate of adoption can be fast, because telecommunications innovations with strong network externalities are expected to have a more pronounced critical mass in their rate of adoption.[87] This is due to the experience good nature of media products which first hampers the rate of diffusion, but accelerates it after reaching the critical mass.

On the other hand, critical mass also implies that the number of network participants drop back if there are not enough of them to turn the spread of a network into a self-generating process.[88] In mobile data communications, WAP and also GPRS have experienced consumers' lack of interest to use these technologies and many consumers' decision to leapfrog them, i.e. to wait and skip this whole cycle of 2(.5)G technology.

Negative externalities can arise when a certain network size has been reached that decreases the marginal utility for its participants with every new entrant. Congestion is one example for a negative externality. For mobile media, the capacity restrictions of cellular networks will turn **peak usage and congestion** into a more pronounced problem than for, e.g., online media. Mobile customers may be easily annoyed when they navigate within a mobile media offer and loose their connection. Already in mobile voice communications, dropped calls as a form of negative externalities of second generation cellular networks are cause of many complaints and offer incentives to migrate to next generation networks.

Value in mobile media markets can most notably be created by the **formation of standards** that reduce uncertainties for all participants in the mobile value chain.[89] Standardization processes in mobile media markets will become important for mobile streaming technologies, mobile payment options, mobile security features, inter-operator DRM standardization, and choice of a mobile Internet program language.

In general, standard formation can be either **market-based or committee-based**. In the latter case, a group of strategic partners assembles in the context of a formal standard-setting effort. This typically involves competition within a standard. Market-based standardization processes, however, involve competition between standards to become the *de facto* standard.[90] Mobile communications standards are developed within **standard-setting bodies** such as the ITU or ETSI.[91] Both ETSI in Europe and IEEE in the US also focus on complementary wireless LAN standardization specifications. 3GPP and the UMTS Forum are in-

---

86   See Shapiro and Varian (1999), p. 13.
87   See Mahler and Rogers (1999), p. 740.
88   See Zerdick et al. (2000), p. 211.
89   Consumers are faced with a high level of uncertainty in purchase situations when no standard has yet gained acceptance. Consumers may react to this situation by delaying their decision in order to ensure that they will benefit from network effects in the future. Also suppliers face challenges of building a customer base and reaching critical mass in the pre-standard phase, see Zerdick et al. (2000), p. 158.
90   See Shapiro and Varian (1999), p. 16.
91   See Werle (2001); Funk (2002a); Hommen (2003); Lehner (2003), pp. 300.

dustry consortia that develop UMTS specifications and establish mechanisms to determine and collect license and royalty fees for UMTS patents (see E-3.21).

Competing standards in the IMT-2000 family of **next generation cellular network standards**[92] and beyond as well as competing standard setting bodies for networks, devices, operating systems, and applications pose significant challenges to further developments in mobile data communications. On the one hand, collaboration at the international level is essential to provide interoperability within and between different global standards. International roaming and its implications for mobile media provision, for example, needs to be addressed (see E-1.22). On the other hand, even agreements on a standard within a committee do not automatically lead to customer adoption. **WAP**, for example, was developed and unanimously approved by a forum founded in 1996 by Ericsson, Nokia, Motorola, and Unwired Planet to set technological parameters for the wireless Internet access market. The standard-setting process was characterized by a strong supply-side orientation with respect to technological development.[93] WAP has neither found widespread market acceptance from content providers nor consumer adoption although a common standard has been adopted by the major industry players.

Cooperative standard setting between firms also raises some public policy concerns, because it can contribute to the danger of monopolization and may collide with antitrust laws. These inherent dangers of a socially beneficial action underscore the **importance of competition policy in network economics** in general and in mobile communications in particular (see E-1).[94] An enforcement of consumer protection measures may be one possibility to solve the conflict from the trade-off between the economic benefits of standardization and its inherent dangers.[95]

1.4.2
System-focused processes and lock-in's in mobile media markets

Mobile media are expected to become an important driver of lock-in's in mobile communications. Mobile operators in particular are constantly trying to reduce churn and to increase the average revenue per user. In both cases, former lock-in's such as handset SIM-lock policies or the lack of mobile number portability have been addressed by policy-makers and don't offer lock-in potential any more. As a consequence, media content, for example hit-driven media events such as the launch of a blockbuster movie, as well as exclusive content contracts, are seen as a means of differentiation from competition and a means of attracting mobile customers.[96] Mobile operators and handset manufacturers are shar-

---

92   See standardization recommendations and information on the ITU-T study group IMT-2000 and
      beyond at http://www.itu.int/ITU-T/studygroups/ssg/index.asp.
93   See Hommen (2003), p. 153.
94   See Picot and Heger (2004).
95   See Feldmann and Zerdick (2004), p. 30.
96   See Feldmann (2005a).

ing this **need for differentiation**; both contract with media companies such as Hollywood studios or music companies for exclusive content provision (see D-4.22).

Exclusive mobile media licenses offer opportunities for the **creation of consumer lock-in's**, because it can be made part of a system good in which, for example, the choice of handset, the operating system, or the exclusive content can contribute to higher switching costs.[97] System goods are strongly related to indirect network effects. The purchase of system goods involves a decision regarding the system architecture and subsequently the choice of components that need to be compatible. The value of the system depends on the **availability of complementary services**. System goods are known from previous ICTs, e.g. videocassette recorders (VCRs) and videotapes, but they become dominant in information technology, e.g., operating systems and application software. Usually, one firm cannot offer all of the pieces that make up an information system and therefore needs complementors. The dependence of information technology on systems creates the need for collaboration and the basis for a multitude of cooperative arrangements.[98]

As a result of system goods, consumer switching costs, e.g. incompatibilities, can be very high and **create lock-in's**. Lock-in arises whenever users invest specifically in multiple complementary and durable assets of a particular information technology system.[99] As a consequence, the costs of switching are greater than the value created through making the switch. Economic consequences of successful lock-in's arise when, e.g., a supplier abuses the lock-in situation in terms of product quality, prices, and an unwillingness to innovate. The European Commission has addressed a number of potential mobile communications lock-in's such as the **SIM lock policy**, digital portal access, and mobile number portability. With regard to mobile data communications, issues such as opening competition to mobile ISP's, open platforms for mobile content providers, or mobile billing service systems need to be investigated (see E-1.11).

The importance of complementary system architectures in information technologies has led to an increase in **business web formation**. Business webs are a form of strategic alliances that integrate the concept of co-opetition (see D-4.1).[100] Firms can focus on their core competencies and contribute to the value creation of the business web that, as a whole, competes on the market. Positive feedback effects are the basis for the success of such a complementary firm cooperation architecture. Mobile operators and media companies have initiated some business web formation for the delivery of content and services, but the positive feedback effects are still marginal.

From a public policy perspective, the creation of lock-ins contradicts interoperability efforts which are essentially in the public and social interest.[101] Due to

---

97 This raises the importance of competition policy in mobile communications.
98 See Yoffie (1997), p. 28; Shapiro and Varian (1999), p. 10.
99 See Shapiro and Varian (1999), p.12.
100 See Zerdick et al. (2000), p. 19; Nalebuff and Brandenburger (1997).
101 See Shapiro and Varian (1999), p.143.

the recognized importance of network effects for mobile media diffusion, mobile operators' threats to block interconnection may not become as powerful and significant. Nonetheless, government intervention, e.g. in the case of **anti-competitive threats,** can become a necessary means to force interoperability. For example, in the case of instant messaging, AOLTime Warner has been forced to open its instant messaging (IM) platform including its mobile IM platform as a condition of the merger approval imposed by the US Department of Justice.[102] Such open systems prevent the creation of lock-in's and can create value. In software markets, for instance, releasing source codes can enlarge the flexibility to respond to the demands of the market. For media companies, open systems are more desirable, because it simplifies and enlarges the potential access of users to their mobile contents and services.

Indeed, a first analysis of the mobile media market shows that there are a number of incentives for media companies to enter these markets: revenue from **mobile paid content models and additional new revenue forms** have the potential to be realized from media companies audiences and advertsing clients. Strategies for the multiple utilization of content, either through content versioning or via content licensing may lead to direct revenues whereas new **opportunities for personalization and interaction** increase user choice and add to a strengthened audience relationship; they may lead to direct usage-related revenues from mobile users and to indirect revenues that derive from brokering customer attention in advertising markets. **Network economics** can support media companies' efforts to exploit these opportunities, but mobile media content and services have to reach critical mass in order for network effects to unfold. After the assessment of the incentives for an engagement in mobile media markets it is indispensable to also analyze barriers to mobile media diffusion and to discuss potential drivers to overcome these barriers.

2
Barriers to and drivers of the diffusion of mobile media

Contrasting the arguments on the potentials of mobile data communications for media companies is the fact that the diffusion of media offers delivered via mobile cellular networks onto mobile personal devices to date is low. Even after the introduction of color screens, higher data transmission speeds, and packet-based billing systems, the acceptance and adoption of media consumption on mobile phones is **far from reaching critical mass.**

Barriers that oppose the incentives for media companies to enter mobile media markets comprise the cost that derives from the discussed strategies such as the **investments into content management systems** which are appropriate to integrate specifications for mobile content or the cost for designing customer personalization systems. They may oppose profitability and economic reasoning for an engagement in mobile media markets and meet with a general risk aversion

---

102 See Faulhaber (2002).

of media companies to invest in digital media provision with uncertain rates of return.

One of the most important investment barriers, however, is the high degree of uncertainty about the **development of user demand** (A-2.1). From a historical perspective, estimations and predictions of demand for innovative media content and services have often turned out to be wrong with different degrees of severity from unintended consequences.[103] Uncertainty also reigns over social implications of new media. Since innovation is increasingly understood as a social process, this influences the assessment of sources of innovation and innovation adoption processes. In media and ICTs that are strongly influenced by network economics, innovation research suggests **user-innovation networks** as emerging paradigms and potential new drivers for innovation which may also prove important for the diffusion of mobile media (A-2.2).

2.1
Uncertainty about innovation diffusion

Demand for media content delivered via mobile cellular networks has been low to date despite availability of WAP-enabled cell phones and packet-based billing models via GPRS-supporting networks. PICOT & NEUBURGER (2002) even diagnose a **usage gap.**[104] The uncertainty about the diffusion of mobile media and potentially innovative mobile applications is not a new phenomenon (A-2.11). Assumptions on successful early applications of new media and ICTs are characterized by high levels of uncertainty on customer demand; on consumer allocation of disposable income on new media infrastructure, content and services; as well as on the social appropriation and the social implications of innovative media and ICT products and processes. This raises questions on the sources of media innovation (A-2.12) and on the determinants of the media innovation diffusion process (A-2.13).

2.1.1
Uncertainty about applications of new media in the history of media and ICT innovations

In the course of media and communication history, **initial assumptions on demand drivers of a new medium** or technology have often been mistaken. Uncertainty about mobile media applications is expressed, for instance, in the broad range of opinions, assumptions, analyses and predictions on innovative mobile applications that vary widely from videophone applications to mobile gaming, mobile payment, or mobile peer-to-peer applications. The unpredicted rate and scope of SMS adoption and the failure of WAP on the other hand raise additional uncertainty in the industry. Yet, in media history too many unknown variables

---

103 See Carey (2005); Compaine (2005); Groebel (2005).
104 See Picot and Neuburger (2002), p. 59; Funk argues the main problem with WAP services was to target them mainly to business customers instead of young people, see Funk (2001b), p. 2.

in the innovation diffusion process - and additionally the "unknown un-knowns"[105] which are the developments nobody even anticipates – underscore the contingency of estimations on successful applications of new media.

Examples for **misconceptions about early applications of new media** can be found throughout the history of media and ICTs. In the nineteenth century, con-temporaries considered the telephone as both a carrier of point-to-point mes-sages to individuals and a medium of multiple address for public occasions of music, theatre, and politics.[106] In Paris, the theatrophone was a popular feature of the 'Paris Exposition International d'Electricité' of 1881. Live performances of the Opéra and the Théâtre Français were transmitted into rooms in the Palais d'Industrie three evenings a week. 'Telefon Hirmondó' prospered in Budapest under a subscription system. In 1883, the first program was transmitted from the central exchange to one thousand regular subscribers.[107] **Telephone enter-tainment** was also extended to the provision of sporting events. Operators such as the 'Cleveland Company' in the US started a service that provided informa-tion on baseball scores and that was always ready to answer questions regarding it.[108] However, efforts to reach extended audiences by telephone required elab-orate logistical preparations and its application to entertainment remained ex-perimental and occasional.

Radio, on the contrary, was expected to become a form of telephony where people could call a radio station and talk to other people equipped to listen.[109] Both radio as well as television broadcasting were thought to be **dialogic media** that would allow unlimited audiovisual dialogues.[110] 'Bell Telephone' projected the future of broadcasting simply as the transmission of important occasions. Initially, it was not seen that wireless broadcasting communication rendered mass audiences an option for electric media by making the delivery of content cheaper and accelerating the development of different kinds of program-ming.[111]

Even applications for new media that have percolated in the public perception as successful from its very beginning, for example in the case of **Minitel,** need a differentiated analysis. Minitel was introduced in France in 1983. However, the strategies used by the French PTT to reach critical mass and to promote a vide-

---

105 Compaine (2000b), p. 475; Compaine (2005).
106 See Marvin (1988), p. 209; Hoeflich (1996), pp. 204. Aronson refers to a 'radio concept of telephony' Aronson (1981), p. 20.
107 See Briggs (1981), pp. 50; Marvin (1988), p. 224; The Telefon Hirmondó was also connected with doctors' waiting rooms, large coffeehouses, hospitals and hotels. It demonstrates that the notion of transmitting regular news and entertainment programming to large audiences existed well before the advent of wireless broadcasting.
108 See Marvin (1988), p. 213.
109 See Marvin (1988), p. 231; Pease and Dennis (1994). In an essay on radio theory, Brecht (1932/33) calls for a democratization of radio broadcasting in such a way that the audience can become the 'sender' and the radio evolves into an apparatus of communication, see Brecht (1992).The radio provided many people with their first experience of owning a piece of technology and it carries considerable weight as a symbol of scientific and technological progress. As the radio became an object of mass consumption, attention shifted from the functional to the symbolic, see Silverstone and Haddon (1998), p. 47.
110 See Flusser (2000), p. 286.
111 See Marvin (1988), p. 231.

otext service that had been unsuccessful in the United States, England, and Germany, included a subsidized price for the service provision, giving away free Minitel access terminals, and refusing to provide paper telephone directories to Minitel users, thus forcing them to use the videotext equipment.[112]

Initial erroneous estimations in the other direction about less influential media applications exist as well. Whereas often new technologies are overestimated, **teletext**, for example, is a medium that has been underestimated.[113] It is an interactive TV application that is not dependent on the difficult introduction process of digital TV. In Germany, it has been introduced in 1980; at the end of 2000 the household reach was more than 82 percent.[114] Teletext is most often used in the mornings, afternoons and on weekends. Users like its instant availability and the information that is provided. News and sports results are among the most popular contents as well as additional information on the TV program and the program contents. Advantages of teletext are that it is free of charge and that it is easy to switch between TV consumption and teletext usage.[115] Even today, SMS applications for teletext such as SMS chats are 'hidden champions' of TV channels use of mobile communications. RTL teletext chat generates an average of 130,000 SMS per day charged EUR 0.20 which translates into a revenue potential of EUR 26,000 per day or EUR 9,490,000 in a year.[116]

The **videophone**, on the other hand, is an application that has been (and is still) expected to arrive since the 19th century. It was first envisioned by the vice president of AT&T in 1889. After the actual invention of wireless communications in 1896, his company's goals for the telephone were to see as well as hear distant friends when communicating with them over the telephone.[117] Since voice could be captured and sent over wires respectively wirelessly, the transmission of pictures seemed to be an obvious next step.[118] Mobile operators continue to praise the videophone as an attractive application of next generation mobile services. LING (1997) observes, however, that the mobile phone context represents the opposite of a desirable video telephone context in many respects such as roaming or carrying out parallel activities.[119]

Uncertainty about user demand also reigns in early mobile data applications. **SMS** was mainly intended to be used to notify phone users that they had voice messages waiting. No one imagined the various ways the users of this technology would appropriate it. These observations indicate a cautious approach to historical analogies and encourage to look for new sources of innovation.

---

112 See Mahler and Rogers (1999), p. 725. Nonetheless, today popular fee-based Minitel applications are weather forecasts, train timetables, and horoscopes as well as games and dating and chatting services. There are even concerns that Minitel's ubiquitous diffusion has been an obstacle to Internet growth in France because some consumers are satisfied with Minitels' online offers, see N.N. (2001b).
113 See N.N. (2001b).
114 See N.N. (2001b), p. 55.
115 See N.N. (2001b), p. 61.
116 See Visiongain (2002), p. 73.
117 See Marvin (1988), p. 157.
118 See de Sola Pool et al. (1981), p. 135.
119 See Ling (1997).

2.1.2
Sources of innovation

The development of mobile media content and services is expected to generate media innovations that, in turn, will lead to mobile media induced revenues for mobile operators, media companies, and other value-creating partners in the mobile media value chain (see D-4.11). Yet, in media markets the notion of innovation can be at risk to be inflated.[120] Often, rather small improvements of existing media are already labeled as innovation.[121] In some tighter definitions, media innovation serves needs that we have not even been aware of before the technologies were available. Drivers for innovation may address latent needs that have not been articulated yet.[122] Innovations in general can be differentiated according to the dimensions **means-induced** (new means for existing purposes) or **purposes-induced** (new purposes that need to be served).[123] Drivers for innovation can also be detected as reorganizations of relationships between different communities. TUOMI (2002) speaks of **recombinatorial innovation** when in this process unintended resources are appropriated.[124] According to these criteria, when applied to mobile data communications the MMS can be classified as means-induced innovation (for instance writing a postcard with a new means), mobile multiplayer games are purpose-induced, and the SMS is a recombinatorial innovation. Yet, the extrapolation from past experiences does not offer support, because innovation is as much about **creating new meanings** as it is about creating novel material artifacts.[125] Therefore, users emerge as new sources of innovation in innovation research.

The dynamics of process and product innovation[126] can be either supply-driven or demand-driven.[127] Recent innovation research in industries that are

---

120 Smits defines an information technology innovation as a "successful combination of hardware, software, and orgware, viewed from a societal and/or economic point of view", Smits (2002), p. 865. In media markets, frameware in order to develop content and innovative productions, e.g. formats, design, or other frames, can be added, see Nausner (2000), p. 119.
121 This may derive from media companies' function to constantly produce something new while preserving to be recognized. Media companies have to differentiate themselves and often simply decontextualize content in order to produce irritation and compete for attention, see Nausner (2000), pp. 120.
122 See Pierce (1977). Kodama calls this process demand articulation when the entrepreneur invents both the need and the product that addresses this need, see Tuomi (2002), p. 24.
123 The differentiation according to the dimensions product innovation (effectiveness gains) or process innovation (efficiency gains) is less useful for service markets or for intangible information goods.
124 In Tuomi's view, mobility of resources defines how easy it is to reorganize motives and meanings linked with new social practices. Mobility of resources, therefore, becomes a central value for societies. In the ideal type of the network society, information technology has increased mobility of resources and has increased the speed of recombination. The space of recombination is an increasingly dominant space for innovation, see Tuomi (2002), pp. 31.
125 See Tuomi (2002), p. 13.
126 The scientific literature on innovation quotes a large body of definitions of innovation. Rogers introduces the perception of newness as the critical element. He defines innovation as an idea or object that is perceived as new by an individual or another unit of adoption, see Rogers (1995), p. 11. Newness is seen as the innovative combination of purposes and means to develop an invention into an innovation, see Barnett (1953), p. 7; Roberts creates the simple formula "innovation = invention + exploitation", see Roberts (1987), p. 3; for a comprehensive discussion of the definitions of innovations see Hauschildt (1997), pp. 6.

characterized by demand heterogeneity as well as innovation theory for network-based technologies focuses demand-driven and user-driven sources of innovation.[128] VON HIPPEL's (1988) seminal research on the sources of innovation challenges the assumption that product manufacturers determine the innovation process. Instead, he suggests the view that the innovation process is distributed among users, manufacturers, and suppliers, depending on where there is the greatest economic benefit to the innovator.[129] CHESBROUGH (2003) suggests a new open innovation paradigm that assumes that firms can and should use external as well as internal ideas and paths to market; he quotes the Hollywood film industry as an example for innovating through networks of partnerships and alliances between production studios, directors, talent agencies, actors, scriptwriters, and specialized sub-contractors such as the suppliers of special effects.[130]

When social appropriation, as in the case of recombinatorial innovation, is such an essential process for media and ICT innovations, the locus of media innovation is likely to move away from the producer and to the user.[131] With this new source of innovation the subsequent questions concern the parameters of the innovation diffusion process.

2.1.3
Innovation diffusion processes

Mobile voice communications has seen an unprecedented diffusion speed. It is an innovation that serves existing purposes more efficiently and that has created new purposes for its use. Mobile data communications, on the other hand, is still far from being adopted into everyday life and has yet to reach critical mass in order to unfold the benefits of network economics. Its slow pace of adoption raises the question if mobile media can be seen as a media innovation already or if, at this stage, it is **rather an invention**.

Mobile service adoption can be viewed from different research traditions such as diffusion research that has its foundations in economics and marketing, or domestication research that has its foundations in sociology. Diffusion research studies the **aggregate outcome of individual adoption processes.** According to ROGERS' (1995) innovation diffusion[132] can be differentiated into three stages: (1) the innovation-decision-process, (2) innovativeness, and (3) an innovation's rate of adoption.[133]

---

127 See Utterback and Abernathy (1975); Geroski (2003).
128 See Adner and Levinthal (2001).
129 See von Hippel (1988).
130 See Chesbrough (2003), p. xxvii.
131 See Silverstone and Haddon (1998), p. 44; Tuomi (2002), p. 24; von Hippel (1988).
132 According to Rogers (1995), the main elements in the diffusion of innovations are: (1) an innovation, (2) which is communicated through certain channels, (3) over time, (4) among the members of a social system, see Rogers (1995), pp. 35. In the history of diffusion research he distinguishes among others opinion leadership, diffusion networks, rate of adoption in different social systems, communication channel use, and consequences of innovation. See Rogers (1995), p. 94.
133 See Rogers (1995), p. 36.

Ad 1: In the innovation-decision process, *re-invention* is the degree to which an innovation is changed or modified by a user in the process of its adoption and implementation.[134] SMS is, again, a good example of **re-invention in mobile communications**. As a result of its user acceptance, many business models in mobile data communications are built on SMS use.

Ad 2: Concerning decisions on the innovativeness, *discontinuance* is one particular decision to reject an innovation after having previously adopted it. Two types can be differentiated: (1) replacement discontinuance, in which an idea is rejected in order to adopt a better one that superseded it, and (2) **disenchantment discontinuance**, in which an idea is rejected as a result of dissatisfaction with its performance.[135] WAP serves as a good example for disenchantment discontinuance. Early adopters who tried the service were disappointed and dissatisfied with WAP offers. Long waiting times and very high cost contributed to the dissatisfaction with the performance. The mobile communications industry reacted with changes, e.g., the packet-based billing based on data volume instead of the circuit-switched billing based on connection time. However, the changes did not yet result in consumer acceptance and adoption.[136]

Ad 3: The innovation's **rate of adoption** is the relative speed with which an innovation is adopted by members of a social system; it is determined by five relevant attributes: (1) relative advantage, (2) compatibility, (3) complexity, (4) trialability, and (5) observability.[137] *Relative advantage* is the degree to which an innovation is perceived as better than the idea it supersedes. *Compatibility* is the degree to which an innovation is perceived as consistent with the existing values, past experiences, and needs of potential adopters. *Complexity* is the degree to which an innovation is perceived as relatively difficult to understand and to use. *Trialability* is the degree to which an innovation may be experimented with on a limited basis. *Observability* is the degree to which the results of an innovation are visible to others. Complexity is negatively related to the rate of adoption whereas the other four attributes are positively related to the rate of adoption.[138]

KRAFFT & LITFIN (2002) analyze whether these so called Roger criteria can be applied to the **adoption of innovative telecommunication services** such as the UMTS standard for mobile phones. They find significant and systematic differences between adopters and non-adopters and suggest that their findings vali-

---

134 See Rogers (1995), p. 202.
135 See Rogers (1995), p. 202.
136 See Sigurdson (2001); Baumgarten (2002), p. 111.
137 See Rogers (1995), p. 36.
138 See Rogers (1995), p. 250. This list of attributes is not exhaustive. Mahler & Rogers suggest that the difference in the adoption of mobile and fixed voice telephony can be explained by differences in network effects, see Mahler and Rogers (1999). The widespread diffusion of 2G mobile telephony in Europe is also related to the regulatory regime, see Gruber and Verboven (2000); Hommen (2003).

date the usefulness of Roger's attributes in the context of innovative telecommunication services.[139]

According to these criteria, however, mobile media cannot yet be perceived as an innovation and can rather be **classified as an invention**. So far, there are only assumed *relative advantages* for mobile media such as independence of location for information access on demand (anywhere on any device) and real-time provision of information services (anytime) as well as location-dependent services that align the personal communication sphere with the current environment. The use of radio in the car, or music on portable devices demonstrates a high-perceived *compatibility* with mobile media use. However, the use of newspapers, magazines, or television has only low degrees of compatibility with mobile communications. Experiences with SMS usage gives positive confirmation that it may be essential to create open mobile data systems that allow users a maximum of *trialability*. It is also unclear if mobile media will be a new means for existing purposes (e.g. repurposing of content), if it can raise new purposes (e.g. location-based services), or if the reorganization of relationships can appropriate unintended resources.

As a result, diffusion research applied to the question of the mobile media diffusion process does not provide results that can be used for further assessment and discussion. Moreover, diffusion research does not pay sufficient attention to the **context of innovation adoption**. These aspects, however, can be found in cultural studies and domestication research that focus the **social use and appropriation of innovations**. On the way to determine potential drivers of innovation for mobile media that can be integrated into media companies' mobile media strategies, the research traditions that focus the social use of innovations may serve as a bridge to context-sensitive drivers of innovation.

2.2
User-innovation networks as potential drivers of mobile media diffusion

Recent developments in innovation theory may shed some light on innovation processes in the network society that also hold relevance for mobile media innovations. The **social use of a new medium** or technology is considered to be a central dimension of innovation diffusion in media and ICT industries; the way consumers appropriate new media into their everyday life is an essential criteria for its adoption (A-2.21).[140] Under the **influence of digitization and the Internet,** innovation processes are further changing. One recent development describes the emergence of networks of innovation (A-2.22). They develop into user innovation networks that offer interesting aligning factors for mobile media innovation diffusion (A-2.23).

139 See Krafft and Litfin (2002).
140 See for example Mansell and Silverstone (1996a); Silverstone and Haddon (1998).

2.2.1
The influence of social use on innovation diffusion

Although the diffusion of the technological capabilities for mobile media use is increasing due to standardized functions in mobile handsets, the use of these possibilities is growing under-proportionally with the exception of the Asia-Pacific region. It has become apparent that **technological availability alone does not create demand**. The sheer technological possibilities to enable data transfers via cellular networks do not justify assumptions on customer adoption and the social appropriation of mobile data offers. As SCHRAPE (2003) points out:

> "Technology readiness is not market readiness; market readiness is not market diffusion; and market diffusion is not usage diffusion."[141]

SILVERSTONE & HADDON (1998) argue that innovation in media and ICTs is a fundamentally social process.[142] TUOMI (2002) extends the argument in saying that **all innovation is about social change**. Innovations emerge and become articulated when they are taken into meaningful use in social practice:

> "New technologies are always appropriated by integrating them into social practice. Indeed, [...] innovation occurs only when social practice changes. Often such change results from appropriation of a new tool which reorganizes the practices of a community. The key to innovation, therefore, is in those social communication and learning processes that underlie change in social practices."[143]

Proponents of innovation as a social complex place users in the home and at workplaces at the center of analysis.[144] SILVERSTONE (1998) observes that **technological change in the domestic field** offers relatively distinct functions and discrete experiences. Over time, these functions and experiences become less distinct and more integrated and interrelated. With every new technology it is uncertain how far, how fast and in what ways it is appropriated into the household. This process is conservative, because new technologies have to be adapted in their adoption, but mostly in the sense that new technologies open new and better ways of doing familiar things.[145]

SILVERSTONE & HADDON (1998) offer a model that they call the **design/domestication interface**.[146] Domestication involves the process of appropriation and conversion. In that process, consumers incorporate new technologies into the patterns of their everyday life while maintaining both the structure of their lives and their control of that structure.[147] In the case of the mobile phone, PALEN,

---

141 Schrape (2004), p. 227 [originally published in German and translated by the author].
142 See Silverstone and Haddon (1998), p. 50; Tuomi (2002), p. 215.
143 Tuomi (2002), p. 217.
144 See Mansell and Silverstone (1996b), pp. 6.
145 See Silverstone and Haddon (1998), p. 66.
146 See Silverstone and Haddon (1998), p. 45; design is seen to have three interrelated dimensions: (1) creating the artefact, (2) constructing the user, and (3) catching the consumer.
147 See Silverstone and Haddon (1998), p. 60.

SALZMAN & YOUNG (2000) show that **new mobile phone users** quickly modify their perceptions of social appropriateness around mobile phone use and incorporate mobile devices into their daily lives.[148] Research on mobile phones also suggests that they are regarded as artifacts through which people express themselves in their identity and in their relationship to others (see C-1).[149] An additional argument for social processes as important determinants of mobile media development is the success of **non-instrumental mobile services** such as ringtone or screensaver downloads.[150]

The social impact of new technologies, however, can also become overestimated. The **perceived revolutionary potentials** of printing press, telegraph and radio, and the Internet have been expected to create novel forms of human community, new standards of efficiency and progress, and newer and more democratic forms of politics.[151] The advocates of electricity in the 1880s, or the aircraft in the first decade of the 20th century claimed these technologies would create a world of abundance, peace, and would eliminate international differences and misunderstandings. Similarly, the television was expected to improve education and enhance democracy. When the videocassette recorder (VCR) was introduced, it was described as a medium that provides a plethora of content options, allows audiences greater communicative choice, participation, and control.[152] CAREY (1992) criticizes the **faith that is attributed to the progressive properties of new media** and its applications to eliminate social disorder and political conflict, and personal alienation between men and machine through user friendliness.[153] POPPER (2000) goes even further and formulates the main task for theoretical social sciences in the assessment of **unintended social repercussions of intended social action.**[154]

In the light of this background, the social use as driver of innovation should not overestimate the scale of innovations that may emerge. It is rather suggested to become the driver for very **small and ordinary innovations** in mobile users' everyday life that also include subtle differences in action which can lead to unintended consequences. Social networks of mobile users are a structure in which these use-driven innovations can unfold.

2.2.2
Networks of innovation

As the Internet has become a key technology in many areas of our everyday life, Internet-enabled innovations can be used to discuss social and cognitive phenomena that underlie technological change. TUOMI (2002) argues that these inno-

---

148 See Palen, Salzman, and Youngs (2000).
149 See Taylor and Harper (2003), p. 31.
150 See Cohen and Wakeford (2003); Pedersen, Nysveen, and Thorbjørnsen (2003); Taylor and Harper (2003).
151 See Carey (1992), p. 190; Standage (1998), p. 211.
152 See Rubin and Bantz (1989).
153 See Carey (1992), p. 116.
154 See Popper (2000b), p. 496.

vations have implications for all aspects of innovative activity due to ongoing **social transformation towards the network society**.[155] In the network society as defined by CASTELLS (2000),[156] presence or absence in the network and the individual dynamics of networks through the architecture of their relationships are the new sources for power and dominance as well as for changes in societies.[157]

Open source, for example, is a new phenomenon of collective production of new technologies that challenges existing economic models of innovation and technological development.[158] Based on these developments, TUOMI (2002) argues that traditional models of innovation will become increasingly misleading in the future. Therefore, he suggests the use of **social and cognitive theories of innovation**.[159] The socio-cognitive basis of innovation leads to a new approach in economic theory where the concept of value has to include the ideas that new meaning and new domains of social practices are created in innovative processes.[160]

In the context of media content development, networks of innovation increasingly support **user-generated content production**. Digital technology has significantly reduced production cost and barriers to market entry which opens new opportunities for amateur content production.[161] The contents of interpersonal communications, e.g., the exchange of messages via instant messaging or e-mail, are hereby not classified as user-generated content.[162] User-generated content needs to be accessible by more than two people on an intranet or the Internet for an extended period of time. **Cooperative publishing**, however, such as weblogs are classified as user-generated content and can enable individuals to compete with professional comments, e.g. from newspapers.[163] These trends originate from the Internet where professionally produced media content offers not only compete intra-medially (e.g., broadcasters online) and inter-medially (e.g., broadcasters and magazines online), but also compete with personal content such as websites created by users.[164] This competitive structure may be trans-

---

155 See Tuomi (2002), p. 3; the traditional linear model of innovation follows Schumpeter's definition of a sequential phase of idea generation, invention, research and development, applications, and diffusion, see Schumpeter (1975).
156 Castell observes that as a historical trend, dominant functions and processes in the information age are increasingly organized around networks. Networks are hereby defined as a set of interconnected nodes.
157 See Castells (2000), p. 500.
158 See Tuomi (2002), p. 3. For example, voluntary special-interest communities provide resources and assistance for fellow community members and their innovation developments, see Franke and Shah (2002); Harhoff, Henkel, and von Hippel (2002); von Hippel and von Krogh (2003).
159 See Tuomi (2002), p. 209. Collective production of new technologies is no more based on an economy of gifts or monetary transactions. Therefore, the economics of innovation require a concept and a theory of value outside the economy itself.
160 See Tuomi (2002), p. 7.
161 See Doyle (2002), p. 144; Feldmann and Zerdick (2004), p. 21; Hass (2004), p. 40. Therefore, low budget productions, for example in the film industry, can achieve critical success such as the film 'The Blair Witch Project' that was made on a shoestring budget and using handheld camcorders.
162 Compaine speaks of conversational content in that regard, see Compaine (2005).
163 Warchalking and WiFi-mapping are forms of cooperative action in 802.11 networks, see Sandvig (2003). Users can produce innovation benefits in a co-op setting which is a loose grouping dedicated to a number of different tasks. From a public policy perspective, co-ops can evolve into important symbiotic infrastructures to commercial wireless infrastructure providers or introduce non-commercial incentives in standardization processes, see Sandvig (2003).

ferred to mobile production as well. In Japan, users are embracing tools to create their own mobile Internet websites. Mobile weblogs or '**moblogs**' capture updated postings in words and pictures with camera-enabled mobile phones.[165] It gives initial evidence that for mobile contents the organization of content production may be complemented by users (see Table A-3).

Table A-3: Selected examples for user-generated mobile content

Forms of user-generated content	Examples
Personal mobile media files	J-Phone's Sha-mail picture messaging users make 60 percent of J-Phone's total subscriber base[a]
Mobile website publishing	TMF music TV channel: digital passport creation, including photograph that is shown on TV screen during SMS chats TVGate: enable TV viewers to produce content, including picture and voice attachment, via SMS/TV interaction[b]
Cooperative mobile publishing	'Moblogs' for mobile weblogs: capture updated postings in words and pictures from camera-enabled cell phones; 'blogmapping': associate entry with hot spot on a map that appears when readers click on the spot, links text and physical world[c]

a.   See N.N. (January 16, 2003).
b.   See Obstfeld (September 25, 2002).
c.   See N.N. (October 9, 2002).

The new information technologies that enable these networks of innovation usher, according to CASTELLS (2001), in a **new technological paradigm**[166] that is based on three major, distinctive features: new information technologies'
1) self-expanding processing capacity in terms of volume, complexity, and speed,
2) their recombining ability, and
3) their distributional flexibility.[167]

Mobile communications' strength may lie rather in **distributional flexibility** than self-expanding processing capacity. However, the interconnection of cellular networks and networks that provide wireless connectivity (see B-2.3) may open an array of new opportunities for innovative recombinations and innovative uses of mobile content and services. They can emerge, spread, and become continuously developed within social networks when wireless and mobile communication platforms are open. BAR ET AL. (2000) speak of a new **user-driven innovation paradigm** that is fostered by open infrastructure development. User-driven innovation processes flourish when users are granted access to a wide

---

164 See Lin and Jeffres (2001), p. 555; Rheingold (2002), p. 121; Feldmann and Zerdick (2004), p. 22.
165 See Denison and Kerber (2002).
166 The notion of paradigm explains the transformation of knowledge by scientific revolutions. A paradigm is a conceptual pattern that sets the standards for performance, see Kuhn (1996).
167 See Castells (2001), p. 160.

range of choices of facilities, services, and network elements. They argue that experimentation by users can then generate a surge of self-sustaining innovations.[168]

2.2.3
User innovation networks

The possibilities of mobile users to repurpose mobile content or to create and distribute user-generated content are still very restricted. However, more autonomy and control at the user level may lead to user-driven innovative uses of mobile media that spring from the diversity of individual needs and let creativity flourish. BENKLER (2005) suggests that mobile operators should rather understand themselves as toolmakers than providers of a mass media content delivery model.[169]

User innovation networks[170] have the advantages that individuals are not restricted to available marketplace choices and that they can benefit from innovations developed by others. Empirical studies suggest that innovation by users tends to be concentrated among lead users. **Lead users** are defined as users of a product or service that combine two characteristics: (1) lead users expect attractive innovation-related benefits from a solution to their needs which motivates them, and (2) lead users expect needs that will become general in a marketplace, but experience them months or years earlier than the majority of the target market.[171] FUNK (2004) suggests that in Japan the lead users in the mobile Internet are young people that are willing to experiment and play with different mobile applications. He criticizes that in Europe, the assumption that business customers will be the lead users for mobile data applications has been the source for their slow adoption. PEDERSEN & NYSVEEN (2003) argue, however, that mobile services adopted by current users such as ringtone downloads do not have to appeal to current non-users; these users are rather driven by instrumental motivational processes and functional mobile services such as mobile parking services.[172] Therefore, lead user driven innovations do not necessarily have to find widespread **imitation in mass markets**.

VON HIPPEL (2002) describes open source projects as an example for user innovation networks.[173] He identifies three situations in which user innovation networks can function entirely independently of manufacturers:[174] when (1) at least some users have sufficient incentive to innovate, (2) at least some users

---

168 See Bar et al. (2000), p. 496.
169 See Benkler (2005).
170 User 'networks' means user nodes interconnected by information transfer links which may involve face-to-face, electronic, or any other form of communication. User networks can but must not exist within boundaries of a membership group, see von Hippel (2002), pp. 2. Other proponents of user-centered innovation models include Tuomi (2002); Benkler (2005).
171 See von Hippel (1986).
172 See Funk (2004); Pedersen and Nysveen (2003).
173 See von Hippel (2002).
174 The concept of mass customization first introduced users as designers of customized products with the aid of standard components and design tool kits, see von Hippel (1998).

have sufficient incentive to voluntarily reveal their innovations, and (3) diffusions of innovations by users is low cost and can compete with commercial production and distribution. However, SANDVIG (2002) critically points out that the reference to 'users' does not necessarily mean **novice user.** It has rather been suggested that a base level of technical expertise is a prerequisite for a user to create a network innovation.[175] MATEOS-GARCIA & STEINMUELLER (2003) also criticize von Hippel's approach in their analysis of **distributed authority in open source systems.** They conclude that the status of users lacking a minimum of technical skill is problematic and their peripheral participation severely limited. Ultimately, they conclude that users' needs are insufficiently addressed or neglected in these types of innovation networks.[176]

However, users that follow lead users in the adopter categories[177] can **innovate by reconfiguration.** VON HIPPEL & KATZ (2002) suggest toolkits for user innovation as an emerging alternative approach in which manufacturers abandon the attempt to understand user needs in detail in favor of transferring need-related aspects of product and service development to users. Toolkits for user innovation tend to benefit product types which are characterized by heterogeneous user demand and changes in market needs towards the creation of markets of one under certain conditions. Effective toolkits have to display five characteristics: (1) enable users to carry out complete cycles of trial-and-error learning; (2) offer users a 'solution space'; (3) enable users to operate them with their customary design languages and skills; (4) contain libraries of commonly used models; and (5) ensure that user designs are producable without requiring revisions by manufacturer-based engineers.[178] These conditions **present challenges for mobile communications environments,** where mobile customers are usually already swamped with manually changing the default settings of their mobile portal.

The **economics of innovation** by users can also differ from the economics of innovation by manufacturers. When users freely reveal their innovation as they do on open source movements, the information becomes a public good. Freely revealing innovations, however, violates a central tenant of the economic theory of innovation.[179] HARHOFF ET AL. (2002) explore the incentives that users might have to freely reveal their proprietary innovations; they demonstrate with a game theoretic model that free revealing pays due to the fact that it improves welfare.[180] Mobile users tend to use the **fixed-line Internet as a platform to re-**

---

175 See Sandvig (2002), p. 13.
176 See Mateos-Garcia and Steinmueller (2003), p. 28. Mateos-Garcia & Steinmueller describe the organizational structure of open source projects as a set of hierarchical layers which encompass a project leader and a core of trusted elite developers. The needs of the larger population of users may offer an opportunity for commercial software firms that have adopted open source business models, see Mateos-Garcia and Steinmueller (2003).
177 According to Rogers (1995), the classification of the members of a social system into five adopter categories comprise: (1) innovators, (2) early adopters, (3) early majority, (4) late majority, and (5) laggards, see Rogers (1995), p. 37.
178 See von Hippel and Katz (2002), p. 9.
179 See von Hippel (2002), p. 12.
180 See Harhoff, Henkel, and von Hippel (2002).

veal their innovative uses of mobile devices. Applications that connect user-generated content stored on the PC with the mobile communication devices are particularly popular. One sample application that particularly worries the media industry is a tool to produce ring-tones from favorite or self-composed MP3-files.[181] These ringtones are also offered on peer-to-peer platforms for trading. Therefore, media companies critically observe these developments that may threaten their mobile licensing revenues.

User innovation networks can – on the other hand – provide beneficial support to media companies' interest of reaching critical mass when they extent to the more general category of **user content networks**. Users can post content that is of interest to others or post questions that seek an answer. In this concept, user content networks offer non-proprietary content in a convenient and accessible form.[182] Such user content networks exist in user-founded and user-run publishing formats such as weblogs or in commercial formats such as specialized websites in the medical field where patients exchange information. Many media companies include this feature on their websites in order to give their audiences a platform to exchange information and opinions. An extension of user content networks on mobile devices already indicates that mobile media content and services can unfold complementary context dependent strengths in a cross-media approach. The implications for public policy that derive from the stronger role of the user as a driver of innovations lie in creating an open environment to enable the emergence of a new innovation commons in media and ICTs (see E-1).

The discussion in this chapter on the incentive structure for mobile media provision is an essential **precondition to understand the rationale for cross-media strategy extensions** (see D). The analysis of barriers and drivers of the mobile media innovation process will become important in the context of the framework for innovation policy design (see E). These considerations, however, have first to be framed by a further and deeper analysis of the mobile communication system that offers insights into the technology push parameters (see B); as well as the investigation on the social use of mobile communications for a more profound understanding of users' demand and the properties of market pull (see C).

---

181 See Federman (2003).
182 See von Hippel (2002), p. 23.

B
The mobile communication system: elements and characteristics

Mobile communications emerges with its data capabilities in next generation cellular networks as a **new distribution channel for media content and services**. Each media channel has specifics and characteristics of its own that influence the syntax and the semantics of media content and that offers distinct usage reasons in relation to space and time. According to DE SOLA POOL (1990) **two critical elements of a communication system** are (1) a series of nodes, or terminals, each of which is an input device, or an output device, or both (B-1); and (2) a transmission medium among the nodes (B-2).[1] These two elements will be used to discuss the technological characteristics of mobile communications as new communications technology for the provision of media content and services and will be extended to a discussion about the characteristics of the mobile communication system (B-3).

1
Mobile devices

Mobile devices are constantly changing with regard to form factors and technological as well as social functions. The design and capabilities of mobile devices **influence the content and services used via the device**; they are important for the further discussion of extending cross-media strategies onto mobile platforms. In order to analyze distinct device classes for mobile media content mobile devices will first be classified (B-1.1). The taxonomy is followed by a detailed analysis of the mobile phone (B-1.2).

1.1
Taxonomy of mobile devices

Mobile transportable and mobile portable media and devices are established and well-known concepts (see I-2.2). Newspapers, magazines, and books are mobile and portable, so are walkmen or MP3-players, PDAs, and notebooks; car radio and other media connected to vehicles are mobile and transportable ICTs. Although they have been excluded from the narrow definition of mobile media (see I-2.2), physical and electronic media will be integrated into the following

---

1   He further includes a switching device and a storage device for some communication systems, see de Sola Pool (1990), pp. 19.

classification system, since a taxonomy refers to classification systems that categorize phenomena into **mutually exclusive and collectively exhaustive sets.**[2] However, for further discussion only electronic IP-enabled and cellular telephony-enabled mobile devices are subject to analysis for the provision of mobile media (B-1.12). For this class of mobile personal devices relevant device characteristics are further systematized (B-1.13). The first step in developing a taxonomy, though, is the choice of differentiating criteria (B-1.11).

1.1.1
Differentiating criteria for the mobile device taxonomy

Mobile device characteristics are important for mobile content and application design, because their size, features and capabilities are important elements of the usage context of mobile media. Since there is a broad array of mobile devices that often have overlapping functionalities, criteria have to be used that differentiate mobile devices as sharply as possible. The criteria for the classification of mobile devices for mobile media provision need to distinguish, for instance, the device's degree of mobility and of portability, its online respectively offline as well as its telephony capabilities (see I-2.2).

RAWOLLE & HESS (2001) offer a **taxonomy of digital media devices.** They differentiate digital media devices into stationary and mobile devices and the transport media into online (network-based) and offline (portable storage). Mobile devices are further differentiated into multipurpose (e.g. PDA) and special purpose (e.g. MP3-player) devices.[3] Together with a differentiation between narrowband and broadband networks RAWOLLE & HESS develop a nine-field matrix and seven device categories.[4]

For a taxonomy of mobile devices in the context of mobile media it is useful to **modify this framework.** The degree of mobility and portability is a crucial criteria for a taxonomy of mobile devices for the use of media, because it involves different user contexts and determines how much attention the user can devote to the mobile device. Therefore, the categories mobile and stationary are transformed into **mobile portable, mobile transportable, and stationary wireless** (see I-2.2).

Also, the transport media differentiation of offline and online is not sharp enough in the context of mobile devices for mobile media use, because it does not pay sufficient tribute to the differences of physical and electronic media or to the differences of nomadic wireless and mobile cellular networks (see I-2.2; B-

---

2   See Doty and Glick (1994), p. 232. This definition goes back to McKelvey (1982). Classification systems thereby categorically assign organizations to heterogeneous groups using a series of discrete decision rules. Typologies, unlike classification systems, do not provide decision rules for classifying organizations or groups.
3   See Rawolle and Hess (2000), p. 90.
4   The seven categories are: mobile information device, mobile information device 3G, online multimedia PC, broadband multimedia PC, offline multimedia PC, online digital TV, and offline digital TV. The combinations TV-based/narrowband and mobile/offline media are not considered, see Rawolle and Hess (2000), pp. 90.

2.21). Digital broadcast networks as transmission media are excluded from the classification criteria, because the devices for nomadic wireless or mobile cellular use only need to be equipped with an additional DVB-T antenna; it adds a different layer for content transmission, but will not be considered for device discrimination. Therefore, differentiating transport criteria for mobile devices are **offline (non-network) physical, offline (non-network) electronic, online (Internet-enabled) nomadic wireless, or online (Internet-enabled) mobile cellular** transport. The differentiation into non-network devices and Internet appliances goes back to EISNER, GILLET, LEHR, WROCLAWSKI & CLARK's (2000) **taxonomy of Internet appliances.**[5] Since non-network and non-IP-enabled devices are not classified as Internet appliances, a portable MP3-player as an example for a mobile device is not an Internet appliance whereas a mobile phone with its WAP capability[6] is classified as Internet appliance. Mobile wireless transport and mobile cellular transport are differentiated to emphasize the specific characteristics of mobile cellular transmission in comparison to wireless connectivity (see B-2.2). The discussed device and transmission criteria can now be used to distinguish mutually exclusive and collectively exhaustive mobile device classes.

1.1.2
Classification of mobile devices

The selected criteria differentiate wireless and mobile devices into nine distinct classes (see Figure B-1). They are discussed in the order that follows the device differentiation into stationary wireless, mobile transportable, and mobile portable.

For stationary wireless devices, two classes are considered:
1) **Wireless electronic devices** are suited for interpersonal communication such as the cordless telephone or they are suited for media transmission such as a DVB-T-enabled TV set. Their use is stationary although these devices can be moved.
2) **Wireless Internet appliances** such as the WLAN-enabled desktop PC allow online and offline computing applications, storage, and synchronous (VoIP) as well as asynchronous (e-mail) communication applications.

Mobile devices that are fixed to an object that is being transported include
3) **mobile transmission devices** such as the car radio or subway TV, and
4) **mobile wireless Internet appliances,** for example automotive or airplane media services.
5) **Mobile cellular communications devices** include, for example, maritime mobile radio communications for interpersonal communication.

---

5   See Eisner Gillett et al. (2000), p. 9. They use the extent to which the device's function is controllable by the end-user as differentiating criteria and design a spectrum from totally fixing the function of devices to automating the configuration of more general-purpose systems.
6   On the WAP model and its comparison with the TCP/IP and OSI models see Lehner (2003), pp. 142.

End device / Transport media	Physical offline (non-network)	Electronic offline (non-network)	Nomadic wireless online (Internet-enabled)	Mobile cellular online (Internet-enabled)	
Mobile portable [connected to person]	Mobile physical carrier (6) e.g. paper	Mobile electronic device (7) e.g. e-book, walk-man, game boy	Mobile wireless personal Internet appliance (8) e.g. PDA, notebook	Mobile cellular personal communi-cations and Internet appliance (9) e.g. cell phone	Mobile personal device
Mobile transportable [connected to object]		Mobile transmission device (3) e.g. car radio	Mobile wireless Internet appliance (4) e.g. automotive telematics	Mobile cellular communications device (5) e.g. maritime mobile radio communication	
Stationary wireless		Wireless electronic device (1) e.g. cordless phone, DVB-T TV set	Wireless Internet appliance (2) e.g. WLAN-enabled desktop PC		

Figure B-1: Classification of mobile devices

Mobile devices that are ported by a person encompass the largest device class; they also have a long-standing history. They include

6) **mobile physical carriers** such as paper,
7) **mobile electronic devices** such as walkmen, e-books, or portable game consoles.
8) **Mobile wireless personal Internet-appliances** include handheld computers, tablet PCs, or notebooks that allow wireless connectivity to the Internet.
9) **Mobile cellular personal communications and Internet appliances** include the cell phone that has mobile cellular two-way communication capabilities for voice and data and that enables computing applications as well as mobile cellular IP access. The form factor is not critical, the cell phone could also be embedded in jewelry or in clothes.[7]

The classes that are the most interesting for the discussion of mobile media are all **mobile portable devices that have a personal character,** that can serve as a

---

7 Laptops that get access to the Internet via a cell phone connection will not be regarded in this respect, because the cell-phone is an access-enabler in that case and voice communication would only be possible via VoIP.

platform for digital media and that are Internet-enabled. These are in particular mobile wireless personal Internet appliances and mobile cellular personal Internet-enabled devices. They will be subsumed under the category 'mobile personal devices' and are subject to the following more detailed analysis. Selected mobile personal devices from these two classes are discussed, because their form, functions and capabilities influence the conditions and requirements for mobile media design.

1.1.3
Evaluation of mobile personal devices

Mobile personal devices as one specific class of mobile devices will be further described and evaluated in order to make more precise statements about potential applications suited for this device class.

Mobile personal devices provide different combinations of functions and capabilities. The evaluation of mobile devices can be based on **technical requirements with regard to transport media** and **device characteristics**. Referring to and extending the framework of RAWOLLE & HESS (2000), three transport media aspects are dominant: (1) the access mechanism (push vs. pull), (2) the number of simultaneous recipients (broadcast-oriented vs. unicast-oriented), and (3) the support of feedback channels (yes vs. no). The relevant device specific requirements are: (4) screen size (small cell phone-sized, medium notebook-sized), (5) data type support (static, time-invariant media types vs. dynamic, time-variant media types), (6) storage capabilities that enable asynchronous download and consumption (supported vs. not supported), and (7) peripheral input facilities (handset, stylus, keyboard).

From a **security perspective**, mobile devices can additionally be grouped into two categories: (8) mobile devices featuring a (removable) security token and mobile devices without removable storage media for sensitive information.[8] This is an essential additional feature, because it enables **user identification and authentification**; in GSM networks, the SIM card contains all essential user data.[9] The trend towards more complex operating systems and applications in mobile devices further asks for security features that are important to deal with viruses, unsolicited messages, and identity theft on mobile devices. Another essential device criteria in the context of mobile media use is the (9) **degree of its miniaturization**, a criteria that affects size and weight of the mobile device and determines if it is a personal light accessory that can be worn on or carried close the body.

---

8   See Freystaetter (2002), p. 452.
9   See Lehner (2003), pp. 220.

Table B-1: Evaluation of mobile personal devices

Requirement	Characteristic	Mobile wireless Internet appliances	Mobile cellular communications and Internet appliances
Transport media aspects			
Access mechanism	Pull	++	+
	Push	++	++
Simultaneous recipients	Unicast	++	++
	Broadcast	++	+
Feedback channel	Supported	++	++
Device specific requirements			
Screen size	small cell phone-sized	0	++
	medium notebook-sized	++	0
Data types	Text	++	++
	Pictures	++	+
	Audio	++	++
	Video	++	+
	3D	0	-
Storage capabilities	Supported	++	-
Peripheral input facilities	Handset	0	++
	Stylus	+	-
	Keyboard	++	-
Security	(Removable) security token	0	++
Miniaturization	Worn on or carried close to body	+	++

Legend: ++ strong support; 0 no support; -- weak support
Source: adapted from Rawolle and Hess (2000), p. 93

Mobile wireless Internet appliances outperform other mobile devices in most categories. Their screen size and more convenient input facilities distinguish them notably from smaller devices. On the other hand, their size and weight, for example in the case of a notebook, do not make them a personal mobile accessory like the mobile phone. With the exception of VoIP, they also don't support synchronous voice communication.

Mobile cellular communications and Internet appliances have weaknesses in the screen interface, peripheral input devices, storage capabilities, and battery power which flaws applications such as browsing the Web. Yet, they offer the most sophisticated means of synchronous and asynchronous communications. Moreover, they carry removable security tokens that enable identification and authentification for mobile services, features that gain importance for more sophisticated mobile transaction, billing, and payment systems that are also interesting for mobile paid content models.

The most essential differentiating criteria for mobile cellular devices, however, is their degree of **miniaturization**. Miniaturization of processors and Internet-enabled communication appliances has led to portable, personal devices that turn increasingly into indispensable personal accessories; mobile customers tend to carry it close to their body similar to a wrist watch. This process is a necessary precondition for ubiquitous availability of mobile content and services.[10] Miniaturization processes can be expanded to forms of ubiquitous computing. **Ubiquitous computing** describes the omnipresence of the smallest, wirelessly interconnected computers that are built invisibly into objects of everyday use.[11] Advances in ubiquitous computing and ambient intelligence[12] include: (1) the integration of ICTs into clothes or accessories such as watches or jewelry; (2) the development of 'smart paper' as a highly mobile input and output medium; and (3) 'smart tags', i.e. transponders that can decode and send out radio signals and make objects 'smart' respectively controllable. In the view of mobile media provision, the concept of ubiquitous computing extends the communication relationship **from person-to-content/organization communication to machine-to-machine communication** and may develop automation processes for pushing or pulling mobile content.[13] The trend towards smaller and more integrated smart devices raises the potential for more, though not necessarily more profound, contact points between users and the media in addition to the often habituated contact with media content at certain times of the day and at certain locations. These developments make personalization of media content more important, because the user has access to relevant context-dependent content via his personalized device independent of location and stationary device availability.

In addition to their personal and ubiquitous nature, mobile cellular devices are also interesting for potential mobile media applications due to their dual communications and (Internet-enabled) data capabilities. Modifying CLARK's (1997) taxonomy of Internet telephony applications, **mobile personal device applications** can be classified with regard to the criteria how much communication

---

10 See Meckel (2005).
11 See Mattern (2004); it is based on the progress in microelectronics, nano-technology, and material sciences.
12 See Ducatel et al. (2004).
13 On the other hand, predictions on the capabilities of emerging technologies are often over-estimated, see Kahn and Wiener (1967); wearable screens that interoperate with their environments still need technological development without even taking issues around their social acceptance into account.

(synchronous and asynchronous) and how much content the applications support.[14] Three basic classes can, thus, be distinguished: Pure communication applications, hybrid communication and content applications, and predominantly content applications. Given the restrictions on screen size, input facilities and storage capabilities, applications that **emphasize communication over content** seem to be more suited for mobile cellular personal devices. The extensive use of messaging services in order to deliver mobile content may serve as an indicator for these mobile application developments.

The discussion of different mobile device classes demonstrates the difficulties connected with exclusively and exhaustively categorizing mobile devices. This derives partially from the fact that the functions and **capabilities of mobile devices are continuously expanding and merging**. Scenarios for the development of mobile electronic devices may include portable game consoles that become equipped with WiFi cards in order to allow their users to engage in multiplayer games in wireless LAN hot spots. The development of electronic paper and its combination with wireless connectivity may soon enable real-time updates of newspapers via WLAN. Next to these potential developments the mobile phone is already integrating ever more functional variants that will be subject to closer investigation.

1.2
The changing concept of the mobile phone

The mobile phone is changing from a pure communication device into a **personal everyday accessory** similar to a watch that is carried close to the body, at least within reach, and that functions as a personal communication and data control center. It has changed from the talkman[15] in the mid-1980s and an emphasis on functional elements to a personal communications device that is rather perceived as a lifestyle gadget (B-1.21). It already includes a number of advanced computing capabilities (B-1.22). Some researchers even envision it to evolve into a universal information and communications device (B-1.23).

1.2.1
The mobile phone as personal and lifestyle device

Mobile phones, their hardware as well as their software elements, are increasingly used to make lifestyle statements. This development strengthens the tie between a user and the mobile phone. At the same time, it is an interesting oppor-

---

14 In Clark's taxonomy of Internet telephony applications, he proposes the distinction between the degree of PSTN and computer-based telephony involvement as most essential criteria for the classification of applications, see Clark (1997), p. 2.
15 In 1984, Nokia Mobira launched its first transportable phone, the Mobira Talkman, with the slogan 'The new talkman does not bind your calls into the car. You can take the phone wherever you go.' The talkman was weighing five kilos, see Steinbock (2001), p. 99.

tunity for media companies to produce mobile media offers that can be used to **express a certain lifestyle.**

The mobile phone is perceived as a very personal device; it is rarely shared with a second person. Although the notion of the personal computer is similar, the degree of connection between object and individual is higher with the personal telephone.[16] Mobile communications supports the personal dimension of relationships and allows a person-oriented **directness**; directness is no longer separated from immediacy that used to be bound to locations.[17] Consequently, mobile phones allow for calling a person instead of calling a location.[18] The Finnish word for mobile phone, *kannyka*, literally means 'extension of the hand' and supports associations of technological artifacts as man-machine symbiosis, in this case the mobile phone as extension of the body.[19]

Radio telephones have already been used in the 1920ies in police patrol cars for public safety. In 1973, Martin Cooper invented the first convenient handheld mobile cellular phone. After first commercial cellular deployment at the end of the 1970s, it was in the 1990s that the mobile phone hit the mass market and **evolved into a fashion accessory.**[20] The desire to give the cell phone a personal flavor and the commercial success of handset-related mobile contents give evidence of the lifestyle-related developments. Screen savers, visual caller IDs, personalized ring-tones and exterior design elements are used to differentiate the cell phone or to demonstrate the affiliation to a certain (lifestyle) group (see C-1.23).[21]

The Finnish handset manufacturer Nokia has pioneered segmenting, designing, and branding its mobile phones.[22] Their approach of lifestyle segmentation - that has thereinafter been imitated by many other handset manufacturers - requires more specific information on user populations and their real life usage patterns than other segmentation variables such as demographic, geographic, psychographic, or behavioral criteria. These new requirements of consumer research demonstrate that the mobile phone is increasingly perceived as a social accessory rather than an instrumental tool; design is beginning to reign over function.[23] Handset manufacturers are increasingly cooperating with media

---

16   See Hoeflich (2001), p. 4. Following up on Bill Gates vision statement from 1975, 'a computer on every desk and in every home', Nokia formulates today 'putting the Internet into everybody's pocket', see Steinbock (2001), p. 306.

17   See Gumpert (1989), p. 245; Lange (1989b) makes the initial distinction between directness and immediacy that is offset in mobile communications.

18   See for example ITU (1999), p. 1. Martin Cooper, the inventor of the portable cell phone at Motorola in 1973, describes their motivation to develop a truly portable phone: "AT&T's vision was to make car telephones. People don't want to talk to cars. They want to talk to people." N.N. (2001a), p.84.

19   Townsend (2000), pp. 91. Initially, mobile phones were called *jupinalle* (yuppie toys), but Finnish teenagers changed that name as mobile phones entered consumer markets, see Steinbock (2001), p. 97. For a discussion of media as extensions of man see McLuhan (2001).

20   See Steinbock (2001), p. 93.

21   In Hong Kong, a new breed of small-sized enterprises is offering to decorate the mobile phones with personal stickers or paintings, see Yen and Ng (2001).

22   See Steinbock (2001); in 2002, Interbrand's annual ranking of 100 of the world's most valuable brands shows Nokia at rank six with a value of US$ 29.97 billion, see http://www.brandchannel.com/ interbrand/test/html/events/WMVB2002.pdf..

23   See Funk (2001b), p. 55; Steinbock (2001), p. 268.

companies in order to use mobile content to **show-case innovative features** of their mobile phones (see D-4.22).

1.2.2
Integration of computing and storage capabilities

Mobile phones tend to incorporate both computing capabilities and storage media that have formerly been primarily associated with handheld computers. For example, Sony has introduced a memory stick for cell phones[24] and handset manufacturers are working towards an **increase of storage without draining too much battery power.** For the provision of mobile media content these developments are important, because processing and battery power as well as software capabilities are a precondition to enable streaming media or Java applications for mobile games on mobile phones; storage media that carries, for example, MP3-files unburden the resources of the mobile phone which can then be used for voice telephony, messaging or other applications.

The technical progress in processing power, commonly referred to as Moore's Law, enables small cheap processors embedded in portable devices to drive multimedia capability into this digital technology.[25] As a result, the **worlds of mobile communications and computing are colliding.** The developments of truly personal computing and communications devices come from two opposite directions. The computing industry, notably Microsoft, is developing special versions of their software for mobile phones that include the operating system as well as its browser,[26] e-mail program and media play-back software. They are starting to contract directly with mobile operators since the leading handset manufacturers develop a competing, open standard in the software consortium Symbian. Symbian members, however, have larger economies of scale than those operators who brand their own mobile phones. Nokia in particular has built a strong brand in downstream consumer markets. Yet, the battle for dominance in the upstream software market has not been decided (see E-3.21).[27]

Increased computing capabilities also enable the development of new applications. Barcode scanning, a technology that has led to efficiency gains in retail industries, is a technology that may lead to interesting applications for the mobile phone. Barcode scanning has enabled the digitized identification of products. **Combining technologies of identification with portable connectivity** may produce new patterns of commerce.[28] Applications at the intersection of scan-

---

24 See Takenaka (June 3, 2002).
25 See Eisner Gillett et al. (2000), pp. 5.; Mattern (2004).
26 For a comparison of different micro-browsers for mobile devices see Lehner (2003), pp. 199.
27 See N.N. (November 23, 2002). In 1998, Nokia co-founded Symbian that provides core software, including the EPOC operating system. See Steinbock (2001), p. 241. Next to Windows CE and Symbian OS there are Palm OS and Linux for PDA operating systems. On their specifications see Lehner (2003), pp. 150.
28 See Swartz (2001); Rheingold (2002), p. 100. Radio frequency identity (RFID) tags may become the successors to the barcode. They contain tiny batteries and send signals up to more than one hundred feet. RFID tag applications of wireless connectivity can change products, places and social interaction.

ning, mobile computing, wireless communications, and the Internet include ticket and mobile commerce services. When barcode scanning capability is added into a mobile device it becomes, e.g., easy to link a web page to a tag that is physically connected to a place or an object. Also, barcodes can be sent via SMS to cell phones for ticket services in transportation, e.g. buses or undergrounds, as well as movie theater tickets or other events.[29] DoCoMo allows its subscribers to pay their monthly invoice at certain convenience stores using a bar code displayed on the cell phone screen.[30] Bango.net, for instance, is a provider for **mobile media barcode transactions**. Users point their handset at a bar code and mobile content is delivered straight to the mobile phone.[31]

Theft of the device and data theft are among the highest risks connected with networked computing capabilities of portable and mobile devices.[32] Data can be extracted from mobile devices even when it is password protected.[33] Also, mobile devices are easily left in taxis and public transportation. In London, mobile phones became the most commonly left item on subway trains in the underground, replacing the umbrella.[34] Nonetheless, for the development of more advanced mobile media applications the increasing computing competencies of mobile phones are a necessary precondition for innovative content design.

1.2.3
Integration of portable media functions

The range of supported functionality of mobile phones, however, is increasing even further. Since many people are carrying a mobile phone with them in any case, the **integration of other portable media functions** may be perceived as convenient. Equipment and handset manufacturers add features into mobile phones such as cameras, radios, and MP3-players. Some mobile phones are also designed to function as game consoles. However, while moving, communicative potentials are minimized; often, they are restricted to speech and audio applications, because the attention of a moving person is devoted to the respective traffic environment.[35] Therefore, **audio media** in particular seems to be a natural extension for mobile communications devices, because headsets are already in

---

29 Mobile parking services make use of barcodes that are placed in the car window; parking site personnel can scan the bar-code and check online if parking has been paid for, see Pedersen and Nysveen (2003), p. 2. For m-commerce, barcode scanning holds some other interesting potentials. For example, users may be able to immediately order a book or CD online that they see on the book shelves of a friend via scanning the barcode with their cell phones.
30 See N.N. (May 15, 2002).
31 Thereby, content providers register a bar code as Bango Number and link it to specific content. International Wireless' CodePoint software reads the symbol, sends a coded number to Bango.net where it is mapped onto a specific URL, see N.N. (July 10, 2002).
32 In the UK, mobile phone theft is considered an increasing problem with more than 700,000 handsets stolen in 2001, according to a government's mobile phone crime report; children under 15 are the most common targets, see Nichols (January 9, 2002).
33 This is a strong argument against efforts of m-payment and m-banking. A lack of trust as well as interest has also contributed to the demise of the B2C-segment of the European company 'Paybox' that developed m-payment solutions and decided in 2003 to concentrate on the B2B sector.
34 See Townsend (2000), p. 91.
35 See Geser (2002), p. 4.

place and the visual senses remain unoccupied for other activities.[36] New audio applications that have been developed for the mobile phone include FM radio[37] or song identification.[38] However, visual elements are also being developed such as interactive 3D graphics for mobile phones.[39] The mobile phone seems to evolve into a **universal device**.

Scholars and practitioners, however, doubt the concept of universal solutions.[40] GOLDHAMMER (2005) calls the tendency towards converged devices a **Swiss army knife dilemma**. CHYI'S (2004) notion of digital content as inferior goods is helpful in that regard. When there is no camera available, chances are that consumers may use the camera within a cell phone that offers low quality pictures. But if they had the choice, they would choose a digital camera over a cell phone. Only in times when there is no other option available, the inferior quality may be accepted. Yet, customers may reject even the option to use the inferior good if the main capabilities of the mobile phone, such as voice telephony, are suffering or **malfunctioning due to over-engineering of the mobile device**. ODLYZKO (2001) is one of the skeptics of mobile media functions for mobile phones. He argues that it is also economically suggestive that the mobile phone will predominantly stay a means for interpersonal voice communications; he supports this assumption with an argument from economic history, namely that consumers historically spent a lot more dispensable income on communication than on content. Along similar lines, also BENKLER (2005) argues for the development of the mobile phone into a toolmaker for users rather than replicating the mass media model on mobile phones.[41]

A study by the German BAT Institute reveals that **psychological boundaries** limit the potentials of a universal cell phone. Among the adherents of a universal solution are mostly young people between the ages of 14-29 years.[42] These developments give further evidence that a **lifestyle segmentation** for the changing concept of the mobile phone will be useful to effectively capture the differentiation in the market.

A newly emerging function of the mobile phone is its capability to mutate into a **wearable remote control device** for the physical world[43] whereby mobile phones can be used to coordinate actions in the physical world. They are already beginning to shape new social power by joining the social networking of mobile

36   See Groebel (2005); Pavlik and McIntosh (2005). See Sawhney (1998) and Sawhney and Schmandt (2000) for a discussion of applications in nomadic audio environments.
37   See N.N. (May 7, 2002).
38   The London-based company Shazam developed a software that allows mobile phones to recognize music. After dialing a certain number, the software checks the played song against a database and recognizes it within 15 seconds. An SMS notifies the caller for the price of 50 pence, see Keegan (April 25, 2002).
39   See N.N. (April 12, 2002).
40   See Hoeflich (1999); N.N. (2001a), p. 86; Doeven (2003), p. 6; Goldhammer (2005).
41   See Benkler (2005).
42   See BAT (2002).
43   See Rheingold (2002), p. xii; Groebel (2005); Kelly (2005). In the US, Verizon Wireless offers a mobile video service that allows to sign up for webcam services, e.g. of certain street crossings to inspect the traffic. Users can also hook up webcams themselves to monitor sleeping children or house entrances, see Pogue (February 27, 2003).

communications with the information processing power of networked PCs (see C-2.42). Remote control functions of mobile phones can be applied to access media content. The consumption process of mobile media does not necessarily have to be linked to the mobile phone. Mobile phones and their two-way communications capabilities allow for **on demand media content ordering via the mobile phone** that will then be consumed at specified locations via different devices.

2
Wireless networks for mobile media transmission

Wireless networks allow the transmission of contents without having a physical link for the 'last mile'. Media content has traditionally used terrestrial broadcast or satellite wireless networks. Next generation cellular networks add two-way transmission of data and cellular Internet access. Low bandwidth characterizes second generation cellular networks at present, but this is expected to change with the **introduction of next generation networks** which will allow advanced multimedia applications (B-2.1). Yet, nomadic wireless access networks such as wireless LAN (B-2.2) and digital terrestrial broadcasting networks may become even better positioned to transmit mobile media (B-2.3). Since each wireless network has its distinct strengths and weaknesses an integrated approach may become the direction of development for next generation wireless networks.

2.1
Next generation cellular networks

Cellular networks are currently in a migration process from second generation digital networks to third generation networks.[44] The migration to next generation cellular networks and the **increase in available bandwidth** enables more advanced provision of mobile text, images, audio, and video. Yet, expectations on the speed at which this is bound to happen has dropped sharply. Numerous problems trouble the vision of a global mobile communications system. Competing standards and issues of interoperability, technological and economic barriers to the network build-up (B-2.11), and policy uncertainties concerning roaming and interconnection agreements for mobile data communications (B-2.12) are only few among the challenges that the wireless telecommunications industry players face.

---

44   For a comprehensive description of third generation cellular networks and their standards see for example Lehner (2003), pp. 62.

2.1.1
Technological and economic challenges for the provision of media content over next generation cellular networks

The provision of mass media content via cellular networks requires higher transmission speeds than the ones that are feasible with second generation networks. Initial expectations on transmission speeds of up to 2 Mbyte/s over 3G networks led to the assumption that not only data types such as text and pictures, but also high quality audio and video could be delivered via cellular networks. The revenues that mobile operators hope to gain with mobile data provision have been an essential argument for the justification of investments into spectrum licenses[45] and into the cost of building 3G networks.[46] However, first introductions of 3G services in the Asia-Pacific, the US, and Europe give evidence of a **significantly lower speed** of approximately 144 kbps/s. This comes closer to the transmission speeds that have been made available with interim solutions named 2.5G transmission capabilities such as GPRS[47] or HSCSD and their enhancement EDGE.

A second argument that rather speaks against the provision of audio and video data types over cellular networks is the cost that arises from the transmission. BROWN (2005) demonstrates that mass media provision over cellular networks is **economically not suggestive.** His calculations compare real-time text, audio, and video delivery via cellular networks and result in prices between $0.20 for the mobile download of 'The New York Times' homepage, $1.28/min for mobile audio and $12.00/min for mobile video real-time delivery.[48] The alternative delivery models he considers comprise

– a reduction of the bit rate via lower bit rate encoding, asymmetric communication, or more efficient spectrum use,
– an increase in capacity using more licensed spectrum, unlicensed spectrum, or more base stations, or
– a broadcasting model that deploys content sharing models with time shifted broadcasting on aggregated demand, or non-real-time delivery.

Brown concludes that the most promising approach for **cost-effective mobile content delivery** is broadcasting, where the marginal delivery cost per user is zero, followed by a low-cost WLAN-based hot spot approach to wireless content.

---

45 The spectrum auctions have resulted in very different outcomes across the world. In Germany and Great Britain, mobile operators have paid up to EUR 50 billion for the spectrum licenses; other countries awarded the licenses in beauty contests. After the telecom bust, the depth-laden operators are now re-negotiating license conditions with regulatory authorities. For an international comparison see ITU (2001a).
46 These cost vary for different IMT-2000 standards. In CDMA networks, the introduction of, e.g, CDMA 1x EV-DO is an upgrade; however, the GSM standard requires a new UMTS network building. As a result, the speed of 3G service introductions vary significantly on a global scale.
47 GPRS is an IP sub-network within a GSM network and therefore suited for mobile Internet access, see Gaida (2001), p. 55; for a description of GPRS specifications see Lehner (2003), pp. 44.
48 See Brown (2005). Also Hampe & Schwabe argue in the context of music provision over cellular networks that mobile cellular music distribution is not technically and economically feasible and reasonable, see Hampe and Schwabe (2002a), p. 3.

This view is supported by DOEVEN (2003) who doubts that point-to-multipoint services via cellular networks will ever happen due to the resulting delivery cost.[49]

Research activities focus on further compression of digital media to develop standards such as audio MP3 and video MPEG4 standards. It has been argued that the provision of clips may be suited for mobile devices in spite of their small screens.[50] However, congestion may still be a central problem when certain media events such as the Soccer World Cup will lead to **peaks in usage**, even if the content in demand consists of only 30-second clips.[51]

THORNGREN (2005) even questions whether speed is the most important characteristic of next generation cellular networks at all. He argues that consumer demand may be satisfied with narrowband applications that are already available today via 2G and 2.5G networks. To the contrary, mobile operators would loose revenue due to the opportunity costs that arise when their customers use data applications instead of voice capabilities. Thorngren suggests that the **always-on capability** of mobile cellular devices will be a more important feature than speed.[52] MECKEL (2005) adds the importance of 'on demand' capabilities to the 'always on' functionality, but puts in question whether there will be social acceptance for these features (see B-3.11).[53]

Packet-based switching technologies are underlying the always-on feature; they have been introduced with GPRS. Contrary to circuit-based switching that measures the time during which a channel is open, packet-based switching measures the data transmitted via a channel. Within this process of implementing a different switching technology, mobile operators have changed their billing and pricing plans from time-based to **volume-based pricing**. This is supposed to lower the cost for consumers. However, consumer confusion over data sizes of different data applications and unchanged high end user cost for mobile data applications has not resulted in a higher acceptance of mobile data in GPRS service markets. Moreover, billing models are an additional challenge of mobile data provision for the migration to next generation networks (see D-2.44). **IP-based billing models** are developed on the grounds of research on IPDR and Ipv6;[54] yet, they are not fully implemented. Nonetheless, **global IP mobility** is a forceful

---

49   See Doeven (2003), p. 7. Doeven quotes estimates from Swedish Radio that compare the costs of providing a radio programming stream per person per day via DAB, GPRS, and UMTS. Their calculations reveal 8,000 times higher cost via GPRS and 15,000 times higher cost via UMTS compared to DAB.
50   Organic light-emitting diodes are emerging as brighter, thinner, and faster than liquid crystal displays. They may become the screen technology of choice for next generations' handsets, see Johnstone (2001). Larger screens might come from a screen that unfolds like a map, see Sherman (2001).
51   Among the technological advances for more efficient spectrum use are developments of software radio and ultra wideband technology, see Lehr, Merino, and Gillett (2002); Iyengar (2002).
52   See Thorngren (2005).
53   See Meckel (2005).
54   See Ericsson (2001); the number of devices that connect to the Internet is growing tremendously and each requires its own address. The IPv6 addressing scheme is suited for a greatly increased number of IP-enabled devices, e.g. mobile phone handsets. See Ericsson (2001); Dornan (March 4, 2002).

vision that is pursued by players across the mobile value chain and that may support the creation of innovative applications and services.[55]

One consequence of the technological and economic challenges for next generation mobile media may be that enhanced messaging services such as MMS will continue to be dominant modes of delivery instead of mobile Internet browsing, streaming, and downloading applications.

2.1.2
Policy challenges for the provision of media content over next generation cellular networks

Interconnection issues for mobile data communication, standardizations for mobile multimedia delivery in IMT-2000 networks, and consumers' health concerns regarding antenna positioning for 3G networks and mobile cellular use in general pose some pressing policy and regulatory challenges with regard to the migration to next generation mobile communication systems.

Interconnection agreements between mobile and fixed-line carriers as well as for international roaming agreements pose a number of problems for the provision of mobile data, because they have to be newly negotiated between carriers, often bilaterally. It is an unregulated area in mobile communications that gives operators a lot of room for negotiations. **Termination charges** are among the most important components; they occur when data is terminated on a mobile operators' network from either another mobile or a fixed network. Media companies that wish to terminate their services on mobile operators' networks are, thus, also affected by the data termination charges that mobile operators set. Roaming has been envisioned as one of the most significant benefits of mobile communications. However, different standards for next generation networks such as UMTS for GSM networks in Europe, or cdma2000 and CDMA 1x EV-DO in Japan and Korea raise problems of **interoperability of mobile data services**.[56] In the case of interoperability, termination charges on foreign mobile operators networks for mobile data services can lead to another set of problems when they impose higher cost on roaming mobile customers than they have been willing to pay, e.g. in the case of mobile data push services.

Mobile operators' and media companies' willingness to invest in the development of mobile media services also relies on the state of standards development. Regional and international standardization committees are working towards **new mobile multimedia standards**. For example, the European standardization organizations ETSI and 3GPP have defined two modes of multimedia broadcast/multicast services (MBMS), that in turn define two services: (1) a cell broadcast service (CBS) is a message-based service allowing for low bit-rate data to be transmitted to all subscribers in a set of given cells over a shared broadcast chan-

---

55 See Steinbock (2001), p. 162.
56 International standardization organizations and committees are working on interoperable specifications of different 3G standards. In Europe, ETSI and 3GPP are driving UMTS standardization efforts.

nel;[57] (2) an IP-multicast service allows for mobile subscribers to receive multi-cast traffic.[58] This **committee-based approach** to set standards (see A-1.42) is contrasted by a market-based approach that is mainly followed in the United States. Qualcomm is one of the US companies that is trying to set **de-facto standards** for mobile multimedia transmissions, e.g. with its BREW platform and affiliated applications that are specifically designed for next generation CDMA networks.

Other policy concerns that affect the 3G network build-out include consumers' perceived health risks through mobile communications. The use of cellular handsets is not the only widely disputed health risk. There are strong disapprovals within, e.g., the German population concerning the installation of antennas for the implementation of next generation 3G networks.[59]

In sum, next-generation cellular networks are facing many challenges and it is questionable whether they are well suited for the provision of mobile mass media due to their technological capabilities and the economics of mobile mass media. An **'always on demand broadcast model' over cellular networks**, therefore, is not a suggested option for media companies or mobile operators. Numerous challenges to policy and regulatory frameworks enhance uncertainties related to the migration to next-generation networks (for a policy discussion of different spectrum regimes see E-3.1).

2.2
Wireless LAN as wireless access networks

Digital media content can be faster and cheaper transmitted via wireless LANs which do not provide ubiquitous coverage such as cellular networks, but which provide nomadic wireless access. Wireless LANs are perceived to be the **next disruptive technology** and pose challenges to revenue sources of mobile data communication (B-2.21).[60] CHRISTENSEN (1997) pioneered the concept of disruptive technologies by identifying the possibility that technologies with inferior performance can displace established incumbents. Wireless LAN are discussed as a potential substitute for cellular data transmission although their characteristics and the implications for content delivery are fundamentally different from 3G networks. Public wireless LAN services in particular may pose threats to 3G data

---

57   Cell broadcasting allows text messages to be broadcast to all mobile handsets in a given geograph-ical area, ranging from a single cell to the whole network. Unlike bulk SMS, targeting particular cells does not require knowledge of mobile telephone numbers. Broadcast channels can be acti-vated from the handset or remotely by the network. This feature as well as its low load on the net-work make cell broadcasting suited for emergency situations when SMS can be delayed or get lost, see http://www.cell-alert.co.uk/cell_broadcasting.htm.
58   For the specifications see ETSI (2002).
59   In its coalition contract, the German government, for example, has dedicated financial research support specifically to potential health risks of 3G networks for the population. For information on the WHO's international research on electromagnetic fields, see http://www.who.int/peh-emf/en/. Taking a historical perspective, electrical phenomena of the late nineteenth century were also regarded as a source of bodily distress and disequilibrium. In 1890, for example, it was reported that the telephone had driven a citizen in Cincinnati insane, see Marvin (1988), p. 132.
60   See Alven et al. (2001); Thorngren (2001); Yen and Chou (2001).

revenues (B-2.22). As a response to the potential threat, mobile operators, therefore, are getting involved in wireless LAN service provision in order to avoid cannibalization of their services (B-2.23).

2.2.1
Wireless LAN characteristics versus 3G networks characteristics

Wireless LAN and 3G networks represent two fundamentally different philosophies. Wireless LAN follows the Ethernet tradition and the **Internet model of communications**. Media content, e.g. provided on a notebook PC, does not have to be adapted at all. 3G networks are operated in the tradition of the centralized **telephony model of communications**. Mass media content has to become repurposed for cellular networks. While the chief focus of mobile cellular has been voice telephony, wireless LANs are principally focused on supporting data communications.

Wireless access to the Internet via local area networks, embodied by the IEEE 802.11x family of standards,[61] differs from access to the Internet via cellular networks which is specified by the IMT-2000 family of standards, because 3G networks offer a **vertically integrated top-down service provider approach** to delivering wireless Internet access, while WiFi offers an **end-user-centric, decentralized approach** to service provisioning.[62]

A key feature of a 3G network is that it offers **ubiquitous and continuous coverage**. The range of a wireless LAN is restricted to up to 100 meters. Mesh network technologies are trying to overcome this limitation by linking wireless LANs with the support of peer-to-peer applications in order to provide continuous coverage over a wider area.[63] Another distinguishing criteria is the bandwidth difference: wireless LAN support data rates up to 11 Mbps; with 3G expected data rates are around 144 Kbps in practice.[64]

Another key distinction between 3G and WiFi concerns **spectrum policy and management**: wireless LANs operate in unlicensed spectrum in the 2.4 and 5.8 GHz band. On the contrary, 3G networks use licensed spectrum (see E-3.1). This has important implications for the **cost of service, quality of service and congestion management** in particular, as well as industry structure in general.[65] Some of the implications of spectrum licenses are that 3G networks provide services that are bound to certain **quality of service conditions** whereas wireless LANs offer access and **best-effort service provision**.[66] For mobile data transmission

---

61 There are several competing WLAN technologies such as IEEE 802.11b, HomeRF, and Bluetooth. IEEE 802.11b (access speeds of up to 11Mb/s) is currently the strongest alternative with upgrade paths to 802.11a and HiperLAN/2 (access speeds of up to 54 Mb/s), see Alven et al. (2001). For a detailed differentiation see ITU (2002b); Lehner (2003), pp. 120.
62 See Lehr and McKnight (2002), p. 2; Tanenbaum (2002), pp. 292.
63 See Werbach (March 5, 2002). Brown demonstrates with a back-of-the-envelope calculation that installation cost for nationwide WLAN coverage in the US can still be calculated to a lower bit rate price mobile media delivery than mobile cellular, see Brown (2005).
64 See Lehr and McKnight (2002), pp. 4.
65 See Lehr and McKnight (2002), pp. 12.
66 See Lehr, Merino, and Gillett (2002).

and the provision of media services, unreliable Internet access can pose a problem, e.g. for streaming applications. The differences in media transmission are also reflected in the ability to put measuring and billing models in place and they influence security in critical network infrastructures. In fact, one of the main disadvantages of wireless LANs are the **deficits in security**. Security tokens in 3G mobile devices such as SIM cards, on the other hand, allow more secure mobile media use, as well as control over user identification, transaction and billing services.

It largely depends on the **perception of mobile users** whether they think of the two access modes as subjectively substitutable. Yet, also their current deployments and business models are still very different. 3G represents the extension of the mobile service provider model and can be bundled with existing services.[67] But while 3G networks see only limited progress with regard to service deployment the base of WiFi networking equipment is growing rapidly. However, WiFi business models from equipment manufacturers, fixed-line and wireless carriers, and independent players are still in their early stages.[68] Particular attention is being paid to business models for the provision of **public wireless LAN access**.

2.2.2
Public wireless LAN services

The **consumption of mobile media in public locations** is one of the main target segments of mobile operators and may become seriously challenged by the spread of public wireless LANs. Local area networks used to be restricted to private or closed spaces, e.g. an office, home, or a university campus. With the emergence of public wireless LANs, Internet access becomes available in public spaces such as cafes or parks for anybody who is equipped with a low cost WiFi card and a respective device.[69]

Although the provision of media services over wireless LAN and 3G networks is quite different, the perceived usefulness of wireless LAN poses threats to mobile operators and their data revenue potentials, particularly when more mobile devices will integrate WiFi cards. In Japan and in the US, for example, handset manufacturers are working on the **integration of cell phones and WiFi cards**. On the other hand, the implementation of viable business models for public wireless LAN access is still difficult. However, in a move of self cannibalization mobile operators next to fixed-line ISPs and emerging players, mobile operators start to integrate public wireless LAN provision into their services. In the US, T-Mobile is the **main hot spot service provider** after the acquisition of the start up Mobile-Star.[70] Public WLAN business models may additionally become challenged by

---

67 See Lehr and McKnight (2002), pp. 9. Even suggestions to differentiate indoor (for wireless LAN) and outdoor (for mobile cellular) use as in Knorr (2001) are not useful in this scenario any more. It rather depends on the device that is at hand when a person is outdoors as well as users' wish to move or to stay in one place.
68 See Carter (2005).
69 See Brown (2001); Werbach (2002).
70 See Carter (2005); Feldmann (2005a).

municipal authorities which are thinking about offering free wireless LAN access to their citizens.[71] Civil attention and enthusiasm accompanies the emerging **FreeNet movement**. Its participants are setting up WiFi base stations and allow open access to any user with suitable equipment. Free community networks are already covering the United States, Australia, Japan, and Korea.[72] However, LEHR & MCKNIGHT (2002) question the long-term viability of the FreeNet movement due to congestion, traffic-variable upstream cost and ISP's prevention methods of user migration from paid access services which results in cannibalization of service provider revenues.[73]

Regulatory authorities around the world are acknowledging the wireless LAN deployments and are freeing spectrum for further use. In Europe, the French regulatory authority ART and the British OFTEL are allowing commercial wireless LAN deployment after initial rejection.[74] In Japan and Korea, spectrum is being freed and in Hong Kong, OFTA is awarding class licenses.[75] When public wireless LAN hot spots in urban environments interconnect and extend their coverage, they may indeed become a preferred wireless access mode for media services such as wireless audio or video streaming applications.

Coming back to the initial argument that wireless LAN are perceived to become the next disruptive technology the question arises if and when this poses a threat to mobile incumbent operators. Research on the **structure of consumer demand and technology rivalry** shows that technologies that offer lower relative power at lower prices become increasingly attractive when consumers face diminishing marginal returns to performance improvements.[76] The disruptive threat can be recognized by
1) the degree of preference overlap between the new technology's existing customers and the incumbent's segment,
2) by preference asymmetries in the firms' differential incentives to compete for new market segments, and
3) by the price at which the invader offers its product.

In the case of mobile media, these conditions apply, if
1) the latent demand for media usage is not the usage of mobile media but of wireless connectivity to online media, if
2) preferences, the relative value of each option, are symmetric to members of different customer segments, and if
3) wireless LAN access is inexpensive.

---

71 London's City of Westminster Council, for instance, provides WiFi connectivity throughout the Soho District of central London for council operatives and remote systems. They consider to extend the service to the public, potentially, however, with a fee-based service provider model see Smith (April 24, 2003).
72 As Nicholas Negroponte states: "The social contract is simple: you can use mine when you are in the vicinity [...]. But I want to be able to use yours when I am near you." Markoff (March 4, 2002).
73 See Lehr and McKnight (2002), p. 10.
74 See ART (2002).
75 See ITU (2002a), pp. 22.
76 See Adner (2002).

In that case, wireless LANs, though inferior in many aspects, have the potential to become the **next disruptive technology**. For the provision of mobile media this can, on the one hand, mean more demand if prices for mobile data can be lowered; on the other hand it can lead to losses in quality and less customer satisfaction. Yet, a more likely development is that multiple delivery modes will augment mobile customers' choices and will enable an integration of heterogeneous context-dependent mobile customer preferences.

2.3
Integration of multiple wireless access networks

The wireless future for mobile media delivery is likely to include a **mix of heterogeneous wireless access technologies.**[77] LEHR & MCKNIGHT (2002) expect that vertically integrated service provider will integrate WiFi into their 3G or fixed-line infrastructure. Moreover, hybrid models of cellular and digital broadcasting networks are being developed to exploit the specific wireless characteristics of each network configured to user needs.

2.3.1
Integration of 3G, wireless LAN, DAB and DVB-T

Next to nomadic wireless and mobile cellular networks, digital terrestrial broadcasting allows a **third layer of wireless transmission networks**. Broadcast systems like DAB, DVB-T, or DVB-H are designed and operated for downstream point-to multipoint services that also allow for mobile reception.[78]

Seamless mobility is a concept that combines the benefits of these different wireless access networks. STAMER (2002) discusses universal access points for media content and its audiences. These **universal access points** can be distributed over a variety of networks.[79] Technologically, software-defined radio will be an important development for the support of multiple wireless technologies on a common hardware platform. It facilitates new interference management techniques that enable more efficient utilization of spectrum.[80]

In the context of mobile media provision, cellular, nomadic wireless, and digital broadcasting networks have **complementary strength** (see Table B-2); the path-independent coverage of mobile cellular and digital broadcast networks,

---

77 See Lehr and McKnight (2002), p. 3; Mansell and Steinmueller (2002), p. 150; Sinn (2002). Tannenbaum suggests to develop tailored communication systems for social and technical networks consisting of wired and wireless systems, see Tannenbaum (1990), p. 126.
78 Digital satellite systems are another mobile communication system that enable voice telephony, navigation services as well as broadcast applications. In the following analysis they will not be further included because in the case of voice telephony they offer expensive niche services for special customer groups; satellite supported navigation systems such as GPS are only subject of discussion for location-based service applications; and mobile broadcasting services are discussed for terrestrial DVB services.
79 Latzer describes the combination of different networks for one application in his mediamatics approach, see Latzer (1997), p. 76. Sawhney points out that in the case of 3G and WiFi, both are feeder technologies that draw traffic into a primarily wireline network. As a result, competition in the wireline-wireless network relationship is limited to the last mile, see Sawhney (2003).

e.g., are complemented by low cost on demand nomadic service delivery of local area networks. Whereas digital broadcast offers low cost for mobile media delivery, mobile cellular and nomadic wireless networks support a greater range of communication types, from engagements with oneself (intimate communication) to on demand application access (choice communication).[81]

Table B-2: Characteristics of different wireless networks

	Mobile cellular	Nomadic wireless	Digital broadcast
Communication distribution	Point-to-point service	Point-to-multipoint connectivity	Point-to-multipoint broadcast
Paths	Path independent (independent of spatial restrictions)	Path dependent (restricted to certain area)	Path independent
Supported communication types (based on number of participants)	Intimate communication (voice, data) Individual communication (voice, data) Group communication (data) Choice communication (data)	Intimate communication (data) Individual communication (data) Group communication (data) Choice communication (data)	Mass communication
Comparative advantage for mobile media provision	Identification, authorization, security for mobile media	High transmission speed and low cost for on demand nomadic media	Low mobile media delivery cost

Source: adapted from Wersig (2000), pp. 24; pp. 167[a]

a.   Wersig offers a number of approaches to systematize ICTs that can be combined according to the intended purpose, see Wersig (2000), p. 24. He uses the criteria path, distribution, and overcoming spatial distance for a typology of new transmission networks, see Wersig (2000), pp. 167.

Mobile operators are already beginning to integrate GPRS and wireless LAN services. However, mobile operators in their role as wireless ISPs experience fierce competition from fixed-line ISPs who are equally combining their broadband services at home or in the office with public wireless LAN service provision.[82] Yet, the combination of mobile cellular and wireless LAN networks has interesting benefits. Security flaws of wireless LAN can be tackled in an integrated cross-network model with **device identification and user authentication**

---

80   See Lehr and McKnight (2002), p. 20. Cooper analyzed how effectively people could use radio spectrum for personal communications starting with Marconi's first transmission. He developed what he calls Cooper's Law, which says that we have essentially doubled the capability of using spectrum every 30 months for the last 107 years, see Cooper (2001), p. 125. Some number crunching reveals that we use spectrum a trillion times more effectively today than Marconi did. With spectrum getting more valuable every 2 1/2 years the regulatory bodies face big challenges in their decisions on allowing new ways to use spectrum more efficiently.
81   For a detailed differentiation of the communication types see Wersig (2000), pp. 24.

mechanisms that are known from mobile cellular. GPRS already supports user authentication, service management, and standardized billing whereas wireless LAN can be used for the physical connectivity to provide high-speed access.

Further opportunities for interconnecting different wireless networks arise with **digital broadcasting technologies.**[83] Digital audio and video broadcasting models are introduced and offer another alternative to the wireless transmission of media. As a matter of fact, BROWN (2005) demonstrates in his analysis of wireless transmission cost, that the broadcasting model is superior for mobile media delivery with regard to the cost of transmission to both cellular coverage and wireless LAN coverage models (see B-2.11).[84]

DVB-T in particular aims at offering a seamless wireless and mobile media experience for any device that is equipped with a DVB-T antenna.[85] GAIDA (2001) suggests counterbalancing the weaknesses of UMTS for point-to-multipoint models of content distribution with DVB-T. **Hybrid models of DVB-T and GPRS** are using mobile cellular Internet access to demand content and DVB-T to economically distribute it.[86] A new **handheld standard for mobile devices,** DVB-H, is being developed that strives for offering 40 video stream programs simultaneously. It takes the limitations of screen size and battery power into account and will restrict bandwidth needs to 384 kBit/s.[87] A **bundling of users** can be envisioned here, similar to the user bundling for online group purchases that enable price reductions in the Internet.[88]

For hybrid DVB-T GPRS (UMTS) services, BISENIUS & SIEGERT (2002) suggest to use broadcasting platforms not only for radio and TV services but also for popular websites, time-critical information updates and teaser services designed as one-click applications. Any personalized pulled interaction based on individual needs can then be fulfilled using telecommunications platforms.[89] Pilot projects that have realized an integration of broadcast and cellular networks and services are the German project ZDFmobil, the Swedish project SABINA, and the European Multimedia Car Platform (MCP) project.[90] Virgin Radio also develops a digital broadcast delivery system that combines DAB and 3G; digital content will be broadcast to users handsets at night and reside in the device's cache.[91] Hy-

---

82   Alven et al. (2001) suggest that an existing broadband ISP is best positioned to offer wireless LAN access and organized sharing arrangements. Alternatively, a private independent entity could maintain a network consisting of access points within a nation. In the US, Boingo is an example for this type of business model.

83   For maps that show the implementation of T-DAB and DVB-T in Europe see Doeven (2003), p. 3. One open question in that regard concerns the universal coverage mission of EBU members and if it applies to T-DAB and DVB-T.

84   For wireless LAN transmission he calculates the cost for a hypothetical nationwide coverage with interconnected wireless LAN, see Brown (2005).

85   See Hirakawa (2002). NEC has developed a prototype of a mobile phone that is equipped with a DVB-T receiver by employing a portable antenna, see N.N. (July 21, 2003). German public commercial broadcasters already plan to expand their public broadcasting license fee onto radio and television enabled mobile phones, see Ott (September 14, 2002).

86   Data transmission speeds are on average 15 Mbit/s for the DVB-T downstream and 40 kbit/s for the GPRS interaction channel, see Gaida (2001), p. 83.

87   See Krempl (2003).

88   For an analytical approach to customer demand bundling see Voeth (2002).

89   See Bisenius and Siegert (2002), p. 72; the rationale of mobile operators is exactly the opposite.

90   For a more detailed description see Gaida (2001), pp. 86; Bisenius and Siegert (2002), pp. 68.

brid services via digital broadcast and cellular networks may be an **intermediate step on the way to interactive TV** and give the long discussion about interactive TV a new twist.

The integration of 3G and wireless LAN is sometimes referred to as **4G**.[92] Generally speaking, 4G is a conceptual framework to address future needs of a universal high-speed wireless network that will interface with wireline backbone networks seamlessly.[93] A further integration of 4G and digital terrestrial broadcast networks may be called **5G** as a future scenario for the development of mobile media access provision.[94]

2.3.2
Implications of an integrated network approach for media content provision

Interconnecting multiple wireless access networks creates new challenges for media content provision and content management systems since different formats and versions of a media offer will be required that can be used for push and pull applications across networks and across devices. It also requires sophisticated selection menus that make it possible to distinguish and to recombine delivery and consumption modi. Similar to hyperlinks that connect web pages on the Internet, **hyperlinks for cross-network content** offers may become an emerging need to relate content in different versions with each other (see D-3.22). Yet, one essential aspect for mobile media provision in a variety of different formats are the costs that are incurred by such a system (see A-1.2). A challenge, hence, is to determine details about the **financial trade-offs from cross-network mobile service delivery.**

An integrated network approach leads the way for more **context specificity in mobile media use.** Multiple access points via multiple devices lead to an increased overlap of wide area networks (WANs), local area networks (LANs), and personal area networks (PANs).[95] Mobile cellular, nomadic wireless, and digital broadcasting networks provide an array of transmission possibilities that offer different opportunities for exploitation dependent on the **users' context and individual preferences.** Interconnected mobile personal devices may soon use wide area coverage for voice and data, local area networks for IP connectivity

---

91   See N.N. (April 19, 2002).
92   There are a number of different definitions for 4G technologies with high-speed data transmission as the common denominator. Mobile Broadband System (MBS) is a '4G' project on high data rates technologies started in the 1990s and overseen by the European Commission; it could offer widespread services in 2020. Multipoint Multichannel Distribution System (MMDS) is a point-to-multipoint fixed wireless architecture that may become a 3.5G solution; IEEE is also working on an MMDS standard called 802.16a. IEEE 802.11b standards as well as Europe's alternative system HiperLAN2 can be integrated with 3G cellular services into a 4G service. 802.11a LANs and High-speed Unlicensed Metropolitan Area Networks (HUMAN) are yet another suggested 4G system. What will be needed in any case is Ipv6 for 4G mobile IP, see Dornan (March 4, 2002).
93   See N.N. (April 4, 2002).
94   Lehner characterizes the integration of fixed, cellular, wireless and digital broadcasting networks as 4G, see Lehner (2003), pp. 79; Zerdick, however, suggests 5G for the combination of UMTS, WLAN, and DVB-T, see Krempl (2003).
95   The free community network movement has additionally created the term neighborhood area networks (NANs) for free shared access to wireless LANs within a neighborhood.

and services, and personal area networks for computing applications as well as (external) storage opportunities.

The combination and integration of a variety of wireless networks can lead to **innovative formats and applications**. For integrated television and online formats, GAIDA (2001) defines three application categories for hybrid DVB-T/GPRS services: (1) broadcast services, (2) interactive broadcast services, and (3) personal services. Broadcast services are provider controlled point-to-multipoint audiovisual and Internet contents. Interactive broadcast services include a bi-directional channel for interaction that can be related or unrelated to the content. 'Quick-hit' applications with interactive hot spots within the TV screen, e.g. click-to-buy or click-to-vote, are examples for program unrelated services. Personal services include video-on-demand applications and Internet video portals that use streaming technologies.[96] In these applications, the **mobile phone provides the back channel**, but it is not used as the transmission device.

When preferences and options for allowed device-to-device interactions are preinstalled by users, many activities can also be executed in the background without a need for user attention. FARATIN ET AL. (2002) introduce a **mobile personal user agent** whose task is to seamlessly manage the procurement and execution of short and long-term connections for mobile users. In a context-dependent manner it dynamically selects the provider that satisfies the user's expected preferences best.[97] This **personal router** is the interface between the user's devices and the Internet. Based on the user's profile and preferences, the personal router chooses the network for a task that the user requested. For example, if the user is asking for the download of songs from a certain artist on his mobile phone, the personal router will determine the available networks, e.g. the cellular 3G service provider and a hot spot wireless LAN service, and will choose the optimal network for the task based on **preset user's preferences** (e.g., price more important than speed).

Along similar lines, the EURESCOM research network suggests a **virtual terminal** that allows user's various devices such as laptop, PDA, mobile phone etc. to act as a single virtual terminal. It provides access to and control of services on any device employing both time based and static user profiles. This enables users to **unify all communication and computing devices** in such a way that they can behave as one device with multiple input and output capabilities.[98]

For the provision of mobile media services, an integration of the capabilities of different networks seems to be a very promising approach, because complementary strengths of networks can be exploited. Wide area networks such as next generation 3G networks provide coverage and instant access to pushed and pulled content and media-related messages; wireless LAN networks allow economically viable downloading and streaming applications; and digital broadcast networks such as DAB and DVB-T enable cost-efficient, potentially user

---

96   See Gaida (2001), pp. 33.
97   See Faratin et al. (2002).
98   See EURESCOM (2002), pp. 4.

bundled on-demand content broadcasts. A personal router that is configured to the individual's preferences concerning quality and price may automatically manage cross-network service provision of wireless and mobile content.

Yet, when media content will be delivered across a variety of networks and devices, the role of the mobile phone may rather remain restricted to serve as a remote control that steers content delivery with its interactive two-way communication capability than a transmission device. Communicative interaction, therefore, may indeed remain its most essential application.

3
Characteristics and usage reasons of the mobile communication system

The increasing miniaturization and personalization of information technologies extends the context of access to media and ICTs, as handheld computers and mobile phones offer a **new kind of nomadic access and media participation, constant availability and an increasing dispersal of information consumption.**[99] Mobile communications offers new dimensions in the relationship between the media and its audiences with regard to space, time, and communication sphere (B-3.1). These new aspects are analyzed in the following chapters and related to the usage reasons the mobile communication system offers (B-3.2). Mobile communications usage reasons are closely related to the users' context such as, e.g., the degree of user mobility (space), the use of interim periods (time), and the desire for virtual accessibility while being unaccessible for the immediate surroundings (personal communication sphere).

3.1
Mobility characteristics in space, time, and the personal communication sphere

CAREY (1992) argues that **communication technologies alter the spatial and temporal boundaries of human interaction** and demand new forms of organization of human relations.[100] Therefore, the characteristics of the mobile communications system in relation to time, space, and the communication sphere will be investigated. Following REICHWALD's (2002) differentiation into Internet characteristics and mobility characteristics, connectivity, location-flexibility, and personal communication sphere will be discussed as relevant dimensions for mobile content and services.[101]

GROSSKLAUS (1997) observes that new technologies and new media usually try to **minimize temporal or spatial distances.**[102] Technological evolutions in miniaturization, synchronicity, digitization, and instantaneousness tend to develop

---

99 See Silverstone and Haddon (1998), p. 70.
100 See Carey (1992), pp. 204.
101 See Reichwald, Meier, and Fremuth (2002), pp. 9. He classifies characteristics of mobile content and services into Internet characteristics and mobility characteristics, the former comprising automation, flexibility of time, interactivity, and individuation, the latter comprising location-flexibility, personal sphere, connectivity, and context sensitivity.
102 See Grossklaus (1997), pp. 7.

a perception of simultaneous spatial proximity and timely concurrency.[103] This observation also applies to mobile communications. Presence becomes the intersection of different temporalities (B-3.11); well-known patterns of spatial orientation are changing (B-3.12); and culturally defined borders between the public and the private are blurring (B-3.13).

3.1.1
Connectivity: always on and on demand

Mobile communications increases users' connectivity to information and communication access in two essential ways: it is **'always on'** in order to receive or demand calls, messages, content and services, including Internet access and it enables immediate reaction; and it is available for **on demand** pulled messages and content.[104] 'Always on' can be defined as a network functionality of providing sustained access to the user or their representatives with no or minimum use of network capacity when no traffic is moving and as a continuous connectivity without the need of any call set-up requirement.[105]

Mobile communications and its relationship to time and the media has yet more dimensions to it. Media production for mobile communication consumption purposes can be published sporadically at a particular point in time or cyclically for a specified period. **Periodicity** meant a new step in media evolution for the new newspapers in the 16th century.[106] However, in mobile communications, periodicity may not be the most essential criteria. Mobile communications does not relate as much to habituation processes as does traditional media consumption (see C-2.22), but it rather leads back to the **sporadic consumption at a random point in time**. Therefore, it is more an occasional than a periodic media. This observation has important implications for the provision of mobile media. Newspapers, for instance, that are implementing SMS services as new mobile paid content models for their readers should, hence, rather think about an **insurance model of mobile media provision** than a periodic mobile media delivery (see Table B-3). Users may be willing to pay an insurance premium to be alerted in the case of breaking news or emergencies, but may also be very satisfied with not being bothered by trivial news in the meantime.

---

103 See Grossklaus (1997), pp. 86.
104 See Funk (2001b), p. 9; Meckel (2005); Thorngren (2005).
105 See EURESCOM (2002), p. 3.
106 See Hoemberg (1992), pp. 90.

Table B-3: Mobile media delivery models from a temporal perspective

Mobile media models from a temporal perspective	Characteristics
Insurance model	No periodicity of mobile media delivery, but pushed breaking news and emergency alerts
Periodic media model	Ex-ante, parallel, and ex-post mobile media offers for traditional media use

BENTELE (1992) suggests that media audiences can perceive time in four different experimental categories: concurrence, sequence, the now, and duration.[107] These categories lead to **different codes and temporal patterns in media consumption**. Mobile communications provides users with more individual choice of the experimental category. Referring to 'the now', for example, the idea of real-time interaction[108] with media content enters the personal sphere through media provision via mobile personal device interaction. Experiencing sequential media time patterns can be supported by ex-ante and ex-post mobile media offers that are additional elements of a traditional media offer and provide options to frame the habituated media consumption process. Mobile media can augment concurrence with audience participation formats via mobile communications, e.g. in TV or radio show formats (see D-2.21).

The exchange of time-sensitive information can also lead to **different patterns of political and economic interaction**. For example, demonstrators in urban political conflict can coordinate their activities with the always updated knowledge about the latest events.[109] Spot markets can be created using real-time exchange of information while people are moving.[110] Historical evidence demonstrates changes and shifts in economic activity through new ICTs as well. Among the main uses of the telegraph was sending time-sensitive information between the Stock Exchange and other locations.[111] It evened out markets in space and shifted speculation and opportunities for arbitrage into another dimension, from space to time, from trading between places to trading between time.[112] Thus, the ubiquitous availability of, e.g., access to financial information via mobile Internet access, pushed messaging services, or FM radio integrated into mobile phones may initiate more shifts towards a competition on time, because it helps to **level information asymmetries**.

---

107 See Bentele (1992), p. 161.
108 See McKenna (1997), p. 6; he defines real-time interaction as characterized by the shortest possible lapse between initiative idea and action.
109 See Rheingold (2002), pp. 157.
110 Plant reports from the creation of spot markets via mobile phone information exchange in geographic areas where fixed-line telephony would otherwise be unavailable or prohibitively expensive, see Plant (2000), pp. 74.
111 See Standage (1998), p. 94.
112 See Carey (1992), pp. 217. The telegraph also had effects on the practical consciousness of time through the construction of standard time zones, see Carey (1992), p. 222.

3.1.2
Location flexibility: ubiquity and location-awareness

Location independence as well as location awareness of ICTs are two new, though different aspects of mobile communications. **Ubiquitous mobile communications** does not transcend space in the way the Internet has brought about a 'death of distance'. Yet, it covers our real-life environment with seamless access points to information and communication infrastructure; it accelerates the **"de-location"**[113] **of communications and media consumption.**

Location-awareness, on the other hand, is a completely different phenomena. KELLY (2005) points out that ubiquity is about 'anywhere', location awareness is about the 'here and now'.[114] New technologies can also create an overlap of different spaces.[115] Mobile Internet access, for instance, implies an overlap of the virtual worlds of the Internet and the real world environment. These **hybridization processes between cyberspace and geospace** are leading to new ideas such as tagging locations with information that can be accessed via mobile devices. Also, an increase in inter-machine communication makes it possible for artifacts to locate themselves in space.[116] Machine-to-machine communication receives new potentials through the development of ubiquitous computing and RFID tags and further supports new combinations of real world environments and virtual spaces. Yet, applications that effectively and productively bridge the gap between virtual spaces and physical places have been slow to emerge. TOWNSEND (2001), therefore, argues that wireless developers should look towards architecture, urbanism, and geography for ideas and inspiration.[117] Indeed, effects of new information and communications technologies on spatial environments are interdisciplinary discussed.[118] For mobile media offers, these discussions gain importance for the development of potential location-based service applications.

Mobile communications extends the range of information and communication exchange beyond fixed locations and directs attention to new, 'here and now' **location-based services.** In a definition of SAMSIOE & SAMSIOE (2002) location-based services need to always include three activities: (1) the location estimation of the mobile consumer; (2) a service produced on the basis of the estimated location; and (3) the service delivery to the mobile consumer.[119] Four categories of location-based services can then be differentiated: safety-related, billing-related, local information-related and tracking and positioning services.[120] An important additional piece of information is the relative location of users that is sometimes more important than absolute coordinates. Also, the con-

---

113 Gumpert (1989), p. 245.
114 See Kelly (2005).
115 See Loew (2001), p. 263.
116 See Mansell and Steinmueller (2002), p. 151; Mattern (2004), pp. 166.
117 See Townsend (2001).
118 See Sassen (2002); Tuomi (2004).
119 See Samsioe and Samsioe (2002), p. 422.
120 See Schilcher and Deking (2002), p. 383.

cept of what is near a person changes with the speed of movement, depending on whether a user is walking, driving, or flying.[121]

Mobile location-based services have to take the user context into account in order to avoid becoming molesting intrusions or privacy violations. To date however, these services raise more technological problems as well as public policy concerns than innovative mobile service dynamics (see E-2.11). The opportunities for **mobile media 'here and now' location-based services** may unfold for local newspapers and city magazines that can offer location-based services on the basis of their editorial content. More interesting mobile media applications may, however, be built on the ubiquitous dimension of mobile data access that enables new media touchpoints at places and times that have not been an option for media consumption before.

3.1.3
Personal communication sphere: hybridization of public and private space

Mobile communications creates new communication spaces of everyday life. It leads to an increased overlap of **two formerly separated communication spheres**, the private and the public. The borders between public and private institutional spheres become more permeable, more flexible, and more interpenetrating.[122]

New ICTs always influence the sharing of space. Where communication occurs, there are usually physical boundaries which can be drawn around participants. New communication technologies differ in their range of access and the area of relevance in the physical world;[123] they thereby influence human action in communicative space.[124] The ubiquitous and instantaneous possibilities of mobile media access and use lead to an extension of the electronically mediated communications space[125] and form **hybrid areas of private and public communications**. Hybridization hereby describes the combination of things that have been previously unconnected, divergent, or belonged to different societal, social, or cultural categories.[126]

SILVERSTONE (1998) suggests that the significance of shifting, extending, transforming, or undermining the boundaries that separate our private from our public lives provides information about the **role of media and ICTs** in everyday life.[127] The telephone was the first electric medium to enter the home and unsettle customary ways of dividing the private person and family from the more public setting of the community.[128] Today, a mediated hybridization of private

---

121 See Werbach (2000).
122 See Feldmann (2002b); Geser (2002), p. 47.
123 See McQuail (1984), p. 22 quoted after Maier-Rabler (1992), p. 358; McQuail (1990).
124 See Graef (1992), pp. 371; McLuhan (2001), p. 180.
125 See Krotz (1995); Krotz discusses the notion of electronically mediated communication spaces which integrate mass communication and individual communication, see Krotz (1995), pp. 454.
126 See Schneider (1997), p. 102.
127 See Silverstone and Haddon (1998), p. 61.
128 See Marvin (1988), p. 6.

and the public space can be observed in television productions of real-people formats. It is the fundamental ambiguity of our increasingly mediated lives to choose what is private and how to present oneself in public.[129] Mobile communications further extends options for personal choices on individual forms of communication and media consumption in public, because voice communication can be executed in public places and media consumption is moving **from household screens in private settings to private screens in public settings** (see C-2.32).[130]

This hybridization of the public and private space through mobile communications also incurs social costs with regard to the social dimensions **verbal versus non-verbal interaction** and **co-present versus remote interaction**. Initial assumptions about psychological barriers of private communication in public spaces[131] have not been demonstrated yet. The ambiguous dimension of **presence and simultaneous absence** in space can, for example, destabilize ongoing face-to-face interactions. Managing two sets of social contexts, the virtual mobile phone context and people in the physical vicinity, raises the question how to include or exclude physically present people in a conversation with a remote partner.[132] Nonetheless, specific rules and codes of conduct are emerging, similarly to the netiquette in the Internet (see C-2.3).

In public spaces the mobile phone can, on the other hand, contribute to defending a private space and the right to enjoy **"civil inattention"**[133]. Yet, compared with other media that are used to create this private space such as newspapers and magazines, walkman, or gameboy the mobile phone is a rather aggressive way of disengagement when used for voice communications, because it disturbs the privacy of others nearby. Whereas it is the individuals' choice to neglect its need for privacy, the public is losing some right to privacy, because people are forced to participate in other people's communication behavior. Therefore, in that sense it is a form of **privacy violation upon the surrounding public's acoustical space**.[134] Mobile media content and services, on the other hand, can add new options for civil inattention in a socially desirable way, because the use of peripheral devices such as headsets can protect the public from sonic disturbances.

3.2
Mobile communications' usage context

Mobile communications and the reasons and situations it offers for accessing media content and services depend to a high degree on the context of the user. In context-aware computing research, context is defined as "any information

---

129 See Imhof and Schulz (1998); Weiss and Groebel (2002).
130 See Silverstone (2004).
131 See Lange (1989b), p. 177.
132 See Ling (2002).
133 Geser (2002), p. 11.
134 See Weilenmann and Larsson (2000), p. 2.

that can be used to characterize the situation of an entity. An entity is a person, place, or object that is considered relevant to the interaction between a user and an application, including the user and the application themselves."[135] Relevant context information for different mobile communications usage reasons comprises if the user is **stationary, mobile** (B-3.21), **or being transported** (B-3.22) which translates into different user needs for mobile applications.

3.2.1
Stationary and mobile usage reasons

Against all assumptions, mobile communications is often **used at home or in the office**, in other words in situations in which the user is stationary.[136] Even in the presence of fixed-line communications opportunities, the mobile phone can be the preferred choice of users. The reasons lie in the **personal nature of the communications situation** and the certainty of reaching the person that a message is targeted at. Even though mobile communications messages, voice as well as data, usually requires a price premium, people are willing to pay for the option to immediately and directly reach a certain person.[137] LING & HADDON (2001) report that, according to a European study, between about a fifth and a third of interviewees always have their mobile phones switched on when they are at home which they count as a sign that these users adopt their mobile phone as a **personal terminal** through which they can be contacted at all times.[138]

Convenience is another reason for stationary mobile usage. FUNK (2001) describes, for example, mobile phone usage at home from the couch while watching TV. Television audience members can use the mobile phone for active intervention in the TV program, e.g. the use of SMS to participate in voting options, or for other parallel activities that take advantage of the 'always on' function of the mobile phone. Yet, although new communications technologies are usually expected to introduce new levels of interactivity, the desirability of interactivity is often misinterpreted. They can also support **rational passivity** (see A-1.32).[139] The more hedonic principle of passively waiting for desired content is a central principle of mass media consumption. Pushed mobile content offers relieve the user from the responsibility to constantly keep up with news or other forms of desired content. This convenience-based usage reason is not connected to mobility, either.[140]

Yet, when people are moving, reasons to use mobile media can be enforced by choosing an audio interface and navigation mode. In many roaming situations,

---

135 Dey (2001), p. 1.
136 See for example France et al. (2001).
137 See Zerdick et al. (2000), p. 217; Funk (2001b), p. 36.
138 See Ling and Haddon (2001), p. 6.
139 See Zerdick et al. (2000), pp. 218; Feldmann and Zerdick (2004), pp. 26.
140 Stationary wireless access to DVB-T transmitted TV content will also offer new usage contexts for users to enjoy rational passivity, e.g. in their garden, on their boat, or in public places. However, in these cases neither content configuration nor media functions are bound to change as in the case of cell media.

the user's hands or eyes are busy. Coordinating foreground activities with mobile communications usage, the **role of speech and audio as the primary interface modality** grows. The management of user's focus of attention can be addressed by wearable audio computing platforms. Nomadic radio, an audio-only wearable interface designed at the MIT Media Lab, provides, e.g., an unobtrusive interface for users combining ambient and auditory cues, synthetic speech, and spatialized audio.[141] It allows for peripheral awareness, spatial listening, and contextual notification while performing other tasks in a user's everyday environment.

Essential for both user contexts, stationary and mobile, in the light of mobile media is the emphasis on personalized media. This development can be captured in the model of **dedicated communications**:[142] users face greater selection possibilities for digital multimedia products in increasing usage contexts, but at the same time they demand an increase in the level of personal experience and relevance and new realms of personal choice.

3.2.2
Captive communications

Another usage reason for mobile media offers can be grounded in a captive situation such as the (short) time periods spent in a means of transportation - bus, taxi, underground, train, elevator - or in preliminary situations, e.g. waiting for the transport to happen. This creates **lock-in situations for mobile users** in which the user can choose to dedicate attention to mobile media to bridge the time spent on being transported.

Captive communications includes the intentional avoidance of communications. Contrary to the perception that mobile communications enhances our possibilities to communicate it can also serve as a means to avoid communication and create personal spheres around a mobile user in public spaces. In public transportations, for example, this is a socially accepted form of de-communication.[143] **De-communication** describes the possibility of periodically withdrawing from the communication system (see C-2.33).[144] In the case of private space creation in public this may include the devotion to the consumption of mobile news and entertainment content and applications. The term captive communications offers a better description for such a mobile media usage situation than the often used phrase 'use of waiting times' that already contains an evaluative component.[145] A train journey, for example, does not have to be considered to be a waiting time, but it can be efficiently used for work or leisure related activities. The captive nature of the situation, however, is a fact regardless of the activities travelers engage in.

---

141 See Sawhney (1998); Sawhney and Schmandt (2000).
142 See Zerdick et al. (2000), pp. 216.
143 See Feldmann and Zerdick (2004), p.26.
144 See Zerdick et al. (2000), p. 220.
145 Often, 'killing time' is described as a usage reason, see for example Plant (2000), p. 62.

Transportable mobile media in a wider definition (see I-2.2) are already a commonly used component in means of transportation. Yet, they can be **augmented via personal mobile cellular services or nomadic wireless connectivity.** Airplanes already have integrated media service for their clients that can choose from a selection of movies to video games and are extended to the provision of wireless Internet connectivity within planes; and wireless Internet-enabled telematics services with ten second screens are introduced in elevators[146] and taxis. **Automotive mobile media services** are emerging for captive situations in cars, offered by automotive telematics service providers. Automotive telematics is thereby defined as the use of computing and communications in vehicles.[147] Auto manufacturers integrate it into luxury car models and are starting to contract with media companies for additional on demand mobile media services for purposes of differentiation. Media content providers such as 'The Wall Street Journal' already syndicate mobile content to automotive telematic providers, e.g. OnStar in the US.[148] In these captive usage situations mobile users may either want fast access to a dense representation of personally relevant media content or mobile content suited for distraction that allows them to bridge the captive situation in an efficient or enjoyable way.

After the discussion of central elements of the mobile communications system – devices and networks – as well as its characteristics and usage reasons for mobile media the question emerges in which ways mobile users take advantage of the mobile communications system. The next chapter, therefore, discusses in what organizational structures and with which motives mobile customers use mobile communications and how these **organizational and behavioral aspects** influence the development of mobile media content and services.

---

146 See Anderson and Voss (2001).
147 See Ehmer (2002); Lawrence (2005). Automotive telematics may become one of the earliest applications of software radio. By moving radio functionality into software, software defined radio (SDR) technology offers more flexibility and reconfigurability for network operations. Upgradeability is especially important in the automotive telematics context, because the product life cycle of trains, trucks, buses, and cars are much longer than the life cycles of information and communications technologies, see Lehr, Merino, and Gillett (2002), p. 10.
148 See Lawrence (2005).

C
The social use of the mobile communications system

The analysis of the social use of the mobile communications system investigates how its channel characteristics are translated into everyday life and social action, because every new medium shapes and controls the scale and scope of human relationship and interaction due to its special physical configurations and capacities.

Although mobile data communications in general and mobile media content in particular have not been widely adopted yet, mobile voice communications has become an essential element in the lives of people around the world. Studies on the appropriation of **mobile voice communications and mobile messaging** into everyday life and their impact on various forms of social networks are conducted and used to form a general sociology of the mobile phone.[1] Since these considerations may serve as **indicators for the development of mobile media adoption**, the discussion of the social use of the mobile communication system – next to system characteristics and usage reasons - is another important, demand-oriented element for the analysis of the **strategic options for mobile media provision**. Therefore, this chapter outlines the structural dimensions of mobile communications use in social networks, mobile users identity and community representation within them (C-1) and behavioral dimensions on communication and media consumption patterns that may be reinforced or changed due to mobile communications use (C-2).

The importance of the social use and appropriation of the media is also supported from a historical perspective. MARVIN (1988) and CAREY (1992) argue that the media is never more or less than the history of its uses.[2] Media are "constructed complexes of habits, beliefs, and procedures embedded in elaborate cultural codes of communication."[3] Thus, new media includes the use of new communications technology for old or new purposes, new ways of using old technologies, and new structures of social relations. In order to assess some of these changes and their relevance for mobile media provision, social network analysis and elements of the cultural studies approach are framing considerations about the social use of mobile communications.

---

1   See Geser (2002).
2   See Marvin (1988), p. 8; Carey (1992), p. 70.
3   Marvin (1988), p. 8.

1
Social networks and mobile communications use

Mobile communications is one additional means of communication in social networks. The study of social networks has been identified as new paradigm to describe and analyze **interpersonal relationships in the network society**. CAS-TELLS (1997) describes the rise of the network society that is characterized by a pervasive, interconnected, and diverse media system,[4] which will further develop with portable, ubiquitous, location-sensitive, intercommunicating devices and their instant access possibilities to the media and ICTs.

For further assessment of the role of mobile communications in social networks RHEINGOLD (2002) identifies **three relevant social scientific areas of observations:**
1) on the level of the individual personality, where cognitive and identity-related issues emerge;
2) on the level of society, where values and power structures are influenced; and
3) on the level of immediate social network formation, where place and community issues emerge.[5]

These areas are taken into account in the following discussion of the concepts of identity (C-1.2) and community (C-1.3) in social networks (C-1.1) and their development under the influence of mobile communications.

1.1
Social network analysis

WELLMAN (1996, 2002) suggests that complex social networks emerge as a **dominant form of social organization**. In his view our social systems are developing from hierarchically arranged, bounded groups into network structures.[6] Mobile voice and data communications can influence social network formation and development with regard to the person-centricity of relations (C-1.11) as well as the intensity of relationships in social networks (C-1.12).

1.1.1
Emergence of personalized social networks

The direct connection to a person via a mobile phone not only affects the personalization potentials of mobile media content but also the personal relationships of users. The Internet supports large numbers of transitory relationships in multiple networks. These networks are evolving with the portability of devices, mobility of users, and increasingly personalized services. Together with evo-

---

4   See Castells (1997), p. 1.
5   See Rheingold (2002), p. 25.
6   See Wellman et al. (1996); Wellman (2002); Wellman, Boase, and Chen (2002).

lutions in mobile communications, they shift the emphasis from place-to-place connectivity to **person-to-person connectivity** and emerging personalized social networks.[7] WELLMAN, QUAN-HAASE, BOASE & CHEN (2002) describe what they call a fundamental transformation in the nature of community:

> "This [wireless connectivity] facilitates personalized communication. The person becomes the target of communication. We call a person and not a place. The person is the node to which communication is directed. [...] The person has become the portal. [...] Each person is a switchboard between ties and networks. People remain connected, but as individuals, rather than being rooted in the home bases of work unit and household. Each person operates a separate personal community network and switches rapidly among multiple sub-networks."[8]

Since the definition of presence within a social network becomes uncoupled from location, mobile phones evolve into "portable places of intimacy".[9] Mobile devices enable a form of networked individualism, being in immediate and direct contact with one's social networks and shifting rapidly between them. According to **Reed's Law**, a network that enhances social networks multiplies even more rapidly as the number of different human groups that can use the network.[10]

Reed's law offers a **new focus for media companies** to actively use personalized social networks. When the person becomes the portal and a potential distributor with mobile and ubiquitous forms of communications, the individual audience member receives a greater weight for media companies. This new role of personalized networks can become incorporated in design strategies of mobile media content and services.

1.1.2
Mobile communication relationships in social networks

Person-to-person connectivity can affect the intensity of relationships and the roles users take in social networks. Mobile communications and mobile services allow for **more intensive forms** of social interaction and instrumentality in social networks. Messaging services such as SMS are used for taking part in social activities, to connect, signal and manage membership in social networks.[11] It supports the sharing of experiences and emotions more immediately and allows for the development of stronger in-group ties.[12] Mobile media's capabilities of ubiquitous always-on and on-demand access to information are one element in

---

7   See Wellman (2002), p. 94; Wellman, Boase, and Chen (2002), p. 160.
8   Wellman et al. (2002), pp. 5; 12; 13.
9   Rheingold (2002), p. 4. See also Geser (2002), pp. 36.
10   See Rheingold (2002), p. xv. Reed's law can be seen as an analogy to Moore's law.
11   See Geser (2002), p. 15; Pedersen, Nysveen, and Thorbjørnsen (2003), p. 3.
12   See Ling (2002), p. 21.

this evolving relationship structure of social networks under the influence of mobile communications.

Research on young people's social practices using mobile communications shows that phone-mediated interactions are viewed as **forms of gift giving**.[13] TAYLOR & HARPER (2003) suggest that the design of new media should consider the ceremonial aspects of mobile gift exchanges and related questions on obligations of reciprocity. Exchanging mobile content is a **means to express relationships in social networks**; it demonstrates ties or rivalries among peers. Mobile communication becomes a legitimate and morally sanctioned mechanism through which young people manage their relationships.[14] Mobile media offers should consider these gift giving exchanges in their mobile content design.

Mobile communications also increases users' opportunities to demonstrate participation in several social networks **maintaining different roles**.[15] When taking a role becomes independent from a person's physical presence at a specific place, previously sequential role involvement can evolve into diachronic role engagement.[16] Mobile media, in that regard, can support users to **meet their information needs** while switching and in order to manage the roles they are taking.

The frequency of contact when relationships and roles are managed and maintained more intensely and the existence of a ubiquitous communications network that supports to be in perpetual contact with (personal) social networks do not invariably mean that there is more or **better discourse and understanding** between social network members. MYERSON (2001) argues that, to the contrary, mobile communications achievements contrast with understanding and discourse. He uses concepts of Habermas and Heidegger in order to discuss the **shortcomings of mobile communications for personal relationships**.

Under the assumption that the vision of a mobile society is about instant, ubiquitous access to exactly the right information to suit immediate needs, mobile communications supports the **acceleration of people's pursuit of their individual goals**. Myerson argues that Habermas' notion of communicative rationality, on the other hand, is not about the competitive pursuit of the individual's own aims and interests, but about the achievement of shared understanding.[17] Understanding, according to Habermas, is the key to true communication; communicative action is the use of language with an orientation to reaching understanding.[18] Mobile communications, however, supports people's communication for the purpose of satisfying other wants. Yet, in Habermas' distinction between pursuing a goal and seeking to communicate, communication means to make a desire understood, not to pursue its immediate fulfillment.[19] Mobile

---

13   See Taylor and Harper (2003).
14   See Taylor and Harper (2003), p. 24.
15   See Pedersen, Nysveen, and Thorbjørnsen (2003), p. 16; Meckel (2005).
16   See Geser (2002), p. 15; Groebel (2005).
17   See Habermas (1995), pp. 28. Habermas distinguishes 'communicative rationality' from 'instrumental rationality', which aims at pursuing a goal.
18   See Habermas (1995), pp. 385; Myerson (2001), p. 23.
19   See Myerson (2001), p. 27.

communications as an exchange of messages lacks the engagement with meaning and ultimately understanding as well according to Habermas. Mobilization then only seeks to improve ordinary (imperfect) communication by **giving it new channels and speeding up the response time.**[20]

Along similar lines, Myerson argues that Heidegger's understanding of communication as a discourse is not met by mobile communications, either.[21] Discourse, in opposition to talk, is in Heidegger's view the way we articulate the intelligibility of being-in-the-world.[22] It is not for the purpose of transmitting messages or getting things done more effectively.

As a consequence, mobile communications' **intensification of communication and messaging in social networks** does not have to invariably be evaluated positively nor does more communication necessarily lead to better communication. This view is also compatible with SILVERSTONE's (2003) argument that **connectedness is not to be confused with closeness.**[23] For mobile media, one potential consequence from this perceived superficiality may be that a broad variety of mobile content is better suited than in-depth content in order to handle many different roles and situations.

1.2
Mobile identity in social networks

TURKLE (1998) suggests that using new technologies always has subjective effects and can change the perception we have of our identity.[24] The use of the mobile phone has evolved from emergency use to routine cases and from specific instrumental to more expressive communications.[25] There is an increase in **socio-emotional functions of mobile communications** that affects the way we perceive and present ourselves in social networks. Identity representation in social networks is one dimension which is affected by mobile communications (C-1.21). It will be argued that mobile communications can support self-identity as conceptualized by GIDDEN'S (1991) and can add to narratives of the self (C-1.22). These observations are essential for the media due to their relevance in the formation of social identities, social relations, and communities.[26]

---

20 See Myerson (2001), p. 50.
21 See Heidegger (1962), p. 204, quoted after Myerson (2001), p. 57.
22 See Heidegger (1962), p. 204, quoted after Myerson (2001), p. 71.
23 See Silverstone (2004), pp.381. This argument is part of his concept of 'proper distance' which is depicted in the cited article.
24 See Turkle (1998), p. 376.
25 See Geser (2002), p. 9.
26 Even from an anthropological point of view mass media are at once cultural artifacts, social activities, aesthetic forms, and historical developments where issues of control over self-representation and expression arise, see Spitulnik (1993).

multiple and collective identities and mobile communications use

ɪne concept of identity in mobile environments contrasts with identity concepts that are developed for virtual worlds of the Internet. In MUDs and chat rooms, users are playing and experimenting with their identities. They use **multiple identities** and representations that are shielded by the (perceived) anonymity the Internet can offer. TURKLE (1998) analyzes the creation of identity in the culture of simulation. She observes that the boundaries of the real and the virtual, the alive and the inanimate, the unified and the multiple selves are blurring in the patterns of everyday life. In real time communities of the cyberspace, users create their multiple selves by moving at the threshold between the real and the virtual.[27] Users create and experiment with their selves in different windows, embracing different roles and different genders and seamlessly move between these identities. Identity as a repertoire of different roles has existed before the emergence of the Internet. However, social groups in real life can exert stricter controls and this can make fast role changing more difficult. In cyberspace, taking multiple virtual identities is connected with less effort.

In mobile communications, role changing is becoming easier as well. Yet, the mobile identity is very closely related to the real world identity. Therefore, Turkle's concept of multiple identities is not very suited to describe identity formation and management in mobile communication. Mobile communications and its use have a lot to do with self-perception and influence on how others should perceive the self. GIDDEN'S (1991) concept of **self-identity** proves to be a useful approach for the analysis of the socio-psychological phenomena that are connected to the **mobile identity**. In his concept of self-identity, the self is reflexively understood by the individual in terms of his or her biography. The identity of the self has to be routinely created and sustained in the reflexive activities of the individual.[28] A person's identity, therefore, is not to be found in behavior nor in the reactions of others, but in the capacity to keep a particular narrative going.

Another identity concept, the **collective identity**, that emerged from the analysis of the network society and that focuses on national identities is not as well suited to the context of mobile communications. CASTELLS' (1997) notion of identity is the process of the construction of meaning on the basis of a cultural attribute or a related set of cultural attributes.[29] He also argues that identities involve a process of self-construction and individuation, however in the context of distinguishing identity from roles and role sets; identities are stronger sources of meaning than roles. In the network society, meaning is organized around a

---

27 See Turkle (1998), pp. 10.
28 See Giddens (1991), pp. 52. Earlier sociological research on the social construction of the self include Mead (1934); Goffman (1959). Also in consumer behavior research the self-expressive use of brands is used as an explanatory concept of consumer attitudes and product consumption, based on the brand's personality associations and self and situation congruity, see Aaker (1997); Reed II (2002).

primary identity that is self-sustaining across time and space; the focus of Castells' formulation of identity is hereby collective rather than individual identity.[30]

CASTELLS (1997) questions Giddens theoretical characterization of identity-building in the network society. He argues that identity grows from communal resistance as new primacy of identity politics in the network society. However, the systematic disjunction between the local and the global in the network society is not as present in mobile communications situations as in Internet communications; the identity construction process as described by Giddens can therefore shed interesting light on the phenomena of mobile identities.

Self-identity is an interesting concept in the discussion of mobile communications, because mobile communications' use can offer means to support the **creation of narratives**. The mobile communication behavior of youth illustrates the construction of self-narratives. As we will see, SMS communication behavior, for example, shows evidence of the strong correlation of identity representation among peers and friends. As mobile media evolves, more advanced content applications may take similar roles. Figure C-1 gives an overview of mobile identity aspects and their potential implications for mobile media. They will be discussed in the following chapters.

1.2.2
Mobile communications supported narratives of the self

Elements from the concept of self-identity such as the creation of narratives of the self can be used to analyze the socio-psychological phenomena that are connected with a mobile identity construct. Self-identity is constituted by the **reflexive ordering of self-narratives**. Narratives of the self are stories by means of which self-identity is reflexively understood, both by the individual concerned and by others.[31] Mediated experience is influencing both self-identity and the organization of social relations. SILVERSTONE & HADDON (1998) argue that it is media and ICTs' distinctively reflexive role in everyday life to display who and what we are through the involvement in consumption.[32] Therefore, also mobile communications' use is related to self-perception and to **influence on how others**

---

29 See Castells (1997), p. 6. Castells differentiates three processes of identity building in the network society that lead to different outcomes in constituting societies: legitimizing identity generates a civil society; identity for resistance leads to the formation of communities; and project identity produces subjects. The main potential source of social change in the network society may lie in project identities that are constructed around collective agents of social transformation, see Castells (1997), pp. 67.

30 See Castells (1997), p. 7. In virtual communities, the choice of names may give some evidence that collective identities are not as important as the individual identity. Nicknames as essential part of the personality and the reputation in a virtual community are often chosen in relation to an aspect of the self or related to the medium, but seldomly related to collectives such as nationalities, see Bechar-Israeli (1995). For our further discussion, the individual identity will, thus, be focused.

31 See Giddens (1991), pp. 243; Mason-Schrock suggests that narrative constructions of a 'true self' by transsexuals may provide resources for fashionable plausible self-narratives, see Mason-Schrock (1996).

32 See Silverstone and Haddon (1998), p. 64.

Aspects of the self-identity (Giddens, 1991)		Aspects of the mobile identity	Potential implications for mobile media
Creation of self-narrative	Reflexively understood by individual	• SMS and MMS as means for identity expression • Performative value of mobile phones	• Mobile media content as social currency
	Social network narrative	• Importance of personal and direct relations within core members of the social network • Mobile 'gift exchange' via SMS and MMS	• Mobile media content as means to demonstrate membership
Life politics	Lifestyle representation	• Linguistic characteristics express membership and demonstrate intimateness	• Mobile media brand community around involving content • Mobile user typologies segmented via lifestyle criteria
	Dilemmas of the self	• Role management and social etiquette in public spaces	• Importance of variety of mobile media over depth of mobile content to handle potential dilemmas of the self

Figure C-1: Aspects of the mobile identity and potential implications for mobile media use

should perceive the self. COHEN & WAKEFIELD (2003) argue that mobile phones as objects that are carried on or near the body become closely involved with the process of self-conscious display; they interpret, for instance, incorporating a digital camera into the personal object sphere as a **remake of the self in day-to-day life.**

The influence of (mediated) communications on self and external perception is also supported by previous communications research. WATZLAWICK, BEAVIN, BAVELAS & JACKSON (1967) formulate in a **tentative axiom of communication** that any communication implies a commitment and thereby defines the relationship between the communicants. This means that a communication not only conveys information, but it also imposes behavior at the same time, and it is a statement about self perception, perception of the other and perception of the other's perception of oneself.[33] In 1959 GOFFMAN observed that people even **improvise public performances** as a way of constructing an identity.[34] In the case of mobile communications, some mobile phone users exploit the presence of third parties as an opportunity to display themselves by **stage phoning,** e.g. to captive audiences in trains.[35] The public display of mobile phone use can also fulfill other social functions such as legitimizing solitude.[36] The **performative value of the**

---

33   See Watzlawick, Beavin Bavelas, and Jackson (1967), pp. 51.
34   See Goffman (1959).
35   See Plant (2000), p. 49.

mobile phone suggests that mobile media content and services should enable some elements of public demonstration.[37] MMS-based services can offer more potential in this regard than current SMS due to its picture and moving image capabilities. PEDERSEN, NYSVEEN & THORBJØRNSEN (2003) show that multimedia messaging services influence identity expression; according to their study results the adoption of MMS is also more influenced by expressiveness and enjoyment than usefulness.[38] This sheds some light on the social character of MMS. When MMS become a more frequently used messaging means for media companies, MMS may be able to deliver where WAP failed, because they allow for more emotional rather than instrumental use due to the **power of images**[39].

Other research on the adoption of mobile services in everyday life contexts emphasizes the importance of **non-utilitarian motivational factors** in mobile service adoption and use.[40] In particular, the motive of self-expression seems to influence service adoption.[41] The analysis of mobile messaging behavior offers first insights into the construction of self-identity. The empirical evidence on mobile communications use is limited; a number of studies, often based on ethnographic research, have been conducted on SMS communication and messaging behavior, but hypotheses are often based on anecdotal evidence. However, in order to set the path for the development of a **sociology of the mobile phone** GESER (2002) suggests that a preliminary synthesis of research on SMS behavior may be fruitful for more generalized theoretical arguments.[42]

In a study on SMS behavior of young people between the ages of 14 and 18, HOEFLICH, STEUBER & ROESSLER (2000) find that SMS messages play a more important role for young people than mobile voice messages or e-mail. First results give evidence of

1) the preeminence of personal and direct communications over mobility as a reason to use mobile communications, and
2) the importance of the self-identity in existing social networks.

Ad 1: The first argument is supported by results that identify **home as the location where SMS communication is often initiated**, a finding that underscores the influence of personalization over the benefits of mobility for mobile communications usage.[43] A supportive argument for the importance of the 'real' instead of virtual identity is that most SMS communication is often conducted within **small groups of people** that already belong to the social network of a person. The exchange of SMS is usually reduced to a core set of people. Numbers in studies

---

36   Plant (2000), p. 42.
37   See Taylor and Harper (2003), p. 29.
38   See Pedersen, Nysveen, and Thorbjørnsen (2003).
39   See Frey (1999).
40   See Leung and Wei (2000); Cohen and Wakeford (2003). Leung & Wei identify the gratifications of mobile phones to be 'fashion/status', 'affection/sociability', 'relaxation', 'mobility', 'immediate access', 'instrumentality', and 'reassurance'. Domestication research presents similar findings, but stresses the importance of self-expressiveness.
41   See Pedersen and Nysveen (2003).
42   See Geser (2002), p. 8.
43   See Hoeflich (2001).

range from predominantly one to three regular SMS exchange partners,[44] often partner and best friend, usually not family members.[45] Research on the sociology of the (fixed-line) telephone already revealed that the telephone is mainly used to care for relationships to already known people and within the geographical neighborhood.[46] Moreover, SMS communication often resembles **quasi-oral communications**. The beginning and ending formulas of SMS are rather short or they do not exist at all, neither in dialogic SMS exchange nor in initial contact SMS sending.[47] This further suggests that mobile communication and messaging relationships are kept with a known set of people. Caller IDs can also give evidence of the sender when they are already stored in the receiver's handset.

Ad 2: Contributions to narratives of the self that individuals offer as part of their self-awareness and self-description to third parties may be found in the choice of linguistic aspects of SMS communications. In mobile messaging, **linguistic characteristics** are a form of meta communication and a means of relationship management. This is due to the utilization of graphostilistic means such as smileys; hybridizations of written and oral language; different syntax conventions, e.g. consequent use of lower-case letters; and ellipses, e.g. the colloquial deletion of vowels or verbs.[48] **User-created communication genres** of abbreviations and shared content creation are used to express social and personal identity in social networks. Multimedia messaging with its ability to include pictures and short audio and video clips is providing users with even more means to create messages and content in form of specific communication genres on mobile devices for identity expression.[49]

In sum, mobile communications is a **powerful reminder of connectedness** within social networks;[50] mobile messaging behavior, the choice of people it is directed at, as well as its linguistic nature provide the first insights into the possible processes of self-narration and self-identity construction. With the advent of more mobile media options, new media-related pieces offer opportunities to become integrated in the messaging exchange processes of mobile users. KELLY (2005) underlines the role of mobile content and services as 'social currency', especially in youth culture.[51] Implications for the design of mobile content and services include that they have elements of self-expression to give users access to social capital by using mobile services.

44   See Schlobinski et al. (2001), p. 28; Rheingold (2002), p. 5.
45   See Hoeflich, Steuber, and Roessler (2000), p. 11.
46   See Dordick (1989), p. 226; Lange (1989a), p. 37. This is also suggested to be a difference to e-mailing which is more often addressed to formerly unknown people, see Duerscheid (2002); however, Wellman acknowledges the importance of local mail with people living within a 50km radius that complements telephone and face-to-face contact, see Wellman, Boase, and Chen (2002), p. 92.
47   See Schlobinski et al. (2001), p. 23; Doering (2002); Duerscheid (2002), p. 17.
48   See Schlobinski et al. (2001); Doering (2002).
49   See Pedersen, Nysveen, and Thorbjørnsen (2003).
50   See Geser (2002), p. 10.
51   See Kelly (2005).

1.2.3
Life politics and mobile communications

The discussion of mobile phone handset personalization (see B-1.21) and the success of ringtone and screen saver download (see A-1.21) already give indications that lifestyle is an essential dimension in mobile media use. The lifestyle component is also essential in Gidden's argumentation on life politics.

GIDDENS (1991) arguments on self-identity result in the concept of **life politics** that he defines as a politics of choice and a politics of lifestyle. He describes a lifestyle as a more or less integrated set of practices which an individual embraces, not only because such practices fulfill utilitarian needs, but because they give **material form to a particular narrative of self-identity**.[52] The narrative of self-identity has to be shaped, altered and reflexively sustained in relation to rapidly changing circumstances of social life. The openness of social life today and the pluralization of contexts make lifestyle choices increasingly important in the constitution of self-identity.[53] MCLUHAN (2001) sees clothing already as an extension of the skin and as a means of defining the self socially.[54] Mobile phones as an intrinsic part of young people's lifestyles can, thus, be viewed as an extension of the self as well.

For teenagers, the search for identity is a key aspect of their lives. The need for autonomy, identity, and a sense of belonging are related to the way they explain their fashion tastes, from clothes over music to sports preferences.[55] The mobile phone as a fashion accessory is becoming an essential element in the identity construction in the distinct teenage lifestyle. Also among college students, new technology is a fashion or status statement; the adoption of new media technologies can project certain social identities. New media technologies are used to make status distinction and to **express membership in well-defined status groups**.[56] In their analysis of gratifications of pager use, LEUNG & WEI (1998) find sociability the strongest intrinsic motive. An essential characteristic of the adopters is that they want to make a statement of being stylish and fashionable, and they want to feel connected to their peer networks.[57] Icons and ring-tones to physically personalize mobile phones are also meant to be displayed and to **demonstrate membership and status in social networks**.[58]

Young people as one particular mobile communications (socio-demographic) user segment also serve as **lead users** for mobile data communications in many ways. FUNK (2001) argues that Japan is so far ahead of the West concerning mobile data use, because Japanese mobile operators have focused on young peo-

---

52 See Giddens (1991), p. 81. Giddens acknowledges that lifestyle choices tend to be segmental for the individual; a lifestyle sector concerns a time-space 'slice' of an individual's overall activities, see Giddens (1991).
53 See Giddens (1991), p. 5.
54 See McLuhan (2001), p. 119.
55 See Wee (1999).
56 See Leung (1998); Tuomi (2002), p. 18.
57 See Leung and Wei (1998).
58 See Rheingold (2002), p. 26.

ple as their main target group from the very beginning whereas mobile operators in Europe and the US first targeted business customers (see A-2.32). From the perspective of the history of the telephone, this assumption seemed to be a natural analogy: early adopters of the telephone tended to be commercial and professional communities that adopted the new means of communication.[59] However, in the mobile (voice) communications market there is a very high diffusion of **new groups of customers who were previously underserved or non-existent** – young people with personal access to communications that limits parental control. Their needs and demands for mobile data communications may be very different from those of business customers which makes extrapolations from the past rather uncertain. The politics of choice and the politics of lifestyle may, therefore, play a more important role, indeed.

The **lifestyle variable** as a central element in consumption decisions is also acknowledged by consumer and media research. Lifestyle is subsumed as a subcategory of psychographic consumer segmentation criteria that attracts interest among consumer researchers. In a move toward an experiential view of consumer research the lifestyle concept includes more explicit considerations on the symbolic, hedonic, and aesthetic criteria of consumption.[60] Media companies, e.g. TV channels, already use lifestyle as a segmentation criteria in order to build **audience typologies.**[61]

However, lifestyle choices can impose difficulties on mobile customers as well. The narrative of the self-identity is inherently fragile in an environment with changing meanings of distance and location and with central importance allocated to the mediated experience. Giddens analyzes the involved tensions and difficulties by understanding them as **dilemmas of the self.**[62]

- The *unification versus fragmentation dilemma* concerns protecting and reconstructing the narrative of self-identity in the face of diversifying contexts of interaction. Mobile communications enforces the fragmentation process, because mobile users can take different roles in a given context, e.g. taking a private call in a business situation or vice versa.
- The *powerlessness versus appropriation dilemma* describes the individual who experiences feelings of powerlessness in time-space distanciations of the social universe. Mobile communications may have counteractive effects, because it tends to provide more power in local activities and mediated experiences within the time-space distanciations of social networks. On the other hand, LING (2002) argues that "forced eavesdropping"[63] may threaten the identity when the forced eavesdroppers feel embarrassment for others, based

59 See Aronson (1981), p. 28; de Sola Pool et al. (1981), p. 131; Silverstone critically remarks that early adopters are individuals with a clearly defined personal agenda when it comes to new technologies. What they may see as exciting hard- or software can be reasons for dissatisfaction with later users, see Silverstone and Haddon (1998), p. 57.
60 See Holbrook and Hirschmann (1982).
61 See Hartmann and Neuwoehner (1999).
62 See Giddens (1991), pp. 187.
63 Ling (2002), p. 8; Geser speaks of the 'colonization' of public space and institutional settings by private communication, see Geser (2002), pp. 42.

on the reflexive process of identification with the soon to be embarrassed person.
- The *authority versus uncertainty dilemma* describes circumstances in which there are no final authorities and the reflexive project of the self must steer the way between commitment and uncertainty. Mobile communications tends to also support choices in the absence of a final authority, because the communications network can be used to mobilize social network resources. Due to a lack of collectively developed routines the complexity of managing two sets of social contexts during private conversations in public spaces can impose uncertainty and discomfort on a person.[64]
- The *personalized versus commodified experience dilemma* is influenced by the standardizing effects of commodity capitalism. Processes of individuation have to be understood in light of the struggles against the commodified influences. Mobile content has potential to support this process of individuation, for example when the public demonstration of mobile content serves as a means to show identification with a media brand.

The lifestyle aspect that is anchored in Gidden's concept of life politics has been the focus of this chapter. Mobile communications adds new dimensions to the politics of choice and of lifestyle that can be experienced both as an enriching component as well as a contribution to dilemmas of the self. Within this **portfolio of lifestyle choices of consumers**, mobile media contents and services can become an additional piece.

1.3
Mobile communities in social networks

Although mobile voice, messaging, and media strengthens the self-identity construction, the **meaning and feedback on self-narratives of identity unfold in communities**. TAYLOR & HARPER (2001; 2003) find that particularly young people use mobile phones to demonstrate participation in social networks and communities and to **define the boundaries of their social networks**.[65] A certain linguistic subculture for mobile messaging can, for instance, be used as 'restricted code'.[66] Concerning the relationship of new communication technologies and communities TUOMI (2002) argues that knowledge and meaning of technology is grounded in communities that reproduce existing social practice.[67] In his argument, new communities and new technological practices can emerge based on **increasing specialization or on combinations of existing** resources. Media companies that form imagined communities around their content and serve as community platforms for users on the Internet may use both re-combinations of re-

---

64 See Ling (2002), p. 20.
65 See Taylor and Harper (2001); Taylor and Harper (2003).
66 See Geser (2002), p. 14.
67 See Tuomi (2002), p. 6.

sources as well as increased content specialization to reach out further to their audiences and community members.

For the discussion of mobile communities the changing nature of community is of particular interest. It is one out of three aspects that INNIS (1951) identifies for changes in communication technology on culture: (1) altering the structure of interests (the things thought about), (2) changing the character of symbols (the things thought with), and (3) changing the nature of community (the arena in which thought developed).[68] Mobile communities can apply to different arenas, from communities of interest to communities of peers (C-1.31), and they can allow for a new form of ad hoc formation (C-1.32) which may evolve into a **community management option for media companies.**

1.3.1
Communities of peers and communities of interest

Mobile communities can unite anonymous members that share a common interest or they can equip an existing community of peers with new communication tools (see Figure C-2). BRINT (2002) offers a very useful **reconstruction of the community concept** that can be used to distinguish mobile community types. Brint's typology is based on identifying structurally distinct subtypes of community using a small number of partitioning variables. The existential basis of relationship among community members divides geographic and choice-based communities. For mobile communications this is an important distinction, because many mobile communities, unlike virtual communities on the Web, can be tied to location. However, even more interesting is the second partition in Brint's model that depicts the primary reason for interaction and differentiates **activity-based and belief-based communities.**[69] Members of activity-based groups share a common interest. Mobile communities around celebrities can serve as a good example for activity-based mobile communities that are characterized by rather weak ties.[70] Belief-based groups, on the other hand, are **communities of peers** or 'imagined communities' in which members are not in face-to-face contact with each other. Mobile buddy lists may serve as an example for belief-based mobile communities. They generally exert a stronger pressure on members to participate in the community and to conform to prescribed norms and values.

Whereas members in belief-based mobile communities may place emphasis on the exchange of self-generated content, **activity-based mobile communities can become organized by media companies** around those media brands that accomplish to raise high involvement with their audience.

---

68   Quoted from Carey (1992), p. 160.
69   See Brint (2001), pp. 10.
70   Peer-to-peer communities can be classified as activity-based communities. In the Napster community, for instance, the personality representations comprised information about the connection type as a basis for other users to make a value judgment; it often contained wrong information about the connection type in order to discourage other users from downloading, see Poblocki (2001). The weak ties between members pose specific challenges to (mobile) community management due free-riding problems, see Adar and Huberman (2000); Feldmann (2005b).

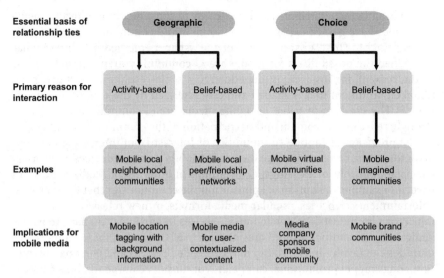

Figure C-2: Activity- and belief-based mobile communities

As mobile communications becomes a new communication form for existing social networks such as personal relationships or community media, geographic proximity increases in importance as compared to online communities where the independence of location of community members is among the defining characteristics.[71] **Location-based information retrieval and creation,** for example tagging locations with remarks and comments, can provide personal relevance, in particular if the people who are posting the information are known and trusted sources. **Mobile buddy lists** have been referred to as closed mobile community models between friends who trust the recommendations of their peers as opposed to anyone else.[72] Distinguishing criteria of mobile communities of peers may be described as concentrated in space, with relatively frequent interaction, and a significant amount of face-to-face contact.[73] As a consequence, the ties between community members can be a lot stronger than in (online) communities of interest.

In communities of interest, relationships can develop on the basis of shared interests;[74] they often evolve around brands. **Brand communities** are specialized, non-geographically bound communities, based on a structured set of social relations among admirers of a brand.[75] They support the social construc-

---

71 On community media under the influence of online communities see for example Hollander (2000).
72 See France et al. (2001).
73 These variables are among a list of subtypes of communities developed by Brint (2001). As such, mobile communities of peers come close to characteristics of Durkheim's conceptualization of communities that feature among other variables dense and demanding social ties, small group size, and perceptions of similarity with expressive style and way of life.
74 See Hoeflich (1995); Wellman et al. (1996).

brands and contribute to a broadening of consumer brand loyalty. Media
nies have gained expertise in building brand communities around their
content since the first subscriber base of a newspaper emerged. The Internet has
broadened the possibilities for **media brand community management**. Online
media content, for instance, is embedded in a social, economic, and organizational environment that is shaped and characterized by the community members.[76] The creation of value in online media brand communities, therefore,
strongly relies on the content and participation of the community members.

The provision of mobile communities of interest is an interesting development for media companies since the use of mobile personal devices allow users
a deepening involvement with specific groups of other users. Media companies
have, for example, the option to **sponsor mobile communities** that form around
entertainment celebrities, popular media formats, or new releases in the book,
music, or film industries. Mobile music services in particular manage to gather
dedicated communities around music and artists. Content in these mobile communities can involve music gossip news, song dedications and personal interaction, song snippet promotional campaigns, or music recommendations from favorite artists. Media companies can **outsource the mobile community management** to application service providers who are entering the mobile marketing
markets as new players. In the US, the new player Upoc forms mobile communities of interest in Manhattan.[77] In Upoc's model there are three distinct ways in
setting up a mobile community, secret, private, or public. Whereas private
groups can restrict memberships and secret groups are not even listed and only
known to their members, public groups can be sponsored by (media) companies. The incentives for the community members to opt into these communities
are free mobile content such as alerts, ring-tones, or coupons for purchasing at
certain locations. Media companies, on the other hand, use the mobile community as **promotional platform** and in part as a new market research tool to reach
targeted audience members. With regard to the common rejection of telephone
direct marketing in the US, however, mobile market research ambitions should
be evaluated and used very carefully, if at all.

Mobile communities of interest exert weaker ties on their members than mobile communities of peers. Yet, one way to expand their scope may become the
strategic use of the social networks of the community members. Media companies who have interest in distributing their mobile promotional contents can
take advantage of mobile communities when they make their mobile contents
available for sharing between mobile devices and when they provide messaging
opportunities for comments so that mobile customers can use **mobile content as
part of their self-identity construction** within their social networks.

---

75   See Muniz and O'Guinn (2001).
76   See Hummel and Lechner (2001).
77   See Rheingold (2002), pp. 165.

1.3.2
Mobile ad hoc community formation

Mobile communications also enables a new model of community formation that takes advantage of **physical proximity and ubiquitous connectedness** to information and communication infrastructure and that influences social etiquette as well as public social and political participation.

Mobile ad hoc social networks are a new form of communities made possible by the combination of computation, communication, reputation, and location-awareness. The notion of mobile ad hoc information systems describes a decentralized and self-organizing network of autonomous mobile devices that interact as peers based on physical proximity.[78] Personal area networks are a special class of ad hoc networks and a potential sphere for the formation of mobile ad hoc communities when mobile devices will take part in people's everyday social interactions. "**Impromptu collaboration**"[79] can arise at the intersection of these technological advances that may promote social relationships among co-located persons during chance encounters. The social context of mobile ad hoc communities is different from online communities because of the short distances of the **community members who are aware of each other.** Time becomes a critical resource in an ad hoc community, too, due to requirements of physical presence and challenges of unexpected interruptions.

In such a model, the **personal media sphere** can become an element of an ad hoc self-organizing mesh network within geographic proximity and provide as well as receive Internet connectivity.[80] Mobile devices could not only share bandwidth but also content and messages. However, automatic exchange of data raises complex issues of privacy and trust. It would require some kind of distributed reputation system as well as a system that prevents spying and monitoring or gaining access to confidential personal data. The design of ad hoc communities, therefore, has to consider how to reward access rights to data and functionality or to group entities such as a set of individuals who are friends.[81]

RHEINGOLD (2002) describes some social applications of mobile ad hoc networking. His notion of '**smart mobs**' refers to swarming tactics enabled by mobile phones that support the coordination of dispersed groups. Loosely linked networks distribute alerts, forward messages, even webcast digital video. Individual group members remain dispersed until mobile communications draws them to converge on a specific location from all directions. Wireless communications and mobile social networks have been used particularly in **urban political conflict.** These network-structured communications hold potential for both enabling democratic forms of decision-making, but also malevolent out-

---

78 See Kortuem et al. (2001).
79 Kortuem et al. (2001), p. 3.
80 See Rheingold (2002), pp. 170; Proem, for example, is a peer-to-peer computing platform for mobile ad hoc networks that enables face-to-face collaboration, see Kortuem (2002). 7DS is a peer-to-peer sharing system that enables the exchange of data among peers that are not connected to the Internet, e.g. for caching popular content, see Papadopouli and Schulzrinne (2001).
81 See Kortuem (2002); Reichwald, Fremuth, and Ney (2002).

comes.[82] The **role of the media** in such cooperative action may be to change the threshold for collective action by information exchanges that may affect the either-or decision to join a collective action.[83]

2
Communication and media consumption patterns and mobile communications use

Mobile communications not only influences the structure and different relationship layers of social networks; it also affects communication patterns and it may affect media consumption patterns. The way mobile communications is appropriated into everyday life (C-2.1) poses new questions on the areas of tension between habituation and impulsiveness (C-2.2), it reorganizes relationships with regard to power and control (C-2.3), and it enables innovative, decentralized uses that may drive innovation processes from a bottom-up rather than a top-down approach (C-2.4).

According to CAREY (1992), communication studies must answer how changes in communication technology influence what we can concretely create and apprehend.[84] The social process needs to be examined, wherein symbolic forms are created, apprehended, and used. **Cultural studies theory as a theoretical framework** thereby reflects the use and contents of media in the light of the conditions of everyday life at the micro-level of personal and household experience. It contradicts technological determinism, but looks for clues to the future of communication in social and cultural fundamentals and trends.[85]

2.1
Appropriation of mobile communications into everyday life

The mobilization of the phone is not only a technological process, but more importantly a cultural one. Technology diffusion is the aggregate outcome of individual choices to adopt new technologies. This can be described as a social and cultural process with an emphasis on appropriation in everyday life.[86] In this sense, the cultural studies tradition emphasizes **media use as a reflection of a particular socio-cultural context** and as a process of giving meaning to cultural products and experiences in everyday life. Cultural studies do not attempt to predict human behavior; rather they attempt to diagnose human meanings.[87]

---

82 See Rheingold (2002), pp. 158.
83 See Rheingold (2002), p. 175.
84 See Carey (1992), p. 31.
85 See McQuail (1999), p. 14.
86 See for example Beck (1989); Silverstone and Haddon (1998); McQuail (2000), pp. 367; Myerson (2001), p. 7; Mansell and Steinmueller (2002), p. 104.
87 See Carey (1992), p. 56; Carey distinguishes cultural studies from Max Weber's notion of 'cultural science' which attempts to provide a phenomenology of industrial science and an analysis of the patterns of dominance and authority typical of such societies. The term studies is more humble than the term science that includes not only taxonomic senses in the interpretation of Thomas Kuhn, but also honorific senses that may confuse the analysis, see Carey (1992), p. 96.

The objectives of cultural studies are, thus, to understand the meanings ¬ dience members have placed on media experience in the process of si¬. specific media use.[88]

It has been argued that the assessment of the social use of mobile communications may be best analyzed with the **uses and gratifications approach**.[89] It focuses on the question of what functions different media types such as the newspaper or television fulfill in the consumers' personal life; in other words it asks what people do with the media ('active audience'), contrasting the previous media effect research paradigm that asked what the media does to the people. BERG & KIEFER (1996) name **five functional uses of media brands**: information, entertainment, education, consultation, and aesthetic enjoyment. Complementary categories drawn from the uses- and-gratifications research comprise identity-formation, social cohesion and integration, and social interaction that can be further distinguished into relaxation, fantasy inspiration, habituation, or escapism.[90] Uses and gratifications studies have been extended to analyze diverse technologies and services such as telephone,[91] VCR,[92] e-mail,[93] online media,[94] pager,[95] and mobile phones.[96] **Unique gratifications that have been found for mobile phone use** are 'fashion/status' and 'immediate access'. However, the uses and gratifications approach assumes that audience members know about the uses and gratifications of the media. Yet, there is no way to verify independently whether these perceived motivations and gratifications apply or not. Functionalist theory is, therefore, often criticized because of its circularity. Moreover, audience motivational theory provides formal models - such as the expectancy-value model of media gratifications sought and obtained -, but it is not easy to translate into a sharp **empirical tool**.[97]

Doubts about the contributions that this approach can deliver have already been cast in relation to online usage and can be applied to mobile communications use as well. TASCHE (1999), for example, questions whether the uses and

---

88 See Carey (1992), pp. 60; McQuail (2000), p. 367. The inability to comprehend what others are saying is, according to Carey, the imperative failure of modern social sciences.

89 See Leung and Wei (2000); for the rationale of uses and gratifications research see Katz & Foulkes (1962), p. 377, quoted after Jaeckel (1999), p. 71; Blumler and Katz (1974); Elliott (1974); Rosengren (1974). Palmgreen (1985) differentiates three phases of gratifications research, the operationalization phase which describes orientation, relief, and entertainment functions of the media; a transition phase in which an insufficient differentiation of individual and aggregate functions is criticized; and an establishment phase that integrates gratifications research with behavioral intention, see Palmgreen (1985). The uses-and-gratification approach is also accused of finalism. The subsequent paradigm shift and the development of the dynamic-transactional approach derives from the intention to replace the finalistic gratifications research and the causal media effect theory, see Frueh and Schoenbach (1982).

90 See McQuail (2000), p. 387.

91 See Nobe (1989).

92 See Rubin and Bantz (1989).

93 See Dimmick, Kline, and Stafford (2000).

94 See Lin (2002).

95 See Leung and Wei (1998).

96 See Leung and Wei (2000).

97 See McQuail (2000), pp. 78; 390. McQuail acknowledges that from the point of view of audience theory the uses and gratifications research has shed light on the nature of audience demands and is helpful for providing the media with guidelines for developing new media services, see McQuail (2000), pp.373.

gratifications approach is sustainable for explanations of online usage. He also quotes the **danger of circularity in gratifications research** where the perceptions of needs and their satisfaction depend on asking questions to the same individual. Also, factors of social desirability and the assumption that users are conscious about the motives for media usage contribute to his doubts.

Research on **new users' perceptions of the applicability of mobile communications** to their life supports the doubts that they may know best about uses and gratifications of a new medium. It is very common that users anticipate instrumental reasons, for instance safety reasons or business-related reasons, as motives for the adoption of communication technology. However, both the landline telephone as well as the mobile phone are widely used for purposes of sociability.[98] PALEN, SALZMAN & YOUNGS (2000) find in their empirical research that new users typically have a **poor understanding of how mobile telephony works and how it affects activities and communication practices.**[99] Therefore, the cultural studies approach is preferred for the following discussion of mobile communications appropriation and its potential consequences for mobile media use.

2.2
Impulsive use of habituation patterns

The space-time related characteristics of the mobile communications system (see B-3.11; B-3.12) allow for impulsiveness that, on first sight, may contradict the largely habituated use of the media (C-2.21). However, **impulsive access to trusted sources of information and entertainment** may serve new audience needs (C-2.22).

2.2.1
Habituation patterns in media use

Time budgets that users dedicate to different media channels are always changing to some extent. Yet, media use is anchored in daily routines and habituated consumption patterns.[100] **Media time budgets** for traditional media display relatively stable patterns of use. In Germany, for example, the time budgets that the average user spends on print and broadcast media offers has remained similar over the past decade with some shifts towards a heavier usage of television and radio.[101] The time spent online, however, is increasing. Users spent 107 minutes per day online in 2001 versus 76 minutes per day in 1997.[102] Hereby, users often visit online media presences of established offline media brands, because they

---

98 See Fischer (1992); Geser (2002), p. 8.
99 See Palen, Salzman, and Youngs (2000).
100 Media use is the individual allocation of time to a media. It can be differentiated into point of time, time budget, and content, see Wilke (1992), p. 257. Beyond the issue how much time people spend on and with the media a problem is to ascertain depth of use, see Stempel III and Stewart (2000), p. 544. On the process of habit formation see Wathieu (1997).
101 See Berg and Kiefer (2002).
102 See Ridder (2002), p.124.

attribute particular **Internet competence to online media from traditional media sources.**[103] Controversial data and arguments on the effects of online use on traditional media use[104] still questions whether online media use is substituting for or complementing established media distribution channels. COLE & ROBINSON (2002), LIN (2002), and GERHARDS & KLINGLER (2003) suggest that a supplementary function of online media - ranging from interactive information retrieval to one-to-one interpersonal, group, and mass communication modes – is not related to any reduction of traditional media use.[105] NIE & ERBRING (2002), on the other hand, find evidence for a displacement hypothesis. The time spent online is spent less with traditional media and interpersonal communications.[106] Recent media time budget studies are increasingly paying attention to the phenomena of **parallel media use.**[107]

Mobile media use, however, may not compete with traditional or online media, but with **face-to-face encounters.** RHEINGOLD (2002) observes:

> "While the Internet competes with television and with face-to-face communication in the home and workplace, smart mob technologies compete with attention to other people who are present in public places and with the users' own idle time between home and work."[108]

The questions that are interesting in the light of mobile media use concern the role of traditional and online media use for mobile media and vice versa. A question that has not been addressed yet is whether Internet experience has any effect on the likelihood of the adoption of mobile media services. Heterogeneous behavior even among experienced Internet users with regard to service adoption does not suggest a linear correlation between years spent online and the formation of other habits.[109] However, **familiarity with browsing and searching** may influence the probability to try mobile data services offered in mobile portals. On the other hand, mobile data users in Japan are largely unfamiliar with the Internet which does not suggest a strong correlation, either.[110]

Moreover, the usage situations of the Internet and potential mobile media offers are substantially different.[111] For example, a mobile data communications session is often restricted to two to five minutes; the **mobile attention span** is less than ten minutes whereas time spent online is at a much higher level and it is in-

---

103 See Ridder (2002), p. 126.
104 See Stipp (2000).
105 See Cole and Robinson (2002); Lin (2002); Gerhards and Klingler (2003), p. 127. To the contrary, Cole & Robinson find evidence for more reading of books, video game playing, and music listening among Internet users.
106 See Nie and Erbring (2002).
107 See Lange (1989a), p. 24; Cole (2004).
108 Rheingold (2002), p. 193.
109 An assessment of the habituation process of experienced online use in Germany suggests two distinct basic user categories, an active dynamic user type and a selective reluctant user type. They differ among other things in PC experience, private and professional motivations of online use and they use online media with different objectives in mind. Online media portals have specific importance for the selective reluctant users who is looking for orientation, see Oehmichen and Schroeter (2002).
110 See Funk (2004), pp 103.

creasing.[112] GESER (2002), however, criticizes that this quantitative perspective on number of minutes of use does not suffice to provide information on: (1) usage intensity which refers to how often mobile services are used; (2) usage breadth referring to the number of visited services; and (3) usage variety measuring the different situations in which mobile services are used.[113] In all of these areas, more research is needed.

2.2.2
Impulse behavior versus habituation in mobile communications

Impulsiveness and habituation do not have to be mutually exclusive concepts. Mobile communications provides opportunities to combine both behavioral modes and to create an **area of overlap** for media use. It, thus, adds a new dimension to media consumption patterns that serves new needs and may attract new audiences.

From the point of view of consumer behavior research KROEBER-RIEHL/WEINBERG (1999) subsume the **concept of impulsivity** under consumer decisions with low cognitive control. In this category, they distinguish habitualized from impulsive consumption decisions. Impulse buying is defined as reactive behavior and often involves emotions as well as an immediate action response to a stimulus.[114] More specifically, impulse buying occurs when a consumer experiences a sudden, often powerful and persistent urge to buy something immediately. It tends to disrupt the consumers' behavior stream. Empirical research shows that these impulses vary in perceived intensity. The mobilization of the phone and its new data capabilities allow consumers to immediately follow an impulse when they wish to communicate or retrieve information or entertainment services. **Clues from the physical surroundings** such as billboards or advertisements for new media product launches in shop-windows, or even stationary uses such as reading a magazine in the bath tub allow for immediate mobile media access and use.

For a more detailed analysis of situations in which impulsive use of mobile media can become relevant, four broad classifications on the nature and significance of impulse buying[115] can be drawn from STERN (1962) and transferred onto mobile media use:
(1) *Pure impulse use* is breaking with habitual patterns. SMS codes in magazine advertisements that allow the user to order samples can serve as one example for pure impulse use.

---

111 Traditional and online media use is already different. Findings on the use of Internet newspapers indicate that reading patterns on the Internet strongly differ from those in the physical world. Reading Internet newspapers is usually more functional and goal oriented and it is concentrated on weekdays, see Dans (2000). This may indicate that mobile media usage will fulfill other needs than traditional and online media as well.
112 See Feldmann (2001b); Funk (2001b), p. 56; Dean (2002); Kelly (2005).
113 See Geser (2002), p. 7.
114 See Kroeber-Riehl and Weinberg (1999), pp. 398; Rook (1987).
115 See Stern (1962).

(2) *Reminder impulse use* concerns information with which the mobile user had prior experience. The use of navigation services in Japan gives evidence of the reminder impulsive nature of mobile data usage. FUNK (2002) reports that train schedule services are used complementarily via PC and cell phone. Peak traffic for PC usage occurs at noon and 5pm. The mobile peak is near midnight when people are checking the latest train to see if they have time for a last drink. Mobile services are used more often at nights and on weekends when many people are away from their PCs in offices and homes.[116]

(3) *Suggestion [by seller] impulse use* depicts the rational or functional use of mobile information and services. Physical world clues can inspire impulsive decisions on mobile data communications use such as billboards or in-store kiosks. The inspiration from locations or events comes close to Baudrillards definition of hyperreal media, generating desire for consumption by manipulating the simulation of the moment.[117]

(4) *Planned [by user] impulse use* can be inspired by presentations in buying locations such as music stores. Mobile users have the choice to intentionally roam shopping locations in order to look for inspirations and purchase online with their mobile device in case of price advantages online. Mobile devices can also be used as a tool for trading mobile media files. Opportunities for small and immediate transactions based on physical proximity can create new spot markets in media content.[118]

The use of mobile text messages already provides some evidence on impulsive use of mobile communications. The character of SMS texts is rather fleeting; they are generally not stored, contrary to e-mails or letters. A high tolerance for SMS typing mistakes, for example, underscores the fleetness of the message system.[119] However, while immediate access gratifications are quoted among the most significant motives for mobile phone use,[120] rather stable and routinized communicative patterns prevail also with mobile technology.[121] A survey on i-mode users' **ringtone purchasing habits** reveals that 20.5 percent of respondents change ringtones after half a month, 30.6 percent within a month, and 25.3 percent after two or three months. Youngsters and female respondents tend to change their ringtones more frequently.[122] For potential mobile media usage this may signal that the existing habituated media use may become pervasive as well.

In sum, the ubiquitous always-on and on-demand feature of mobile communications supports impulsive behavior regarding access to communications, information retrieval, and information interaction and processing.[123] Although it

---

116 See Funk (2002b), p. 6.
117 See Baudrillard (1995).
118 This argument goes back to Plant (2000), pp. 74.
119 See Duerscheid (2002).
120 See Leung and Wei (2000).
121 See Geser (2002), p. 16.
122 See N.N. (2003b).

contrasts media use behavior that mostly forms habituation patterns impulsive use can enforce the audience-media brand relationship via multiple touch points in **situations where media access and use has not been possible before**. Yet, until now there is no evidence that cellular media use has any potential of developing habitualized communications patterns. It rather allows for impulsive use of established media use patterns. Therefore, **fast access and efficient navigation tools** may become far more important for mobile media offers than efforts to establish regular cell media usage such as daily news alerts.

2.3
Changing politics of power and control

Next to the space-time related characteristics of mobile communications there is the personal communication sphere (see B-3.13) that undergoes changes in power and control. Personal communication and Internet appliances such as mobile phones that are used in both private and public spaces shift control over content consumption to 'personal screens'. According to ZERDICK (1990) socio-psychological factors of the power and control related to telephone use can also influence the **evaluation of new services**.[124] Against this background, new mobile content and services can be seen in the context of changing power geometrics as well.

2.3.1
Shifts of power and control in private spaces

MARVIN (1989) argues that since communication patterns always express social patterning, any perceived shift in communication strengthens or weakens familiar structures of association. New media alters **real and perceived social distances** between groups, making some groups more accessible and other groups less so.[125] Mobile communications is empowering in the sense that it enlarges the range of options available to individuals and social groups. On the other hand it **increases social control**, because it raises expectations of connectedness. The pressures to accept or reject, or to modify a new technology such as mobile communications can come from the conflicts between domestic and public values, e.g. in the case of young people from the competing claims of parents and peer groups.[126]

A new communication technology such as the mobile phone can, for example, introduce disruption into the security of familiar routines and rituals.[127] Mobile communications devices provide household members who share newspaper, ra-

---

123 See Geisselbrecht and Fotschki (2002), p. 238; Geser (2002), p. 46; Reichwald, Fremuth, and Ney
     (2002), p. 528.
124 See Zerdick (1990), p. 11.
125 See Marvin (1988), p. 234.
126 See Silverstone and Haddon (1998), p. 65; Carey (2005).
127 See Silverstone and Haddon (1998), p. 64; France et al. (2001).

dio and TV sets, and often also PCs with a new means of individual and personal communication and content access. ITO & DAISUKE (2001) have coined the term **power-geometrics** with respect to the impact of the mobile phone in the home. The family as a social system can be affected and potentially weakened on a normative and cognitive level. Young people can circumvent the control of their parents when they use their mobile phone instead of the family fixed-line connection. Thereby, personal communications is individually received and not influenced by the presence of other family members. The mutual knowledge about each other's communication network decline.[128] Teens can communicate without the embarrassment of revealing their peer relationships; or when other family members are already asleep; and without the monitoring of parents and siblings.[129] With regard to media consumption a shift can potentially be perceived **from household screens such as the TV screen to personal screens such as mobile phone screens.** It may also explain mobile users' early devotion to adult content formats for mobile media.

New forms of communication put communities like the family under stress, because contacts between its members and outsiders become difficult to supervise. Using two mobile handsets for different personal relationships, for example, avoids problems in situations where mobile phone use needs to be explained or is being controlled.[130] Often, energetic efforts are made to limit opportunities for new instruments of communication to **create new secrets and to protect the old ones** they put at risk.[131] The reconfiguration of patterns of use, therefore, involves both regulation and re-regulation in households as well as the management of conflicts over access and use.[132] One example in parent-child relationships is how children make trade-offs about how to spend their allowance and how they use messaging and future mobile media services.

In other areas of personal relationships mobile communications also **widens the social sphere.** SMS communication, for example, supports the initiation phase of interpersonal relations without the risk of embarrassment.[133] Texting is perceived as a means to communicate about feelings and thoughts without having to voice them. For teenagers, in particular, this is an essential asset of SMS and it is used for initiating, sustaining, and managing personal relationships, e.g. to constitute a co-presence with a loved one. This increase in control over communication relationships is also described as 'Cyrano de Bergerac'-phenomena of SMS.[134] GROEBEL (2005) argues that mobile media services can add **new dimensions to emotional communications** when, for instance, mobile music can be transmitted during a conversation or sent to a loved one and hence opens new dimensions of mood management.[135]

---

128 See Plant (2000), p. 59; Geser (2002), pp. 32; Rheingold (2002), p. 4.
129 See Ito and Daisuke (2001), p. 9.
130 See Plant (2000), p. 55.
131 See Marvin (1988), pp. 69.
132 See Silverstone and Haddon (1998), p. 69.
133 See Geser (2002), p. 22.
134 See Plant (2000), p. 57; Ito and Daisuke (2001), p 11.
135 See Groebel (2005).

2.3.2
Shifts of power and control in public spaces

Mobile media use in public spaces can be a lot less intrusive than mobile voice communication that can incur a social cost in public spaces among an anonymous crowd. Power is shifted towards the individual who can significantly intrude into the privacy spheres of third parties that are present. Not only the conversations, also the ringing of mobile phones are **changing the sonic environment** and alter the background noises in public places.[136] There is a wide array of impersonating tones and melodies that disrupt and irritate people, because an incoming call provokes a sense of urgency[137] and often more than one person within a public place feels compelled to answer when a phone is ringing. **Mobile audio and video applications** that are used without headsets will further contribute to a sonic intrusion of the public sphere. But mobile voice telephony, indeed, creates a lot more dysfunctional results. Public use of the mobile phone leaves people within earshot powerless to intervene and forces them to eavesdrop. GOFFMAN (1966) explains the difficulties to overhear just one side of a conversation with boundary-maintaining tendencies that neither fully admit nor fully exclude third parties.[138] Mobile communications use in public also conflicts with proprieties of presence[139] towards the person who is calling, because telephone conversations in themselves already display inherent hybrid characteristics between intimacy and distance.[140] As a result, there are **conflicts of social spaces** and it is the user's decision to honor the norms of the physical space or the norms of the conversational space.[141] Similar conflicts can arise with **pushed mobile media delivery.** It can be an unwelcome threat which interrupts activity or it can result in turning away from the communication partner in the real-world environment.

Mobile communications, thus, requires new management skills of social interaction in public spaces. LING (2003) describes **disengagement rituals** that help people extracting themselves from the pre-existing social situation to answer a mobile call and manage front and back channel interaction.[142] PLANT (2000) identifies three options upon the receipt of a public call: flight, suspension, and persistence. People either absent themselves from their social situation, they stop current activities, or they stay put and engaged with the actual world as far as possible.[143] All three responses leave people present at that time abandoned and the etiquette of handling these situations is becoming an important social skill.

---

136 Plant (2000), pp. 29; Ling (2002), p. 7.
137 McLuhan (2001), pp. 268.
138 Quoted after Plant (2000), p. 47.
139 See Marvin (1988), pp. 87.
140 See Zerdick (1990), p. 11.
141 See Palen, Salzman, and Youngs (2000).
142 See Ling (2002), p. 11.
143 See Plant (2000), p. 31.

Social etiquette in public spaces disapproves, for example, of listening too loudly to music as expressed by signs in public transportation that ask passengers to be conscious of the volume of their walkmen. It is therefore surprising that there is not more resistance against public telephone conversation. Certain locations have already been deemed inappropriate for mobile use; **'no mobile' policies** have been introduced in hospitals, air planes, theatres, some restaurants and even in quiet cars in trains.[144] The purpose of mobile phone usage other than telephony, for example data usage, are **more discreet and inoffensive**. Mobile media use may counteract some of the described social cost since its consumption can be insulated from third parties.

2.3.3
Tele-presence and de-communication

With rising expectations on **tele-communicative omnipresence** through mobile communications, ubiquitous availability and connectedness can also turn into a burden for the individual.[145] The active choice to resist and the ability to neglect these expectations emerge into **new signs of power and control**.

De-communication describes the possibility of periodically withdrawing from the mobile communication system. It is expressed by the capability to resist the omnipresence of mobile communications and create zones of communicative absence (see B-3.22).[146] ZERDICK (1990) also coins the term 'selected aloofness' in the readiness to initiate or accept telephone communication.[147] Whereas the option of reaching others anytime and anyplace is evaluated positively, the opposite case to be available for everybody anytime anyplace is evaluated ambivalently to negatively. The former symbolizes influence, control, and power. The latter is not a symbol of power. To the contrary, access barriers such as, e.g., a secretariat are usually seen as a symbol of power.[148]

Mobile data communications can, on the other hand, be **actively used to de-communicate**. People in urban settings traditionally use mobile media in the wider definition (see I-2) to evade interaction with surrounding strangers, for instance reading a newspaper, using a walkman, or engaging in mobile messaging and mobile service applications. Thus, mobile phones contribute to the strategy of individuals to **defend private space in public**, a rational behavior that is not only socially accepted but sometimes also socially desirable.[149]

Mobile media delivery, for example location-based services, on the other hand provide a lot more information on the **movements of users in public spaces**. When voice calls are incoming, users have the choice to give information about the context that may be intentionally false.[150] PLANT (2000) observes an in-

---

144 See Plant (2000), p. 36.
145 On the distribution of power between caller and receiver see Baumgarten (1989), p. 195; Hoeflich (1989), p. 206; Lange (1989a), p. 33.
146 See Zerdick et al. (2000), p. 220.
147 See Zerdick (1990), p. 15.
148 See Zerdick (1990), pp. 15.
149 See Geser (2002), p. 10; Feldmann and Zerdick (2004), p.26.

clination to lie about location, feelings and intention that is made easier by the use of mobile phones. With mobile data, on the other hand, de-communication in public spaces can add new information on users' roaming habits (see also E-2.11).

2.4
Micro-coordination, collective action, and user-driven innovation in mobile communications

The discussion of the social dimensions of mobile communications use already shows some potential implications for the use of mobile media. Social use that develops specifically in the mobile communications system, however, may provide the most **innovative reasons to embed mobile media into everyday life.** In addition to further developments of habituation, power, and control patterns, mobile communications also supports the formation of new communication patterns. Micro-coordination (C-2.41) and collective action (C-2.42) are not new concepts in themselves but develop into unique functions and usage reasons for mobile communications (C-2.43) and may unfold relevance for the properties of and the provision of mobile media (see Figure C-3); they will be discussed in the following chapters. According to MARVIN (1989), new uses based on novel technological properties and new social groups that form audiences can serve as **indicator for the dawn of a new medium:**

> "When audiences become organized around these uses, the history of a new medium begins. [...] Here, the focus of communication is shifted from the instrument to the drama in which existing groups perpetually negotiate power, authority, representation, and knowledge with whatever resources are available. New media intrude on these negotiations by providing new platforms on which old groups confront one another."[151]

Hence, these emerging social uses of mobile communications can be followed as potential indicators if mobile media evolves into a new medium.

2.4.1
Micro-coordination with mobile communications

It has been argued that mobile media serves as an ingredient in a number of lifestyle choices. When the mobile device is not used for consumption or social network interaction processes, **instrumental functions** can gain in importance next to the socio-emotional functions of mobile data communications. Mobile media use in this scenario is only initiated by the mobile device. LING & YTTRI (2002) describe instrumental functions of mobile phones as **micro-coordination.** SMS are a popular tool used for the micro-coordination of leisure activities.[152] Mobile

---

150 See Geser (2002), p. 26.
151 Marvin (1988), p. 5.

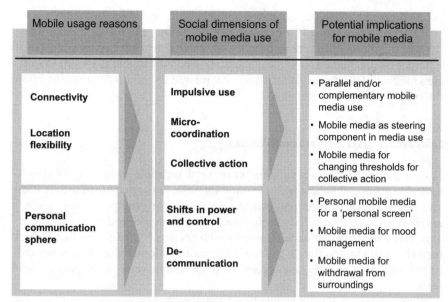

Figure C-3: Potential implications of the social use of mobile communications for the provision of mobile media

phones allow one to flexibly arrange and rearrange schedules specifically en route, to give real time updates on social events, and to maintain a social and emotional band with peers via SMS communication.[153] It not only reveals information about the embeddedness of a person within a social network, but about **changing norms and lifestyles**. Timeliness is loosing value as a virtue; the new vice is to forget the mobile phone or let the battery die. The option of micro-coordination with mobile phones reduces the need for temporal planning and shifts the focus from ex-ante agreements to a more current and ad hoc coordination or 'approximeeting'. Scheduling becomes a constant stream of negotiations and reconfigurations.[154] However, this lack of commitment to the appointment in mobile sociability may lead in the long term to a loss of efficiency rather than a gain of efficiency.

Micro-coordination may also extend to **interactions within the physical space** as well as virtual spaces. Ubiquitous computing, smart locations, and digital cities are beginning to turn the mobile phone into a remote control for the physical space.[155] But also hybrid models for mobile media delivery such as GPRS/DVB-T models (see B-2.32) take advantage of the micro-coordinating

152 See France et al. (2001).
153 See Hoeflich, Steuber, and Roessler (2000), pp. 13; Schlobinski et al. (2001), p. 26.
154 See Plant (2000), p. 64; Townsend (2000); Horx (2001), p. 103; Geser speaks of a deregulation of agendas, see Geser (2002), p. 23.
155 See Rheingold (2002), p. 28; Groebel (2005). Spy cams that control property such as the entrance of a house can already be transmitted on a mobile phone, see Pogue (February 27, 2003).

point-to-point function of the mobile phone. With regard to the mobile phone as the **"connective tissue"**[156] **between offline, online, and on-air media** offers, the mobile phone can serve as functionally interdependent between the use of different media. Audiences can use the mobile communications system to initiate a media consumption via a different device and transmitted via another than the cellular network.

2.4.2
Collective action via mobile communications

Mobile communications is yet another network technology with capabilities to assemble groups of people with common interests to **participate in the creation and use of common resources.** Among teenagers, for example, mobile phones are often used collaboratively in that they share messages and contents and engage in collaborative action with co-present teenagers.[157] **Ad hoc social network formation** and interaction in mobile communities allows for instantaneous collective action which may be designed through mobile voice, messaging or contents.

Wireless devices enable people to act together in new ways and in situations where collective action was not possible before.[158] These situations can comprise both social control and means of resistance. Many-to-many mobile communications empower cooperative bands of intercommunicants, for example in urban spaces. Here tactics of **distributed control and lateral cooperation** create new leverages.[159] Decentralized communications within groups offer potential for informal organization and also empower users to circumvent prescribed rulings.[160] RHEINGOLD (2002) remarks on the **role of the media for 'the power of the mobile many':**

"Mobile media that can augment the informal, mostly unconscious information exchanges that take place within the interaction order or affect the size or location of the audience for these changes, have the potential to change the threshold for collective action."[161]

Collective action and ad hoc community formation can be based on a form of **collective intelligence.** LÉVY (1997) defines collective intelligence as an intelligence that is distributed, perpetually created, coordinated in real time, and that is effectively mobilizing competences. Its grounds and objectives are mutual recognition.[162] Decentralized self-organization supported via mobile devices can become astonishingly intelligent. It is in this perception of connecting and com-

---

156 Kelly (2005), p.112.
157 See Weilenmann and Larsson (2000).
158 See Rheingold (2002), p. xviii.
159 See Rheingold (2002), p. 156.
160 See Geser (2002), p. 32.
161 Rheingold (2002), p. 175.
162 See Lévy (1997), p. 29.

municating in social networks that RHEINGOLD (2002) speaks of collective intelligence.[163] This collective intelligence that emerges from collective action can be used to create new means and forms of communication and may spark innovative uses of mobile communications.

Also real world entertainment formats that promote collective action **combined with mobile ad hoc coordination** can emerge as new promotional tools for media companies. Local radio stations, for instance, often engage in fun activities within their communities to attract attention from (potential) listeners. For them, real world activities such as scavenger hunts that get combined with mobile ad hoc coordination[164] can be used for sweepstake activities. Device-to-device communications via peer-to-peer networks is another option that links social networks into cooperative ventures.[165] GESER (2002) critically remarks, however, that relationships become more bilateral and individualized with mobile communications. Thus, he concludes that mobile phones are not potent instruments for a fast build-up of large-scale collectivities and collective actions.[166] Yet, for mobile media, ad hoc sharing and the collective use of content, for example in relation to entertainment content such as mobile multiplayer games, can provide new means for collaborative use.

2.4.3
User-contextualized content and user-driven innovation

User-generated and **user-contextualized content** (see A-2.32) is an interesting area for mobile communications, both in the context of creating a self-narrative of the mobile identity and gaining a reputation in mobile communities.[167] A host of new digital appliances encourages users to create their own digital content such as digital images, web sites, sounds, and film sequences. In Japan, people who create personal media files such as digital images, text or video can post this content directly on the Web from a mobile phone.[168] On the other hand Japanese mobile users are also building **mobile websites** with personal contents that can be accessed via a mobile phone. Magic Island, for example, is a popular provider of mobile homepage creation services.[169]

More importantly however, software and technologies that enable users to contextualize (or manipulate) professionally produced content are gaining in popu-

---

163 See Rheingold (2002), p. 179.
164 See Feldmann (2001b).
165 See Rheingold (2002), pp. 76 .
166 See Geser (2002), p. 31.
167 The decomposition of the traditional separation between consuming audiences and producing media content providers under the influence of new ICTs may contribute to realize the demands of Brecht's (1967) radio theory. Enzensberger (1970) calls these participation possibilities and further collective production and self-organization capabilities (then of electronic media) emancipated media usage versus traditional repressive media usage, see Brecht (1992); Enzensberger (1997).
168 See Funk (2001b), p. 30; Rheingold (2002), p. 169
169 See Funk (2001b), p. 30; Funk even suggests to regard the percentage of i-mode subscribers who are creating and maintaining i-mode sites as a measure of i-mode's popularity rather than the total number of subscribers.

larity. The most popular function of **mobile map services** in Japan, for example, is sending maps in mail messages. Clicking on an icon automatically creates a homepage for the map and integrates the link into the mobile message. Setting up meeting places is a popular application for this service. Users pay 200 Yen a month for this ability; simple maps of the different providers are offered for free.[170]

Facilities that allow users to impact programming in traditional media are, for example, fast forward or replay functions in video programming that transfer value from the programming provider to the viewer.[171] Online media offers many opportunities to contextualize content, for example online newspaper articles that can be commented on and sent to third parties. In mobile communications **sending branded media content contextualized with a personal message** may become a successful proposition. They could be embedded in mobile blogging applications. Weblogs are a form of collaborative publishing where editorial content is commented and linked into a personal context of the user. Blogs are self-published web-surfing diaries that link to favourite sites and include commentary on the mentioned sites. The power of blogging lies in **reframing issues**. A message gains authority by the power of the media, but bloggers act as intermediaries in reframing the contents for different publics.[172] The blogging sub-culture that has been created in the Internet is already extended on mobile platforms. Mobile users can use their cell phones to immediately add new postings to their weblog. Mobile phones hereby offer an innovative function of **audiologs**, i.e. voice SMS that can be posted on the weblog as MP3 file.[173] Other forms of **mobile collaborative publishing** may emerge with the proliferation of mobile ad hoc communities.

A higher degree of **selection and modification possibilities** for mobile data communications transfers power to the user who can decide what actual level of participation she prefers.[174] With open access to contents and users' ability to freely change and contextualize it, opportunities for innovations driven by users can emerge.[175] LESSIG (2001) considers a subtext of the advertisement from Apple Computer, "Rip, mix, burn", to explain how digital technology can enable people to become part of the creative process and innovate.[176] Reputational gains are quoted by HARHOFF ET AL. (2000) and TUOMI (2002) as incentive for users to innovate and to freely reveal their innovations which supports arguments on

---

170 See Funk (2002b), p. 9.
171 See Benkler (1998), p. 193.
172 See Rheingold (2002), p. 121.
173 See Gongolsky (May 20, 2003).
174 The level of participation can be related to the notion of interactivity. Goertz (1995) definition of interactivity for the media is useful in this context. Interactivity in his understanding is dependent on the degree of selection possibilities, modification possibilities, and linearity. The higher the values of these parameter the higher is the degree of interactivity, see Goertz (1995), p. 485.
175 Consumer empowerment requires firms to give up some control over key marketing variables in exchange for an increased degree of consumer responsiveness, see Wathieu and Zoglio (2001). Integrating the customer into the development process is practiced by a number of firms that are already taking advantage of potential users' innovative capabilities. New ICTs are adding capabilities, e.g. web-based methods, for customer input into product development processes, see Dahan and Hauser (2001). Mobile communications can also complement traditional market research. Mobile community platform providers, e.g., are using mobile communications and their mobile community members for product testing of their commercial clients.
176 See Lessig (2001), p. 9.

the relevance of the construction of the self-identity within social networks. Also RHEINGOLD (2002) is convinced that people who are using mobile phones, pervasive computing and location-aware technologies will eventually invent new forms of social interaction including entertainment, commerce, communion, and conflict.[177] One small example from SMS communication is the array of new acronyms that creative SMS users produce and that they share similar to a secret code among their friends.[178] A critical issue for **mobile user-driven innovations** for mobile data communications concerns the design of mobile operator's pricing plans; they should encourage experimentation by users in order to reap the benefits of positive feedback effects.[179]

When mobile data communications confers power on consumers to create, publish, broadcast and debate their own point of view, mobile users challenge mass media content and content dissemination.[180] On the other hand, media companies can aim at **turning user innovativeness into an opportunity**. The possibilities for such a win-win situation lie in the expansion of their cross-media strategies and the integration of traditional and online media with mobile content and mobile communications options (see D-4.13).

For media companies and their approach to integrate mobile communications platforms into their strategies at audience and advertising markets, the observations on the characteristics as well as the social use of the mobile communication system are **relevant parameters in the design of mobile media contents, formats, content-related communities,** and the integration of mobile media with their existing media content. These challenges and opportunities for cross-media extensions are the subject of the discussion in the following chapter.

---

177 See Rheingold (2002), p. 182.
178 See Duerscheid (2002).
179 See Funk (2001b), p. 68.
180 See Rheingold (2002), p. 197.

D
Cross-media and cross-network strategies for mobile media

Media companies that consider extending their activities onto mobile communications platforms need to analyse how they can reflect the characteristics of the mobile communications system and its social use in their cross-media strategies (D-1). With the emergence and the diffusion of the Internet, cross-media strategies have been adopted by a majority of media companies. A **differentiation of platforms for digital media** also leads to further extensions of cross-media strategies. A new medium involves shifts in functions as well as content and service developments. As such, it usually does not substitute for another medium, but complements existing media. **New mobile media categories emerge** that have distinct formats and contents and that can use different models of bundling and pricing (D-2). However, a stand-alone model for mobile media does not exploit the strengths of cross-media strategies. It is the **integration of content and services** not only across different media but also across different networks that creates value for media customers, both audiences and advertising clients (D-3). This **process of value creation** is the objective of all players in the value chain. However, competition between media companies and mobile operators to participate in the revenue generation is strong and co-opetition is the prevailing competitive strategy paradigm for mobile media markets (D-4). Figure D-1 provides an overview of the structure of the chapter.

1
Extensions of cross-media strategies

Cross-media strategy development is one essential characteristic of traditional media companies' strategy under the influence of the Internet (D-1.1); mobile communications platforms create new opportunities for cross-media extension. The objectives for such an extension onto mobile platforms provide the direction for the formulation of strategic options (D-1.2).

1.1
Definition and historic development of cross-media strategies

Cross-media strategy definitions focus for the most part on **media content development**, either from a diversification strategy point of view or from a media

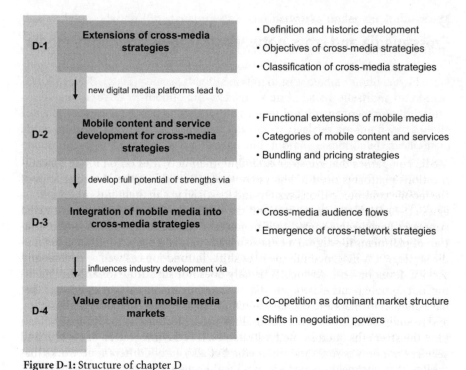

Figure D-1: Structure of chapter D

brand extension strategy point of view; other definitions relate specifically to the **cross-promotion opportunities** of a cross-media brand.

SJURTS (2002) defines cross-media strategies as **diversification decisions** of media companies which target other media markets.[1] In this definition, different media markets relate to traditional media markets such as newspaper, magazine, broadcasting, satellite and cable markets as well as new media markets such as Internet and mobile communications. This definition also distinguishes itself explicitly from definitions of cross-media strategies that mean a combination of different advertising measures.[2] The **economic reasoning for cross-media strategies** as diversification decisions can be explained through two streams of theory in business management. The market-based view underlines competitive strategy and competitive advantage.[3] In this line of argument, diversification can strengthen media companies' bargaining power against suppliers and

---

1   See Sjurts (2002a), p. 5. In addition to diversification strategies, Caspar considers market expansion strategies as a type of cross-channel media brand strategy as well. For details on the typology see Caspar (2002a), p. 60.
2   Mueller-Kalthoff suggests a separation into cross-media publishing and cross-media marketing to integrate both concepts, see Mueller-Kalthoff (2002a), p. 19.
3   See Porter (1980); Porter (1985).

customers. The resource-based view explains competitive advantages via unique resources within the firm.[4] Content repertoire of media companies can be regarded as a unique resource that can lead to competitive advantages when content is used across platforms.[5] Yet, since the following analysis focuses on media companies' strategic options in mobile communications markets, the definition of cross-media strategies as diversification decisions of media companies which target other media markets does not offer sufficient potential to define cross-media strategies *within* a certain media market.

CASPAR (2002) takes a **brand extension strategy perspective** on cross-media strategies. His definition of cross-media brand extension strategies comprises a more differentiated approach to cross-media strategies, because diversification strategies are only one option among several. He defines a cross-channel media *brand* - the term cross-media brand can be used synonymously - as a media brand that extends its offer over several media channels.[6] Cross-channel media *branding strategies* are defined as the **management of a portfolio of content in different channels under the same brand** or as the corresponding brand extension strategies onto new channels.[7] Hereby, he defines a cross-channel media *brand extension* according to the marketing-theoretical literature on brand extensions as the introduction of a new media product in a new product category.[8] A new media product is classified along the criteria content of the offer, qualitative and quantitative scope, and newness. This implies that the pure communicative support of media or advertising content via a different channel is not included in the definition of cross-channel media brand extension.[9] For the remainder of the book, the definition of Caspar will be followed.

Cross-media strategies are not a recent phenomenon. In Germany, **inter-medial cross-media extensions** have been pursued since the 1970s. For example, publishing houses have created TV shows around magazines in the '90s, and radio channels have produced TV shows. Typically, **intra-medial cross-media extension** has been more successful, e.g. the extension from one print product onto a print brand family targeted at different audiences.[10]

Cross-media diversifications have increased over time and gain in significance with newly **emerging digital distribution platforms**.[11] One significant effect of digitization is a progressive expansion in distribution outlets for the media.[12] Hereby, new media are often emerging with the technological platform as the dominant feature of their identity.[13] Digital compression techniques multiply the potential number of broadcast channels; the Internet provides an unlimited forum for publishing, broad- and narrowcast transmissions, multimedia

---

4   See Wernerfelt (1984); Barney (1991);Grant (1991).
5   See Sjurts (2002a), p. 14.
6   See Caspar (2002a), p. 10.
7   See Caspar (2002a), p. 18.
8   See Caspar (2002a), p. 29. For research on brand extension see for example Hätty (1989); Aaker and Keller (1990); Farquhar et al. (1992); Loken and Roedder John (1993); Erdem (1998); Simonin and Ruth (1998); Caspar (2002b).
9   This distinguishes cross-channel brand extensions from marketing communication.
10 For an overview and examples of cross-media strategies in Germany before 1984, in the 80ies and 90ies see Sjurts (2002a).

and different interactive services; and mobile communications allows an increase in multiple utilization of content and personalization (see A-1.2; A-1.3). The increasing demand for content and the changing interests of different cohorts of media users provide creative and commercial opportunities for media content producers.[14] The **exploitation of digital media content** raises questions on how to manage the digital assets effectively and efficiently. Hereby, content management systems need to be able to capture, store, manage, and protect digital content and provide flexibility for later stages of editing, manipulation and packaging.[15]

The Internet initiated large-scale cross-media extensions. Today, almost all media brands have an online presence. Online media offers can differ significantly, based on the cannibalization potential of the online offer, and on various copyright agreements, for example with picture or moving image copyright owners. The **importance of the Internet for media companies** has led to the development that new media products often are already launched as cross-media offers. In 1999, the launches of new media offers in the German TV and print markets, for instance the TV news channel N24 and the German edition of Financial Times, FTD, were cross-medial from the beginning.[16] The real-people format 'Big Brother' is an often-quoted example of the successful exploitation of an integrated TV and online format.[17] In general, a transfer of user's expectations and media brand images requires media companies to offer online media in the context of their original media offer but with medium-specific added value.[18]

However, a large number of cross-media brand extensions have not been successful. Strong and recognizable media brands have several advantages when it comes to the exploitation of digitally induced economies of scale. Yet, using many channels is connected with **high costs and leads to different losses due to dispersion.**[19] CASPAR (2002) observes that only a few media brands possess the capability to establish new media offers in new channels that are independent from both the economic and the publishing point of view.[20] Since the classifica-

---

11 For a discussion on integrated TV-online media offers see for example Neuberger (2000); Raff (2002); Reitze (2002); Sewczyk (2002). In this discussion there is dispute about the role and scope of online activities of public commercial television. The functional tasks of public commercial TV only justify the financing of online media activities that contribute to the basic supply ('Grundversorgung'). However, there is no formal or legal explanation what is included in the basic supply. Therefore, online media activities are subject to interpretation. Not surprisingly, the arguments of public and commercial TV providers differ. For a discussion of the needs and limitations of public television online see Steemers (2001); Rueter (2002). Cross-media brand extensions with regard to financing mobile media offers also have to be assessed in view of the public service character.
12 See Karmasin and Winter (2000a), p. 28; Advani and Choudhury (2001); Doyle (2002), p. 143. In the economic and financial print news sector brand extensions onto the Internet have contributed to international growth potential, see Arrese and Medina (2002).
13 See Dennis and Ash (2001), p. 31.
14 See Doyle (2002), p. 144; Dreier (2002), p. 58.
15 See Schumann and Hess (1999a); Doyle (2002), p. 145; Hess (2004), pp. 67.
16 See Neuberger (2000), p.106.
17 See Trepte, Baumann, and Borges (2000); Glotz (2001); Hass (2004), p. 56.
18 See Ridder (2002), p. 130.
19 See Dreier (2002), p. 53.
20 See Caspar (2002a), p. 10.

tion and success factors of cross-media strategies depend on the system of objectives of a media company, cross-media extension objectives will be discussed next.

1.2
Objectives of cross-media extensions onto mobile platforms

Media companies can pursue economic and psychographic objectives with cross-media extensions onto mobile platforms. Psychographic objectives of cross-media extensions onto mobile platforms are tightly related to media companies' brand management and customer relationship management. Economic objectives comprise expanding existing and generating new revenue sources (see A-1.1) as well as striving for cost savings. The **realization of synergy effects** is an argument that is often used when the extension of cross-media strategies is considered.[21] However, in the case of cross-media extensions onto mobile platforms, the potential for cost savings through synergetic effects is unclear. Building mobile applications requires specific knowledge and the cost for the application service provider, mobile distribution cost, and using the database resources of the mobile operator can constitute a large part of the value creation process. Synergy effects between the provision of online media and mobile media are also low for media companies due to the characteristics and specifics of the content distribution.[22] Mobile operators may be better positioned to realize synergy effects for the bundling and marketing of mobile content with their mobile portals.

For media companies, therefore, **psychographic objectives gain in importance,** even though ultimately they also result in the objective to increase profits and they also have to be subsumed under economic objectives. Opportunities for media companies lie in strengthening both brand awareness and brand loyalty of audiences and advertising clients (D-1.21). Media brand extension strategies on mobile platforms pose opportunities to augment or form new relationships with media audiences and advertising clients (D-1.22). Figure D-2 provides an overview of the system of objectives; they will be discussed in the following chapters.

1.2.1
Media brand development

Media organizations as well as media content can be perceived as brands that have to be managed in audience as well as advertising markets.[23] **Media brands** offer orientation and support selection decisions of media audiences and advertising clients in the allocation of the scarce resources attention respectively ad-

21 See Englert (2002); Sjurts (2002a), p. 3; Hess (2004), pp.64.
22 See Englert (2002), p. 215.
23 See Chan-Olmsted and Kim (2001); Feldmann (2001a); Siegert (2001).

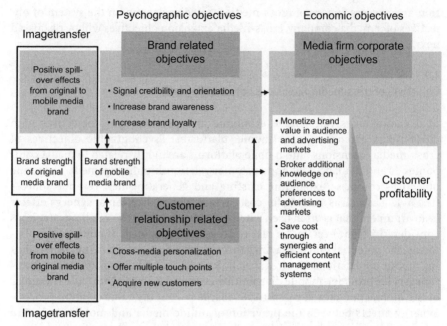

Figure D-2: System of objectives of cross-media extensions onto mobile platforms
Source: adapted from Caspar (2002a), p. 50

vertising budget.[24] These roles become even more important for media brands on the Internet with its abundance and diversity of authorship and publishing forms; yet, the functions of gate-keeping, editorial intervention and validation of authorship remain.[25] REICHWALD & MEIER (2002) argue that mobile devices in general are suited to be the carrier of a brand promise.[26] German media brands such as 'FAZ', 'Financial Times Deutschland', 'Spiegel online', 'Sueddeutsche Zeitung' and 'Kicker' are among the 73 content providers that started mobile media offers for the i-mode Germany launch in April 2002.[27] It is important to note, though, that mobile media extensions bear not only opportunities but also threats from **spillover effects**[28] **for the media brand** when the mobile media offer does not meet users' expectations of the brand.

The dominant paradigm for media brand management is the **identity-driven branding** approach.[29] Hereby, the inner perception of the brand philosophy and the outward perception of the brand image are differentiated. The objectives of

---

24 See Feldmann (2001a), pp. 17; Siegert (2001), p. 121.
25 See McQuail (2000), p. 119.
26 See Reichwald and Meier (2002), p. 221.
27 See Lauff (2002), p. 197.
28 See for example Aaker and Keller (1990); Farquhar et al. (1992); Erdem (1998); Simonin and Ruth (1998).
29 See Kapferer (1994); Meffert and Burmann (2002).

identity-driven brand management are to create a strategic fit between the inner and outer characteristics of the brand and to create and sustain a **consistent brand identity**. Media brand integration across different platforms particularly requires a consistent and congruent brand image for the media brands' product, communication, price, and distribution policies.[30]

For cross-media strategies, the **meta-media function of media brands** is particularly essential. Media brands can be understood as institutions that signal credibility and orientation. This meta-media function becomes important in the pre-communicative phase of the media selection process, in particular because media contents are an experience good.[31] The brand signaling capability is certainly an element that supports cross-media consumption decisions as well as processes of habituation in media usage. Also, digital environments favor strong and recognizable media brands, because they support customers in making choices.[32] Media brand transfer strategies onto new distribution channels such as mobile communications strive for extending the meta-media function onto new usage situations and **multiple touch points with the media brand** throughout the day.

Brand transfer strategies can take two different forms. Brands can be transferred within the same product category (line extension). The second form extends a brand onto a different product category (brand extension).[33] **Brand extension strategies** describe a management process in which the name and values of an existing brand are used for new products with the objective of a positive image transfer.[34] Positive spill-over effects support the new product in the market entry phase and may influence image perceptions of the original brand. Yet, in general, the risks of a brand extension are very high in comparison to its opportunities such as positive image transfers. The risks include negative spill-over effects such as brand dilution when the translation of the brand promise into the core competencies of a new medium fails and the failure is reflected on the mother media brand.[35]

The omnipresence of a media brand in a 'one brand all media' approach may lead to an augmented customer relationship and ultimately higher customer **brand loyalty** although it may not be appropriate for every media brand due to high investment cost. Media brands strive for accompanying the user through-

---

30 See Meffert and Perrey (2002); Meffert, Bierwirth, and Burmann (2002).
31 See Siegert (2001), p. 226. In online purchase situations, brands serve as a proxy for a retailer's credibility with regard to non-contractible aspects of product bundles such as shipping time. Branded retailers also hold significant price advantages which reveals the brand as an important determinant of customer choice in online environments, see Brynjolfsson and Smith (2000).
32 See Doyle (2002), p.145.
33 Among numerous examples for line extensions in the German media industries are the extensions of the German magazines 'Spiegel' to 'Spiegel Reporter', or 'Focus' to 'Focus Money'. Examples for brand extensions comprise the extensions of the magazine 'Spiegel' to 'Spiegel TV', the radio format 'Eins Live' to 'Eins Live TV', the TV soap opera 'GZSZ' to the magazine 'GZSZ' to name just a few. Brand transfer strategies in the media industries are subject to failure in many cases; so are some of the quoted examples such as 'Spiegel Reporter' or 'Eins Live TV'.
34 See for example Hätty (1989); Keller (1998); Meffert and Heinemann (1990); Anand and Shachar (2001).
35 See for example Loken and Roedder John (1993); Kapferer (1994).

out the day with their media content in different usage situations via different networks and devices.[36] A media brand extension onto mobile distribution platforms and potentially ubiquitous points of contact with the media brand gives media audiences **more options for brand interaction** and may attract new audience members as well.[37] Users can follow any impulse to access media offers.[38] In this respect, impulsive mobile media usage leads to a **manifestation of established media usage habits** (see C-2.2). Research on brand loyalty indicates that attitudinal loyalty can also influence brand performance parameters such as market share and relative price.[39] Under this perspective, mobile media can have positive spill-over effects for traditional and online media offers.

Since negative spill-over effects from a brand transfer failure also bare risks for the mother brand, the decision about a media brand extension needs criteria for the decision process. CASPAR (2002) argues that **brand strength** is an essential parameter to be assessed for cross-channel media brand strategies. His conclusions suggest that a media brand transfer onto mobile distribution platforms require, among other factors, strong media brands in order to attract attention and potential for revenue models that allow a sustainable brand extension.

1.2.2
Customer relationship management development

Mobile media extensions provide opportunities for deeper audience relationships that may be monetized in advertising markets. **Individuation** of mobile services is the basis for a sustainable customer relationship and **digitization** is the basis to efficiently manage this process.[40] On the other hand, mobile services bare the risk of being too intrusive and to shy customers away. Therefore, new forms of permission marketing[41] are being developed specifically for mobile services (see E-2.1).

Relationship management is the active management of customer contacts and relations. It is based on the combination of the objectives profit maximization and customer value creation.[42] Relationship management aims at **increasing customer loyalty**. It attempts to involve and integrate customers and other partners into a firm's developmental and marketing activities that can result in interactive relationships. The advantages of relationship marketing include transaction cost advantages, an improvement of customer satisfaction, and higher profitability. In media markets, **subscription relationships** may be seen as a first customer relationship. Emerging distribution channels allow for ex-

---

36   See Dreier (2002), p. 44; Englert (2002), p. 221.
37   See Reichwald and Schaller (2002).
38   See Geisselbrecht and Fotschki (2002); Lauff states that, for example, the success of TV shopping
      formats relies on impulsive consumer purchase decisions, see Lauff (2002), p. 107.
39   See Chaudhuri and Holbrook (2001); Anand and Shachar find that multiproduct firms and their
      profile affects brand loyalty. These findings can also be reflected in brand extension strategies and
      channel spillover effects, see Anand and Shachar (2001).
40   See Mueller, Aschmoneit, and Zimmermann (2002); Reichwald and Schaller (2002).
41   See Godin (1999).
42   See Wirtz (1999); Reinartz and Kumar (2000); Winer (2001); Day and Van den Bulte (2002).

tending and intensifying this relationship. The Internet offers new dimensions in this regard, e.g. because they enable interaction and two-way communication.[43]

Suitable mobile content and services for customer relationship management have recently raised attention, because they offer multiple access points for customer relations.[44] Cross-media offers intend to reach one customer over a variety of channels. This multiple customer relationship allows the customer to choose freely and context-specificly from different contact options with the content. STEMER (2002) uses the notion of **multi-touchpoint services.** It includes a function that allows customers to start and finish a certain application on different devices and via different networks without loosing data in between.[45] In this scenario, the user can personalize certain content across devices including specific interaction patterns, and push and pull services (see D-3.2).

On the other hand, cross-media offers also aim at **attracting new audiences.** For example, television channels that attract mainly older audiences that are not (yet) of interest to advertising clients, hope to bind younger user groups to their media brand with online media.[46] Media companies that target a **young customer group with their mobile media offer** may also be able to win new customers. Mobile media content is interesting for pure Internet brands as well that can initialize contacts to users that have no online experience. In Japan, for example, the mobile Internet is said to be the first contact many people have with the Internet in general.[47] These new users typically do not have PC access in their offices and homes. The investment in a mobile handset differs significantly from the investment into a PC. Therefore, a new user group is entering the Internet via mobile devices and their Internet experience differs from those with PC Internet experience. However, online media offers can reach out to these audiences with mobile services and attract new customers.

Media companies' customer relationship management can benefit from mobile media offers that tighten the linkages between media organizations or media content and their audiences and offer multiple forms of customer retention.[48] Mass media companies want t develop closer relationships with their customers in order to gain **deeper insights into users' preferences** and behaviors that can be brokered to advertising clients and that can be used to augment the personalization of media content offers. In the light of this background, data mining techniques and the building of a database with customer information has gained importance (see A-1.11). For integrated media companies it becomes an option to integrate customer data to be able to offer **cross-media personali-**

---

43 See Siegert (2000), p. 190; although this allows for the provision of online services, community building, and feedback, a study by Dutta and Segev shows that large companies across industries do little to exploit the customer relationship management potentials, see Dutta and Segev (2001), p. 8.
44 See Silberer, Wohlfahrt, and Wilhelm (2001).
45 See Stamer (2002), p.111.
46 See Reitze (2002), p. 137.
47 See Funk (2001b); the music and video online service Tsutaya, for example, has more mobile than fixed-line Internet subscribers see Funk (2001b), p. 37.
48 See Wirtz (2000); Funk (2001a); Hampe and Schwabe (2002b); Reichwald and Meier (2002).

zation.[49] The integration of useful content linked to specific audiences with great precision is seen as a theme in the future of digital media.[50]

One often neglected piece of analysis is the value of customer relationships in terms of **customer profitability.** It needs to be taken into account, though, in order to evaluate mobile content and services and their contribution to the brand management and extension of the customer relationship (see Fig. D-1). The **customer value** is a central construct in the evaluation of the individualization performance.[51] REICHWALD & MEIER (2002) suggest a relationship between the resource input needed for mobile services and a 'return on customer'.[52] They characterize customer value as a multi-dimensional construct that integrates the potential and the actual customer value as well as the objectives of the firm. Mobile services can influence potential customer value from a revenue perspective but also from a communication perspective. Here, the potential for customer integration into mobile services is stressed (see A-2.3), because of the greater reach via users' social networks compared to other direct marketing forms of customer relationship management.[53]

1.3
Classification of cross-media strategies and their mobile extensions

Cross-media strategies relate to different dimensions and can have different specifications. For the discussion of cross-media extensions onto mobile distribution platforms it is, hence, useful to develop a classification system for a systematic discussion of media companies' strategic options. A classification of cross-media strategies requires the determination of relevant dimensions and their specifications.[54]

1.3.1
Classification systematization for cross-media strategies

Under the definition of cross-media strategies as diversification decisions of media companies one approach towards a classification of cross-media strategies can be made using the criteria (1) relatedness of resources, technologies, and risks (related versus unrelated) and (2) relationship between original and targeted media market (horizontal versus vertical diversification).[55] Based on these criteria, SJURTS (2002) distinguishes **intra-, inter, and extra-medial diversifications.** Among the inter-medial diversifications are related, unrelated and conver-

---

49 See Stamer (2002), p. 109. Online business models already allow for targeted advertising and one-to-one marketing, see Fox and Wrenn (2001), p. 114. Digital technologies make it also more economically feasible to produce content aimed at narrow audience segment, see Doyle (2002), p. 144.
50 See Dennis and Ash (2001), p. 31.
51 See Weiber and Weber (2001).
52 See Reichwald and Meier (2002), p. 210.
53 See Reichwald and Meier (2002); von Hippel and Katz (2002).
54 For a general introduction to classification techniques see Bailey (1994).
55 See Sjurts (2002a), p. 5.

gence-oriented diversifications. The market entrance of media companies in Internet or mobile communication markets is classified as **convergence-oriented diversifications**.[56] As such, the classification does not allow a further specification of different strategic options for mobile media extensions.

The definition of cross-media strategies as brand extension strategies onto new channels used in this book spans the classification of cross-media strategies along the dimensions of **product innovation and product variation** or differentiation.[57] It builds upon a corresponding classification from the strategic management literature, ANSOFF's (1966) product/market matrix.[58] A diversification strategy according to Ansoff is the introduction of new products into new markets and corresponds with a product innovation. A market development strategy is the introduction of existing products into new markets. In the latter case, CASPAR (2002) suggests that media products differentiate if the semantics of the media product remain or if they change in the new channel.[59] The characteristics of a new media product are its degree of newness, the content, and its scale and scope.[60] The degree of product newness is dependent on the perception of the media user. A product innovation generates a **perceived new value** while a product variation is similar in the basic functional value and contributes a **value added service**. The product newness can be further specified into autonomy of the media product[61] and the semantic space of the media product.

A mobile media offer that is not autonomous but strongly related to the original media product and semantically similar can then be classified as a **marketing support strategy**. Although it is a very weak form of a cross-media brand extension it is an important strategic element in media management, because media companies extensively use tools for the self-promotion of their content.[62] Therefore, it will be included in the cross-media strategy classification. An autonomous mobile media offer that is similar to the semantics of the original media product (product variation) is classified as **market development strategy**. An autonomous mobile media offer that opens a new semantic space (product innovation) is classified as **market diversification strategy**.

Mobile extensions of cross-media strategies can be referred to as **promotional media** content in the case of marketing support cross-media strategies, **repurposed media** content for mobile media market development strategies and **cell**

---

56 See Sjurts (2002a), p. 7.
57 Caspar uses this differentiation to specify the horizontal brand strategy dimension for a general classification of cross-channel media brand strategies, see Caspar (2002a), pp. 51. The dimensions product innovation respectively variation are also consistent with the cross-media strategy definition of Sjurts because both categories relate to a diversification into another - the mobile - media market.
58 See Ansoff (1966), pp. 132.
59 See Caspar (2002a), p. 55.
60 See Caspar (2002a), p. 26; for the discussion of product innovation and product variation strategies see Hätty (1989), pp. 33; Meffert (1999), p. 295.
61 Autonomy can refer to the content and the economic context of the media product; the consumer perspective on the autonomy of the content will be regarded as the necessary condition for autonomy, the economic autonomy will only be regarded as the commensurate condition. Online media offers, for example, have been largely without economic autonomy although media companies are working hard towards implementing self-sustaining online business models.
62 See Siegert (2000), pp. 186.

media content (see I-2.2) for mobile media market diversification strategies (see Fig. D-2).

1.3.2
Mobile marketing support cross-media strategies

Mobile marketing support cross-media strategies offer particular opportunities for the communication management of media organizations. Media organizations use their ability to manage consumer attention for purposes of self-reference. SIEGERT (2001) differentiates five forms of **self-referential communication elements** for media organizations: media advertising in other media, e.g. outdoor advertising for TV shows; cross-promotion in different media of the same organization via cross-ownership; media PR aimed at other media organizations, investors, or political institutions; self-promotion such as trailers; and cross references within the editorial media offer that direct to other contents of the same media brand.[63] Mobile communications is an interesting emerging platform for **self-promotion of media organizations** (seeTable D-1). It favors concise and targeted messages and content; mobile alerts or mobile trailers can cross-promote traditional and online media of the same brand whereas cross-

Strategy type	Properties		
	Autonomy	Semantic space	Mobile extension
Marketing support	Not autonomous	Equals original media brand	Promotional media content
Market expansion	Autonomous	Equals original media brand	Repurposed media content
Market diversification	Autonomous	New semantic space	Cell media content

Figure D-3: Systematization of cross-media strategies and their mobile extensions
Source: adapted from Caspar (2002a), p. 60

---

63   See Siegert (2001), pp.179.

references in editorial media can raise attention for mobile subscription services of the media brand.

Table D-1: Selected examples for mobile self-promotion of media organizations

Brand	Self-promotion form
NBC	Promotion of the fall show launches: 3-minute audio/videoclips of five new NBC shows (comedy and drama) for handheld devices[a]
MTV	Wireless promotion of MTV Music Awards[b]
Simon & Schuster	Excerpts (350 to 400 words) from the newest Stephen King short story collection for handheld devices via telephone kiosks on the streets of Manhattan[c]

a. See N.N. (June 13, 2002).
b. See McDonough (August 22, 2001).
c. See Elliott (2002).

In Japan, many radio and TV stations are promoting their programs on **mobile Internet sites**. Information on actors as well as advertised products in and around the program may be the next step in mobile TV-related promotional services. However, TV stations also go further than pure mobile promotion. 'Fuji Television', for example, is selling **TV-show related products** such as theme songs as ring-tones via the mobile sites of the content and site management provider index.[64]

Magazines in Japan are also expanding the reach of their advertisers by providing **product codes** that readers input into their mobile phones in order to obtain more information or product samples. The trading house 'Itochu' partners with women's fashion magazines and makes advertised products available for purchase via the mobile phone. The leading Japanese mail-order company 'Senshukai' discovered that more than 80 percent of its users order only from their mobile phone.[65] This observation also supports the hypothesis that convenience and the mobile phone as a form of remote control that is preferred over the PC – if one is available – can be more important for its use than any argument concerning the mobility of users.

Purchases that follow promotional mobile content may be of particular interest. Music purchases as a result of sample mobile music listening has been very popular in Japan. 'Tsutaya Online' is realizing higher sales with this mobile approach and also manages to direct mobile users into its stores after sending discount coupons on mobile phones.[66] **Mobile discount coupons** are among a number of new marketing support elements. They can be cheaper and more effectively distributed over mobile phones when users opt into this possibility.[67]

---

64 See Funk (2001b), p. 138.
65 See Funk (2001b), p. 140.
66 See Funk (2001a), p. 14.

Mobile marketing supports cross-media strategies that may increase usage intensity of media brands or recruit new customer groups for an established brand. As such, they aim at creating an **audience flow** for a media offer in its different representations across different channels (see D-3.1).

1.3.3
Market development cross-media strategies

Product variations of media offers provide different functions and add complementary value to existing media offers. Autonomous mobile media offers that are similar to the semantics of the original media product are a form of **versioning** that adapts to different transmission networks, devices, functions, and usage contexts (see A-1.21). Content is not newly created, but repurposed. Versioning strategies are suited for market development cross-media strategies, because digitization allows for a **dis- and re-integration of media content** and an integration of customer demands via personalization.[68] Therefore, new degrees of content configuration allow for quantity-, quality-, or time-based versioning strategies (for examples see Table A-1). Furthermore, **multiple use of content licenses** enables an efficient exploitation of popular media content and lowers the risk for content producers, particularly when licensing strategies as a means of media financing are already implemented before the media production process starts (see A-1.22).[69] Mobile media extends usage options for media audiences, offers alternative access possibilities to a service, and meets impulsive user needs (see B-3.2; C-2.22).[70]

Print media such as newspapers can overcome some of their inherent structural weaknesses by using mobile media. SMS alerts for breaking news can direct their readers to the online offer and provide a new time-related versioning strategy with acceleration – not delay – as its main feature. In the case of news alerts, this can be called a **forward integration of news delivery**. Otherwise, the next physical newspaper contact would be on the following day and audiences may turn to news updates delivered via broadcasting and other online media.[71] LAUFF (2002) suggests that newspapers can also use their **local core competencies** for location-based mobile services such as traffic news, event news, or information about sales.[72]

Mobile media characteristics such as the short mobile attention span need to be taken into account for the **design strategies of mobile content**.[73] In an international comparison, the time users dedicate to a mobile screen is below five

---

67   See Funk (2001b), p. 79; for example, the movie and video store Tsutaya Online convinced seven percent or 16,000 out of 240,000 mobile users to use discount coupons between May and July 2000, see Funk (2001b), p. 147.
68   See Hass (2004); Hess (2004), p. 77.
69   See Dreier (2004), p. 95.
70   Dreier argues that multiple access points to media content in more user contexts also support that media keeps its important societal function of integration, see Dreier (2002), p. 58.
71   See Feldmann and Zerdick (2004), pp. 28.
72   See Lauff (2002), p. 117.
73   See Feldmann (2001b); Dean (2002); Kelly (2005).

minutes on average with high variability reaching to only 1.5 minutes average mobile data usage per session in Japan. However, mobile users with more experience tend to increase the usage time.[74] Versioning strategies for mobile media, thus, suggest a **reduction of content** that is displayed on a mobile device; information provision - news or entertainment related – can, for instance, be restricted to headlines. However, it can be combined with on-demand and interaction options such as additional print, audio, or audiovisual content that users can opt into 2G or 2.5G networks are already used to directly **link mobile media offers** to other media content offers. For example, text-based headlines can be followed by a telephone number that will contain more extended audio news. Hyperlinks can lead to a WAP page with more information. Voice-links can also direct the user towards a call center. For next generation networks, mobile media offers are generally expected to develop from predominantly text-based to **predominantly video-based** because of the higher bandwidth in next generation networks (see B-2.1). In fact, the "intimate distance"[75] created by moving pictures may relate well with the hybrid of intimacy and anonymity of the telephone[76] as well as the personal nature of the mobile phone. However, pictures instead of video sequences may fulfill these functions as well and contribute to the argument that narrowband mobile content is not only more reasonable from an engineering and economic point of view (see B-2.11), but also from the user's perspective.

From an **organizational perspective**, the provision of mobile media as market development cross-media strategies can strongly rely on existing media production units. This is similar to online strategies of traditional media companies that are often closely related to the offline content in order to realize synergy effects. Online media provision is often not a core activity, but is integrated into existing (offline) business units.[77] Hereby, content management systems that support offline and online publishing formats need to be upgraded to also support mobile content production.

Easy organizational integration is particularly true for another option of mobile media distribution: the distribution of media content exactly as it is. **Audio content types** can use this possibility as a viable option. Cell phones can already be used to receive radio channels in exactly the same form as a radio set. Also, digital media files can be fully replayed as the mobile phone and MP3 players begin to merge. It is convenient for the user to carry only one portable device and it does not disrupt any foreground activity such as walking, driving, reading or other activities that requires the visual senses. Mobile devices could also allow for the download of audio books that is, for example, a fast growing segment in the German media market.[78] Media contents and formats that have previously worked well as mobile media in a wider definition (see Introduction-2.2) without a cell phone connection can continue to be successful even when they start

---

74 See Dean (2002), p. 255.
75 Frey (1999), p. 101.
76 See Zerdick (1990).
77 See Arrese and Medina (2002); Vogel (2001); Chan-Olmsted and Park (2000).
78 See Fey (2001), p. 237.

to **use new mobile devices.** The limitations of 'traditional' mobile media use with a mobile device, however, lie above all in **battery power** as the new emerging bottleneck. It is the users' choice to make the trade off between using the battery life of one session for mobile media applications or to save it for outgoing and incoming telephone calls.

1.3.4
Market diversification cross-media strategies

Autonomous mobile media products and services that open a new semantic space (product innovation) are classified as constituents of market diversification cross-media strategies. A mobile product innovation often has the representation of so called **small format content.**

Small format or cell media content requires the adaptation of content design towards the specific characteristics of the transmission media and the interface of the device. It also needs to take into account the different usage contexts of stationary and mobile users as well as their reasons for mobile media use. A push-delivery is often executed via SMS or MMS messaging services; pulled small format content can be accessed with a WAP browser or via mobile operators' portals such as i-mode, EZWeb, or T-Zones. However, the failure of WAP due to long connecting and downloading times, pricing models and overall disappointed expectations does not indicate that there will be high future user demand for a new WAP version.[79] Innovative mobile media offers in mobile operators' portals space may attract more attention, because of their prominent position and a common effort to overcome the deficiencies of WAP.

Personal relevance of content is essential for the acceptance of mobile (cell) media offers, because the attention span of mobile users is restricted and a lot shorter than in many other screen interaction situations.[80] Personalization reduces the complexity of a mobile media offer and reduces search and navigation costs for users.[81] It also means that media companies will have to develop more advanced **filtering systems** for personalization of content than the ones that are used for, e.g., personalized Internet newsletters. Collaborative filters may evolve into one option that can be developed for mobile contexts. They create the infrastructure for users to relate their preferences to the preferences of others and develop personalized recommendations based on a customer's purchase or consumption pattern and tastes.[82] Mobile filtering systems, however, need to additionally take different user contexts into account. For example, a user should be able to repress a service when it may be inappropriate or inconvenient to receive it (see B-3.13). Mobility is one of the most obvious reasons for the necessity of such an 'off-function'. When users are in public or when they are traveling, for

---

79 See Sigurdson (2001); Lauff describes the relationship between information utility and waiting time as inversely proportional, see Lauff (2002), p. 81.
80 See Feldmann (2002b); Groebel (2005).
81 See Rawolle, Kirchfeld, and Hess (2002), p. 341.
82 See Zerdick et al. (2000), p. 192.

example, they may not be willing to pay for the international roaming fees put on top of a mobile media service.

In terms of content strategies, the personal nature of cell media is likely to support a further diffusion of **adult content services**. In the Internet, among the major media providers only two types of information providers had early success in finding substantial revenues from subscribers: one area was adult content sites with sexually explicit material; the other area was financial information.[83] Evidence for popular media content for mobile phones demonstrates that financial information is not as successful as expected, but that erotic content services generate the largest mobile media revenue proportion.[84]

Mobile media as market diversification cross-media strategy can also stimulate the development of **new offline media format and content**. In Japan, print magazines such as 'Nikkei Mobile' are emerging that provide information on unofficial i-mode sites and other mobile content screening. In that regard, cross-channel extension also happens to some extent from mobile media offers towards traditional media.[85]

Mobile media may furthermore drive **voice-activation in media content development**. Nomadic environments and users' mobility in them often require that the attention is directed towards activities in the real world. Therefore, audio cues from the user to the mobile device and vice versa are likely to further develop in order to allow for a seamless integration of media consumption and mastering real-world tasks. **Audio content** is already uniquely produced for mobile devices, e.g. the 'Financial Times Deutschland' audio news. Storage for audio content in mobile devices could also allow for the download of personalized radio shows.[86] The market for audio books in Germany is a fast growing segment;[87] in the US, audible.com is a new player for audio content who offers subscription services to mass media content in audio files including 'The Wall Street Journal', 'The New York Times Audio Digest', 'Forbes', or 'NPR's' daily radio newsmagazine.[88] The main restriction to extensive listening to audio content via cell phones, again, is battery power.

The production of cell media requires specifically tailored production tools for mobile platforms to comply with content design criteria for cell media. The **economics of cell media** and its potential to become a profitable business largely depends on media firm internal decisions such as the bundling and pricing of cell media (see D-2.4) and media firm external factors such as the number of companies that participate in the mobile media value creation and that compete for revenue shares (see D-4.).

---

83   See Compaine (2000b), p. 451.
84   See Benninghoff (2003).
85   See Funk (2001b), p. 124.
86   See Kelly (2005).
87   See Fey (2001).
88   See www.audible.com.

2
Mobile content and service development for cross-media strategies

Mobile media can develop content into new areas as every new medium adds a new (re)combination of space-time configurations that influence the media. The assessment of the strategic options to extend cross-media strategies onto mobile platforms requires an analysis of this mobile content and service development. Similar to Internet or online media that **adds new functionalities** to print and electronic media, mobile media serves different functional needs (D-2.1). In order to systematize the evolving mobile formats, MCQUAIL's (2000) **distinction of new media categories** is useful to relate the social use of mobile communications to mobile format, content, and service development (D-2.2). Furthermore, the aggregation economics of new mobile media content must be considered to compare and evaluate various forms of bundling and pricing strategies (D-2.3).

2.1
Functional extensions of cross-media strategies and typology of mobile media categories

The question of the functional and format developments of mobile media for media audiences is essential for the evaluation of the design of mobile media offers. If, for example, an important functional development of online media consists in the creation of interaction opportunities between audience members - such as adherents of a certain TV format - the design and strategic development of online communities around media brands may be more important for media companies than the provision of streaming media. It also demonstrates that dimensions for functional and format developments lie in both the characteristics of the new media (see B) and its social use (see C).

2.1.1
Functional extensions of cross-media strategies

Mobile media, as every new media, differs functionally from traditional and from online media.[89] In order to describe the complementary dimensions of new media, research on cross-media strategies asks for both **functional similarities as well as differences** of different media.[90] Users expect online media, for example, to be related to the offline content and to the offline brand image. However, it should serve different functions such as independence of regional limitations or sovereign audio-visual media use independent of given time frames of radio and TV channels.[91] The emergence of new media can also lead to a **shift**

---

89   See Dreier (2002), p. 58; Caspar stresses that cross-channel media brand strategies have to be a
       functional, not just a communicative, enhancement, see Caspar (2002a), p. 29; for the discussion
       of the WWW as functional alternative to TV see Ferguson and Perse (2000).
90   See Ferguson and Perse (2000); Wolf and Sands (2000).
91   See Ridder (2002), p. 129; Reitze (2002), p.137.

of functions. One of the many effects of television on radio has been to shift radio from an entertainment medium that families used to gather around into a "kind of nervous information system"[92] for news, traffic data, and weather reports. For the effect of the Internet on radio SCHRAPE & TRAPPEL (2000) expect, e.g., a increase in segmentation of radio formats.[93] New digital media also offer value added services for traditional media.[94] In print markets, 'daily-me' papers[95] have not replaced newspapers and e-editions are often used complementarily, for example, to serve a specific market segment such as foreign markets. But functional shifts can also be rather subtle. Print-online cross-media strategies of newspapers with their immediate reaction capabilities to breaking news, for instance, challenge traditional TV and radio news formats that may loose some of their audience to online newspapers.[96]

Mobile media place different weight on functions known from online and traditional media and also provide opportunities for additional functions. Mobile cross-media extensions open innovative opportunities to **integrate mass media and interpersonal communications**; to create new communication spaces for audience members, e.g. SMS chat or match making services; to develop the communication links between media producers and media audiences such as remote participation formats; to personalize media offers; to create mobile brand communities around media brands; and to offer new forms of cross-promotion to advertising clients that may arouse attention for other advertising formats.

Two new functionalities are conceivable for (1) mobile coverage and (2) nomadic connectivity. The **always-on functionality** of mobile communications (see B-3.11) differentiates mobile media offers from media accessed with portable computing devices via nomadic wireless connectivity. Instantaneous readiness for use is self-evident for non-electronic media, e.g. print media, as well as for broadcast media that simply needs to be turned on or interpersonal communication media such as the telephone. Internet connectivity is usually only awarded after setting up a PC and an Internet connection; it requires some effort as well as time.[97]

In addition, media offers that use nomadic wireless connectivity can provide new functions such as **hot spot-based updates**. They can add value to mobile publishing services if they provide updates of digital information whenever a user is within the reach of a nomadic wireless network. For the newspaper industry, a combination of wireless connectivity with electronic paper would, for

---

92 McLuhan (2001), p. 298.
93 See Schrape and Trappel (2000). A substitution of broadcasting media through online media is also not plausible from a supply-side point of view even with high-speed Internet access and broadband media applications. Online content provision is dependent on the speed of data transmission, quality of service and access cost to the underlying infrastructure. For a back-of the envelope calculation of data transmission rates for live streams see Reimers (2002).
94 See Glotz (2001).
95 See Negroponte (1995).
96 See Oehmichen and Schroeter (2003), pp. 382. Feldmann & Zerdick, however, observe that in times of emergency broadcast media still outperform online media, see Feldmann and Zerdick (2004), p.28.
97 See Lauff (2002), p. 128.

example, create new opportunities while retaining the cost advantage of elec-tronic distribution.[98] Whenever the user is within the reach of a hotspot, the electronic paper could automatically request an update for the latest news.

The acceptance of mobile communications for audience participation for-mats has led to a revisited discussion of **interactive TV** in Europe. The mobile phone initiates more interaction with and among audience members than any complex interactive TV application that has been developed so far. It, again, sup-ports the argument of the mobile phone as a connective tissue between media brand, media organization, and media audience. In this case, it functions as in-teraction provider with its capabilities for synchronous and asynchronous two-way communications.

In media communications, the **uses-and gratifications approach** addresses the functional use-oriented positioning of media offers (see C-2.1).[99] It is a ver-sion of individualist functional theory and research that seeks to explain media use and gratifications from the motives and self-perceived needs of the audience members.[100] However, it is criticized, among other things, that typologies of 'motives' often fail to match patterns of actual selection or use. Despite the many difficulties of the uses and gratifications approach it still seems useful for some **purposes of description.** MCQUAIL (2000), for instance, combines audience moti-vations' influences on media choice into a heuristic model to understand the process of audience formation.[101] The functional use of a media offer as the core use dimension may, thus, be acceptable for descriptive purposes of mobile me-dia content and service models as well. For the **development of a heuristic** that combines influences of the mobile communication system and the social use of mobile communications into a model to understand the process of media con-tent and service development, the functional use can be further differentiated into the distinction between **experience use and symbolic use.** Experience use is related to the channel characteristics of the communications system while sym-bolic use relates to social functions that are grounded in the social use of the communication system.[102] These two sets of factors, the experiential and the symbolic use, are introduced in the following chapter to distinguish new media categories for mobile media formats.

2.1.2
Typology of mobile media categories

Mobile content and services are often grouped into categories such as news, en-tertainment, database query, or advertisement. The UMTS Forum, for example, distinguishes eight 3G service categories: rich voice (simple and enhanced), lo-

---

98   See Compaine (2000a), p. 475.
99   See Blumler and Katz (1974); Rosengren (1974); Rosengren, Wenner, and Palmgreen (1985).
100 See McQuail (2000), p. 504.
101 See McQuail (2000), pp. 391.
102 See Caspar (2002a), p. 101; Siegert uses functional use and symbolic use in the discussion of media brands. While the functional use asks for the core competency of the media brand, the symbolic use offers a psychological added value in her differentiation Siegert (2001), pp. 122.

cation-based services, multimedia messaging services (consumer and business), mobile Internet access, mobile intranet access, and customized infotainment.[103] Yet, these categories **fail to capture the new properties of mobile, interactive, network-based media,** because they only enumerate a number of services that could be enlarged or reduced as mobile media technological development, services, and audience taste changes.

For a more systematic description that is not as volatile as these service enumerations, the **proliferation of different categorical types** can be useful. Typologies are more abstract and represent a unique combination of attributes that are believed to determine the relevant outcomes.[104] In search of a possible basis for a 'new media theory' MCQUAIL (2000) argues that it is very difficult to distinguish the channel (or medium) from the typical *content* that it carries or the typical *use* that is made of it or the *context* of use (for instance home, work, or public place).[105] Due to the diversity of the category 'new media' and their continually changing nature he suggests distinguishing **four main categories of 'new media'** that share certain channel similarities and types of use:
1) **interpersonal communication media,**
2) **interactive play media,**
3) **information search media,** and
4) **collective participatory media.**

Under the assumption of **mobile media as a form of new media** this typology is transferred onto mobile media categories. For the systematic discrimination of mobile media categories, experiential use (channel characteristics, see Chapter B) and symbolic use (social use, see Chapter C) will be reduced to **four central dimensions.** The time-space dimensions connectivity and location flexibility are the characteristics of the mobile communications system that discriminate best, because every new medium introduces unique time-space relations. Concerning the social use of mobile communications, the arguments on self-identity and community formation are subsumed under relationship management; the notion of micro-coordination depicts a central social function of mobile communications and can enclose the mobile communication patterns of impulsive use, tele-presence and de-communication (see Fig. D-4).

Interpersonal communication mobile media includes mobile messaging and telephone services; mobile games are an example of interactive play mobile media; information search mobile media comprises a diverse range of information retrieval; and collective participatory mobile media includes collective action via mobile phones and user-contextualized content. All four categories will be analyzed in detail in the following chapter.

---

103 See UMTS Forum (2002b).
104 See Doty and Glick (1994), p. 232.
105 See McQuail (2000), pp. 126.

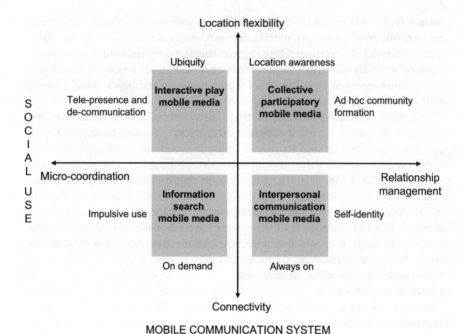

Figure D-4: Typology of mobile media categories

2.2
Categories of mobile content and services

Mobile media categories share certain types of content and services. For the further discussion of mobile content and services, COMPAINE's (1986; 2000) differentiation of **content (or substance), format, and process** is introduced. It is useful, because it abstracts from traditional boundaries of media industries, e.g. the newspaper or the television industry, that do not suffice for digital media any more. He distinguishes content, process, and format as several discrete types of activities that the media covers.[106] *Content* is gathered, stored and transmitted in a certain *process* and displayed for the user in a certain *format*. Digital media requires a re-evaluation of distinct industry boundaries with regard to formats; a virtual community format, e.g., can be run by both a news magazine or a TV channel. For a discussion of what content may be suited for integrated cross-media offers, various formats for mobile content and services will be analyzed.[107] They are subsumed under the four distinguished mobile media categories (see Figure D-5) and discussed in the following chapters.

---

106 See Compaine (2000a), pp. 542. For example, videocassette and cable are both displayed in a television format; yet they are alternative forms of delivering substance and they are television although they are not broadcasting. Thus process and format should not be confused when defining a medium.

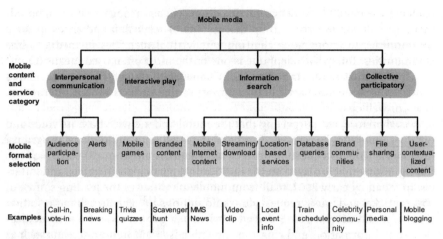

Figure D-5: Differentiation of formats for mobile content and service categories

2.2.1
Interpersonal communication mobile media

Interpersonal communications is among the most essential usage reason for mobile voice communications. Its combination with media offers is particularly interesting, because users have ubiquitous access to mobile content and mobile messaging services; mobile users can also evolve into distributors of mobile media when they receive forwarding and sharing opportunities. Formats for this mobile media category can take advantage of the **always-on functionality** of mobile devices (see B-3.11) and the mobile content offers as support for mobile **users self-identity in social networks** (see C-1.2).

Audience participation: Media organizations or existing media content offers can use mobile communications to engage in a communicative relationship with their audiences. One prominent communication-related format is audience participation. Audience participation has been integrated into media offers already in the 1960ies when audience members formed groups that gathered and jointly participated in the media consumption process.[108] HESS-LUETTICH (1990) characterizes phone-ins as **dialog-form of communication within mass media**.[109] It is the interactive back-channel for the audience to communicate with the media

---

107 Format refers to the form in which the substance is made available to the users. A format depicts a set of syntax and semantics. For example, hypertext is a central syntax feature of the World Wide Web that has stirred new format developments for web-based publishing, see Caspar (2002a), p. 24.
108 See Cassirer (1959); experiences range from group listening in Great Britain over farm forums in India to teleclubs in Japan.
109 See Hess-Luettich (1990), p. 282.

content providers.[110] Audience participation also has a long tradition in broad-casting.[111] It ranges from group discussions of television audiences in local communities to anonymous chatting with virtual identities in media online communities. Today, the telephone is one of the most often used means for audience participation, e.g. in radio and TV shows; additionally the Internet allows a variety of audience participation opportunities such as e-mail interaction, chats, or weblogs.[112]

It is, therefore, not surprising that the mobile phone with both its voice and texting capabilities has emerged as a tool to (1) call into audio-visual programs, (2) vote via SMS on a question posed within a media program, (3) place requests for, e.g. a song that is played on the radio, or (4) participate in games and lotteries. In Japan by early 2002, mail from mobile phones was the leading source of concert ticket and music requests for radio stations.[113] The British radio station 'Capital Radio' develops SMS-driven services using short codes for song dedication, song information, and ring-tone downloads.[114] Moreover, screens such as the **TV screen** can now be used as a **platform for interpersonal communications**. For example, viewers of the music channel MTV are able to send messages to their friends that are publicly displayed on the TV screen and seen by a wider than targeted audience. It is an example for the hybridization of private and public spaces in media worlds[115] (see B-3.13) and resembles in part the 'stage phoning' that some mobile phone users display in public (see C-1.22). It demonstrates that mobile messaging can support not only communication between media organizations and audiences, but also between audience members. Teletext is another medium that encourages the TV audience to use the TV screen as interaction interface between audience members. SMS teletext chats are popular interactive TV applications that are using the mobile phone.[116] Other forms of interpersonal communication-related audience participation formats include mobile letters to the editor or other forms of audience feedback.[117]

Alerts: Mobile messaging, in fact, generates an additional avenue for direct communication to and with media audiences, even though personalized pushed services are a form of one-way communication. A range of (interactive) text, graphic, audio and audio-visual content can be integrated with messaging services to create **alternative platforms for audience access to news, information, and entertainment**. Traditional media increasingly use alerts for the delivery of mobile content. These are time-critical pieces of information that are pushed to the users who have opted into the service. Newspapers use mobile alerts to deliver headlines of **breaking news**; a functionality that traditionally radio – which

---

110 See Beck (1989), p. 62.
111 See Cassirer (1959).
112 See Glotz (2001), p. 5.
113 See Funk (2005).
114 These SMS-services cost between £0.25-2.50, see N.N. (September 23, 2003).
115 See for example Weiss and Groebel (2002).
116 See Bisenius and Siegert (2002), p. 29.
117 See Plant (2000), p. 81.

remains the most pervasive medium worldwide – held as a carrier of news and disaster information.[118] Radio is immediate, informative, and credible. However, mobile media may also **functionally augment radio** through the implementation of additional pushed alerts to cell phones. Next to news services, entertaining formats from print to TV use mobile alerts to distribute personalized entertainment news. These can, for example, be related to a certain program or to a certain celebrity. Alerts are predominantly text-based in 2.5G networks, but are including pictures and may include more media types from video to 3D graphics in next generation wireless networks.

2.2.2
Interactive play mobile media

Interactive play mobile media can make use of the location flexibility of mobile services and create formats that extend interactive play applications from purely 'location-bound' to 'ubiquitously available' (see B-3.12). They can be used to establish a **continuous tele-presence in the media offer** and allow for micro-coordination of, e.g., game passages on the move. On the other hand, they can be used to create a virtual private space in the public and de-communicate with immediate surroundings (see C-2.33).

Mobile games: Mobile gaming applications are of particular interest, because handheld gaming is a successful mobile application for non-IP enabled portable electronic media devices (see B-1.12); moreover, game consoles as well as PC-based video games are increasing their popularity.[119] News content providers such as Asahi News and Nikkei News in Japan are experimenting with mobile quiz games designed to attract subscribers and provide market research potential in the long run. Users can accumulate points to win prizes while advertisers can include questions about products and commercials, e.g. to test the effect of TV advertising.[120] **Interactive TV SMS games** include trivia quizzes or on-screen multiplayer games such as WaterWar, an SMS-controlled game developed by the Finnish company 'Frantic Media'. Up to 30 audience members control on-screen characters via SMS commands, similar to a capture-the-flag game.[121]

However, mobile games are not a successful proposition in any case. In 2001, the Japanese online trading company 'DLJ Securities' developed a mobile trading game that simulates the stock market.[122] The 30,000 users of the game were 22 years old on average in contrast to the average of 40 years of DLJs customers. DLJ hopes to convert the young mobile Internet users into customers. Yet, mobile stock trading, an application that has been envisioned as a driver of mobile Internet use in order to transact in real-time from mobile phones, does not turn

---

118 See Pease and Dennis (1994).
119 See McInnes et al. (2002); Jones (2004).
120 See Funk (2001b), p. 110.
121 See Obstfeld (September 25, 2002), p. 4.
122 See Funk (2001b), p. 98.

out to be particularly suited for roaming or even stationary mobile user situations. DLJ offers analysis on the PC and transaction via mobile phones. However, the PC requires three pages to buy or sell stocks while an i-mode pone requires eight pages. A telephone call to announce the planned transactions to an operator would be a lot more convenient and context-suited. In this case, the **design of a mobile game may not prove helpful** in the long run to inspire users for real-world applications.

Branded content: For advertisers, interactive play mobile media is an interesting option to transfer the concept of branded content onto mobile platforms (see A-1.12). Media companies may co-brand that type of content to increase spill-over effects into both directions.[123] Mobile content that lends itself to become mobile branded content can be **fun-oriented applications** such as mobile multiplayer games or mobile scavenger hunts. Since it is in the interest of the advertising company that the mobile branded content spreads and that it exploits the opportunities of mobile network effects, mobile peer-to-peer communities can be used to allow users to **swap mobile branded content.**[124] For mobile operators and potentially media companies as mediators the increase in traffic with mobile multiplayer games can lead to an increase in revenues. Depending on their negotiation power, media companies could additionally participate in these revenues as a new form of advertising revenues.

2.2.3
Information search mobile media

Mobile users who value immediate access to content services upon any impulse (see C-2.22) may value the opportunity to take advantage of information search mobile media. If this form of content pull is not sufficient, on demand requests of push services (see B-3.11) can also be used.

Mobile Internet content: A widespread assumption about potentially successful mobile media content is the **use of mobile media for the dissemination of news.**[125] Evidence from the Asia-Pacific region on mobile information usage supports the doubts on an essential role of mobile in news and information retrieval. Data from Japan reveals that news is not among the most wanted mobile content services. Entertainment-related content is more desirable to the majority of mobile users. In Japan, particularly the unofficial i-mode sites show a **strong affinity towards entertainment,** 77 percent of the registered unofficial sites can be classified entertainment-related.[126] FUNK (2001) suggests that simple

---

123 See Siegert (2001), pp. 175; Mueller-Kalthoff (2002a), p. 25.
124 See Feldmann (2005b).
125 Glotz, e.g., argues that typical radio service such as financial information will be disseminated via personalized devices and UMTS and challenge the radio industry, see Glotz (2001), p. 4.
126 See Funk (2001b), p. 33; in this statistic, individual and communication/dating sites, ringing tones, games, screen savers, and adult content are considered entertainment related, while phone information and restaurants are not.

content is most appropriate for information search mobile media offers. In Japan, content such as weather and general news, information about music or concert tickets as well as entertainment applications are far more successful than business news, car sales, or rental information that have been expected to provide useful real-time and location-specific information.[127]

Mobile Internet content can include **on demand messaging services** that push mobile content to users upon request. Examples of current MMS service offerings include MMS slide shows that are used for weather reports, sports and entertainment highlights, and adult content services.[128] A trial version of T-Mobile's MMS news in July 2003 in Germany featured the popular (print) media brands 'Stern', 'Sport Bild', and 'Gala'.[129]

Streaming and download services: Next generation networks will allow the **mobile streaming and download of audio and video files.** Media services such as music downloads are envisioned as are replays of a best-of collection of soccer goals. A number of trials have been implemented across Europe and Asia. In Germany, T-Mobile already purchased the mobile rights to offer mobile video coverage of the national soccer league. A live goal ticker with video sequences is scheduled to start with the Bundesliga 2003/04 season. In the meantime, T-Mobile customers can order 20-second news, entertainment, and erotica video clips priced between EUR 1.99-2.49 per message. In Finland, 'Soprano MobileTV' service allows consumers to watch movies and other television programs for EUR 1.70 per week.[130] In the UK, the customers of the mobile operator 3 have access to specially formatted ITN video news bulletin that are typically 90 seconds long.[131] In Japan, NTT DoCoMo launched the one-to-many video streaming service M-Stage V-Live for 3G 'Freedom of Multimedia Access' (FOMA) phones. The 'Free Channels' for V-live subscribers and the 'Member Channels' for customers of content providers as well as corporate users which enable users to download or stream live and archived content.[132]

Location-based services: Location-based services are another carrier of great expectations for information search mobile media. In general, location-based services can be differentiated into four categories: safety-related services, billing-related services, local information-related services and tracking and positioning services (see B-3.12).[133] For media companies, **local information-related services** may become of interest, because local expertise could be translated into new audience services. Local newspapers and magazines or travel guides,

---

127 See Funk (2001b), p. 52; Funk (2001a); he also observes that young people tend to put more emphasis on reach and a variety of contents whereas people over 30 with more specialized interests appreciate rich information more, see Funk (2001b), p. 53; Funk (2004), pp. 122.
128 See Pedersen, Nysveen, and Thorbjørnsen (2003).
129 See N.N. (July 7, 2003b).
130 See N.N. (September 25, 2002); the service has been developed by Nokia, the communications firm Soprano Communications, the software provider Oplayo, and the film distributor FS Film.
131 See N.N. (February 25, 2003).
132 See N.N. (April 25, 2003).
133 See Schilcher and Deking (2002)

can consider providing mobile local information and editorial content on certain locations. However, these services are difficult and costly to implement and require user information that can easily conflict with data protection legislation.[134] The difficulties of implementing location-based services and transaction management models are among the reasons for the low acceptance of location-based services in Japan.[135] Media companies may consider collaborating with municipalities or cultural institutions such as museums to offer location-based mobile information services.[136]

Mobile database queries: Databases are often neglected as one essential element that can provide value when users are disconnected from their usual information sources. Database queries such as finding information about the last train departure at night enjoy popularity in Japan in opposition to map-based navigation services that suffer from low resolutions and small displays.[137] Contextual, impulsive needs to look up numbers, addresses, tips, timetables and the like create usage reasons for mobile applications and provide value that users may be willing to pay for, e.g. on a per usage basis.[138] However, media companies have to reorganize their content management to **give access to databases and archives** that add value to their mobile audiences.

Mobile music order services are one example for potentially attractive **mobile media database applications**. A 'music over mobile' trial version by MTV, BMG and mmO2 already functions via 2.5G networks. Customers select a 'get new music' option and receive a selection of top chart hits presented by MTV for a twelve second trial listening and a subsequent purchase option. Selected tracks can be downloaded within 90 seconds on a mobile MP3-player that can be clipped to a mobile phone.[139]

2.2.4
Collective participatory mobile media

Ad-hoc collective participation options for mobile communications (see C-2.4) represent some of the **user-driven innovation mobile services** (see A-2.3) that have the potential to develop bottom-up with social use. They can evolve into interesting options for both activity- and belief-based communities (see C-1.31).

Mobile brand communities: MUNIZ & O'GUINN (2001) introduce the concept of brand communities that can be applied to the management of (mobile) media brand communities (see C-1.31).[140] Particularly in the entertainment world,

134 See Freytag and Neumann (1999).
135 See Funk (2001b), p. 52; Funk (2001a); he also observes that young people tend to put more emphasis on reach and a variety of contents whereas people over 30 with more specialized interests appreciate rich information more, see Funk (2001b), p. 53; Funk (2004), pp. 104.
136 For a prototype of a mobile situated documentaries see Pavlik and McIntosh (2005).
137 See Funk (2001b), p. 105.
138 See Geisselbrecht and Fotschki (2002), p. 238.
139 See N.N. (March 14, 2003).

consumers turn to media brands as intermediaries that can aggregate content and audiences.[141] HUMMEL & LECHNER (2001) suggest virtual communities as a model for media content management. Hereby, interaction with and among users is part of the creation of content.[142] **Community-related mobile media platforms** can be used to expand these virtual community models of media brands. The admirers of a media brand or a media featured celebrity receive the option to multiply their contacts with the brand community. **Repurposed mobile media content** can be pushed regularly such as daily quotes or program teasers, or irregularly as breaking news. For example, music magazines can offer their readers to keep them updated on a favorite band or singer. Television formats that create high emotional audience involvement such as soap operas or real people formats may deliver motives for the audience to participate in mobile community offers and express opinions and emotions. The Netherlands' music TV channel TMF provides an example for a **cross-media brand community** that aligns the TV channel brand and its online communities with the use of a mobile device. It allows its audience to register in TMF's online community with a digital photograph. The picture is shown on the TV screen when the user sends an SMS to the channel, a service that allows TMF to outperform MTV in the SMS service market.[143]

Mobile media can also be used as platform for ad-hoc communities to inform users who are planning spontaneous collective actions. RHEINGOLD (2002) describes these **swarming tactics** that use the mobile phone for purposes of microcoordination and may base decisions of group formation based on information derived from mobile media offers (see C-2.4).

Mobile file sharing platforms: Instant and ubiquitous access to virtual storage or ad hoc community formation for both social network-based mobile communities and anonymous members of an activity-based mobile community may offer incentives for **file and information sharing**. Mobile file sharing in ad hoc communities can take advantage of social networks of mobile users, social aspects of physical proximity, and new interaction patterns.[144] **User-generated content** such as digital pictures, sound greetings, or video recordings may become popular properties for sharing within small world social networks. Since the mobile phone is increasingly used as a means of self-expression, its nature suggests personal file sharing as well as using mobile peer-to-peer platforms as a means of **virtual storage**. Professionally produced media content, on the other hand, may be shared in the form of links that point towards files that will be available for

---

140 See Muniz and O'Guinn (2001).
141 See Wolf (1999), p. 218.
142 See Hummel and Lechner (2001). For a discussion of virtual communities as business models see also Timmers (1998), p. 6; Kannan, Chang, and Whinston (2001). Online communities can exert a powerful influence on a product's adoption, both favorable and unfavorable; for example, investment experts who provided advice in online communities as a special service have in some cases been forced publicly to acknowledge errors in recommendations when community members pointed them out. See Rangaswamy and Gupta (1998), p. 16.
143 See Obstfeld (September 25, 2002), p. 2.
144 See Feldmann (2005b).

later download on a different device or via a different network. The distinct role of mass media providers can hereby lie in the community platform provision and management of mobile peer-to-peer communities.

User-contextualized content: A hybrid between user-generated and professionally produced content is user-contextualized content. Consumers increasingly become **co-creators of value.**[145] They actively participate in generating the value they derive from a product. On the mobile Internet, consumers can, for example, provide reviews on experiences with local business entities. Experiences from the Internet where they can forward editorial content such as newspaper articles via e-mail to interested friends may also be transferred to mobile settings. **Forwarding capabilities together with personal messaging services** can make use of the social networks of mobile customers and can evolve into interesting revenue drivers, mainly for operators though through an increase in network traffic. When a media brand community is able to generate a lot of additional traffic based on the media content, this should become a proposition for new revenue sharing agreements with mobile operators.

2.3
Bundling and pricing strategies in mobile media markets

Users' adoption of mobile media is not only dependent on the content and services that are developed, but also on the **bundling architecture and the options for price discrimination**. The aggregation form and the pricing of mobile media is an important incentive structure for mobile media use across mobile media categories. Therefore, supply-side and demand-side economies of aggregation have to be considered as well as alternative pricing models that provide sufficient transparency and have their origin in user needs.

In media markets, bundling strategies are an **essential element of delivering media content** to consumers.[146] Media products are offered bundled in print media subscriptions, compilations on a music CD, or program bundles in a pay TV bouquet. They can also be made accessible in an unbundled way such as in some paid content models, e.g. for online media, or in free TV channels where the user has no lock-in effect to stay with a particular program. Digital media production and distribution has **altered options for bundling strategies**. Yet, mobile cellular media distribution brings changes about, again.

---

145 See Senge and Carstedt (2001), p. 32.
146 The discussion of bundling strategies in economics builds upon the seminal work by Adams and Yellen (1976); Schmalensee (1984); McAfee, McMillan, and Whinston (1989). For an economic introduction to bundling see for example Varian (2000a), pp. 444.

2.3.1
Economies of aggregation for mobile media offers

Mobile media are subject to distinct **supply-side economies of aggregation** that differ from online media. Hence, bundling strategies as discussed for digital media provision in the Internet may not be appropriate for digital media provision via mobile cellular networks.

Cost characteristics of digital information goods comprise high first copy costs and marginal costs of reproduction that are close to zero. These cost characteristics lead to economies of scale that are supported by network effects and can be exploited for network goods. BAKOS & BRYNJOLFSSON (2000) introduce the notion of **economies of aggregation** for digital information goods and suggest that pure bundling strategies are the optimal form of bundling.[147] Their argument is based on the assumption that aggregation and pricing strategies are dependent on the delivering medium. Since the Internet has significantly reduced the marginal cost of distributing digital information, large scale bundling can create economies of aggregation for information goods. The aggregation of information bundles also entails several types of cost such as production, distribution, transaction, binding, and menu costs. Therefore, the decision to aggregate information goods is based on the trade-off between these costs and the benefits of aggregation.

This view is contrasted by CHUANG & SIRBU (1999) who suggest that in cases of **heterogeneous customer demand** mixed bundling strategies for digital information goods can outperform pure bundling. The underlying assumption is that consumers only value a subset of the bundle components, i.e. that consumer preferences are multi-dimensional.[148] In the case of academic journal publications, for example, customers may well be interested in one particular article only. In these cases, mixed bundling reaps the rents from price discrimination best.[149] Both types of aggregation can be observed in traditional and online media markets. Mixed bundling strategies are increasingly used by online media providers who offer free services to their subscriber base and paid content models for either premium content or archival requests as well as online subscription services.

---

147 See Bakos and Brynjolfsson (2000); in an earlier paper they differentiate bundling as aggregation across different goods, site licensing as aggregation across different consumers, and subscription pricing as aggregation across different time periods, see Bakos and Brynjolfsson (2000).

148 In the model of Bakos & Brynjolfsson (1999), consumer valuations of goods are independent and identically distributed, therefore it can only capture consumer valuations for the bundle in its aggregate. Chuang & Sirbu (1999) advance this view on the aggregate willingness to pay by asking for the correlation of values for the components in the bundle. In their model, the choice of the optimal bundling and pricing strategy is affected on the demand side by the component rank in order of preference and the fraction of articles that have one-zero value to the consumer.

149 By offering both mixed bundling and unbundled services, the publisher can extract consumer surplus more completely via consumer self-selection. However, super-bundles of multiple journals and site licensing can expand the product mix as well, see Chuang and Sirbu (1999). Olderog & Skiera (2000) show that the degree of benefit conferred by the bundling strategies depends essentially on the relation between consumers' reservation price for the product and variable costs, see Olderog and Skiera (2000).

Bundling examples for mobile media offers can be drawn from NTT DoCo-Mo's experiences with the i-mode service. I-mode offers a range of **mobile content subscriptions** that users pay for on a monthly basis in addition to the usage-dependent traffic fees. Whereas the subscription services in Japan are well received they still lack mobile user acceptance in the European i-mode extensions. However, for next generation services, DoCoMo may change the subscription model that already faces less adoption for 3G FOMA services. In mobile media markets, the **revenue sharing models** between mobile operators and content providers for bundled mobile media offers are an additional important element. NTT DoCoMo has introduced a 91/9 sharing model for content providers and operators in Japan and a modified version, an 86/14 sharing model, in Europe.[150] The large share of revenue participation in bundled subscription services may be an argument in favor of mobile bundling from the perspective of the media content provider. Yet, the supply-side economics will change in next generation service models and may also change mobile operators' willingness to share revenues.

2.3.2
Mixed bundling of mobile media offers

Aggregation of digital information goods is less attractive when marginal costs of production and distribution are high or when consumer demand is very heterogeneous. If marginal costs are non-trivial, then **dis-aggregation can economize on these costs** by allowing users to opt out of elements of the bundle.[151] This argument applies to 'bandwidth-hungry' mobile media content and services in next generation networks. Also, mobile customers may perceive the flexibility dimensions that are inherent in mobile voice communications bundles as useful for mobile data communications bundles as well and, thus, develop heterogeneous customer demand structures.

Although mobile voice services have profited from bundling[152] and have contributed to new subscriber growth and more extensive usage, mixed bundling strategies may become the **dominant bundling strategy for next generation mobile content services** due to
1) distribution cost for the delivery of mobile media offers,
2) heterogeneous and multi-dimensional consumer preferences regarding personalized mobile data services, and
3) the option value of bundles.[153]

---

150 Reportedly, this difference is due to more service provided by European mobile operators such as call center services in case of customer questions or complaints and other services.
151 See Bakos and Brynjolfsson (2000). This holds also true when customers are characterized by heterogeneous maximum consumption levels, see Wu, Chen, and Anandalingam (2002).
152 See Alleman (2005).
153 See Feldmann (2002a).

Ad 1: For mobile media, the distribution costs can be significant unlike in fixed-line Internet models. For a cellular real-time delivery of mobile media content, **marginal costs of distribution cannot be modeled as close to zero;** hence, they decrease potentials for economies of aggregation. BROWN (2005) analyzes the cost of delivering mobile mass media content for text, audio, and video using three alternatives to reduce the initial real-time delivery high quality costs: reducing the bit rate, increasing capacity, and searching for alternative delivery models (see B-2.11). As a result, he suggests that significant cost savings are only possible in a broadcasting delivery model since here the marginal delivery cost per user is zero.[154] One way to achieve such a content sharing delivery model is to aggregate content demand requests. **Demand aggregation** is an emerging area of marketing research that is gaining significance with new possibilities via digital ICTs.[155] Advantages for buyers lie in reduced cost, for sellers in the potential to capture more buyers and enlarge market share.[156]

Ad 2: In order to offer attractive pricing models, unbundling of mobile media services can also better meet consumer demands due to **more options for price discrimination.** The opportunities to react on impulses via mobile communications (see C-2.22) support the argument that user needs for mobile content do not follow habituation patterns and are not as dependent on bundling models as in traditional media offers. To the contrary, **context-specific mobile media** offers are difficult to plan for from the content provider point of view. For customers, mobile content offers do not provide similar functions of traditional media bundles such as newspapers that can serve as an insurance against communicative isolation in society. Therefore, multidimensional consumer preferences can be used as an argument for unbundling mobile media as well.

Ad 3: Yet, there may be willingness to pay for the **optional value to use mobile data services.** In this case, consumers may prefer a small monthly subscription and higher per use costs when they decide to use a mobile data offer. However, subscription models are more likely for text-based mobile media offers than audio-visual content types due to the bundle price that also needs to balance the transmission cost and network management.

The argument that unbundling options and mixed bundling strategies for mobile media distribution outperform the former pure bundling strategy can also be regarded as consistent with evidence from the **success of bundling strategies in early market phases.** FUNK (2001) argues that fixed-term paid subscrip-

---

154 See Brown (2005); in broadcast markets such as Germany an on demand broadcasting model is currently not viable due to restrictions in media law.
155 See Voeth (2002).
156 Voeth demonstrates that a formal optimization for sellers and buyers is not congruent and reveals potential for intermediaries, see Voeth (2002). Zerdick critically observes that sellers can circumvent price reductions in initial setting of high prices (personal conversation from May 6, 2003). From a theoretical perspective of new institutional economics this problem can be interpreted as a misuse of information asymmetries in a principal-agent relationship between buyers and sellers.

tion services are the initially important business model for mobile content providers.[157] However, as consumers learn about potential benefits through bundled content offers and the mobile data markets are advancing and maturing, more differentiated bundling strategies will be able to meet heterogeneous consumer preferences best. Thus, mixed bundling strategies are emerging as the optimal form of bundling for mobile media offers.[158] Customer bundling models may become an option for future digital wireless broadcast delivery of audiovisual content.

2.3.3
Value-based pricing strategies

Pricing of media and entertainment as well as telecommunication services is a very essential and **sensitive parameter in the design of bundling strategies.**[159] It gets even more complicated when an innovative service is introduced into the market such as next generation mobile services.[160] Pricing designs have to take into consideration the still unknown information needs and use behavior patterns of the mobile communications customer. Under uncertainty, **differentiated pricing structures** allow more effective market segmentation and the capturing of additional market share. On the other hand, consumers show strong preferences for **simple pricing schemes,** in particular for their individual spending on media and information and communications technologies.[161]

Generally speaking, pricing schemes for mobile data can be differentiated into metered and unmetered pricing. **Unmetered flat-rate pricing** promotes greater usage of services because it guarantees an upper limit, but it can possibly create conflicts when network loads during peak hours become too heavy.[162] **Metered pricing systems** can be differentiated into time-based, data volume-based, location-based, and value-based metered pricing.

In mobile data communications, time-based pricing strategies in circuit-switched networks and volume-based pricing strategies in packet-switched networks have neither been accepted. **Time-based pricing schemes** have failed for

---

157 See Funk (2001b), p. 64.
158 If media companies or new mobile data service providers can enter the mobile media market with unbundled services or as a one-product company, market entry barriers rather consists of implementing billing systems than receiving access to the mobile distribution channel.
159 See Odlyzko (2001a), p. 30; Edquist (2003a), p. 29. In Germany, consumer protection measures include that value-added SMS service providers using a 0190 service number are not allowed to charge more than EUR 3 for ringtone and logo downloads that are advertised in youth magazines, see N.N. (August 9, 2002).
160 From a marketing research point of view, a conjoint analysis is one possible method to analyze consumer preferences on bundles of properties and willingness to pay for alternative bundles. Analogies are sometimes used as a tool to base extrapolation methods upon them. The results can, however, be misleading due to different assumptions and contexts.
161 In the 19th century, simple pricing plans already showed results: when the pricing structure of the telegraph in Paris was changed to fixed prices within the Paris tube network independent of the message length, the volume of the messages being passed around the network almost doubled in the first year, see Standage (1998), p. 101.
162 The strong public preference for flat-rate pricing is based on risk avoidance and overestimation of usage, according to Odlyzko who quotes Bell System studies, see Odlyzko (2001a), p. 20.

WAP-applications and even data **volume-based pricing** for GPRS does not unlock the market potential so far that initially has been targeted. Consumers are uncertain about the size of applications that they consider using on cellular networks which inhibits usage.[163] Two potential pricing strategies have found widespread acceptance in mobile communications to date: for voice services, **bulk minute plans** give users more certainty on their spending for communications expenses and drive traffic into the networks. At the same time, operators have a calculated steady income basis. Block pricing plans as, e.g., implemented for wireless voice services in the US also have potential to make usage-based pricing plans for mobile data communications simpler.[164] For SMS communication and content services that are delivered in a messaging mode, **value-based pricing** is an option that consumers are familiar with.

While flat-rate pricing is the preferred option from the consumer perspective[165] and data volume-based pricing from the network engineering perspective, value-based pricing is the preferred option from a marketing perspective, because value-based pricing captures consumer rents best. Hereby, differentiated pricing is based on the **perceived value of a service or application** and on the basis of customers' willingness to pay. Starting from the perspective of the consumer it calculates how much the provision of a service is allowed to cost and what margins can be achieved. Value-based pricing is very common in the media industries, that typically use a mix of different sources for media financing in order to achieve intended margins (see A-1.1). Value-based pricing also simplifies billing models that do not have to implement measurements of volume or time. The accepted price may only change in international roaming situations. But also for international clearinghouses, value-based pricing for mobile content would be beneficial, because it relieves them from measuring individual volume and time use in roaming situations.

For media companies, the degree of price differentiation from a revenue perspective and the cost-saving potential from economies of aggregation from a cost perspective will be relevant parameters for decisions on pricing models. More so, however, the **sensitivity for the mobile user contexts** will contribute to acceptance of pricing strategies. Thus, pricing systems for mobile data services should aim at being flexible in order to optimize revenue streams and to take advantage of price differentiation opportunities. Yet, in the discussion about sophisticated dynamic pricing schemes for **real-time mobile content** based on val-

---

163 However, Funk suggests that in Japan users appear to be more aware of content charges than of packet charges. As a consequence, mobile operators strategy towards content charges should not destroy incentives for content providers to develop new mobile services. Instead, mobile operators can increase their revenues via packet charges while supporting positive feedback effects for the provision of mobile content. See Funk (2001b), p. 41.

164 The introduction of AT&T's 'Digital One Rate' pricing plan for wireless voice services in 1998 marks an essential caesura in the US wireless voice market. It featured a single payment for a large block of time and has been widely imitated; subsequently, wireless usage surged, see Odlyzko (2001a), p. 21; Alleman (2005). Alleman as well as Carter critically reflect the consequences for the wireless telecommunications industry in which wireless voice has become a commodity, see Alleman (2005); Carter (2005).

165 Odlyzko argues based on historical evidence that even tiny charges based on utilization decrease usage substantially due to user preferences for simple pricing plans, see Odlyzko (2001a).

ue, customer demand, and network capacity, one potential challenge of dynamic price management may be to update users in real-time on pricing changes.

2.3.4
Mobile billing and payment systems

Mobile billing and payment systems that customers trust are an important pre-condition for the sustainability of mobile media offers. Media companies and other mobile content providers are facing a significant challenge when they have to build billing and payment systems themselves. Mobile operators are the **most natural billing aggregators and payment intermediaries** (see Table D-2). They have billing systems in place but make their micro-payment systems often only available to a limited amount of partners. Alternative micro-payment systems for mobile content providers can include bank transfers, credit cards, pre-paid cards, fixed-line telephone accounts and portal sites.[166] Many content providers are using a **premium rate reverse-billed SMS model** as a standard way for simple content to be paid across mobile operators' networks. Mobile operators as well as other mobile ASPs that contribute to value creation receive revenue shares from the premium rate that is charged. Another possibility is the retail sale of vouchers for **prepaid mobile entertainment services.**[167] Consumers can use these vouchers, e.g. retail scratch cards, to download icons, ringtones, and games directly to their handsets.[168]

Table D-2: Selected mobile billing and payment options

Billing aggregator and payment intermediary	(Dis)advantages	Mobile user perspective
Network operator	(+) Existing customer relationship	Convenient
ASP (third party)	(+) Prepaid services (retail) (-) M-wallet applications	Integrated in everyday life User investment for configuration, lack of trust
Credit card company	(-) No micro-payments	Security concerns

As cell phones develop from a communications into a transactions device, billing systems need to handle **pre-paid, post-paid, and passed-off to third party**

---

166 See Funk (2001b), pp. 73; the Japanese Government was pressuring NTT DoCoMo in 2001 to open its service for all content providers. One problem to that suggestion that DoCoMo put forward, however, is that they cannot inspect all contents beforehand, see Funk (2001b), p. 73.
167 Funk reports that a regulatory challenge arises from pre-paid services. Mobile operators have to inform their pre-paid customers about the remaining time before making a call, but problems arise when they have to ensure that the remaining number of packets will suffice to complete a data transaction, see Funk (2001b), p. 181.
168 See McDonough (May 24, 2002). The mobile ASP Digital Bridges uses mobile prepaid services for its games 'Star Trek: First Duty' and 'Men in Black II' and forms relationships with music companies to offer prepaid mobile music. Vouchers can also be integrated in artists' CDs or DVDs.

data services. Two competing systems, m-wallet capabilities on the front end and billing software at the backend, have not found acceptance in the market yet.[169] Technical challenges in m-payment comprise issues of authentication; authorization; confidentiality to protect payment against the monitoring of details; and non-repudiation, a guarantee that the consumer cannot falsely claim not to have participated in the transaction. Security challenges include encryption, digital signatures, Public Key Infrastructures, and Secure Electronic Transactions. Other challenges include the role of payment service providers and trusted third parties. But more challenges lie ahead of mobile operators that struggle to migrate from circuit-switched to packet-switched IP billing systems. The lack of appropriate micro-payment systems is a current barrier to the introduction of **demand-oriented IP billing models**. These models need to integrate database marketing and customer relationship management systems to implement price differentiation strategies. Since the value proposition of mobile media offers may vary significantly, billing systems should be able to price them differently according to their functional value. Further, billing systems have to be compatible with a broad variety of different handsets and third party application providers.

As mobile operators start integrating services across networks, **customer profitability across networks** may also become an interesting parameter for the choice of pricing and billing strategies. Pricing for IP delivered information may vary depending on the network that is chosen. For mobile operators as well as for the mobile content providers this means that customer profitability may have to be re-defined across networks as well. The **billing complexity will further increase** with the need to consolidate billing data from heterogeneous IT environments, geographically dispersed sources, multiple business partners and the responsibility to communicate charging information to customers in real-time for event-driven pay-per-view services. Alternatively or additionally to mobile operators' billing systems an independent third party clearing house model may be more promising for specified billing services. In any case, an outsourcing of billing and payment functions can be helpful for media companies to concentrate on their core competencies, i.e. mobile content production and bundling.

From the perspective of a media content provider, mobile content is unlikely to be a stand-alone business proposition, but it can add value to audiences and advertising clients when integrated in existing cross-media strategies and managed across the variety of next generation networks.

3
Integration of mobile media into cross-media strategies and emergence of cross-network strategies

The analysis of the mobile communication system and its social use have shown that media content transmission via next generation cellular networks poses significant economic and political challenges and that relationship management

---

169 See Sabat (2002), p. 521.

and micro-coordination are essential criteria for the social use of mobile communications. Therefore, an **integrated approach of offline, online, and mobile media** is suggested to exploit the functional complementarities in a better way than a stand-alone mobile media model.

Cross-media strategies become particularly powerful when they integrate the different existing formats and processes of media content, because they can exploit the complementary strengths and functionalities of each medium (3.1). Furthermore, the variety of wireless networks - which each offer distinct characteristics with regard to parameters such as speed of data transfer or directionality modes of communication - suggest to deliver media services across different networks (3.2).

3.1
Cross-media audience flows between traditional, online, and mobile media content

The integration of stationary offline and online content with forms of mobile media are meant to secure competitive advantages in both audience and advertising markets.[170] It can exploit the **benefits of different distribution modes and of users' demand for personalization degrees**, mobility, and their relation to physical environments.[171] From the point of view of media audiences, integrated traditional media, online media, and mobile media can create a meta-narrative across different media (3.11); cross-media audience flows can become of interest for media companies' advertising clients and their cross-promotion activities (3.12); within the integrated offer the role of mobile media can also be to serve as a remote control for steering interactive involvement with traditional or online media (3.13).

The **audience flow concept** has its origin in television program management. Here, the sequences of programs and the way they hand over to a subsequent program are chosen and designed to lead audience members from one program into the next one and to prevent them from channel surfing. For individual television viewing choice, RUST & ALPERT (1984) develop an audience flow model incorporating considerations of utility, audience flow, and audience segmentation.[172] With the growing numbers of media distribution platforms, media companies are developing audience flow concepts **towards a cross-media audience flow**.[173] Audience flow effects such as lead-in's to a network's subsequent programs are now transferred to cross-media lead-in's.

---

170 See Mueller-Kalthoff (2002a), p. 19.
171 See Ahy (2001); Rawolle, Kirchfeld, and Hess (2002); Reichwald and Schaller (2002).
172 See Rust and Alpert (1984). Genre-specific explanations based on expectations and cognitive demands have been identified as factors that can hold attention to a television program, see Hawkins et al. (2002).
173 See Mueller-Kalthoff (2002a), p. 22; Englert (2002), p. 221.

3.1.1
Meta-narrative creation

CASPAR (2002) suggests that cross-media offers should not be organized according to the distribution channel but according to the media semantics. This argument supports the perception of media offers as semantic space and as meta-narratives that span with complementary functions across different media channels. KELLY (2005) defines **meta-narratives** as the provision of story details and character information over different media. He views meta-narrative creation as a focus for the integration of mobile content into traditional content.[174] Storytellers can use each media channel to communicate different kinds and levels of narrative information. Star Trek is a good example for the creation of a meta-narrative having developed TV series, movies, novels, comic books, CD Rom and online games, and various other spin-offs that influence the content characteristics. MURRAY & JENKINS (1999) describe these characteristics of the Star Trek narrative in new digital media as encyclopedic, spatial, kaleidoscopic, participatory, and procedural.[175] Mobile communications' immediate access to digital media and virtual environments as well as the possibility of combining those with location-specific objects give storytellers **new experimental space for the creation of nonlinear and interactive narratives.**[176]

Since meta-narratives derive their value from the abstraction from one medium, the creation of new forms of cell media can relate to existing media content. The **media brand identity and its central brand promise** have to be transferred onto an innovative cell media format. Entertainment content offers opportunities to create meta-narratives that span a narrative over a variety of platforms, formats, and media types (see Table D-3). Video games, for example, can deliver different parts of their story to different media. The Japanese mobile game provider *Bandai* offers game players to continue playing the same video game on their mobile phone when they have to leave the home.[177]

The brand identity of the content thereby spans like an umbrella over the media platforms that each contribute a media-specific part of a narrative. RAWOLLE, KIRCHFELD & HESS (2002) suggest to create an **integrated service portfolio** in which mobile services are characterized by low complexity but high time- and location- dependence whereas stationary services are suited for high complexities but low context sensitivity.[178] Experience from Japan demonstrates that content providers already complement and integrate their fixed-line Internet offers with mobile services. Mobile customers use integrated accounts for PC fixed-line andcell phone mobile use, e.g. for (financial) news or ticket services. Preferences

---

174 See Kelly (2005).
175 See Murray and Jenkins (1999); Jenkins (2001).
176 See Murray (1995); Pavlik and McIntosh (2005).
177 See Funk (2001b), p. 136.
178 See Rawolle, Kirchfeld, and Hess (2002), p. 342; Funk also stresses the importance of design principles such as simplicity and mobile devices as complements, see Funk (2001b), p. 51.

Table D-3: Selected examples for mobile narratives as part of cross-media meta-narratives

Media brand	Mobile narrative
MTV	MTV videos, footage from live performances and MTV programming clips, e.g. Jackass clips for 3UK's mobile video services[a]
Men in Black II	SMS, WAP, and Java games with four different plots featuring locations and aliens from the movie: players take control of an MIB agent; alien activity investigation; and two sets of MIB agent training[b]
Popstar	Java-based mobile game: users are challenged to become a star and have to build fame by rehearsing, touring etc. (Kiloo) Separate versions are developed with additional mobile licenses from the singers Christina Aguilera and Nelly (Legend Mobile)[c]

a. See N.N. (September 23, 2003).
b. See N.N. (May 23, 2002).
c. See N.N. (July 2, 2002).

are typically customized via the PC.[179] FUNK (2002) provides an interesting example about a **cross-medial event application**: information access about the New Year's weekend 2001-02 peaked in magazine sales about *a month* before New Year's Eve with the December issue, about *half a week* before in PC Internet access, and on the *actual weekend days* in mobile site access (see Table D-4).[180]

Table D-4: Example of a cross-media use for event information in Japan

Media	Access time
Magazine	Magazine sales peak with the December issue about a month before New Year's Eve
Online media	Internet access peaks about half a week before New Year's Eve
Mobile media	Mobile site access peaks on the New Year's weekend

One essential question is which medium captures the initial user's attention and can serve as a **lead-in medium** for further cross-media consumption. Cross-media audience flows can have a variety of initial points that lead into the cross-media experience. For traditional media it has become a common strategy to use their content representation to direct users towards additional online content. Newspaper articles end with a reference to a URL; anchormen on television provide audiences with URL information of their program brand or TV channel brand. Analogous, cross-media audience flows that encourage audiences to use the mobile content offer can be **originated in traditional media**. Increasingly, media organizations additionally provide information on mobile media offers such as SMS short numbers that work similar to a fax services, WAP pages, or alert services.[181]

---

179 See Funk (2001b), p. 7; Funk (2001b), p. 136.
180 Funk (2002b), p. 14; Funk (2005).
181 See Reichwald and Meier (2002), p. 220.

However, mobile media may also become an initializing point for a cross-media experience and may develop into a source of new audiences. In this scenario, mobile media can serve as a **means to arouse attention**. The actual consumption of the desired content may be executed later with a different device and via a different network. Mobile media then takes the form of a teaser that refers the user to the content offer in other media. However, a mobile teaser ad is positioned differently from other teaser ad forms. For example, research on teaser ads suggests that music and interactive audio-visual images play an important role in the meaning viewers attribute to teaser ads. Specifically, music connects with and accentuates selective visual elements.[182] If integrated into mobile teasers, however, forms of music-visual connectivity of mobile teaser ads can increase the public disturbance and privacy intrusion we experience with a broad variety of cell phone ringing tones today. Thus, mobile lead-in's need creative and medium-specific teaser formats.

Meta-narratives can also span over an array of media to respond to the evolving **parallel media usage behavior** (see C-2.21). From the demand-side, users increasingly split their attention, multi-task, and use different media simultaneously. Research on Internet use and its relationship to traditional media that spans between rivalry and complementarity reveals that many users are using these media in parallel. Parallel media use is a phenomenon often observed with younger age groups who use the Internet, e-mail or chat with friends while listening to music, the radio, or watching TV.[183] Additionally, they are using the cell phone to simultaneously send personal messages. Parallel media behavior is an interesting development for cross-media strategies, because it can affect the formats of the offline and online content that can already be designed for **parallel or sequential use**. Media organizations have responded to this trend by designing bi-medial or multi-medial program formats. For example, the German TV program 'GigaTV' was designed to encourage parallel TV-Internet usage. Concepts for real-people soaps such as 'Big Brother' include simultaneously serving different functions of audience participation with different media such as choosing camera angles in the live web-stream and chatting with other audience members during the time slot of the TV program.[184] Mobile media as a very personal form of media can be **embedded in parallel usage formats**, for example with respect to interactive TV shows. More advanced forms of bi- or multimedial formats apart from mobile messaging combinations have yet to be developed.

Mobile media content design hereby has to create a compelling experience. Lessons can be learned from the design of online media content. Early research on the design of online environments suggests that an important objective for websites is to provide **flow opportunities**. Flow is defined as a cognitive state experienced during online navigation which is (1) characterized by a seamless se-

---

182 See Hung (2001). Groebel suggests to integrate music bits and pieces into mobile voice conversations as a form of mood management, see Groebel (2005).
183 See Cole (2004), pp. 82.
184 See Trepte, Baumann, and Borges (2000).

quence of responses facilitated by machine interactivity; (2) intrinsically enjoyable; (3) accompanied by a loss of self-consciousness; and (4) self-reinforcing.[185] To further understand the specific activities during which consumers have these experiences, two distinct categories of consumption behavior are differentiated: goal directed and experiential customer behavior. NOVAK, HOFFMAN & DUHACHEK (2002) suggest that particularly for goal directed online activities the flow construct is of importance, contrasting prior research that suggested its main importance for experiential online behavior. Under the assumption that mobile media use will be rather goal directed, the flow concept may gain importance for the design of meta-narratives as well, for instance for the choice of **navigation and selection modi** of mobile media. Mobile media use is in many cases inferior to other parallel use options, therefore an inter-medial flow becomes as important as the intra-medial flow. Since media brand loyalty is an essential parameter for advertising clients, cross-media audience flows may also affect arguments on media agencies' pricing strategies in advertising markets.

3.1.2
Cross-promotion with mobile media

For advertising clients, a cross-media audience flow becomes an interesting concept that extends existing cross-promotion communication strategies; from integrated traditional mass media and online advertising to mobile advertising. [186] A strong umbrella brand, e.g. the Financial Times (FT) Group, can be used as a selling argument for clients who want to advertise in different media across the FT Group.[187] TANNENBAUM already suggests in 1956 that a message conveyed via different media **increases the probability for consumers' attitudinal changes.**[188] However, it is still a challenge to determine which media type to use with what intensity and for what price in order to increase advertising effectiveness. Research on the relationship between radio and television advertisement, for example, suggests that cross-promotion enforces the effectiveness of the ad message, because the radio reaches audiences often immediately before a purchase decision whereas television can use additional visual effects to support brand recall.[189] Combined TV and online advertising strives to enhancing the advertising effectiveness by raising attention via TV and provide additional information online.[190] While the Internet as advertising medium has been recommended for

---

185 See Novak, Hoffman, and Yung (2000), p. 23.
186 See Mueller-Kalthoff (2002a); cross-media advertising models within a vertically integrated media company are not further differentiated, although they can take two different forms: (1) cross-media advertising within one media brand, e.g. an integrated TV and online advertising campaign with Disney's TV channel ESPN or (2) cross-media advertising across different brands, for example and integrated advertising campaign across AOL TimeWarner's brands such as AOL, Time Inc., Warner Bros. etc.. Big consumer goods manufacturers such as Procter & Gamble prefer the latter in order to negotiate bulk discounts.
187 See Alline (2002), p.22.
188 See Tannenbaum (1956).
189 See Domke and Wild (2002). Within one medium, it has been suggested that visual content in print advertisements also affects the effectiveness of inserted coupons, see Leclerc and Little (1997).
190 See Domke and Wild (2002); Riedel and Schoo (2002), pp. 149.

products that require high involvement[191] additional mobile advertisements may be better suited for low involvement products that do not require complex explanation.

Branded content, e.g. in the form of mobile multiplayer games, can be among the future forms of mobile advertising as well as **sponsoring of mobile media content** provided by media companies (see A-1.12). Here, the waiting times before a mobile video stream, for instance, can be taken as an ad slot for sponsoring, an unobtrusive mobile advertising form that could gain acceptance among users. Branded content offers value to the user itself and is, thus, suited to be developed for mobile devices as well. Mobile marketing tries to make use of the social networks of mobile users because it encourages users to share branded or sponsored mobile content as an opportunity for constructing a self-narrative (see C-1.2), e.g. via sponsored mobile animated greetings.[192] In Japan, media companies not only engage in mobile advertising but also in facilitating **mobile product ordering** based on traditional advertising forms. 'Magaseek', which is a joint venture between a magazine publisher and a leading trading house, offers mobile services for readers who can order advertised products via their mobile phones; 'Magaseek' acquired 36,000 users for such a service within six months.[193] A mobile affiliate revenue model for media companies, however, is a rather difficult proposition (see A-1.12).

Personalization of mobile advertising is based on the idea of **permission-based marketing**. Once a user has allowed the advertiser to establish a relationship with them, marketers may collect, profile, and track user data. New developments in data mining techniques on the Internet have alarmed privacy advocates and enlarged the privacy debate around real-time personalization (see E-2.2).[194] Some evidence from Japan suggests that there is a higher click-rate on mobile advertisement than on PC Internet ads.[195] However, **novelty effects** can blur these statistics. There is still a high probability that most mobile users will regard mobile advertising as a privacy intrusion.

3.1.3
Micro-coordination functions of mobile devices

Mobile devices do not necessarily have to be used for any kind of content consumption in an integrated cross-media approach. To the contrary, it is more and more likely that they will serve as a **means for interaction with other media content**.

Integrated mobile and TV services have some interesting potential, because they provide interactive services that have long been suggested for interactive TV but have never been implemented. TV channels currently expand their in-

---

191 See Yoon and Kim (2001).
192 See Brand and Bonjer (2002).
193 See Funk (2001a), p. 11.
194 See CDD (2001).
195 See Funk (2001b), p. 82.

formation services about their programs onto mobile platforms and increasingly interact with their audiences via mobile devices. The emotional qualities of the lead medium television can be combined with communication and transaction possibilities of an interactive voice telephony and Internet-enabled device such as the mobile phone.[196] Along the same lines hybrid GPRS (UMTS) DVB-T applications make use of the micro-coordinating functions of the **mobile phone for back-channel services** (see B-2.32).

In opposition to growing acceptance of mobile interactive applications mobile commerce appears to have been strongly overestimated; its adoption does not indicate that mobile media will rely heavily on related **transaction services**. However, technological advances in ubiquitous computing are promising with regard to an integration of barcode scanning and RFID tags into mobile communications applications. Potential applications may be barcodes that are integrated into print advertisements, for example, and that allow the user to scan ads with a mobile phone which may lead to the delivery of a product sample or the purchase of the product. In a simpler form, advertisements in traditional media can carry product codes that users send via SMS to the retailer. In these cases, the media company has proof of its mediation and could participate in the generated revenue in the form of a commission fee (see A-1.1).

If **micro-coordination of media use evolves into a central function of mobile phones** even in next generation networks, mobile data communications use may remain low. However, there are also proponents of the argument that **mobile voice communication** will continue to be the dominant mobile application.[197] More spectrum and more bandwidth in next generation cellular networks could abstain from dedicating bandwidth to mobile data services and instead use it to tackle the overload of 2G wireless networks and improve mobile voice telephony performance,[198] although 3G networks are not necessarily designed to provide an incremental improvement in voice services. Cross-media offers would in this case rely on mobile content and services as 'connective tissue' between cross-media offers.[199]

3.2
Emergence of cross-network strategies

The multiplication and differentiation of networks that arise as new distribution channels for media content as well as the miniaturization and multiplication of mobile devices (see B-2.31) suggest that digital media content and services will not only be delivered in various formats across different media, but that **a single media service may be delivered across different networks and devices** (see Fig. D-5).[200] LAUFF (2002) argues that media content and services and their different functionalities need to be detached from a prime device and prime network.[201]

---

196 See Funk (2001a), p. 12; Stamer (2002), p. 114.
197 See for example Odlyzko (2001b).
198 See Odlyzko (2001b); Cooper (2001).
199 See Reichwald, Ney, and Wagner (2002), p. 325; Kelly (2005).

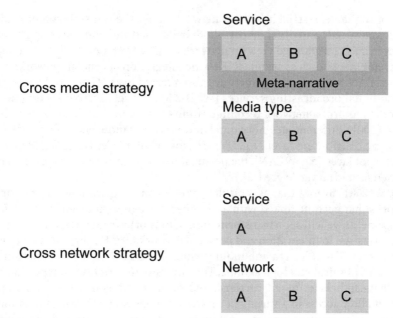

Figure D-6: Cross-network service delivery

NOESEKABEL & LEHNER (2002) stress the importance of few 'media breaks' for users, which means that, e.g., usage preferences should be available across networks and devices.[202] The **network choice** can depend on user preferences about quality, price, or time constraints. The device choice will largely depend on the user context. A configuration of these user preferences is a **specific user investment**, but it can lead to an increase in flexibility, convenience and ubiquitous service quality of digital media (D-3.21). Hyperlinks that connect hypermedia today may serve as a model for the design of **cross-network service interconnection** (D-3.22).

3.2.1
Reconfiguration of fixed-line and wireless networks

Cellular networks are one means of voice and data delivery among many wireless and fixed-line networks. Wired networks such as fiber-optic cable, and heterogeneous wireless networks such as wireless WANs, MANs, LANs, PANs, sat-

200 See Feldmann (2001b), p. 3; Buhse (2002), p. 174; Geisselbrecht and Fotschki (2002), p. 242; Mansell and Steinmueller (2002),p. 4.
201 See Lauff (2002), p. 206.
202 See Noesekabel and Lehner (2002). Mueller, Aschmoneit & Zimmermann also suggest that the Internet may be the input facility for mobile preferences, see Mueller, Aschmoneit, and Zimmermann (2002), p. 366.

ellite, or digital terrestrial broadcast networks, offer the transmission of media at different speeds and different costs both in licensed and unlicensed spectrum. However, such a **separated view on networks** can be overcome with technological developments such as seamless IP, or the integration of cellular networks and wireless LAN, known as 4G, sometimes also referred to as 5G due to the integration of digital broadcasting services (see B-2.31).[203] Yet, interconnecting these networks requires a **network reconfiguration** to allow the handover of services. LEHNER (2001) differentiates horizontal and vertical handovers in five different layers: the distribution layer (e.g. DVB-H), the cellular layer (e.g. 3G networks), the hot spot layer (e.g. WLAN), the personal network layer (e.g. Bluetooth), and the fixed (wired) layer (e.g. ADSL).[204]

NOAM (2001) argues that as a result of the dynamic environment of multiple networks that become linked with each other through various interconnection arrangements we will see a **transformation of networks** from interconnection to modularization to integration and personal networks.[205] He suggests that interconnection will first lead to unbundling which creates a modularity of networks in terms of physical and logical units. This diversity in turn leads integration efforts that can be user-based, carrier-based, or provided by new system integrators that allow access to a variety of services in a one-stop fashion. System integrators aim at putting together customized networks for personal use. These **personal networks** are tailored virtual network arrangements that suit personal communication needs and that package and price bandwidth-on-demand from different carriers.[206] Cross-network media services can be envisioned to use the latter form of personal networks in order to increase user satisfaction with media content and services.

Also MANSELL & STEINMUELLER (2002) identify enormous variety in possible network configurations for delivering new services.[207] The **virtual home environment** (VHE) concept, for example, describes the provision and delivery of personalized services across network and terminal boundaries with the same design characteristics so that users are constantly presented with the same personalized features, user interface customization and services, independent of network, device, or location.[208]

Advantages from a multiple network approach lie predominantly in the different **network specifications for mobile multimedia applications** that can be combined.[209] For mobile media provision via wireless networks, digital mobile

---

203 See Lehr and McKnight (2004), pp. 188; the concept of 4G extends to the integration of even more wireless networks including satellite, broadcasting, cellular, wireless local loop, LANs and indoor networks, see Lehner (2001), p. 18; Bisenius and Siegert (2002), p. 74.
204 See Lehner (2001), p. 18. IP can be used over any network including broadcasting networks without protocol conversion. Therefore, IP-based transmissions facilitate the convergence between telecom and broadcasting networks, see Doeven (2003), p. 7.
205 See Noam (2001), pp. 248.
206 See Noam (2001), p. 251; thus system integrators link the network of networks with software-defined application systems to a system of systems.
207 See Mansell and Steinmueller (2002), p. 4.
208 See Hommen (2003), p. 137.
209 See Bisenius and Siegert (2002), pp. 49.

radio systems, wireless local networks, or digital broadcasting systems offer distinct specifications available for combination. Mobile radio systems allow always-on connectivity, mobility up to approximately 250 km/h receiver speed, integrated IP transmission and security features such as terminal identification and subscriber authentication. Wireless LANs have high transmission capacities, for example up to 11Mbit/s within the IEEE 802.11b standard. Yet, they are quasi stationary. Digital broadcasting systems offer the best synchronous transmission services and support MPEG transmission; however, they lack a return channel and are unsuited for telecommunications services. Consequently, mobile media services have to make use of the **complementary advantages of broadcasting and telecommunications platforms**. While broadcasting systems can excel in strongly asymmetric, high data rate point-to-multipoint or simulcast transmission, telecommunication systems offer point-to-point transmissions possible at different times. For the decision on the **network choice** for wireless content delivery SABAT (2002) suggests four critical dimensions: geographical area covered, content transmission rate, mode of synchronization of content with the source, and user interface or device capabilities.[210] Depending on the context of the user, these dimensions can receive a weight that determines which network is best suited for which media applications in which situation.[211]

A first step for cross-network services can be seen in the **integration of WiFi into 3G networks**. With their distinct advantages wireless LAN would allow content and service providers a wider set of services under disparate conditions of quality and price. It provides the opportunity to offer local hot spot connectivity in high demand areas which could offset the capacity limitations of 3G. The billing and wide-area network management capabilities of 3G networks such as authentication, and resource allocation could address some of the shortcomings of WiFi. Innovative services may include scheduled high speed file transfer when near a hot spot, or adaptive power management strategies such as a switch to 3G to conserve battery power.[212]

For a systematization of wireless networks, MCKNIGHT, LINSENMAYER & LEHR (2002) designed a **wireless grid** that spans between the poles of 'best effort unlicensed nomadic wireless' and 'spectrum market-based mobile wireless'. The wireless technologies and spectrum management regimes of the grid encompass ultra-wideband (wide-area shared spectrum), Wi-Fi (local area shared spectrum), 2G (licensed spectrum), 3G MVNOs (secondary spectrum markets), and 4G (service level agreement and trading).[213] This wireless grid still lacks the integration of digital terrestrial broadcasting and can further be extended to fixed-line networks. Therefore, cross-network services don't only imply a reconfiguation of networks, but also a combination of different devices. In the "post-

210 See Sabat (2002), pp. 510.
211 See Zeglis (2001), p. 25.
212 See Lehr and McKnight (2002), p. 18.
213 See McKnight, Linsenmayer, and Lehr (2002) p. 5.

PC age"[214], many devices are becoming connected to (IP-based) networks and increasingly communicate (wirelessly) from **machine-to-machine**.

Cross-network and cross-device strategies not only support the delivery of personalized mobile media content[215] but are also useful because different quality levels that can be reached. They enable **content modality** to vary according to the device. A cell phone will display a hyperlink, a title or short text and only video key frames whereas other mobile appliances with bigger screens, and stronger computing capabilities and battery power are better suited for the consumption of full texts, high dissolving pictures and high audio and video quality. This requires the transcoding of content formats and representation for multiple devices. The degree of integration and the quality of service is hence also dependent on the infrastructure and the available **financial resources**.[216] The question about allocation of financial resources should also be viewed in the light of media brand management. Consistent quality of a media brand representation across networks and devices only be assured via the format and the content. Consequently, a major challenge of cross-network strategies is to **maintain a quality frame for format and content across channels**.[217]

Although the vision of a seamless IP experience across different networks offers attractive perspectives, it is unclear who will act, for instance, as the **cross-network Internet service provider**. When fixed-line access, wireless access, and mobile access are bundled together the national incumbents may well be in a comfortable position to offer integrated services. In many national markets the telephony incumbent is simultaneously the largest ISP and is in addition usually among the top mobile service providers. It would be difficult for competitors from both the mobile communications industry as well as the independent ISP industry to offer competitive services. Another barrier to any form of cross-network mobile media service delivery lies in spectrum policy. Mobile operators who have invested in licenses for third generation networks and services are carefully observing the development of DVB-T and may enter a political battle that will determine who will be able to develop and implement any type of business model of cross-network mobile content services.[218]

3.2.2
From hypermedia to hypernetworks

For cross-network media consumption users will need means to **navigate between the different networks**. For the navigation and the selection of the appropriate content module designed for a certain network access condition a **meta communication architecture** needs to be developed that allows for either on de-

---

214 Mattern (2004), p. 160.
215 See Funk (2001b), p. 153. Other visions of an embeddedness of ICTs, including wireless and mobile content and communication services, refer to ambient intelligence that will surround us in everyday life, see Ducatel et al. (2004).
216 See Noesekabel and Lehner (2002), p. 134; Reichwald, Ney, and Wagner (2002), p. 324.
217 See Caspar (2002a), p. 23.
218 See Lauff (2002), p. 190.

mand or automated content services. In the case of online media, hypermedia is one distinct navigation characteristic that adds value in comparison to traditional media offers. Websites and documents can be linked and the user can navigate through the plethora of hyperlinked information. In analogy, cross-network services need hyperlinks between different networks for the navigation and selection of media services. A link that connects a cellular network to a wireless LAN or a wired network can point towards a media service that is initialized from the cellular network but executed via another network. Therefore, **hyperlinks for cross-network navigation**, for example established via one-click buttons on the display of a mobile phone, have to be developed. One potential barrier to hyperlinked cross-network services is that IP-based services are not yet the common standard for all mobile applications although mobile data developments indicate the tendency to view mobile networks as an extension of the Internet. The backbone of GPRS and 3G networks is already a de facto IP-based network infrastructure. The crucial challenge for the migration from cellular 2G to 3G networks is upgrading the over-the-air link and the mobile devices.[219]

When the isolated view of different (wireless) networks evolves into an innovative reconfiguration of existing and next generation networks it will require **new service categories** to describe the seamless delivery of a media service. According to BISENIUS & SIEGERT (2002) the **service reconfiguration can start on three levels**: at the user, the terminal, and the protocol level.[220] User level network reconfigurations refer to services that are delivered via one medium, e.g. a URL information given on television, and processed via the 'human interface' of the user who turns toward the PC in order to follow the link. Terminal level network configuration allows a shift between networks and may become more interesting if, for example, DVB-T-antennas or WiFi cards become integrated in mobile phones and laptops. Protocol level network reconfigurations, e.g. on the basis of IP, enable automated dynamic network management that can be based on user profiles and personal preferences.

The instant mobile music purchasing prototype Catch-Your-Song (CYS) can be viewed as an early example of a user-level network configuration. It combines a mobile access component for "catching a song" and a web-based component for the individual music archive. Users register their favourite radio stations and personal interests on the Web; when they listen to the radio they can buy songs via a WAP-enabled mobile phone. The current song is displayed on the mobile phone screen and can be purchased with one click; once users return to their desktop PC they will find a personal library with the songs they ordered. Subsequent options on both the cell phone and desktop PC interface include ordering the single, the album, downloading the song on the cell phone or send a greeting e-mail with the song attached.[221] In this scenario, **one paid media service is completed using multiple networks,** it gives the user the option to immediately follow an impulse while at the same time enjoying the lower download price of

219 See Freystaetter (2002), pp. 451.
220 See Bisenius and Siegert (2002), p. 66.

the wired network in comparison to the wireless one. Another user-driven service re-configuration can be developed around virtual storage that combines fixed-line and mobile Internet. In this concept, media content as well as personal media files such as pictures can be stored virtually on a website and ca be accessed via any wired or wireless network and any IP-enabled device. In Japan, more than 10,000 different outlets of 'Photo Net Japan' already offer a photoloading service on i-mode compatible home pages in 2001.[222] **Virtual web-based storage counteracts device storage constraints**; music files, for example, that have been downloaded on a personal web account could be accessed and viewed via a mobile Internet appliance without the constraints of limited mobile storage.[223] Web-based interaction and mobile access to it is also a viable model for mobile search engines. It is more convenient for users to perform and store a search using a PC with a keyboard and a big screen and be able to access the results later on other potentially smaller (mobile) screens.[224] These examples demonstrate that the delivery of media content and services across networks is heavily dependent on interoperability and standardizations and on routers that can read and execute on users' preference profiles for network choices. The integration of one application across multiple networks and devices would also favor the **integration of various databases** that need to exchange and store information about, e.g. address books and calendars, bookmarks or downloads.[225]

Developments of interoperability and integration enable a further navigation performance towards automated cross-network navigation. Navigation between networks can also become automated. A **personal router** (see B-2.31) is an agent that coordinates cross-network applications on behalf of the user.[226] It knows some of the user preferences and can also learn from previous experience. The personal router decides which network is most appropriate in which user situation. The agent supports starting a transactions on one channel and ending it on another channel. A personal router would also have to integrate different user profile databases in order to offer media and network overarching personalization services.[227] The criteria for the network choice can depend on cost of data transmission and users' willingness to pay, speed of data transmission and users' willingness to delay the consumption, as well as new models of spectrum

---

221 See Hampe and Schwabe (2002a), pp. 8. Other examples include a pilot project of IBM and Core Media. They test 'multi-touchpoint transactions' such as receiving information on a radio song or ordering the CD of the artist via the mobile phone. This can be done via a one-click-option with an SMS or via a voice portal, see Stamer (2002), p. 118.
222 Photo Net Japan had acquired almost one million users for this service as of early 2001 who paid between $3 and $4 for the service, see Funk (2001b), p. 75.
223 See Cooper (2001), p. 121; Funk (2001b), p. 75; Laats (2001), p. 166; Sony, for example, is integrating its memory stick into mobile phones to enhance their storage power, see Funk (2001b), p. 155.
224 See Funk (2001b), p. 12.
225 See Noesekabel and Lehner (2002), pp. 130; Geisselbrecht and Fotschki (2002) also stress the importance of an integrated database management; in content management systems, XML/XSL modeling is used as a solution to separate content and layout, see for example Noesekabel and Lehner (2002); Rawolle, Kirchfeld, and Hess (2002); Hess (2004).
226 See Clark and Wroclawski (2001); Faratin et al. (2002).
227 See Stamer (2002), p. 109.

and bandwidth trading that introduce marketplaces and dynamic pricing models into network transactions (see E-3.12).

Furthermore, navigation between networks may change from text-based to **voice-based interaction.**[228] In mobile wireless media environments voice and audio technologies often provide a better user experience and user interface than text or image-based user interfaces. Voice and audio may therefore be used to extend the reach of Internet content and applications from Web servers to mobile appliances. Moreover, voice recognition and more intelligent search procedures are reducing specialized skills needed to use mobile devices. With reliable voice recognition the degree of skill that is needed to be 'computer literate' will be reduced to **'telephone literacy'.**[229]

4
Value creation in mobile media markets

The strategic developments of media companies towards extended cross-media and cross-network strategies take place in a dynamic market structure that is constantly evolving and changing. Within the market structure, the relationship between media companies and mobile operators is particularly interesting, because it is characterized by **both cooperation as well as competition** (D-4.1). In an emerging content market for mobile media, mobile operators and media companies are competing for the revenues generated via mobile media consumption as well as for the customer relationship. However, they have to cooperate in order to create value for the customer. As the mobile media market is evolving, negotiation powers are shifting between all players that contribute to the mobile media value creation; yet, different perceptions of the value of their strongest assets - the customer billing relationship in the case of the mobile operator and the media brand relationships in the case of mass media companies - lead to interesting shifts in negotiation power for revenue sharing models (D-4.2).

4.1
Co-opetition as the dominant structure of mobile media markets

The concept of co-opetition describes the process of value creation in mobile media markets best. It provides new insights into the discussion of mobile media markets, because it integrates the role of complementors in value nets that may be taken by social networks.

Co-opetition is about **creating value and capturing value.**[230] Whereas creating value is an inherently cooperative process, capturing value is inherently competitive. In information and network industries, this concept has gained in

---

228 See Laats (2001).
229 See Compaine (2000a), p. 474.
230 See Nalebuff and Brandenburger (1997).

importance, for example with the emergence of business webs that are characterized by relationships of mutual complementarity.[231] Therefore, co-opetition is used as a framework for the discussion of expanding existing and developing new mobile media markets.

4.1.1
From value chains to value nets

The concept of value creation in strategic management is associated with value chain analysis.[232] The **mobile *data* industry value chain** comprises a large number of players that can be categorized into infrastructure suppliers, software suppliers, network operators, and service providers. Infrastructure providers comprise network and handset equipment manufacturers; software suppliers provide operating systems; implementation services for back-end network management-oriented and front-end customer-oriented services; as well as application development. Network operators can be owners of spectrum licenses or they can enter the market as mobile virtual network operators (MVNOs). MVNOs are mobile value added service providers that buy access to a mobile network on a wholesale basis and offer retail services similar to full network operators (see E-3.12).[233] In the service-oriented components of the mobile data value chain, content and application development providers and enablers for the implementation of mobile services are included as separate entities.[234] They are regarded to be separate, because mobile content and application development and implementation require specific investment and specialized skills. Media companies, for example, have to consider how far they intend to vertically integrate or outsource these specific competencies.

With a narrower focus on the provision of mobile media content and services important players in the **mobile *media* value chain** are

- **infrastructure suppliers** for access devices such as handset manufacturers whose screen and input facilities design as well as their choice on the operating system affect decisions on content creation;
- **network operators** who acquire spectrum rights, build infrastructure and provide QoS, payment systems, and security for mobile media transmission;
- **mobile service providers** who provide mobile ISP services or who resell airtime as MVNOs and may acquire exclusive content rights as sources for their differentiation;

---

231 See Zerdick et al. (2000), pp. 176; Chan-Olmsted & Chang observe an increase of competitive-cooperative relationships between leading global media conglomerates, see Chan-Olmsted and Chang (2005).
232 See Porter (1985). Value chain analysis has evolved into a variety of models that either use the value chain as analysis tool to identify competitive advantages within a firm or to describe the value creation process within an industry that can also be interpreted as linking firm-level value chains of an industry. For the following discussion we refer to the latter understanding of value creation within an industry.
233 See for example Ulset (2002).
234 See Maitland, Bauer, and Westerveld (2002), p. 489.

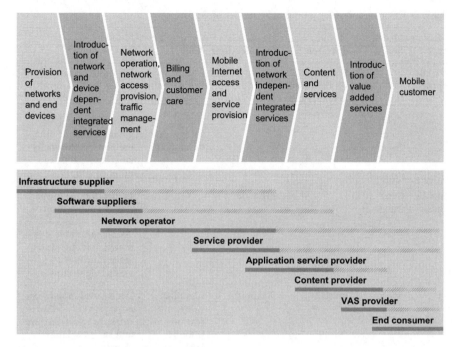

Figure D-7: The mobile media value chain

- **mobile interface application service providers,** who provide messaging and WAP gateways, mobile browsers, and software for mobile applications such as J2ME;
- **content providers** who produce and package mobile media content; and
- **value added service providers** who offer navigation services in mobile portals, personalized or location-based services (see Fig. D-7).

At all layers of the mobile value chain there is **fierce competition over the developments of standards.** For example, the operating systems (OS) for mobile computing devices such as Windows CE, the Symbian consortia or Qualcomm's CDMA-bound OS are competing among the players in the software supplier layer. Media companies are dependent on the outcome of these standard wars. Before they **invest specifically into one system,** they now have to cooperate with many players which drives cost and limits innovative activity. Media companies are also dependent on application service providers in the service provider layer for the provision of mobile media services. Mobile ASPs have core competencies in areas such as **SMS and MMS gateway management** or they have contracts with different mobile operators on the use of certain short numbers which are a scarce and hence a valuable resource. Table D-2 provides some examples for joint mobile service creation.

Table D-5: Cooperations for joint mobile service provision

Media type	Media brand	Mobile operator	Handset manufacturer	Developing ASP	Mobile service model
Mobile games		Vodafone Global Content Services		Digital Bridges (game developing)	WAP and Java mobile games for Vodafone live! customers[a]
		Columbia Pictures		Digital Bridges (game developing)	SMS, WAP, and Java games with four different plots; additionally ringtones, icons, and other graphics[b]
Mobile music	Sony Music		Ericsson		M-Use, mobile music download platform (planned launch: fall 2003); paid content model for songs and artist information as well as video clips[c]
	MTV, BMG	mmO2	Siemens	Chaoticom (file compression), SDC (mobile DRM)	'Music over mobile' trial service via 2.5G networks to select, retrieve and store the latest chart hits[d]

a.   See N.N. (March 3, 2003b).
b.   See N.N. (May 23, 2002).
c.   See N.N. (February 19, 2003).
d.   See N.N. (March 14, 2003).

The scale and scope of players that are involved in delivering mobile media services to the end consumer build **barriers to profitability**. There is potential for conflict when all players in the mobile value chain want to be compensated in an environment where consumer prices have to be determined demand-driven and not cost-based in order to find acceptance in the market.

Hence, media companies have to think about their **scope of vertical integration** in the mobile value chain. Depending on the scale of the mobile media engagement, forward or backward integration may lead to increased profitability. These decisions depend on the objective the media company pursues. A backward integration may only be profit-maximizing when media companies plan to enter the MVNO market.

If media companies do not intend to increase the degree of vertical integration, horizontal integrations can gain in importance and suggest the creation of a **mobile media value net**. With the emergence of the Internet and greater attention to network economics, value nets emerge as a new paradigm for cooperation in network industries. NALEBUFF & BRANDENBURGER (1997) conceptualize the value net as a net of customers, suppliers, competitors and complementors of a company. It integrates PORTER's (1998) five competitive forces that determine industry profitability when potential entrants and substitutes are classified as either competitor or complementor and it adds a dynamic perspective on creating new markets through the perspective of game theory. The perspective of value nets creates **linkages between value chains and the network of relations between firm networks and industry structure**. Horizontal linkages between players in the value net and the roles they take are important for the value creating process and reflect the importance of inter-firm relations in the development of an emerging industry.[235]

Next generation mobile data services are expected to be characterized by a multi-faceted mobile data value net.[236] The broadening of the value chain concept to that of a value net is important for the value creating process of mobile content services, because the value net partners add specific competencies while lowering the overall risk.[237]

4.1.2
Players and roles in the mobile media value net

Complex interdependencies between players who create value in mobile media markets characterize mobile media value nets. The value net describes all the players of an industry and analyzes the elements of competition and cooperation among them. It thereby provides the conceptual scheme for applying game theory to business.[238] In the view of business as a game, the players involved are customers, suppliers, competitors and players who provide complements, so called complementors. Their interdependencies are determined by their roles. However, players can also have multiple roles. From the point of view of a media company a player is a **complementor** if customers value the media offer more when they have an integrated offer and if suppliers find it more attractive to provide resources to both. A player is a **competitor** if customers value the media offer less when they have the other player's product and if it is less attractive for a supplier to provide resources to the media company and the competitor than to the media company alone.[239] Business webs that have become increasingly the norm in network industries incorporate the idea of using complementors to en-

---

235 See Maitland, Bauer, and Westerveld (2002), p. 502.
236 See Funk (2001b), p. 63; Maitland, Bauer, and Westerveld (2002), pp. 486; Steiner (2002), p. 76; telematic provider, for example, need strategic media industry partners for portal services, see Ehmer (2002), p. 471.
237 Business webs display some of the potential benefits of vertical integration within an industry that can accelerate the rate of information exchange, lower capital and operating costs through integration economies and thereby overcome entry barriers of an established industry. However, both market and bargaining power are intransitive and temporary. As a result, the need for vertical integration changes as an industry evolves and as a firm's position within it changes, see Harrigan (1983).
238 See Nalebuff and Brandenburger (1997), pp. 8.
239 See Nalebuff and Brandenburger (1997), pp. 16.

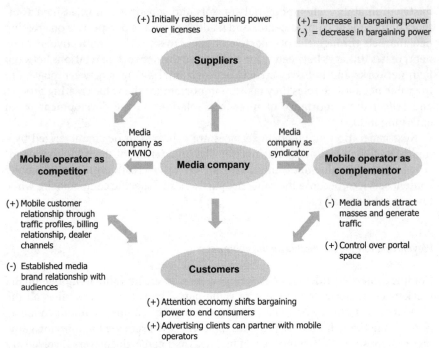

Figure D-8: Players and roles in the mobile value net

hance the value of one's own product.[240] Additionally, research and development costs and high upfront investments can be spread.

In mobile media markets, **mobile network operators** (MNOs) can be both
competitors and complementors for media companies (see Figure D-8). They
both compete for a relationship with the mobile customer. Mobile operators are
in a strong position, because they have **key assets such as a large customer contract base,** access to personal data, traffic profiles, location information about
mobile users, and billing relationships with the customer. Moreover they have
an established mobile brand, dealer channels and the network infrastructure itself.[241]

Media companies, on the other hand, have **cognitive and emotional relationships with their audiences** that they establish with the support of their brand
identity and their brand promise. Media brands are promoting usage habits that
they can build on with expanded functions of personalization and communicative interaction. Strong media brands have the ability to attract mass audiences
and create incentives for an expansion of existing media usage onto new plat-

---

240 Incentives for the formation of business webs between network and content provider are partic-
     ularly relevant to online information product markets since the information product demand is
     significantly affected by the quality of network delivery, see Oh and Chang (2000).
241 See Maitland, Bauer, and Westerveld (2002), p. 491; Steiner (2002), p. 78; Maitland (2005).

forms.[242] In order to attract audiences and create mobile data revenue streams, mobile operators have to rely on these media brands, they do not have the core competency to produce their own content.[243] However, **co-opetition between conduit and content** is not a new phenomenon. A historic perspective on the wireless communications industry reveals an interesting parallel to the invention of the telegraph. In the 19th century, telegraph companies, both in England and the US, failed when they tried to enter the news agency market based on the capabilities of their extended telegraph network capacities; they were quickly outperformed by emerging news agencies. Western Union, the world's biggest company at the turn of the century, saw in its network of telegraph agents the natural base for the business. However, the editorial service provided by the Associated Press's and Reuters news was better than Western Union's.[244] In analogy to the historical evidence, mobile operators and media content providers need to **cooperate to create value**, but they **compete when it comes to sharing the generated revenues**.

Different objectives of media companies can **shift the recognition of mobile operators as complementors or competitors**.[245] When media companies syndicate content to mobile operators' portals, the interdependencies are strong and both players have incentives to expand the pie. However, their relationship can evolve into a stronger degree of co-opetition when media companies develop their own portal strategies or when they enter the mobile communications market as MVNO. In the latter case, mobile operators are competitors for the provision of mobile media at the retail level. At the same time, though, mobile network operators are complementors in the function as wholesale service provider.

Bertelsmann considered an MVNO entry in 2000,[246] but decided against it although the company's experiences in direct marketing and club management would have been useful for a mobile retail strategy. MTV Europe, on the other hand, is entering the Swedish mobile telecommunications market with a prepaid service that targets their core audience and relevant target groups for their advertising clients. Mobile services include music news, premium ringtones, program information as well as special numbers to contact MTV's VJ's and featured artists. The branded mobile service 'Hello MTV' uses Telia Mobile's GSM network and has subcontracted the mobile virtual network enabler Spinbox to provide network management, billing, and customer care.[247] In pursuing this

---

242 See Sjurts (2002a), p. 16; Caspar stresses the importance of the media brand strength as an essential element of a cross-channel strategy; an advantage of established media companies is the existing knowledge about customer preferences that can be transferred onto new channel offers, see Caspar (2002a), p. 47.
243 Given the complexity of content development strategies mobile operators may focus on building new infrastructures although this is sometimes referred to as a 'bit pipe strategy' which limits the diversity of revenue streams. See Maitland, Bauer, and Westerveld (2002), p. 491; Freystaetter (2002), p. 454.
244 See de Sola Pool (1990), p. 73.
245 For a discussion of the different strategic options that emerge for media companies see Feldmann (2002b).
246 See N.N. (November 28, 2000). Bertelsmann negotiated with all German UMTS license holders except for Vodafone who already pursued an exclusive agreement with Vivendi at that time.

MVNO strategy MTV can use its **brand value** of $6.08 billion, according to Interbrand's 2002 ranking.[248] Also Disney has considered offering prepaid services in the evolving US mobile pre-paid market.[249] Virgin Mobile is an example of a successful MVNO strategy that **specifically targets the youth market** with its brand and its entertainment-oriented services.[250] Handsets carry names such as 'The Party Animal' or 'The Super Model' and are equipped with 'VirginXtras'. MTV is one of Virgin's content partners to supply these mobile entertainment contents. Additionally, Virgin Mobile can take advantage of an existing retail structure, the Virgin Megastores and Our Price shops that supports their direct customer relationship.[251]

Whether facilities-based network operators will voluntarily make their services available to MVNOs will depend on the net effect of the potential loss of profits from retail sales and the potential increase in profits from wholesale revenues.[252] **Media companies' as MVNOs** could potentially serve incremental customers although that is rather unlikely given the high penetration of mobile communications particularly in youth markets. Yet, media companies may hesitate to challenge mobile operators with an MVNO model in the near future. Since user acceptance for mobile media offers is low, the timing of market entry does not play the same role as in Internet markets, where first mover advantages have often been claimed to be critical to success. To the contrary, **first movers in mobile media markets have higher risks** because they have to build mobile media markets and because they are facing high investments with uncertain returns.

New entrants in the mobile media market can also introduce a new arena of competition for media companies. Although they may lack a strong brand, innovative performance, a higher inclination to take risks, or targeting a new customer group can lead to growth and potential economies of scale effects.[253] In general, the advent of a new technology promotes the growth of new generations of intermediaries that develop core competencies with regard to the new needs of producers and consumers.[254] In Japan, for example, mobile content is provided by a host of emerging players. The mobile offers of established media companies such as Nikkei or the renowned Asian Wall Street Journal are not nearly as popular as contents from new, predominantly entertainment-oriented content providers.[255] New mobile intermediaries can function as complementors to media content producers; today they often facilitate SMS and MMS gateway services including collecting revenue shares from mobile operators. In the case of RTL's SMS teletext chat service, the new mobile ASP also **moderates and censors**

247 See Phillips (June 2, 2003).
248 See N.N. (August 16, 2002). According to the Interbrand ranking, MTV is one of the world's most valuable media brand.
249 See N.N. (July 28, 2003).
250 See N.N. (June 21, 2002).
251 See Ulset (2002), p. 546.
252 See Maitland, Bauer, and Westerveld (2002), p. 491.
253 See Christensen (1997); Adner (2002).
254 See Sarkar, Butler, and Steinfield (1996).
255 See Funk (2001b), p. 35.

the **SMS traffic** as value added service. These censoring revenues help to make the business feasible for the ASP.[256]

Media companies also have to analyze their investments in mobile media content against the background of the **proliferation of wireless LANs** and the use of unlicensed spectrum as potential substitutes for cellular media use. Wireless LANs do not pose the same threat to media companies as they do to mobile operators. Although the provision of media services in licensed and unlicensed spectrum is fundamentally different from a technological perspective (see B-2.2), market definitions are based on the subjective substitutability from the point of view of the customer. If customers view cellular and WLAN offers as substitutable, they are hence competing with each other. Media companies' engagement in the wireless LAN arena is different, because existing Internet content does not have to be repurposed just because the access mode is wireless. Pursuing a **portal strategy** with different wireless LAN Internet Service Providers (WISPs) is a lot more interesting for media companies: from (1) a financial perspective because the investment risk is significantly lower and (2) when they want to **retain control over the selection and navigation** of content offers in opposition to mobile content provision for mobile communications where the operators will try to dominate the mobile portal space.

Traditional suppliers of media companies, for example a production company that delivers TV show productions to a TV channel, can gain in bargaining power in the short-term when they own the copyright to their produced content and when they begin to contract directly with mobile operators on mobile content licenses. However, media companies may change their contracts concerning property rights of the content they acquire in such a way that they **include mobile rights as an element of digital rights**. In that case, it is in the interest of suppliers that media companies deliver content to mobile distribution platforms, because it increases the value of the licenses and the rights they are trading.

The **mobile consumer** may reap the biggest economic benefits, because the (un)willingness to pay is an essential parameter in the business models of mobile market players. Moreover, **consumer's attention** is acknowledged as a valuable resource in the media industry. The short attention span that consumers dedicate to the small displays of the mobile phone, for example, increases this value and makes the cell phone screen to one of the most valuable pieces of 'real estate'.[257]

Advertising clients to whom media companies broker the attention of their audiences in traditional media models also gain in bargaining power. On the one hand, they can expand cross-promotion strategies with media companies. On the other hand, **mobile operators and independent ASPs** are starting to compete for their advertising budgets as well. Mobile operators can offer to provide more detailed information on the mobile communication behavior of their customers and they can **provide positioning information**. This can be of interest to adver-

---

256 See Visiongain (2002). This report quotes EUR 0.06 – 0.10 per SMS as payout rates for censoring services.
257 See Noam (2005).

tisers who want to integrate location-based services and link mobile advertisements with real world interaction. In this respect, media companies and mobile
operators are competing on yet another level. Evidence for the severity with
which mobile operators are developing their own advertising models can be
found in Japan. Here, the mobile operator NTT DoCoMo has founded a joint
venture with the advertising agency Dentsu already in 2000 to develop innovative mobile advertising campaigns.

4.1.3
Integration of social networks as complementors

Social networks and mobile customers' roles within them play an outstanding
role in mobile communications (see C-1.2). Therefore, possibilities to integrate
these social networks as complementors in mobile media value nets may become a **new source of value creation**. A complement to a product or service is a
product or service that makes the first one more attractive; this process is recip-
rocal.[258] Thus, thinking about complements is about expanding the pie rather
than dividing it. In order to enlarge the pie in mobile media markets, social networks can be viewed as complementors in the mobile value web. Social networks
can provide the context for mobile media and thereby contribute to the creation
of social and economic value. The contributions of social network members may
consist of messages that are related to media content, similar to messages that
are attached to, e.g., a newspaper article that users forward via e-mail on the Internet. Personal relevance is hence not only created by the media company, but
it is an option users can create. Media companies that design their mobile media
offers after consideration of their mobile users' identity and its role in social networks and that **let users actively shape the social context of mobile media** can
create a win-win situation that expands the market and makes their own content
more attractive from the perception of users. Moreover, mobile communications
allows an **efficient integration of the individual customer as a co-producer** in
the process of content and service production due to the inherently personal nature of the mobile phone (see B-1.2).[259] **User-driven elements** are essential to
identify latent user needs with regard to new features of mobile content and
services such as location- and context-sensitivity.[260]

Taking advantage of social networks of users and supporting users to create
self-narratives around their mobile identities will therefore also be important
against the background of **profit maximization**. Paid content models and the
generation of new revenue sources such as time-and usage- based fee-sharing or
termination rate-sharing are of media companies' particular interest.[261] However, the realization of economies of scale for mobile media offers will be deci-
sive for the generation of profit. Since many players in the value chain contribute

---

258 See Nalebuff and Brandenburger (1997), pp. 10.
259 See Reichwald, Ney, and Wagner (2002); Reichwald and Meier (2002); von Hippel and Katz (2002).
260 See von Hippel (1986); Reichwald, Ney, and Wagner (2002), p. 326.
261 See Englert (2002), p. 218.

to delivering mobile media value to customers and want to be reimbursed, **margins are low and initial investments are high** due to the specificity of the investment. One consequence for media companies is to try to unlock network effects that favor economies of scale. Social networks as complementors have the potential to develop into one essential driver of network effects.

4.2
Shifts in negotiation power in mobile media markets

Mobile media markets are dynamically changing as they mature. The intended shift in next generation networks towards an increased sophistication in mobile data communications leads to changing negotiation powers between the players of the mobile value net (D-4.21). Media companies will receive more options to challenge mobile operators and handset manufacturers (D-4.22).

4.2.1
Shifts in the relationship between media companies and mobile operators

The growing importance of mobile media as a mobile data revenue source and the increasing dependence of mobile operators on strong media brands that attract a critical mass of mobile customers **shifts negotiation power towards media companies**. Media companies can also raise customer satisfaction with mobile media when they design **cross-media narratives** which will give them more leverage in negotiations with mobile operators. Mobile operators will have to increase their **customer segmentation** activities in order to serve a wide variety of customers and extract the optimal consumer rent. It has been a common strategy to use different handset designs for different customer groups; corporate customers are offered handsets with more office application integration capabilities whereas youth customers can choose handsets that are specifically designed for extensive texting or gaming applications. Media content and mobile portal selection priorities that feature more information or more entertainment content can become further means of segmenting customers and serving them in a very targeted way. Mobile operators will need a broader variety of media contents in order to pursue **customer segmentation strategies based on content provision** in mobile portals. This will increase media companies' bargaining power and it may also be used to make bundled media content offers to mobile operators which can increase the content profitability.

Another aspect of an increase in customer segmentation based on content offers is that **emerging players in the mobile media market** receive opportunities to even become more popular with mobile users than established media brands. CHRISTENSEN (1997) introduced the concept of disruptive technologies to explain incumbent failure in the face of radical technological change. FUNK (2002) applies this concept to the mobile Internet. He argues that **new mobile content creators** have a better understanding of mobile customer needs and therefore excel in the production of mobile content. Contrasting the framework of Christensen's work on incumbent failure in the face of disruptive technological change, leading media incumbent brands manage to convince Internet users with their online presences.[262] In analogy to media companies' online activities, they can also utilize their **credibility and users' trust in their editorial competencies** in mobile media environments and use their assets in negotiating higher and/or more revenue sharing opportunities with mobile operators.

4.2.2
Shifts in the relationship between media companies and handset manufacturers

Media companies find **new customers** for their content licenses in handset manufacturers (see Table D-6). Competition in the mobile handset arena is fierce and handset manufacturers are actively striving to **differentiate themselves in the perception of the mobile consumer**. For example, Nokia has started early on with implementing a 'Club Nokia' concept, followed by Siemens who is offering club concepts as well. One means by which to **demonstrate technological superiority**, e.g. display size and screen brightness, is to direct users' attention to attractive mobile video contents. Consequently, handset manufacturers are contracting with major film studios to exclusively offer mobile movie previews. For movie producers mobile content becomes an increasingly interesting option, because licensing agreements are a **means of financing major media ventures**. This is one reason why they may be inclined to sign exclusive content deals instead of striving for a maximum spread on all mobile devices. If the upfront exclusive license revenue is higher than the expected revenue from, e.g., paid content modules available on all mobile devices media companies have an incentive to close deals with handset manufacturers.

Table D-6: Selected examples for handset manufacturers' interest in mobile media

Media brand	Handset manufacturer	Mobile media offer
James Bond 'Die another day'	Sony Ericsson	Limited edition product packages and premium mobile content; polyphonic ringtones and colorful MMS messages showcase the capabilities of SonyEricsson's new mobile phone models[a]
MTV	Motorola	MTV-related content such as ringtones and screensavers is preinstalled on Motorola devices; joint international MTV show 'MTV Mash' that integrates the mobile content[b]

a.   See N.N. (October 28, 2002).
b.   See N.N. (July 7, 2003a).

---

262 See Kueng (2002).

In 2003, for instance, MTV and Motorola closed a three-year $75 million marketing alliance that includes MTV content pre-loaded on Motorola handsets as well as joint marketing collaborations for new MTV shows and MTV/Motorola events and retail promotion. Their lifestyle-oriented approach targets the youth segment that they hope to attract with the strong MTV brand and Motorola's mobile phone design that includes mobile entertainment functions such as **mixing capabilities for users** to create unique ringtones.[263]

Another benefit of the relationship between media companies and handset manufacturers is that media companies are likely to retain more **control over their content**. Mobile operators tend to strive to become content aggregators and therefore negotiate for the right to decide where to place content within their portals and how users can navigate the bundled offer of the mobile operator. Handset manufacturers on the other hand may be willing to give more exposure to the content they contracted for, in part because they are likely to offer less variety in content; media content is only one means for them to attract customers and bind them to the mobile phone brand. Nonetheless, the interest of handset manufacturers in mobile media also **strengthens media companies' negotiating position** with mobile operators, because it increases demand and competition for mobile media brands.

This chapter discussed the extension of existing cross-media strategies; the development of new functions, formats, and services of mobile content; and their integration through cross-media audience flows and new cross-network strategies. It has been argued that the social use of mobile communications plays a dominant role in the process of value creation in mobile media markets. However, in order to leverage mobile media, a policy and regulatory framework is needed that fosters innovation and innovative cross-media strategy development under the influence of mobile communications. It will be developed in the next chapter.

---

263 See Motorola (March 12, 2003).

E
Innovation policy for mobile media

In the first four chapters, this book has discussed incentives for media companies to consider entering mobile media markets; it has analysed the mobile communications system and its characteristics as well as the social use of mobile communications and how users appropriate it. Taking these elements into account we have translated the results into a systematisation framework that distinguishes strategic options for media companies to extend their cross-media strategies onto mobile platforms and to integrate and develop them with emerging mobile media content and services. The understanding of social networks as complementors to mobile media value nets is one strategic element to promote bottom-up user-driven innovation that acknowledges new innovation paradigms in network economics (see A-2.3). However, the question of what kind of policies may support **fostering innovation in mobile media markets** remains.

BAR ET AL. (2000) suggest that innovation policy for mobile communications should strive to **creating incentives** to upgrade existing networks and build next generation network infrastructures and services in order to **stimulate innovative competition among users.**[1] Extending these thoughts to mobile media, further questions raised by media development under the influence of mobile communications have to ask what rationale there may be for regulation in order to promote mobile media development.[2] They do not only relate to telecommunication policy, but also to information and media policy issues in the wider context of the information society.

MANSELL & STEINMUELLER (2002) argue that interconnection and interoperability are key issues of the regulation for the information society infrastructure and services.[3] SAMUELSON & VARIAN (2001) name security, privacy, content regulation, and intellectual property as fundamental information policies.[4] Among these issues, three areas of public policy emerge as specifically relevant to **leverage in-**

---

1   See Bar et al. (2000), p. 507; on the objectives of public innovation policy see Kuhlmann (2001) p. 954.
2   The rationale for regulation can have two foundations: regulatory intervention to protect against market failure and regulatory intervention in the public interest. Two complementary paradigms can be their basis: the political economy approach to regulation emphasizes the impact of interest groups on policy; the public interest approach looks at market failures as a motivation for government intervention, see Laffont and Tirole (2000), p. 16. Regulation failures have to be considered in the second approach as well, although it usually assumes that governments are benevolent.
3   Mansell & Steinmueller define the vision of the information society as the idea that the information revolution opens a path to new opportunities for sustainable growth and development, new potential for social inclusion and representation, and new ways to achieve social and cultural expression, see Mansell and Steinmueller (2002), p. 9.

novation for mobile media: competition policies that emphasize open access[5] and interconnection (E-1), consumer protection policies that include consumer and data protection as well as privacy issues (E-2), and wireless commons policies[6] that focus on innovation capabilities through spectrum policies and mobile IPRs[7] for the promotion of innovation for mobile media (E-3).

1
Access and interconnection policies for mobile media

Access and interconnection policies for mobile media as a specific type of mobile data communications are essential for the development of mobile content and innovative approaches to its use.[8] ANTONELLI (1997) argues that access to new information and communication infrastructure is essential if potential **marginal users** are to be induced to adopt new technologies. Moreover, the reduction of final prices in mobile retail markets that are dependent on interconnection charges in mobile wholesale markets is essential if the adoption of ICT innovations is to be encouraged.[9]

Mobile customers should be able to freely choose and access mobile media content which raises questions on portal space allocation, navigation and selection tools, and control over content (E-1.1). In mobile data business-to-business markets termination rates for voice and data in packet-switched networks will have to be defined for next generation mobile content and services. Interconnection charges in mobile communications markets have been fairly unregulated so far but may need to be revisited - for example in the wholesale termination market - if they turn out to become a **barrier to the adoption of innovative data communications services** such as mobile media (E-1.2).

---

4   See Samuelson and Varian (2001); Werbach further enumerates Internet governance and standards, see Werbach (1997); Mansell & Steinmueller include regulatory developments related to liberalization and universal service as key institutional issues underlying the growth of the information society, see Mansell and Steinmueller (2002). Yet, in the context of mobile media development these issues won't be subject to discussion.

5   See Maitland, Bauer, and Westerveld (2002); Noam (2005).

6   See Lessig (2001); innovation policy for the Internet is related to the perception of the Internet as an innovation commons.

7   See Benkler (2005).

8   Access and interconnection are defined as separate concepts. Access, e.g. to mobile networks, means the making available of facilities and/or services, to another undertaking, under defined conditions, on either an exclusive or non-exclusive basis, for the purpose of providing electronic communications services. Hence, it does not refer to access by end-users, but to 'inter-operator access'. Interconnection means the physical and logical linking of public electronic communications networks used by the same or a different undertaking in order to allow the users of one undertaking to communicate with the users of the same or another undertaking or to access services provided by another undertaking. Interconnection is a specific type of access implemented between public network operators, see European Commission (2002); Intven (2000), p. 3-2.

9   See Antonelli (1997), p. 41.

1.1
Open access to mobile platforms, portals, and content

Mobile media production, aggregation, distribution, and consumption is dependent on the **bottleneck of mobile operators networks, platforms, and services.** Open access to mobile platforms, portals, and content is an essential policy objective, because it can lead to an increase in competition and users' choice (E-1.11). Mobile communications markets are generally considered to be competitive, yet with strong features of a "natural oligopoly"[10] that allows only a limited number of operators with possibly different coverage to interact competitively in equilibrium.[11]

Opening telecommunication bottlenecks to competition involves the setting of access charges, defining the notion of service, and the monitoring of compliance of access policies.[12] Potential for anti-competitive abuse arises when appliances are tied to services provided by operators that occupy a (near-) monopoly position in the value chain (E-1.12).[13] For mobile data this situation can be particularly relevant when a mobile service provider effectively gains control over what content and services appear on what handset in whose portal (E-1.13).

1.1.1
Open access to mobile platforms

Open access to mobile platforms sets incentives for a variety of media content providers to invest into content expansion and development. Mobile media formats need to be compatible with mobile platforms. Therefore, open access to them for all media companies that want to invest into mobile content production is an **essential design requirement.** RHEINGOLD's (2002) arguments arise from a social use point of view:

> "If today's mobile telephone morphs into something more like a remote control for the physical world, social outcomes will depend on whether the remote control device's software infrastructure is an open system, like the Web, or a closed, proprietary system."[14]

The Internet is often considered to be an open system due to its end-to-end architecture.[15] In this view, the intelligence is at the end nodes of a network, i.e. in the devices that are connected to it. This enables users to **innovate at the device level** without being dependent on the decisions of the providers of the net-

---

10 Valletti (2002), p.1.
11 In general, competition policy is recently given a more prominent role in telecommunications and it is substituting certain areas of ex ante regulation with ex post remedies, see ITU (2003a).
12 See Laffont and Tirole (2000), pp. 137. There is generally a trade-off between promoting competition to increase social welfare and encouraging the incumbent to invest and maintain infrastructure.
13 See Eisner Gillett et al. (2000), p. 17.
14 Rheingold (2002), p. 96.
15 See Saltzer, Reed, and Clark (1984); Blumenthal and Clark (2001).

work on what kind of applications are or are not possible. LESSIG (2001) argues that the end-to-end architecture of the Internet has a positive impact on innovation. Therefore, he suggests **transferring the principles of end-to-end architecture to other information and communication industries** in order to achieve dynamic industry development.

Such arguments can be transferred to the mobile data industry, for instance on **opening the mobile ISP market.** MAITLAND (2005) observes that one of the main differences between Internet and mobile data markets is the absence of ISPs in mobile markets; these functions appear to fall into the domain of the network operators.[16] This circumstance is considered to be a problem, e.g., in Japan. Here, the regulatory authority MPHPT is taking measures to open mobile Internet service provision to competition and foster a dynamic mobile ISP market.[17] In DoCoMo's i-mode business model the mobile operator offers services such as access to content, user authorization, and billing over a common mobile infrastructure; the operator's gateway is the only Internet access route. Upon pressure from the MPHPT, DoCoMo agreed to open up its network for other mobile ISPs. Japan's largest ISP, Nifty, is preparing its mobile service launch backed by industry and government pressure.[18] Also the Korean regulatory authority is working towards opening gateways and portals. Their approach is composed of three stages: (1) the opening of operator portals to other content providers; (2) the opening of the operators' gateway to other ISPs; and (3) opening the Inter-Working Function (IWF), a function unique to CDMA2000 networks that allows, for example, independent content provision and billing to other operators, ISPs, and content providers.[19] Even in these Asia-Pacific countries with the worlds' most developed mobile data markets it will be crucial for further expansion to **foster open platform policies** that will allow competing and new players market entrance.

Open platform policies can also refer to **addressing and numbering schemes.** Mobile operators use GPRS, for example, as a means to exert control over content providers. GPRS has a **private Ipv4 addressing scheme** and operates within a **.GPRS top level domain.** GPRS networks are separated from the Internet by a Network Address Translator (NAT). Mobile operators use this characteristic to charge for services such as telling ASPs the International Mobile Equipment Identity (IMEI) handset ID, IP address, or geographical location of their customers.[20] The benefits and drawbacks of introducing a dedicated Top Level Domain (TLD) within the UMTS environment are discussed within the UMTS Forum.[21] Mobile content providers do not have a sufficient lobby in these fora, yet, and mobile operators will be interested in cementing their control powers.

---

16   See Maitland (2005).
17   See ITU (2002b), p. 82.
18   See ITU (2002b), p. 54.
19   See ITU (2002b), p. 84.
20   See INTUG (2002a), p. 8; INTUG (2002c), p. 6.
21   See UMTS Forum (2002a).

The **allocation of short codes** for value-added messaging services is another element for mobile service provision that develops into an emerging issue for regulatory authorities. For the provision of mobile media services or interactive instant response services, messaging continues to be a preferred distribution mode for mobile content providers. The Catalan public broadcaster Televisio de Catalunya (CCRTV) uses, for instance, a channel branded short phone code for its daily interactive SMS TV game shows.[22] Yet, **numbers for value-added services that have marketing value are scarce** and access to receiving them is one important precondition for the installation of new mobile media services. The Irish Office of the Director of Telecommunications Regulation (ODTR) developed a framework for value added SMS services that proposes a 5-digit short code access system and the development of a new range of short codes to allow both network operators as well as third party service providers **equal access** to the mobile market for the delivery of value-added SMS services.[23] In Australia, the Australian Communications Authority (ACA) raised even more questions with respect to **future numbering arrangements for premium rate SMS and MMS services**. The ACA requests industry comments on the question if SMS and MMS should be treated equally or if they require different solutions due to the fact that there are important technical differences between SMS and MMS: MMS use a network's traffic channel whereas SMS uses the control channel. Issues also include setting aside **specific number ranges for different categories of SMS services** such as freecall, standard, premium, and restricted access as well as length of SMS and MMS numbers, in particular short and simple numbers that have marketing value.[24] A differentiation of these services via different numbers could become a signal to consumers of **when to expect premium charges**. The intended transparency can serve as a means of consumer protection, because mobile content and service providers with differing objectives can be distinguished through the numbering policies.

Another crucial case in point is **opening the access to handsets**. NOAM (2005) demands open access to handsets in the US market to provide consumers with increased choices. In Europe, such an approach has been pursued since 1996, but **SIM lock policies** are currently being revisited. In 1996, the Director-General for Competition (DG IV) of the European Commission intervened in the case of the SIM lock feature on mobile phone handsets.[25] It could be used as a theft deterrent, but at the same time effectively locked a particular handset and subscriber to a single mobile operator, thereby preventing subscribers from changing their service provider. DG IV notified handset manufacturers and network operators that it considered the SIM lock feature as having anti-competitive effects. As a result, manufacturers agreed to include the ability for subscribers to unlock the

---

22 See Obstfeld (September 25, 2002).
23 See ODTR (2002).
24 See ACA (2002); most respondents agreed upon a distinct number range required for premium rate messaging services. However, they suggest to use a new range of numbers that are not associated with adult or chat services, see ACA (2003).
25 See Intven (2000), p. 5-29.

SIM lock feature. However, for **UMTS SIM (USIM) cards** the SIM lock system has been reconsidered. The UK regulator OFTEL, for example, considers twelve months as sufficient USIM lock period for initial cost recovery.[26] It is questionable, however, if SIM lock policies will be beneficial for the introduction of next generation services or of they will damage these emerging markets in the light of restricted consumer choices.

1.1.2
Open access to mobile portals

Mobile customers need to be able to locate mobile media offers. The **small portal space** on mobile phone screens is an essential bottleneck and a strategic asset of mobile operators; the screen of a mobile phone is valuable real estate.[27] There is support for the argument that media companies should consider building competitive mobile portals themselves (see D-4.12).

In developing their mobile portals, mobile operators have increasingly adopted the role of **content aggregators** and even content creators. Due to their ownership of the network infrastructure and direct customer relationships they exert a strong influence on the market for mobile portals, content and services. Mobile operators are attracted to **walled garden portals** that include content selection as well as discriminatory billing. 'Walled garden' structures are closed platforms that control supply and demand within their offer. In the case of DoCoMo, the control DoCoMo exerts via the walled garden structure implies a **price cap for official content providers** on their subscription charges as well as **advertising restrictions.**[28] The MPHPT is exerting pressure on DoCoMo to open their portal space as well as the contractual benefits they offer to selected content providers.

In Europe, policy-makers and regulators are also working towards ensuring that portals are as open to competition as possible. The European Commission paid attention to the concern about open portal access in their decision on the portal Vizzavi. In 2000, Vodafone, Vivendi and Canal+ created Vizzavi, a **multi-access Internet portal** with a seamless environment for web-based interactive services across platforms such as fixed and mobile telephony, (handheld) PCs, and television sets. The European Commission concluded that the joint venture would lead to **competitive concerns in markets for TV-based and mobile phone-based Internet portals.** It approved the creation of the Vizzavi Internet portal joint venture only after the companies submitted commitments to ensure rival Internet portals would have equal access to the parent companies' set top boxes

---

26   See ITU (2002b), p. 87. The SIM lock policy becomes particularly relevant if handset subsidies will be restricted and thereby handset cost constitute a pre-use user investment.
27   See Eisner Gillett et al. (2000), pp. 17; Noam (2005). When display size is becoming more valuable, competition in display size may change mobile phones form factors again, e.g. to folding phones such as clamshells or other forms, see Funk (2001b), p. 156.
28   See Funk (2001b), p. 72.

and mobile handsets.[29] In another example from France, the Commercial Court ruled against France Telecom's attempt to lock users into its own WAP portal.[30] When access to portals is restricted, though, mobile content providers raise the question of **securing transparency in the selection of portal content** and the question of ensuring equal portal selection. In Japan, content providers claimed that the screening standards of mobile operators required to be accepted as an official content provider are non-transparent and that the treatment of official sites is discriminatory. In 2001, the telecommunications ministry MPHPT recommended that content providers and ISPs jointly set up an organization to decide the criteria for selection of mobile sites. It further recommended to expand DoCoMo's collection of subscription fees and billing process to unofficial content providers as well in order to set incentives for mobile content development.[31] In China, the 'Monternet' program of China Mobile claims to ensure open portals to content providers.[32]

The issues for disagreement go even further, however, when it comes to determining which layer of the portal space content is placed, how many clicks mobile customers need to access mobile content offers and what navigation tools are offered to mobile customers. Analogies to the competition policy concerns on mobile portals and **how entries are listed** can be found in the regulatory discussion about Electronic Program Guides (EPGs) for digital TV portals and Customer Reservation Systems (CRS) in the airline industry.

As a result it is in media companies' interest to **lobby for open access** to mobile operators' portal if they decide to develop their own mobile portals. In this case, open access to handsets becomes important so that users are able to change default settings and choose the media companies' portal offer. If media companies decide to remain syndicators for mobile operators' portal space, a set of additional questions on the control over content arises.

1.1.3
The distribution of control over content

The distribution of control over mobile media content affects the relationship between media companies, mobile operators, and users. The question is how respective levels of control need to be balanced in order to achieve an outcome that fosters innovation best. BENKLER (1998) argues that the two most important **social effects of communications regulation** are to be found in (1) the impact it exerts on the distribution of control over the flow of information on the level of society and (2) in the way that distribution of control affects individual autonomy and

---

29 See European Commission (2000).
30 See ITU (2002b), p. 85.
31 See ITU (2002b), p. 54.
32 Under the Monternet program, service providers can access China Mobile's network at any place to provide nationwide service. It is also known as the 'one-stop shop, China-wide service' arrangement. China Mobile keeps nine percent of the traffic revenue, information service providers receive 91 percent which has generated incentives for many service providers, see ITU (2002b), p. 109.

political discourse. As a result, he demands that communications infrastructure regulation should focus on attributes that (1) make digital information technology a potential vehicle for achieving broad distribution of access and (2) that enable participation in the social process of knowledge production.[33] These arguments support the assumption that open access to mobile platforms, portals, and content can foster bottom-up user-driven innovation.

The influence of carriers on content and the distribution of control over content provision is is particularly interesting in the light of the background of co-option between media and telecommunications companies (see D-4.1). Differences in network architectures can affect the provision of content to consumers and can lead to the question of the **network provider as editor**. MACKIE-MASON, SHENKER & VARIAN (1996) differentiate two competing visions that affect content provision: one model is based on the application-blind architecture of the Internet, the other is based on the application-aware architecture of online services, among which some are content aware and some are content blind. They describe two ways in which the network provider can play an editorial role which affects content provision: through technological and institutional delivery cost that vary across architectures; and through the extent to which the architecture permits the network to differentiate transport prices for different goods.[34] They find that **content aware networks favor mass market** over niche goods and reduce clutter when they exercise their editorial capability. On the other hand, the emergence of multiple networks with multiple architectures and different content menus demand **interoperability which favors the blind architecture**. Customers who want to avoid clutter may be willing to pay for editorial services provided by competing sellers over blind networks.[35] In a multiple network environment for next generation mobile data services, opportunity could therefore arise for mobile editorial services that provide orientation in a content blind architecture. Currently, mobile operators have control over content in their portals, similar to application aware online service providers in Mackie-Mason, Shenker and Varian's model. First experiences confirm that operators favor mass attractive media brands over niche content. As a result it is essential for the promotion of mobile content variety that independent media content offers can be accessed. Yet, mobile operators may remain in control of the application even if their architecture is content blind. They can potentially use this control to delay or hinder mobile media content to become accessible. Cross-network service provision of mobile media (see D-3.2) will hence be dependent on mobile operators' willingness to cooperate.

But even in the case of multiple interconnected networks that would favor a blind architecture in Mackie-Mason, Shenker and Varian's model and release control over content the **information flow** does not necessarily have to be free. NOAM (2001) describes the problem:

---

33 See Benkler (1998), pp. 183.
34 See McKie-Mason, Shenker, and Varian (1996), p. 4.
35 See McKie-Mason, Shenker, and Varian (1996), p. 22.

"What impact will an interconnected network of networks have on content? Would information flow with greater ease or with more restrictions? What would be the effect on the complex web of traditional content rules that apply to different types of networks?"[36]

For a discussion of these issues, Noam distinguishes **five legal regimes for information flow**: the constitutional, the privileged trustee, the private contract carriage, the common carriage, and the arbitrage model.[37] In the constitutional model content flows are governed by fundamental speech rights. The privileged trustee model ties the flow of content to special rights granted by the state. The private contract carriage model focuses contract and property and exercises general commercial freedoms. The common carriage model is traditionally underlying telecommunications users' access to the public networks for the flow of information over telephone networks. Segregated content flow rules become impossible as networks interconnect; thus, an **arbitrage model** may emerge. This model proposes a system that strives for achieving the goals of common carriage in a private carriage system and that provides third-party neutrality. Noam argues that **third-party neutrality** ensures nondiscriminatory flow of information and provides substantial freedom of contract for carriers.[38] Ensuring the **free flow of mobile media across different interconnecting networks** (see D-3.2) may favor the arbitrage model. Carriers in this model cannot discriminate against their customers' customer. The implications for content provision are that control over content cannot be extended on all networks, similar to the 'first sale'-doctrine in intellectual property provision.[39] In the arbitrage model, mobile carriers can contract freely with other mobile and fixed-line network operators, information can flow freely over mobile cellular, wireless, and fixed-line networks, and users obtain some degree of control over how they can use purchased mobile media content for use in different networks.

While the arbitrage model for the free flow of mobile information is applicable to telecommunications operators in cooperation with media companies, further models for content providers and the **control over content they share with users** still need to be discussed. BENKLER (1998; 2005) distinguishes **three communications models** that have different functions concerning the distribution of control over content between content providers and users:[40]
1) the **broadcast model** concentrates communicative functions in the hands of broadcasters and gives end-users relatively little control over programming as components of their personal knowledge environment; in mobile media environments he speaks of the 'Glorified Car Radio' (GCR) model that is available only for push content delivery selected by the content provider;

36   Noam (2001), p. 211.
37   See Noam (2001), pp. 211.
38   See Noam (2001), pp. 212.
39   See Noam (2001), p. 226. This doctrine grants copyright owners the right to control only the first sale of their work.
40   See Benkler (1998), pp. 187; Benkler (2005).

2) the **telephony model** reflects a broader distribution of the capacity to originate the intelligence flowing over channels; it provides end-users with greater
incentives to collect and process information. For mobile data communications Benkler speaks of a modified 'Mobile High-Speed Internet Access'
(MHIA) model that promotes a user-controlled environment but that introduces constraints on the flexibility of users, e.g. in order to privilege certain
content through preferential delivery;
3) the **Internet model** reflects a high degree of individual control over communication flows and also distributes broadly many other communicative functions; for high-speed mobile Internet access this could be an MHIA model
based on open wireless networks that is built purely of collaborating end-user
devices.[41]

For the provision of mobile media, Benkler argues that the broadcast or mass
media model would not be beneficial, because from the point of view of copyright policy mobile content providers would probably not be treated like terrestrial broadcasters whose services are covered by a compulsory license with a
statutorily-fixed royalty; instead they would have to negotiate appropriate licensing fees. He suggests the **Internet model as the preferred choice for users**
who receive free choices to use mobile content. He further suggests equipping
users with tools for communication in order to exchange their own cultural ex-
pressions. This implies a shift of direction from license-based control over content to a **user-controlled environment** that promotes rather than curtails interactivity and choice.[42] Benkler suggests that communications policy decisions
will best serve the democratic values of self-governance, both in the sense of individual autonomy and in the sense of political participation, when the adopted
policies are likely to lead to a **broad social distribution of communicative functions**.[43] Therefore, the core of mobile data provision should be the provision of
Internet access through equipment that enables license-free, network-owner-in-
dependent communication.

Figure E-1 shows the three models of control over mobile content distribution. Each model involves differences in control over content on the part of the
mobile operator, the media content provider and the mobile customer.

Ultimately, releasing control to users can turn out to become beneficial for
media companies and their objectives when users can exploit the full opportunities and strengths of their social networks. Yet, it remains a **joint effort of media companies and mobile operators** in which both have to agree on what level
of control they can afford to give away and what they need to retain.

---

41 See Benkler (1998), pp. 187.
42 See Benkler (2005).
43 See Benkler (1998), p. 195.

	Control over content of		
	Mobile operator	Content provider	Mobile user
Broadcast model	Control over handset capabilities (hardware limitations) and dedication to a set number of content providers	Control over programming	No control over content
Telephony model	Control over handset capabilities (hardware limitations) and portal (e.g. portal defaults)	On-demand content delivery, user control content pull	Equipping users with tools
Internet model	Any device can connect to any infrastructure, free choice of content providers	On-demand content delivery, user control content pull	User-controlled environment

Figure E-1: Three models of mobile content distribution

1.2
Interconnection policies for mobile data communications

Interconnection charges can constitute a major part of the total operating expenses for providing telecommunication services and they can create a type of **barrier to innovation.**[44] This barrier will also affect media companies' mobile content offers. High interconnection charges can influence the profitability of mobile media and reduce incentives for mobile content development. NOAM (2001) describes interconnection as the glue that holds the network of networks together.[45] In mobile data communications, the major interconnection issues concern **termination charges for fixed-to-mobile interconnection as well as international roaming.** The early stage of mobile data provision provides little empirical research on mobile data termination. Interconnection arrangements are developing between individual mobile operators and providers of GPRS Roaming Exchange (GRX) services. Arrangements on traffic exchange between operators in a 3G environment have yet to be developed.[46]

---

44 See Bourreau and Dogan (2001), p. 176.
45 See Noam (2001), p. 1. The first interconnection treaty was signed on October 3, 1849, between Prussia and Austria in order to be able to send messages between Berlin and Vienna. Then, it was an inefficient system in which a special joint telegraph office was constructed, staffed by representatives of each country's telegraph company, who were connected to their respective national networks, see Standage (1998), p. 68.

Particularly in competitive markets regulatory intervention is suggested to be kept to a minimum. Mobile communications markets are considered to be competitive. Yet, regulation of interconnection represents one of a **small number of exceptions** to the general rule. The new EU regulatory framework draws attention to mobile markets with regard to call origination and call termination on public mobile telephone networks and national markets for international roaming services. The case for regulation may be based on a **combination of rationales** such as potential monopolies in mobile communications, externalities, information inadequacies, anti-competitive behavior and predatory pricing, or unequal bargaining power.[47] An open question is if regulatory intervention in 2G mobile wholesale termination markets can have effects on an increase of competition in 3G mobile data markets.

1.2.1
Termination charges for mobile data communications

Media companies that want to offer services via a mobile operator platform have to pay for the termination of these offers in mobile networks. The **level of wholesale interconnection charges** affects the profit margins of media companies; it is, therefore, a new area of telecommunication policy that is put into the focus of media companies.

The role of mobile services in telecommunications has changed in recent years. On a global scale, mobile subscribers have overtaken fixed-line subscribers, traffic to and from mobile phones is steadily increasing and in some countries such as Germany the **revenues from mobile communications are almost overtaking fixed-line communications revenues.**[48] In the light of that background, an increased regulatory interest and attention is paid to mobile-to-mobile, but in particular fixed-to-mobile interconnection agreements on termination charges.

Opinions on the extent of competition in mobile retail and wholesale markets vary significantly. The discussion about mobile wholesale markets focuses on the question if each mobile operator owns a bottleneck with regard to termination due to the fact that these services cannot be substituted. In Europe, the factor between mobile and fixed network termination can differ significantly. In 2001, the EU average for the fixed-mobile termination charge difference was a multiple of 15.58, i.e. mobile termination was more than 15 times higher than fixed network termination.[49] For example, fixed-mobile interconnection charg-

---

46   One issue of contention is who should pay for incoming calls and messages on mobile devices. In the US, the receiving party pays (RPP) model dominates for wireless calls. In Europe, the calling-party-pays (CPP) principle is in place; it enables the mobile carriers to charge incoming callers high prices, see Noam (2001), p. 47.
47   See Baldwin and Cave (1999), p. 17.
48   See ITU (2003b). In 2002, mobile communication revenues constitute 33 percent, fixed-line revenues 36 percent of total telecommunication revenues in the German market that has a volume of EUR 61 billion, see RegTP (2003), p.3,
49   See Freund and Ruhle (2002), p. 32.

es in Germany (0.1491 to 0.1849 EUR/min) were substantially higher than mobile-fixed interconnection charges (0.0186 EUR/min) in 2001.[50] In order to address this issues, mobile operators are evaluated with regard to the criteria of **significant market power** (SMP) that refer to the ability of a firm to independently raise prices above market levels for a non-transitory period without loosing sales to such a degree as to make this behavior unprofitable.[51] Moreover, the concepts of **parallel pricing behavior and collective dominance** by joint alliances of operators have been introduced in the new EU regulatory framework as new criteria for measuring market power. Mobile operator's price increases on commercial SMS in Europe could, for example, be interpreted as testing the price and demand elasticity of the market and may even serve as evidence for parallel pricing and exercising joint dominance.[52]

In targeting mobile operators with significant market power, **defining the relevant market** is the first crucial step. The relevant market analysis for an identification of potential *ex ante* regulation includes the exploration of the relationship between different functional levels of competition at the wholesale and the retail level, and the application of consistent distinctions and indicators to the separate processes of market definition and market power assessment. Possible market definitions differentiate one single national mobile market versus each network as a market of its own and they differentiate wholesale and retail levels. One essential question is if there is a **mobile call termination market** for call termination in individual mobile networks. The European Commission refers to call termination on individual mobile networks as a service market. According to this definition, all mobile operators are dominant regarding the termination of calls on their networks.[53] The subsequent questions that may arise concern future 3G services such as **value added SMS or MMS services** and ask if they need to be treated as markets of their own as well.

The discussions about **SMS origination and termination as a market of its own** may serve as an early indicator for services introduced in next generation networks. The supply of SMS origination and termination is technically different from mobile voice telephony. The text message is carried in the signalling channel with a low priority. High priority messages are used for signals associated with call set-up and inter-cell call transfer. As a consequence SMS delivery, which has distribution cost that are close to zero is subject to different economics. These characteristics may serve as an argument for analyzing SMS as separate market from voice telephony.[54] As a consequence, mobile operators would be considered to be monopolists in these markets which would affect the way

---

50 See Kurth (2002a). Further regulatory problems arise, because fixed-line competitors of the former incumbent protest against integrated telecommunication companies such as Deutsche Telekom who are thought to receive special fixed-mobile interconnection rates for their fixed-line business unit.

51 See Intven (2000), p. 5-11.

52 See INTUG (2002a), p. 6.

53 See ITU (2002b), p. 77; in the Japanese mobile market, all personal digital communications and CDMA mobile phone operators are designated as one relevant market. In Korea, only the dominant mobile operator, SK Telecom, is designated as significant market power operator in the mobile service market, see ITU (2002b), p. 77.

they set prices. For media companies these prices for termination are one component reducing their profit base. As such, a regulatory intervention in order to **prohibit monopolist pricing** would be in the interest of media companies. Since media companies set the prices for mobile media offers according to target costing principles that originate from consumers' willingness to pay and that are not necessarily cost-based, a reduction in cost of service delivery means an increase in profit for media companies. Alternatively, media companies could try to negotiate participation in interconnection revenues from traffic that is created due to their media brand attractiveness (see A-1.11).

For mobile operators, the **effects of potential regulatory intervention** could be substantial. Mobile operators revenues are driven by SMS, call termination, and international mobile roaming revenues. According to a Goldman Sachs Research Report from May 2002, estimates of Vodafone's, T-Mobile's and MMO2's revenues from incoming calls and international roaming range from a revenue share between 13 and 19 percent for mobile termination and 5 to 14 percent from roaming.[55] Thus, the effects of regulatory intervention in call termination and roaming markets for European operators are estimated to lead to **sudden sharp drops in income**.[56] It could also make next generation data services less attractive for operators when termination charges would become regulated. Since the rationale for regulation will depend a lot on the definition of the relevant market, it underlines the importance of relevant market definition as an essential element of competition policy in network economics; it may allow inadequate options when chosen too narrow.[57]

Concerns on regulatory intervention are in particular that it will harm competition in mobile markets. HAUCAP (2003) argues that the **high specific investments and sunk costs** in building next generation cellular networks justify prices above cost to set incentives for taking the risks connected with investment.[58] However, OFTEL (2002), for example, concludes that regulating call termination on mobile networks in wholesale markets will not weaken competition in mobile retail markets. To the contrary, they argue that the regulation of termination charges might promote **vigorous retail price competition** and would be desirable for consumers.[59]

The discussion demonstrates that the potential regulation of interconnection fees plays a crucial role in the development of prices in mobile retail markets.[60] Therefore, the **adoption of ex-ante regulation for 2G mobile services** may affect the development of next generation mobile data content and services. A loss of revenues in the traditional mobile termination market may pressure mobile in-

---

54 See INTUG (2002a); SMS is not carried on the mobile data network and is thus not part of the mobile data market, either.
55 See INTUG (2002c).
56 A 10 percent cut results in revenue losses between 1.4 and 2.7 percent; a 30 percent cut results in revenue losses up to 8.2 percent, see INTUG (2002c), p. 3.
57 See Picot and Heger (2004),pp. 345.
58 See Haucap (2003); he characterizes an ex post sector-specific regulation as a government hold up.
59 See OFTEL (2002).
60 See Freund and Ruhle (2002), p. 40.

cumbents to set more incentives for mobile content providers to develop new mobile data services in 3G and beyond.

1.2.2
International roaming and mobile media services

The issue of interconnection pricing extends to international roaming, which is perceived to be one of the greatest benefits of mobile communications in general. An issue of inquiry is whether mobile operators use their dominance in their domestic call termination market as a **lever to exercise power** in the call origination markets of foreign countries. There is no regulation of international roaming and mobile operators have considerable bargaining power which leads to charges within the EU that are up to five times higher than for national mobile calls.[61] INTUG (2002) presents some evidence on **excessive pricing behavior** of mobile operators in Europe regarding wholesale cost of call termination.[62] It is used in the European Commission's inquiry whether international mobile roaming is potentially less than fully competitive and whether parallel pricing behavior distorts competition.[63]

The monitoring of international roaming costs for voice communications is now expanding to the **termination of SMS and data traffic.** International SMS roaming charges are a growing necessity, but since they are negotiated among mobile operators they tend to be high as well. International roaming charges, thus, can evolve into a **barrier to the mobile data communications market growth.** Regulators may have to intervene to establish cost-oriented roaming charges.[64]

Interconnection principles such as those set out in the **Reference Paper**[65] for the WTO's Agreement on Basic Telecommunications or the European Interconnection Directive[66] require interconnection charges to be cost-oriented. Without a cost-based standard for setting interconnection charges a dominant operator would have an incentive for high termination rates for calls that originate on a competitor's network. As a result, the competitor's customers will have to

---

61   See Sutherland (2001), p. 5; ITU (2002b), p. 88.
62   See INTUG (2002c), p.11. Differentials around EUR 0.14 per minute are reported to translate into price differences up to 14 times between mobile and fixed call termination cost. For consumers, the difference in price within the EU can be up to 500 percent, see Sutherland (2001), p. 9.
63   See INTUG (2002c), p. 9; higher charges for roaming are usually justified by the higher value to the caller; Vodafone New Zealand, however, allows its customers to make international calls in Australia without a roaming premium which questions the roaming schemes that prevail in Europe or the US, see INTUG (2002c), p. 9.
64   See ITU (2002b), p. 88. No institution will act as arbitrating body in case of disagreement; consumers have no institution to whom they can direct their complaints about international mobile roaming issues. An expansion of mobile data communications will increase international mobile roaming problems.
65   See WTO (1996).
66   Also, following Article 7 (1) and (2) of the EU Directive 97/33/EC (as amended by Directive 98/61/EC) the principle of cost orientation for interconnection charges is only applicable for firms with significant market power in the interconnection market. Only few European operators are subject to significant market power for interconnection. Otherwise, for non-dominant operators a regulation based on appropriate or reasonable tariffs is applied, see Freund and Ruhle (2002), pp. 21.

pay for excessive termination charges. Also, a dominant firm can use the roaming termination fee revenues to subsidize losses from predatory pricing actions to drive competitors out of the national market.[67] Signatories of the WTO GATS Reference Paper have not enforced implementation of these commitments on the interconnection of international calls to mobile cellular networks so far. But even if mobile operators are not considered dominant the question on reasonable tariffs remains. Media companies who offer mobile subscription services that are pushed to the user should have an interest in the extent of these roaming charges that will burden the mobile roaming customer.

To date, mobile operators have started negotiations on next generation international roaming charges with the introduction of GPRS services. The market for **international roaming services with GPRS** can potentially extend to all networks and countries that use one standard. However, mobile operators have to solve the **billing details for GPRS roaming**, which includes cross-border processing of data traffic including Calling Line Identification (CLI) data that raises new data protection issues. The data being processed for GPRS billing will further include, among others, handset number, subscriber identity, IP address, identity and transactions of the services being used, and personal data submitted such as credit card numbers or home addresses. Operators may also exploit uncertainty about the regime for data protection to prevent third party providers from accessing the international roaming service market. INTUG argues that mobile operators seem to aim at staying in control of both traffic and billing information.[68]

The costs of international roaming are a serious concern to consumers and businesses such as media companies. Overhead and operating costs are de facto incurred in roaming and should be recovered. Currently, however, consumers seem to be over-charged.[69] As **global roaming in next generation networks** becomes an issue, a more open and competitive regime is essential if prices are to be driven down to levels that users accept. One means of consumer protection on the device level could be mechanisms that automatically select the cheapest available option. Another means to introduce more competition in roaming charges may be to license MVNOs. Here, another option for media companies emerges to enter the mobile communication market (see D-4.12; E-3.12).

The discussion of access and interconnection policies for mobile media that are traditionally an important element in telecommunication policy demonstrates that they become a **new policy area of interest for media companies**, because the provision of mobile media content and service benefits from open access to mobile wireless platforms and from a decrease in interconnection rates, particularly for national and international termination charges.

---

67   See Intven (2000), p. 3-9.
68   See INTUG (2002b). Within GPRS roaming the resolution of a URL into an IP address can, e.g., be performed locally or taken back to the home operator.
69   See Sutherland (2001).

2
Consumer and data protection and privacy policies for mobile media

As mobile communications becomes a platform for mass media provision, media companies are facing difficult decisions on the **degree to which they should collect and use information about individuals' intellectual habits and preferences**. Technological advances such as mobile communications are creating an unprecedented potential to use aggregated data on consumers for purposes ranging from the protection of national security to achieving commercial competitive advantage. The ability to locate a person can be beneficial in the case of an accident or an emergency, but may be regarded as a threat to individual welfare in circumstances of commercial exploitation.[70] Media companies have to be very sensitive to the latter issues in order to find acceptance for their mobile media offers.

> "The dream of perfect ceaseless information flow can slip so easily into a nightmare of perfect perpetual distraction. Our technologies don't just empower us: they also harass us [...]. [...] And every new channel of information is a potential intruder with a sales pitch. [...] So one of the questions about ubiquitous technology becomes: [...] How do you anti-spam-filter your life?"[71]

Mobile media offers that implement DRM technologies will also stand for more control over access and use of digital files and implicate the privacy interests of their users. COHEN (2003) argues that the **connections between consumer protection and information policy** can no longer be ignored in digital environments in which mass-distributed information goods are increasingly bundled with complex licenses of DRM technologies that require fair information practices.[72] Interrogating the relationship between mobile media and consumer protection (E-2.1) and privacy (E-2.2) raises deeper questions on the nature of location-based services (E-2.11), security (E-2.12), and unsolicited messages (E-2.22).

2.1
Consumer and data protection policies

Personalization and location-specificity of services not only opens up a range of new business opportunities, but also an array of consumer and data protection concerns. When people, rather than artifacts, are tracked, it includes additional issues such as the security of the mobile communication system.[73] **Data protection laws** for telecommunications-based information and communication services comprise three different levels: telecommunication infrastructure (trans-

---

70 See Mansell and Steinmueller (2002), p. 339.
71 Gleick (2001), p. 1.
72 See Cohen (2003), p. 18.
73 See Mansell and Steinmueller (2002), p. 156.

port layer), information and communication services (application layer), and content exchange (content layer).[74] Different laws on each of these layers regulate when a third party is eligible to collect, analyze, and use consumer data. These aspects of regulation are necessary to limit the extent to which risk derives from the use of mobile data communications in general and mobile media content and service in particular.

2.1.1
Location positioning technologies and location-based services

Location-based services rely on mobile awareness services such as position acquisition, geocoding, reverse geocoding, spatial search, mapping, and routing.[75] **Lifestyle media brands** may consider offering location-based services for their audiences or brand communities (see C-1.3). However, there is considerable threat of negative spill-over effects if consumers feel either monitored and/or threatened by abuse. The 'monitoring of everyday life' may become an **unintended consequence of wireless emergency systems.**[76]

Initially, the emergence of location-based services was driven by government regulation of emergency services rather than commercial location-based service applications. Network-based solutions such as triangulation or handset-based solutions, e.g. GPS, can be used to provide the emergency services with the latitude and longitude of the caller's location. The rules of the FCCs wireless 911 service or the European commission's E112 initiative include the provision of precise automatic location identification (ALI).[77] Regulatory efforts hereby aim at incorporating wireless systems into the existing emergency response framework. Essential implications of these plans concern the question of whether or not the disclosure of locational information is limited to emergency calls or whether locational data are subject to secondary use as a **source of funding for the wireless emergency infrastructure.**

Even permission-based marketing approaches that reach a user agreement to apply locational information to location-based one-to-one marketing services raise a number of jurisdictional concerns. The crucial point with **opt-in services** may become that consumers do not realize potential privacy implications at the time they consent to use a location-based service. One suggestion to address this problem is to create opportunities for limitations of user agreements concerning the scope of space, time, and matter.[78] Overall, **consumer information policies** become crucial; currently, they are in the responsibility of mobile operators. Location-based service providers are not eligible to collect location-based data, they are dependent on the information of the mobile operators. The problem be-

---

74 See Kaeding (2002), p. 197; for the German market these laws are: Telekommunikationsgesetz, Telekommunikationsdatenschutzverordnung (transport layer), Teledienstedatenschutzgesetz, Mediendienstestaatsvertrag (application layer), and Bundesdatenschutzgesetz (content layer).
75 See Pflug and Meyer (2002), p. 402.
76 See Bennett, Phillips, and Regan (2002).
77 See ITU (2002b), p 130.
78 See Gasser (2002), p. 22.

comes aggravated if, for instance, mobile operators are obliged to inform users on the collection, storage, and usage of the sensitive data which is a challenging task due to small displays of mobile phones. Mobile service providers further need the users' agreement to use such information.[79] Such an electronic agreement has to meet the same requirements than a written one, e.g. the requirement that it is always available to consumers. A possible solution for meeting this requirement may be the **introduction of a toll-free number** that users can call to obtain the critical piece of information. However, large amounts of text of consumer information policies still pose a challenge for any kind of mobile location-based services. But regardless of all challenges: the essential underlying principle for all personalized and location-based services is that users keep control over sensitive data.

Commercial location-based services also raise concerns regarding information on the pricing of these services, e.g. of premium rate SMS messages,[80] as well as the **liability risk for both consumers and service providers**. Network system failures or technological incompatibilities that delay, for example, the time critical delivery of information can cause harm in the case of critical decisions and consequently lead to liability risks.[81] For mobile media delivery this issue will become pronounced with the evolution of mobile picture and video applications that will be priced higher than current SMS services and, thus, bear more potential for conflict.

Even in situations that tend to be perceived as particularly suited for location-based services such as in international roaming situations these services pose another set of challenges. National and international **geo-data markets** are characterized by a lack of technical and legal interoperability, a lack of international geo-data clearinghouses, and a lack of transparency of services offered. Consumer protection, therefore, also becomes an important issue for **international roaming and cross-border mobile data provision**. Existing international laws and conventions are not particularly designed to handle cross-border disputes that arise from relationships built through mobile services. Applicable law needs to be determined in cases, where, e.g. the mobile service provider delivers erroneous or misleading information to the mobile phone of a customer in another country which results in a financial loss for the customer.[82] Media companies have not made extensive use of location-based services until now. The political difficulties connected with location-based services indicate that a fast market entry may not become the preferred strategic option.

---

79 See Kaeding (2002), pp.199.
80 In Denmark, the regulator asked the industry to ensure that consumers receive price information on premium rate SMS and to inform consumers actively about the possibility of barring premium rate SMS messages, see ITU (2002b), p. 83. The ACA remarks that there may also be issues in relation to billing and credit card management for premium rate messaging services. Existing industry codes need to be expanded to adequately cover these new services, see ACA (2003), p. 7.
81 See Gasser (2002), p. 28.
82 See Sutherland (2001), p. 17; Tschoepe (2001), p. 212.

2.1.2
Security concerns in mobile data communications

Security concerns with regard to mobile media provision can relate to the mobile media transmission as well as to the use and payment mechanisms for paid mobile content models. **Streaming or downloading mobile media** as paid content services require stability of critical network infrastructure in order to ensure security for transmissions and payment. The proliferation of mobile communications as critical infrastructure for sensitive data transfer or money transactions means that **security and encryption policy** takes on new importance. Security services such as mobile authentication, securing payments and protecting customer data are crucial components of any value-added mobile content and service offer.

Existing security features are considered to be insufficient in the light of the proliferation of wireless networks and mobile services.[83] Authentication using public key infrastructure (PKI) is more difficult to implement on mobile handsets than on PCs.[84] A lack of security in **mobile operators' locational data** offers new potential for abuse with different degrees of severity.[85] The introduction of more complex operating systems in portable devices introduces even more security concerns that are usually associated with the Internet such as viruses, identity theft, and file manipulation. One approach is the development of **mobile file system security** as a set of measures to selectively access protected information in the case of more complex microprocessor-controlled portable devices.[86]

Not only software but also hardware components are crucial elements of mobile security. Mobile devices can be grouped into two categories from a security perspective: mobile devices featuring a security token and mobile devices without removable storage media for sensitive information. A **security token** is a removable piece of hardware that stores confidential information such as private keys and subscriber details. In the GSM system, the introduction of the SIM concept was the first effort to secure over-the-air communication with mass-implementing cryptographic measures. The GSM system design further incorporates authentication, speech encryption, IMEI checking (verification of the mobile phone's equipment number), and user confidentiality. WAP security features comprise a WAP Identity Module (WIM) and wireless transport layer security (WTLS).[87] Problems arise when mobile operators do not uniformly execute security services. The verification of the mobile phone's equipment number, for example, which is intended for barring stolen or illegal devices has been

---

83   See Freystaetter (2002); Geisselbrecht and Fotschki (2002); Hirsh (2002).
84   See ITU (2002b), p. 92.
85   Irritation may occur when unsolicited advertisement is sent, but more seriously criminals may determine the right time to intrude on a mobile operators' subscribers house, see Steinfield and Kim (2002).
86   See Freystaetter (2002), pp. 452.
87   See Freystaetter (2002), pp. 445. From a historical perspective, the main impetus on mobile security came from the cryptographic community with public key infrastructures (PKI) and their implementations for electronic information exchanges and transactions in the financial industries.

switched off by several mobile operators. A stolen mobile phone can thus still be used in networks that do not perform the IMEI check.

A **lack of standardization in mobile security** that protects both data and consumers poses a barrier to the development of next generation mobile services, particularly for mobile transactions. Media companies from the music and entertainment industries that are working towards payments for digital mobile entertainment services may want to constitute a lobbying force that could enforce a common standard of mobile security.[88]

2.2
Privacy concerns in mobile data communications

Mobile customers can perceive pushed mobile media content and services as a form of privacy intrusion even with an opt-in approach when there is a lack of personal relevance (E-2.21). The problem increases with the growth of mobile spam and poses a serious threat to the overall adoption of mobile media (E-2.22).

2.2.1
Threats to liberty and quality of life

Telecommunication networks, as NOAM (2001) observes, have brought "marvels of convenience but have also created jeopardizes to privacy"[89]. The definition of privacy refers to the state of being undisturbed, the freedom from intrusion or public attention, and the avoidance of publicity. A major challenge is to establish and enforce boundaries between what is public and what is private. This can, e.g., be addressed through social conventions, legal sanctions, or technological methods.[90]

With regard to mobile communications, RHEINGOLD (2002) identifies three distinct **threats of the always-on vision:** threats to liberty with ubiquitous surveillance, threats to quality of life through an erosion of sanity and civility, and threats to human dignity as more and more people turn to symbiotic interactions with machines.[91] **Mobile data-mining techniques** that media companies may use to collect more information on user preferences can be perceived as a threat to liberty and to quality of life. With regard to ubiquitous surveillance, mobile operators are able to collect far more data than media companies. However, mobile media usage can contribute to an erosion of civility and etiquette in public spaces (see B-2.3). Depending on the way media companies handle sensitive data, mobile media provision thus can influence users' perception on mobile communication as a threat to quality of life.

---

88   See Freystaetter (2002), p. 457.
89   Noam (2001), p. 240.
90   See Mansell and Steinmueller (2002), p. 338; the literal translation from the Latin word 'privatus' means 'apart from the public life'.
91   See Rheingold (2002), p. 185.

A particular privacy concern with regard to mobile media is the collection of name-linked data. **Name-linked data** is data about an individual or an individual's behavior that is clearly identifiable with that individual; financial transactions or healthcare records provide some examples. There may be a public interest in the use of this data. Yet, it offers many potential abuses especially when the means by which such data is collected is out of the direct control of the individual.[92] The advances of mobile data communications which include the collection of name-linked data are likely to raise growing concern about the extent of what is legally known about individuals and who is allowed access to that information.

In addition to data about individuals there is also data that displays patterns of individual interaction with electronic networks and services. These **tele-metadata** are data transmitted as part of the set-up, progress, clear-down, billing, and network management of a message through a public telecommunication network. The spectrum of interests in protecting the collection and analysis of that data is polarized between arguments on beneficial social outcomes such as tracking fraud and arguments on the promotion of marketing purposes.[93] Privacy abuse through the manipulation of name-linked data and tele-metadata can have serious **implications for user confidence** and the take-up of new services. Due to the potential value loss and concerns that self-regulation models are rather unlikely to be successful it lies in the interest of all parties involved in mobile content value extraction - carriers and content and service providers - to work towards governance solutions.

Additional privacy concerns arise with the implementation of mobile DRM technologies. The control they exert over access and use of mobile media files conflicts with the privacy interests of users of information goods. The **monitoring capabilities of DRM** create the potential for a vastly increased collection of information about individuals' intellectual habits and preferences. The relevant question in this context is whether information about intellectual consumption is gathered and stored in a form potentially accessible to third parties.[94] Media companies are likely to be subsumed under the label of third parties, because mobile operators will have an interest to be in charge of installing mobile DRM technologies in order to obtain that information and gain in their bargaining power in compaison to media companies (see D-4.1).

Some consumers, however, may voluntarily trade their privacy for various enticements from media companies such as bargains or the latest ring-tones.[95] **Establishing markets in privacy** is a possible response for these types of demand. Negotiations, transactions, and markets as a way to establish and protect privacy is a non-traditional policy approach – next to the traditional policy approaches of centralized general protection, decentralized ad hoc protection, and self-regulation. NOAM (2001) suggests a system of personalized access charges between

---

92 See Mansell and Steinmueller (2002), p. 377.
93 See Mansell and Steinmueller (2002), p. 380; tele-metadata exclude the content of the call itself.
94 See Cohen (2003).
95 See Rheingold (2002), p. 187.

individuals to set the level of privacy protection.[96] Along similar lines, FELDMANN & ZERDICK (2004) suggest **inverse value added services** as a concept that allows users to get paid for their attention. Mobile media content can serve as such a 'reward payment' in future advertising models when mobile users consent to advertising in exchange for popular mobile entertainment contents.

2.2.2
Mobile unsolicited commercial messages

Mobile media content in 2G and 2.5G cellular networks is mainly delivered in the form of messaging services. But messaging also offers attractive delivery models for next generation mobile services. Therefore, the growing problem of mobile unsolicited commercial messages becomes an issue for media companies as well. Mobile unsolicited commercial messages are likely to increase and may **turn customers completely off mobile services**. Therefore, media companies have to be careful what kind of cross-promotion activities they may offer as part of their self-promotion activities or to their advertising clients.[97] It may be better to **resist generating revenues via mobile advertising** in order to secure customer acceptance for the original mobile services.

Japan can serve as a deterrent example: according to the Daily Yomiuri newspaper in Japan, more than 950 million e-mails are sent and received on mobile phones every day with more than 84 percent of them consisting of spam. The Japanese government passed first legal measures which forces spammers to put a special identifying character in the subject line of each ad message.[98]

Mobile spam mail that is unsolicited by receivers is typically sent for advertising purposes. Both mobile telemarketing calls and messages are not only often a nuisance to the called party, but it can also cause negative externalities and carry cost for both network providers and users. In a receiving party pays (RPP) environment, for example, mobile spam is harmful for users in that it incurs cost to the receiver and it is unlikely that the mobile subscriber will be able to recover the cost of an unwanted call or message from a direct marketer.[99] For mobile operators spam mail puts an **extra burden on network capacity management** and on the user's capacity of the mobile mailbox. Due to network capacity constraints mobile spam is likely to lead to even greater financial consequences than PC spam mail.[100]

---

96 See Noam (2001), pp. 242; Feldmann and Zerdick (2004), p. 27. The system of markets in access such as the idea of a Personal-900 service is theoretically grounded in Coases's argument that in a conflict between the preferences of two people the final outcome will be determined by economic calculus regardless of the allocations of rights, see Noam (2001), p. 244.
97 SMS are even used as a new viable means for political advertisings in election campaigns, see Mills (November 4, 2002).
98 See Farrell (2002); an analogy can be found in US legislation against fax spam: to control unsolicited fax transmissions, there is a law that requires sending fax machines to attach their phone numbers for identification, see Blumenthal and Clark (2001), p. 116.
99 See Rohlfs (2002).
100 See ITU (2002b), p. 93.

A legal countermeasure against spam is the **opt-in approach** where consumers specify that they are willing to receive messages. European Members of Parliament voted in favor of a single opt-in policy for unsolicited commercial e-mail and SMS messages across Europe.[101] In opposition to Germany and Italy, France and the UK had implemented an opt-out approach. In an opt-out approach, service providers may send messages unless consumers request them to stop. However, the EU legislation calls for a harmonized opt-in policy. In Hong Kong the six mobile network operators incorporated the prohibition of unsolicited promotional inter-operator SMS in the terms of contract with customers and take action against senders of spam.[102] Yet, these first legal measures do not offer sufficient leverage against mobile spam providers.

One recent measure taken in Japan is the rule to display the full header of mobile mail that also shows the routing information from mail senders. Content providers are obliged to show 'mi-syoudaku-koukoku' (non-agreed advertisement) in the mail header so that users can delete these messages without opening them. DoCoMo additionally changed its system of giving its customer an e-mail address from '(phone number)@DoCoMo.ne.jp' to new addresses containing alphanumeric characters, because they hope to create a barrier to the generation of random 8-digit e-mail addresses. The current most significant technical countermeasure used is **filtering**. Yet, new ways to **circumvent these filters** are continuously being developed as well.[103] Filtering also involves the systematic deletion of messages containing specific words or sender addresses. Thus, questions should arise on who sets the rules for these filters.

Unsolicited mobile messages can turn into one of the **biggest threats to mobile messaging, mobile content,** and all business models that center around it. Spam is already perceived as a form of digital plague for PC-based e-mail. Small displays of portable mobile devices and the danger of perpetuous interruption and nuisance is making spam an even more serious threat for mobile devices. Mobile operators as well as mobile content providers are advised to take this concern seriously as customers with bad spam experiences may turn away from any kind of mobile interaction apart from telephony.

3
Towards an innovation commons approach for mobile media

Innovation commons as defined by LESSIG (2001) support creativity and allow bottom-up innovation to flourish. The commons[104] are a resource to which anyone in a relevant community has a right without obtaining the permission of anybody else. Innovation commons in that view constitute a **space where crea-**

---

101 See McMahon (May 30, 2002).
102 See Ofta (2002).
103 See ITU (2002b), p. 94. An increase in filtering techniques may also lead to an increase in spam messages.
104 The classic 'tragedy of the commons' refers to the fact that a resource can be overused if it is not protected by property rights, see Hardin (1968).

tivity can flourish. Yet, Lessig argues that they are not only formed by norms but also by the technological architecture.[105] For the provision of mobile media, both spectrum policies (E-3.1) and IPRs (E-3.2) are relevant areas in which wireless innovation commons can be established.

Spectrum policies and IPRs can also be identified as essential institutions in the **systems of innovation approach.** Systems of innovation (SI) is a framework for the study of innovations that aims at incorporating all important economic, social, political, organizational, and institutional factors that influence the development, diffusion, and use of innovations.[106] The main elements of systems of innovation are organizations and institutions. **Organizations** - the players or actors - are formal structures that are consciously created and that have an explicit purpose. **Institutions** are a set of common habits, routines, established practices, rules or laws that regulate the relations and interactions between individuals, groups, and organizations.[107] Innovation policy in that view has to focus on the relations between organizations and institutions to ensure that negative lock-in situations are avoided and to proactively support emerging new product and service areas and new sectoral systems of innovation.[108] Spectrum regimes and IPR policies are **essential institutions for mobile media provision.** The way they are designed and the way they relate to the organization of mobile media production, bundling, and distribution will be important for the development of innovative mobile media content and services.

In the SI approach, interactions between different organizations are the basis for the development of innovations; they include market-based transactions as well as non-market-based collaborations. In this sense, systems of innovations also **integrate a user-centered model of innovation** that regards social changes as origins for distributed innovation processes and as sources for innovation.[109] The SI approach can, thus, be used as a framework to discuss the potential of innovation commons for mobile media.

3.1
Spectrum policies for wireless technologies

Mobile media can be delivered in different **spectrum regimes** which compete for dominance in the wireless data communications market. Spectrum policies and regulatory frameworks evaluate arguments on the necessity to license spectrum[110], to trade spectrum, and to compete among different wireless technolo-

---

105 See Lessig (1999); Lessig (2001).
106 See Edquist (2003a); innovations are defined as new creations of economic significance, including both product and process innovation, see Edquist (2003a), p. 2.
107 See Edquist (2003a), p. 2; the origins of these definitions lie in the seminal work of new institutional economists such as North (1990).
108 See Edquist (2003a), p. 6.
109 See Tuomi (2002), p. 10.
110 In general, there are three approaches to authorizing telecommunications operators and services: individual operator licenses, general authorizations (which the British refer to as class licenses), and no licensing requirements, i.e. open entry. The licensing regime determines how much control network operators retain over technological developments, see Intven (2000), p. 2-7.

gy models. For mobile media provision, unlicensed spectrum may provide the highest user-controlled environment (3.11); spectrum sharing models in cellular networks may provide the highest degree of competition (3.12); and digital broadcast networks may provide the most economic mode of mobile media delivery (3.13).

3.1.1
Wireless commons and open spectrum

In the disputed discussion on the development of spectrum regimes proponents of an expansion of unlicensed spectrum in relation to licensed spectrum favor wireless commons and open spectrum approaches. Media companies are in a good position to make use of either spectrum regime although their investment decisions on the degree of mobile media development are likely to be influenced by the outcomes of the political spectrum decision.

The spectrum commons approach is one of **three typological approaches to spectrum policy**: administrative spectrum management, market-based approaches, and commons approaches. In a comparison of these spectrum management regimes, BAUER (2002) identifies two distinguishing criteria: the way these approaches design property (exclusive or non-exclusive rights) as well as the disposition rights over spectrum (allocation, assignment, and dynamic adjustment). While in administrative spectrum management government planning dominates both allocation and dynamic adjustment, market-based approaches rely on transactions. Commons approaches concern **non-exclusive rights** and focus on the user for **dynamic adjustments and sources of innovation**.[111] Commons regimes establish a framework that grants rights to groups of users rather than the individual. This is different in open spectrum approaches that advocate open use by anyone.[112]

The spectrum commons approach regards **bandwidth as a common resource** that all equipment can call on and that is subject to sharing protocols rather than being under the control of government agencies or property owners. Its proponents argue that technology - more precisely smart radio equipment (see B-2.2) - has rendered the old dichotomy between government licensing of frequencies and property rights in frequencies obsolete.[113] Historically, the basic assumption underlying spectrum management is that spectrum is a scarce resource. Therefore, government spectrum allocation in the public interest is the best way to avoid radio interference and pursue public interest goals such as national defense, public safety, and critical infrastructure. However, NOAM (1998) questions why control of spectrum is constitutionally permitted. He regards spectrum as speech and the regulation of spectrum as regulation of free speech. Advocates of the open spectrum or commons approach go even further in their argument that

---

111 See Bauer (2002), p. 3.
112 See Raja and Bar (2003), p. 5.
113 Thus, the choice is between a market in infrastructure rights and a market in equipment, not between a market approach and a non-market approach, see Benkler (2002), p. 41.

the assumptions underlying the **dominant spectrum paradigm of scarcity** no longer hold due to technological advances. They argue that open spectrum would allow for more efficient and creative use of spectrum, enable innovations, reduce prices, foster competition, and bring communications policies closer to democratic ideals.[114] It is suggested that regulatory intervention **focus on the device** in order to create the conditions for entrepreneurial innovation.[115]

Mobile media provision that refers to services in unlicensed spectrum bands currently describes online media accessed wirelessly, e.g. over WiFi networks via (handheld) PCs. As soon as WiFi cards are integrated into mobile phones more options for mobile media and cross-network service delivery choices will emerge. Mobile media in open spectrum environments can pose problems to paid content models for mobile media due to a **lack of quality of service requirements** (see B-2.21). However, an expansion of open spectrum as well as more opportunities to combine services in licensed and unlicensed frequency bands that exploit the core competencies of the licensed and unlicensed regime will certainly serve media companies' interests; it will give them the opportunity to create product and price differentiated offers.

Using mobile media over unlicensed frequency bands may be a means to reduce prices for content transmission and **give users more freedom to share content**. It can also be an incentive to use mobile media, because it provides users with more options, e.g. to deliberately choose licensed spectrum for secure transactions or quality of service transmissions.

Wireless commons are also perceived to promote **bottom-up innovation processes**. Under LESSIG's (2001) argument that the principle of innovation in the Internet is the openness and simplicity of the network, open wireless systems have even better characteristics for innovation. The flexibility of open spectrum that supports the mobility of resources for existing and novel purposes also supports recombinatorial innovations that emerge when social practices are recombined (see A-2.12).[116] Open wireless systems contribute to foster innovation and social welfare, because **consumers with rapidly evolving preferences can dynamically utilize wireless networks**.[117] For example, ad-hoc, self-organizing mesh networks use automated processes to dynamically use mobile devices and to enhance the efficiency of spectrum use as the number of devices increases (see B-1.1).[118] Each node can serve other users simultaneously as infrastructure; the network of devices can cooperatively distribute the available bandwidth. A number of security concerns are connected to the fact that mobile

---

114 See Benkler (1998); Werbach (2002); Raja and Bar (2003); there are three primary techniques for magnifying the efficiency of wireless devices: spread spectrum systems, cooperative networking, and software-defined radio.
115 See Rheingold (2002), p. 152. User-driven innovation is suggested to be a perceived benefit of the end-to-end network design; flexibility at the lowest levels of the system permits applications that cannot be anticipated. Sandvig criticizes the use of technical arguments as a proxy for normative arguments and suggests to define the legitimate public policy role for government as regulating transparency and participation, see Sandvig (2002), p. 24.
116 See Tuomi (2002), p. 31.
117 See Benkler (2002), p. 45.
118 See Werbach (2000); Rheingold (2002), p. 149; Werbach (2002).

phones become routers in ad hoc networks. On the other hand, users can find new ways of using high bandwidth with mobile devices in combination with mobile content and services.[119]

As a policy recommendation for the evolution of spectrum regimes, BENKLER (2002) as well as LESSIG (2001) favor a combined property and commons approach even though they suggest that open wireless networks will be more efficient, because it is not yet clear which approach is more socially valuable.[120] NOAM (1998) advocates for the combination of open access to spectrum with the utilization of market forces, i.e. the introduction of market-based fees to reflect the opportunity cost of spectrum. This model proposes the establishment of a **futures and derivates market in spectrum.** However, no workable mechanism so far can master the collection of spectrum fees.[121] Mobile content provision can only benefit from the advocacy of wireless commons. For example, media companies can consider developing services for an integrated 3G/WiFi network approach (see B-2.3) that supports higher speed wireless access and may encourage the development of mobile broadband content.

From the user perspective, familiarity with wireless access also increases with greater unlicensed spectrum service opportunities and may **stimulate cross-network services as well as mobile media use.** As a result, media companies can benefit from the expansion of transmission networks for mobile media and should have an interest in supporting open spectrum initiatives.

3.1.2
MVNO models for spectrum sharing and trading

Media companies can also benefit from new **spectrum trading models.** MVNOs will increase competition for attractive media content, but moreover, media companies with strong brands can consider becoming MVNOs themselves.

MVNOs are mobile value added service providers that buy access to a mobile network on a wholesale basis and offer resale services similar to full network operators.[122] New agents in the MVNO market can pursue various business models that cover different elements in the mobile communications value chain. In a **pure MVNO model,** the MVNO is an operator which provides mobile services to

---

119 However, non-exclusive rights regimes such as open spectrum do not allow a user to protect an innovation through exclusive control, see Bauer (2002), p. 11; thus, commons models may be more appropriate in situations with lower innovation costs and risks, see Bauer (2002) p. 12.

120 See Lessig (2001), p. 230. In his analysis, Benkler draws on the problem of social cost as introduced by Ronald Coase. Benkler's evaluation of the social cost of communication in either system includes the equipment cost that enable the communication, the displacement effect on other communications, and the overhead in terms of transaction and administrative cost, see Benkler (2002), pp. 23.

121 See Noam (1998); he suggests a token system for using scarce spectrum. These tokens fluctuate in price as the demand for spectrum changes. Noam was the first to point out that even if one doubts that radio technology eliminates scarcity spectrum property rights are obsolete and should give way to a dynamic real time market in spectrum clearance rights. According to Benkler, economists' responses to this approach range from mocking disbelief of economists such as Hazlett (1998) to the serious evaluation of tradeoffs between property in spectrum and open wireless networks, e.g. Faulhaber and Farber (2002), see Benkler (2002), p. 5.

end users in a similar way to MNOs but without having frequency bands assigned; the **enhanced service provider model** focuses mainly on marketing, customer care, and billing, but also allows some control over some network elements; in the **service provider model,** the MVNO has no control of network elements. Branding and customer services are the most important elements for differentiation from competitors.[123] Internationally, there are considerable disparities in policies governing MVNOs with regard to allowing or prohibiting this practice and in terms of regulatory intervention.[124]

MVNO models are feasible, because spectrum policy that has typically parceled spectrum in space is now turning to facilitate access to spectrum in the time dimension.[125] From a technological perspective, software-defined radio allows licensees to dynamically rent certain spectrum bands when they are not in use by other licensees. From an economic perspective, **secondary markets** provide a mechanism for licensees to create and provide opportunities for new revenue streams and services in distinct slices of time.[126] The development of secondary markets is one approach to increase the **efficiency of spectrum use.** In this model, licensees are able to trade unused spectrum capacity either by leasing it on a long-term basis or by selling spare capacity during off-peak periods. This allows for the development of new services and introduces economic incentives to develop efficient technologies that increase the secondary market's flexibility.[127]

In general, the MVNO model is open to companies from many industries, including banking, retail, and the media. Media companies have been very cautious to enter the mobile communications market. High investment even without license costs, network build-out and clearinghouse costs and a lack of core competency in providing telecommunications services make an MVNO model a high-risk media expansion. Bertelsmann, MTV, and Disney have considered MVNO models (see D-4.12). They are encouraged by the successful exploitation of the Virgin Mobile brand, which has prompted media companies to enter **mobile prepaid markets.** A number of internal and external factors that influence

---

122 See for example Ulset (2002). In the German mobile market, new types of market players in emerging MVNO markets have a conceptual but no legal definition, yet. German telecom law only distinguishes 'operators of telecom networks' and 'provider of publicly available telecoms services'. MVNOs who own fixed network infrastructure and only use the mobile component of a mobile carrier cannot be classified as service providers from a regulator's perspective. Yet, MVNOs cannot be classified as network operators, either. Other issues concern roaming agreements: according to German law before the implementation of the EU new regulatory framework, only the licensed mobile operators can sign roaming agreements, MVNO's who do not have a mobile network cannot, see Kurth (2001).
123 See McKnight, Linsenmayer, and Lehr (2002), p. 9; Pérez Saiz, De Sande Caldera, and Castejón Martín (2002); OFTEL has established a layered competition model for the mobile service market that underlies the distinction above. A higher layer implies greater freedom of network control.
124 See ITU (2002b), p. 80; in Ireland and Hong Kong, for instance, MVNO offerings are a mandatory condition for 3G operators.
125 See Powell (2002).
126 The new EU regulatory framework explicitly provides possibilities of spectrum trading in Article 9 of the Framework Directive, see Stumpf and Nett (2003), p. 3.
127 See McKnight, Linsenmayer, and Lehr (2002), p. 6. For a model of real-time secondary spectrum markets where the license holder runs an admission control algorithm based on QoS requirements see Peha and Panichpapiboon (2003).

External factors

		Opportunities	Risks
I n t e r n a l	**Strengths**	• Media brand • Customer relationships in audience markets • Relationship with young customer segments (heavy mobile users)	• Retail outlet relationships • Peak-load traffic and network management challenges • Similar target groups compared to MNO
f a c t o r s	**Weaknesses**	• Billing relationships and direct marketing activities • Network management, billing, customer care	• Subscriber acquisition and monthly subscriber cost, bad debt • Risk allocation for network build-out, spectrum reclaim

Figure E-2: Analysis of external and internal factors for MVNO decisions of media companies

media companies' decisions for or against an MVNO strategy are illustrated in Figure E-2.

When media companies estimate the investment cost for an MVNO entry strategy, **performance metrics** that they must include comprise subscriber acquisition cost, churn rates, monthly cost per subscriber per month and bad debt on the costs side as well as monthly ARPU on the revenue side. Due to their inherent opportunities for cross-media extensions of their content they are in an interesting position to drive ARPU with their mobile media services. Yet, potential open access obligations to allow other content providers onto their platforms and into their portals apply to media companies as well. As a result, media companies that seek, for example, a branded and integrated approach for youth-oriented media content which allows for bundled cross-media offers for advertising clients, may become, in analogy to Vizzavi (see E-1.12), subject to competition concerns about **leveraging market power in neighboring markets.**

Spectrum license holders on the other hand need to calculate the trade-off between increasing revenues by driving MVNO traffic into their networks and loosing revenue through MVNOs with strong brand names that may cannibalize customers from the license holder. In order to assess the financial MVNO viability for both the network operator and the MVNO it is crucial to consider the **sim-**

ilarity or disparity of the targeted customer segments as well as the spectrum requirements of the MVNO.

Regulatory intervention may be needed when MNOs do not (temporarily) have excedentary capacity for providing MVNO access services and would have to invest in their access network.[128] Risk allocation is another specification difficulty in MVNO models. It increases with the cost for network building and with revenue risk due to uncertainty about consumer acceptance of mobile content and services as well as profit margins. It increases the difficulty of a regulatory design of secondary spectrum markets that should seek a **fair allocation of risks** in a manner optimizing incentives for both the license holder and the franchisee. Other risks that may require regulatory intervention relate to the entry and exit rights of buyers and sellers to secondary spectrum markets, risks of investment when spectrum may be reclaimed, standardization of spectrum trading contracts, and responsibility requirements for content on licensed frequency bands.[129]

Media companies have to decide if they are willing to take a share in these risks and to **invest specifically in licensed cellular mobile services.** They have the freedom to choose between this option and an increase of activities in unlicensed frequency band content models. Since commons models and licensed spectrum models can co-exist they do not face an either-or question but rather decisions on the scale and scope of activity.

LEHR & MCKNIGHT (2002) suggest that continued progress towards secondary spectrum markets can benefit both 3G and WiFi models. For 3G, secondary markets allow more flexible management of property rights.[130] For WiFi, congestion issues may be addressed. They argue, however, that secondary spectrum market mechanisms for WiFi could operate better in a licensed band with clear property rights, a potential future spectrum policy that is likely to raise a controversial debate.[131] Secondary markets as well as license flexibility may also be useful in **integrated cross-network approaches** that link different wireless technologies, for example for integrated services that use 3G for control channel and WiFi for high speed file transfer when available.[132] Although cross-network service offers are an emerging market for media companies (see D-3), it is questionable whether media companies have to take the risk of being MVNOs in order to use the opportunities of mobile media cross-network services. Their

---

128 See Pérez Saiz, De Sande Caldera, and Castejón Martín (2002), p. 19.
129 See McKnight, Linsenmayer, and Lehr (2002), p. 8; Stumpf and Nett (2003). A critical regulatory question regarding the introduction of MVNO models is if it is appropriate to force operators that purchased 3G licenses to disaggregate their network in favor of other entrant operators. Therefore, the evaluation of associated investment risk when access to the MNO network is obliged is particularly challenging, see Pérez Saiz, De Sande Caldera, and Castejón Martín (2002), p. 13.
130 Valletti suggests a model of coverage differentiation, analogous to price differentiation, for efficient spectrum use. He develops a model of competitive interaction between mobile operators that vary coverage and the size of their networks according to heterogeneous customer demand, see Valletti (1999).
131 See Lehr and McKnight (2002), p. 19.
132 See McKnight, Linsenmayer, and Lehr (2002), p. 7.

range of options between MVNO, portal provider, or syndicator allows them a differentiated risk-reward assessment.[133]

3.1.3
Mobile broadcast media versus mobile cellular media

Digital terrestrial broadcast is emerging as a third option for the delivery of mobile media. It may pose significant threats to mobile operators' expected data revenues and may, therefore, lead to **policy battles between telecommunication regulatory authorities and media regulatory authorities**. Despite the promise of next generation mobile cellular networks for the delivery of mobile broadband content, DVB-T is a more efficient and more economic solution for mobile content distribution (see B-2.3) and, thus, may cannibalize perceived revenue sources of mobile operators.[134] Ideas to integrate DVB-T-antennas into mobile phones are hence taken up with resistance or at least skepticism from mobile operators. In Germany, public commercial broadcasters, on the other hand, are actively pushing mobile and hybrid broadcasting models.[135] For media companies in general, these transmission alternatives can enable more differentiated pricing models and will as such serve **heterogeneous customer demand**.

The combination of digital terrestrial broadcasting and next generation mobile cellular services allow for two alternative modes of content services: (1) broadcast services with an interactive component and (2) telecommunications services with a broadcast component. In either case, this development allows broadcasters to leverage their content across a range of delivery networks. However, **sector-specific horizontal regulation** may influence the possibilities these options will provide. In Germany, public commercial broadcasters are not allowed to provide on-demand interactive broadcasting services that use mobile cellular networks for the initiation of mobile media provision and DVB-T networks for content distribution. Telecommunications services with a broadcast component may also need regulatory support for interconnection requirements and agreements.

Differences in regulatory objectives for mobile media in cellular and broadcast networks can also result in regulatory conflicts. One example is the principle of **technology neutrality** that the EU has introduced in the new telecommunication framework in order to support widely accepted regulatory objectives of telecommunications such as fostering competitive markets to promote the efficient supply of telecommunication services, good quality of service, advanced services, and efficient prices.[136] This principle requires that services are regu-

---

133 See Feldmann (2002b).
134 Digital broadcast can also pose a competitive threat to fixed-line broadband ISPs. In the US, Disney is planning a wireless video-on-demand service, MovieBeam, that takes advantages of datacasting via digital broadcasting infrastructure as a cheap alternative to broadband Internet delivery, see Olsen and Hansen (April 7, 2003).
135 Private commercial TV broadcasters are still holding back with their investments in DVB-T; mobile operators are joining pilot projects on hybrid models although their objectives for being part of them could also derive from trying to hamper the process.

lated in a comparable manner, irrespective of their means of delivery. The European Broadcasting Union (EBU), however, opposes the idea of technology neutral regulation and remarks, for instance, that the **introduction of secondary markets for radio spectrum is not appropriate for the broadcasting sector** since it does not take into account such general interest objectives such as pluralism, cultural diversity and public service,[137] nor does it recognize the specific character of the audiovisual media.[138]

The integration of non-TV services into the DVB-T service bundle poses further regulatory challenges. Many proponents of DVB-T suggest the integration of non-TV services into the DVB-T service bundle. Non-TV services comprise program-related and program-unrelated services as well as radio broadcast; under German law, all of these options can be differentiated into media services and tele-services. This differentiation is essential in order to determine which law is applicable. Whereas the delivery of an electronic newspaper via DVB-T is classified as a media service, the delivery of a video clip is classified as a tele-service. However, neither media nor tele-services are 'broadcast' which opens a **regulatory vacuum for the allocation of spectrum for these services.**[139] GAIDA (2001) criticizes the fact that the media authorities in Germany erect market entry barriers for new DVB-T media and tele-service providers due to these lacks in spectrum policy. It may become an obstacle to the market acceptance of DVB-T that could use these services as a means for differentiation from cable TV and satellite networks. The implementation of hybrid DVB-T-GPRS (UMTS)-multimedia services, therefore, remains a challenge. For media companies this implies that digital terrestrial broadcasting may develop into an option in the long run, but that their **short-term efforts for mobile media content and service provision** better focus on mobile cellular and nomadic wireless networks.

In sum, the discussion demonstrates that **spectrum management regimes** can affect industry development. Spectrum policy decisions on the interplay of next generation cellular networks, wireless LAN, and digital broadcast networks **influence the investment that media companies have to undertake** for the provision of mobile media services (entry costs), the number of players and their bargaining power in mobile media markets (market structure), and the generation and sharing of profits among players in the mobile value net (appropriability of profits).

---

136 Other regulatory objectives of telecommunications include promoting increased telecommunication connectivity for all users through efficient interconnection arrangements; protecting consumer rights including privacy rights; and optimizing the use of scarce resources such as radio spectrum, numbers and rights of way, see Intven (2000), p. 1-2.
137 The core objectives for content-based services are plurality of voice; impartiality; diversity of content; high quality of content; and taste and decency, see Zerdick et al. (2000), p. 257.
138 See EBU (2000).
139 See Gaida (2001), pp. 182.

3.2
Mobile intellectual property rights

Repurposing existing content and developing new mobile content for new mobile distribution platforms has the potential to become a profitable value proposition for media companies (see A, D). Yet, the challenges associated with **access, usage, and redistribution rights of digital content** apply in mobile environments as they do for the Internet. Media companies are using their intellectual property rights in part to issue exclusive license agreements. They are also pushing mobile operators to develop and implement mobile DRM systems. Both developments may harm potential mobile innovation commons and may also not evolve into the value maximizing strategy for media companies.

Mobile intellectual property rights are one of the key issues for the development of mobile media. SHAPIRO (1999) calls intellectual property the sword and shield of the information economy.[140] They are among the heatedly discussed issues that become **increasingly relevant for media economics**. MCQUAIL (2001) describes IPRs and DRM as part of the **widened scope of media policy concerns** due to the arrival of new media.[141] Concerns about rights management have become predominantly attached to the issue of copyright violation. A common view in media industries is that existing protection of digital intellectual property is either insufficient or that stronger measures are needed to ensure penalties for infringement. However, reinforcing and extending historical decisions on conflicting interests in the enforcement of intellectual property rights without reopening a discussion of the social trade-offs of such changes is - in the view of MANSELL & STEINMUELLER (2002) - inappropriate.[142] In the case of mobile media, the social appropriation of mobile communication and changes in media and communication consumption patterns (see C) require such a re-evaluation of social trade-offs with regard to IPRs (E-3.21) and DRM (E-3.22).

3.2.1
Intellectual property rights for mobile media

IPRs comprise copyrights, trade secrets, as well as trademarks and patent protection and exploitation.[143] They can be viewed from two perspectives with respect to mobile data communications:
- from the infrastructure perspective that analyzes the role of essential IPRs and
- from the content perspective that analyzes the role of exclusive IPRs.

---

140 See Shapiro (1999), p. 3.
141 See McQuail (2001), p. 224.
142 See Mansell and Steinmueller (2002), pp. 289.
143 For an introduction to the theories of intellectual property see Fisher (2002); on the philosophical background of IPR see Stengel (2004); Siegrist (2004) depicts the historical evolution in power shifts between creator, publisher, and user; Towse analyzes incentives for artists in digital media compensation patterns, see Towse (2002).

Essential IPRs in the process of standardization in the telecommunications industry are defined as protected knowledge that is indispensable for a product that has to comply with a certain standard.[144] BEKKERS, VERSPAGEN & SMITS (2002) investigate the **role of IPRs in the GSM standardization process**; they argue that essential GSM IPRs have changed the standardization process in the telecommunications industry, because firms started to recognize the strategic importance of IPRs. At the level of the public interest, however, the intensification of patenting activities in hopes of obtaining essential IPRs for future standards is not necessarily a positive development. Their resulting policy recommendations are targeted at (1) a clearer operationalization of the concept of a 'suitable and fair reward' for holders of IPRs that are relevant to a standard such as public license agreements and conditions or a limit on the cumulative license fees for essential patents and (2) a further push within the European Commission towards a technology-neutral policy that will require IPR-holders to be more modest, because alternative standards could be embraced.[145] Standardization processes for cellular networks are a **precondition for mobile media development**. When they are slowed down due to patent issues, uncertainty about the development of mobile data standards also affect downstream innovation, for instance mobile media content.

In the mobile communications industry **patent thickets** are another evolving competition policy issue concerning intellectual property rights. A patent thicket is an overlapping set of patent rights; it requires firms seeking to commercialize a new technology to obtain licenses from multiple patentees.[146] **Cross-licenses and patent pools** are methods that are used to deal with the patent thickets. SHAPIRO (2001) demonstrates that package licensing can be desirable for complementary patents, particularly in the telecommunications industry, which is characterized by formal standard-setting for the launch of new technologies (see A-1.4).[147] Yet, innovators can also be forced to **share rents under cross-licenses** which reduce incentives for innovation and fast market entry.[148]

Patent pool issues also apply to **mobile application-enabling software compression technologies and mobile streaming services**. The MPEG video compression technology provides an example of a recent IPR issue that relates directly to the provision of mobile media. MPEG LA is the licensing agent who manages the MPEG patent pool. **Patent licensing issues for mobile video delivery services** arose in June 2003 when MPEG LA announced the collection of royalties not only from equipment manufacturers but also from content providers at the rate of two cents per hour of MPEG-4 encoded streamed content.[149]

144 See Bekkers, Verspagen, and Smits (2002), p. 173.
145 See Bekkers, Verspagen, and Smits (2002), pp. 186.
146 See Shapiro (2001); Fosfuri (2003).
147 This is particularly relevant in the case of hold-up risks, the danger that new products will inadvertently infringe on patents issued after the product launch. Thus, when cross-licensing is desirable Shapiro argues that antitrust law and its suspicion of cooperative activities between direct competitors can have the perverse effect of slowing down innovation, see Shapiro (2001), p. 4.
148 See Bessen (2003).
149 See Honma (June 2, 2003).

MPEG-4 Visual is currently employed for DoCoMo's 'i-motion' service and KD-DI's 'Ezmovie' service to compress video content. These companies as well as content industry groups such as the Mobile Content Forum (MCF) or the Association of Media in Digital (AMD) oppose MPEG's licensing policy and warn that the **additional royalty burden** threatens the emerging mobile content provider business. Another implication from MPEGs licensing policy may be that content providers turn to the alternative standard H.264 or to a Microsoft video codec that requires fees for decoders and encoders but no usage fees.

In the competitive market for **mobile streaming audio and video players**, the big three Internet players, RealNetworks Real Media Player, Microsoft's Windows Media Player, and Apple's Quicktime Player are competing to deploy their software in the wireless market. RealNetworks, for example, is licensing its mobile RealPlayer for the streaming of music and videos on handsets to major wireless operators such as Vodafone.[150] However, they have been accused of **excessive pricing** for its software. Market leverage through agreements with the leading carriers may force mobile content providers to license RealNetwork's software in order to distribute their mobile content. RealNetworks has received a lot of support from the mobile communications industry regardless of the conditions of their licensing agreements; handset manufacturers, among others, support Real in order to combat Microsoft's efforts to achieve control over mobile computing markets.[151] Mobile operators' **exclusive contracts with software providers** tend to create another bottleneck and investment obligations for media content providers and potentially users who have to comply with the software decisions of mobile operators.

From the point of view of mobile content providers, **exclusive IPRs** in the realm of copyright are an essential issue. The history of copyright policy has not been subject to the application of consistent policies across functionally similar areas.[152] Each new technology offers a **new battlefield for copyright licensing and royalty regimes** and so does mobile media.

"The contours of the license requirements and the rate of royalty are generally determined by the political jockeying rather than by specific application of general principles." [153]

The objectives that may be served by strengthening and extending property rights protection include: (1) promoting invention and authorship of new work; (2) safeguarding the rights of creators from others copying; (3) encouraging the dissemination of ideas; and (4) protecting the rights of authors to be recognized

---

150 The global partnership will serve 119.7 million cellular subscribers in 36 countries, see Goltzsch (June 30, 2003); Markoff (June 30, 2003). Also the Ericsson Content Delivery Solution is based on RealNetworks Helix Media delivery technology that allows streaming and controlling media in every 3GPP-compliant format, including MPEG-4, see N.N. (February 20, 2003). Apple Computer Inc. develops wireless multimedia content delivery via QuickTime, also based on an MPEG-4 solution, see Apple (February 12, 2002).
151 See Markoff (June 30, 2003); Longino (July 17, 2003).
152 See Benkler (2005); Siegrist (2004), pp. 314.
153 Benkler (2005), p. 266.

and to receive income from their work.[154] Yet, limitations on the use and copying for social purposes raises difficult questions about the **trade-off between private and public interests** and incentives for innovation. NOAM (2005) argues that selectivity over content would be particularly troubling as the wireless medium becomes a mass medium.[155] The exclusivity of intellectual property rights may create the basis for the accumulation of market power and reduce consumer choice and plurality of voices.

Many large publishing and media companies have achieved a significant incumbent position through a long history of building market reputation and controlling intellectual property rights to their stock of titles. The partial loss of control over their key assets on the Internet has led to strong reactions to securing digital rights. For mobile platforms, media companies want to **retain control over their content** from the very beginning. Therefore, they are building mobile DRM systems in order to protect their assets.

3.2.2
Digital rights management for mobile media

DRM systems are often a prerequisite for media companies to make their content accessible on mobile platforms. **Forward lock policies** are already in place for ring-tone downloads. More rigid DRM systems for mobile media are either developed by mobile operators, handset manufacturers, or the media companies themselves. The restrictions in use and potential user manipulation, however, are inhibiting innovative uses as well as the integration of social networks into mobile media strategies. Mobile media as part of an **integrated cross-media strategy** may provide incentives to open mobile media DRM systems.

Mobile content providers distinguish two sets of DRM technologies: DRM systems for the encryption of their digital content and DRM distribution platforms that manage the overall process related to the distribution of both access and the associated rights. When mobile carriers choose a specific DRM platform this can have far-reaching consequences for mobile content business models, because mobile media creators have to specifically produce in that format. It can become a **barrier to mobile media creation** when different mobile operators choose different DRM systems. If carriers want to encourage choice in media offers they may have to be ready to initially support multiple content formats and DRM technologies.[156]

DRM administrates the operation of a control system that can **monitor, regulate, and price each subsequent use of a digital file** that contains media content such as video, audio, photos, or print.[157] DRM systems encompass the compo-

---

154   See Mansell and Steinmueller (2002), p. 294.
155   See Noam (2005).
156   See Buhse (2002), p. 173; Bechtold (2004).
157   The trend of technology regulating digital copying and redistribution of content began in the US with the Audio Home Recording Act (AHRA) of 1992, both AHRA and DMCA have no exemption for fair use, see Greenstein (2001), p. 379.

nents of access, usage, and redistribution control by using underlying technologies, for example encryption, watermarking, or metadata identification. The main rights in a DRM model are render rights (e.g. print, view, or play); transport rights (e.g. copy, move, or loan) and derivative work rights (e.g. extract, edit, or embed).[158]

Whereas forward lock policies in mobile DRM systems follow a delivery control principle, alternative control mechanisms focus on usage control. **Superdistribution** is a mobile DRM architecture that **distributes mobile content and mobile right vouchers separately.** The fundamental idea is to allow free distribution of mobile content while controlling access to usage. New business opportunities emerge from this model, because users can forward mobile content within their social networks. The object metadata includes the information on purchasing the rights; upon receiving a mobile content object other users can purchase the related right voucher with one click.[159] With this usage control concept, mobile users can recommend and share files across wireless and fixed networks, using e-mail or mobile messaging.

Despite the promises of DRM to enable a secure electronic marketplace for mobile media and to provide media companies with adequate renumeration for mobile content creation DRM systems can lead to an over-protection that not only restricts the interests of users and the society at large but that could also lead to a new "privatized property right"[160] that undermines copyright limitations. This new **conglomerate of protection** from technology, contracts, anti-circumvention regulations, and technology licenses has potential to supplant copyright law.[161] In the case of (mobile) DRM, the technological development should acknowledge the most noticeable limitations to copyright protection, the concept of fair use as well as the circumvention of technological protection measures.

Yet, the persisting drift of institutional change towards a stronger IPR protection system is altering the balance between private rights and the public domain.[162] The **doctrine of fair use** is a central element in the discussion over the role of DRM technologies. The debate mirrors the fundamental disagreement over the definition of fair use and the question of whether or not consumer copying is fair. LESSIG (2001) demands that law that protects software engineered to protect copyright has to acknowledge fair use as well; otherwise in this argument, the **law is the instrument through which a technological revolution is undone.**[163] Also BECHTOLD (2002) argues that DRM technologies must be sure not to erase the **important range of access and use rights traditionally protected under copyright law.** KU (2003) suggests the recognition of fair use as creative destruction rather than market failure. The Schumpeterian notion of creative de-

---

158 See Fetscherin (2002), p. 166;
159 See Nokia (2001); Buhse (2002).
160 Bechtold (2002), p. 10; Bechtold (2004), p. 340.
161 See Tuomi (2002), p. 220. He suggests that there will be increasing demand for processes that integrate technology development with policy.
162 See David (2003).
163 See Lessig (2001), pp. 188; 265.

struction depicts a process that incessantly revolutionizes the economic structure by incessantly destroying the old one and creating a new one; thereby it effects the foundations of firm outputs and profits.[164] Ku argues that the combination of digital technology and Internet networking have creatively destroyed copyright. As a result, consumer copying must be built into DRM technologies. When legal restrictions are understood as the creation of new rights for copyright owners and the destruction of rights previously enjoyed by the public they are not justified by copyright.[165] For mobile media, the discussion over fair use **extends the borders of the mobile device**.[166] Fair use for digital media such as consumer copying has to be tackled across devices and across fixed-line and wireless networks. Therefore, arguments on the design of DRM systems have to encompass all digital platforms for digital content, including mobile platforms.

With the proliferation of mobile devices' computing capabilities, also the **circumvention of technological protection measures** used by copyright owners to control access to their works becomes a relevant issue. The anti-circumvention provisions, e.g. of the DMCA, are seen as a battle between Hollywood and Silicon Valley. Hollywood is seeking the strongest possible ban on the act of circumventing a technical protection system while Silicon Valley is restricted in their ability to engage in **lawful reverse engineering**.[167] SAMUELSEN (2003) criticizes that the prohibition of reverse engineering through the DMCA of 1998 both undermines the preservation of fair use and harms competition and innovation in the information technology sector. The DMCA's provisions are significantly broader than the WIPO treaty requires and they violate the goal of imposing predictable, minimalist, consistent, and simple regulations on the digital economy.[168] With the **shift of control from users towards copyright owners**, e.g. via the DMCAs limitations on fair use or the anti-circumvention rules, the creative use of content is severely limited. It also undermines arguments by wireless spectrum commons proponents on regulation at the device level and the creation of a user-controlled environment, because they impair the creative use of mobile content and services.

Of course, there are cases in which mobile content will not be subject to copyright protection. **Mobile user-generated content** is not (yet) copyrighted work. There are also examples from professionally produced content that provide users with control over use and distribution. No direct copyright protection will apply to mobile content when providers have an explicit interest in distributing and sharing information without direct payments, e.g. when they expect to increase their future revenues. Advertising purposes, limited functionality trial versions as a purchasing incentive, or post sale support are among the innovative uses of mobile ICT infrastructure that require only a **selective application of copyright enforcement**.[169]

---

164 See Schumpeter (1975), pp. 82.
165 See Ku (2003).
166 See Hampe and Schwabe (2002a).
167 See Samuelson (2003), p. 2.
168 See Samuelson (2003).

For copyright protected mobile media an interesting short-term issue is who will be responsible in the future for the negotiation of mobile licenses and contracts. Currently, carriers, content aggregators, or mobile marketing companies that want to integrate any form of mobile content have to negotiate licenses directly with the copyright owners.[170] This may change as mobile licenses will become an integral part of other forms of licensing agreements or as independent royalty collecting entities for mobile content emerge.

The open question remains about how to design policies for mobile media in a way that frees innovation, promotes competition and allows people to adopt, appropriate, transform and reshape new media.[171] In the fight against power and income losses through the sharing of digital media, media companies have strongly voted for the protection of copyrighted content in digital environments through DRM systems. In mobile communication environments, however, opportunities arise when users contextualize and share content within their social networks and innovate around mobile content; overall, it can result in **beneficial outcomes for media companies,** e.g., when paid content models and revenue generation are considered across different digital distribution platforms. The strategic consequences for media companies from mobile DRM systems that allow flexible uses can be twofold: **fostering upstream innovation** by building strong media brands to create customer lock-in and support customer willingness to pay for cross-network services; and **fostering downstream innovation** by open access to and free use of mobile media content and services.

---

169 See Mansell and Steinmueller (2002), p. 304.
170 See Buhse (2002), p. 178.
171 See Rheingold (2002), p. 202.

Conclusion

The book 'Leveraging mobile media. Cross-media strategy and innovation policy for mobile media communication' analyzes the influence of mobile communications as an emerging distribution channel for the provision of media content and services on the media industry. It takes two different viewpoints on potential levers for the developments of the media industry and mobile media:
from a corporate strategy point of view it assesses the potentials for an **extension
of cross-media strategies**; from a public policy point of view the book investigates **demands and requirements for an innovation policy** that fosters innovation in mobile media markets and comprises three central elements: competition policy, consumer protection and privacy, and intellectual property rights.

The discussion about the extension of cross-media strategies is based on the
analysis of the **social use of mobile communications**. It acknowledges the technological opportunities and constraints of mobile personal devices and next
generation wireless networks. Within this framework, it develops a demand-oriented federated approach towards the integration of mobile media with existing
cross-media strategies by asking how to translate the social use of mobile communications into competitive strategy for media companies.

A **user-driven innovation paradigm** underlies the discussion of the design of
innovation policies for mobile media. It asks how to foster user-driven innovation and aims at identifying potential bottlenecks and leverages for mobile media development.

1
Summary of the major findings

Mobile media markets offer a number of **incentives for media companies** to enter or expand their engagement within them. Paid content revenues, which are
obtained straight from the user offer interesting revenue potential for mobile
media as do licensing revenues in the context of multiple content utilization
strategies. Licensees can be mobile operators, handset manufacturers, or emerging mobile content players. Yet, the uncertainty over customer demand remains
high. In order to overcome **barriers of uncertainty**, a user-oriented approach to
innovation development that is based on the social use of media and ICTs and
user innovation networks as an emerging innovation paradigm in network-ori-
ented societies is suggested.

The **constraints of mobile devices** and the numerous technological, economic, and political challenges of the migration to next generation networks do not suggest a near-term provision of mass media content delivered to mobile handsets. However, the new characteristics of the mobile communications system such as connectivity, location flexibility, and the hybridization of the public and the personal sphere offer a number of **emerging usage contexts and usage reasons**. Contrary to many expectations, the stationary use of mobile communications is a strong reason for usage due to the direct connection to a person, not to a location. But also mobile and captive user situations lend themselves to the use of mobile media.

The social use of mobile communications, predominantly among young people, is closely connected with the **construction of a mobile identity in social networks**. The self-identity construct of GIDDENS (1991) is used to analyze the creation of self-narratives with the support of SMS and MMS messaging services and potentially with more advanced mobile media offers. But also the **impulsive access to trusted media brands** offers new opportunities for media companies. However, an insurance model of mobile media delivery that only disrupts mobile users in cases of breaking news or emergencies may be an alternative to consider in opposition to attempts to build new habituation patterns for mobile media, e.g. via the daily SMS or MMS media content delivery.

Cross-media strategies, classified into mobile marketing support, market development, and market diversification of cross-media strategies, can extend their scope with new mobile content and services. Four **new mobile media categories** are developed: interpersonal communication, interactive play, information search, and collective participatory mobile media. These mobile media categories can become integrated into existing cross-media strategies via the creation of meta-narratives. The main functions of mobile media in an integrated approach relate to either **micro-coordination**, using the mobile phone as a remote control device, or relationship management within social networks. Social networks can serve as **complementors in media companies' mobile media value net**. In this scenario, mobile users evolve into distributors of mobile media offers when it fits their lifestyle choice and when it supports their self-narrative creation in their social networks. Further, cross-media strategies can develop into **cross-network strategies** when media companies begin to deliver one service across a variety of (wireless) networks including cellular, wireless LAN, and digital broadcast networks. Network choice can be based on consumer preferences and can be executed via a personal router.

The profitability of mobile media offers is a challenging issue for media companies since many players in the mobile media value net contribute to the value creation process and, therefore, want to be compensated. In the **negotiations for revenue sharing models** between mobile operators and media companies, however, there may be a shift in bargaining power towards media companies due to their competencies in attracting mass audiences with their strong media brands; moreover handset manufacturers who are fiercely competing for differentiation increase the demand for mobile media. Mobile operators face increasing competition for mobile data revenues from MVNOs in cellular networks, through WLAN providers and due to DVB-H developments. Media companies, on the other hand, can exploit their brand strengths to attract mass audiences and signal credibility and orientation.

Innovation policy for mobile media that intends to strengthen **bottom-up innovation approaches and user-driven innovations** fosters user choice and is intended to build user experimentation with mobile media. This policy approach will require **open access policies** to mobile platforms, portals, and content, for example with regard to open access to handsets without new SIM lock policies; free choice of the mobile portal; and opportunities to forward, contextualize or manipulate mobile content. Pricing of mobile data in retail markets is an essential precondition for the extent of user experimentation. In that context it is helpful that interconnection charges in wholesale markets, e.g. in the mobile termination and international roaming markets, may become subject to regulatory intervention. Regulation of 2G termination rates may potentially foster 3G mobile data innovation. Media companies should be interested in low interconnection charges since it increases their potential profit margins.

The design of new spectrum regimes, such as an increase in frequencies dedicated to unlicensed spectrum that allows user-controlled environments as well as more flexible use of licensed spectrum via secondary spectrum markets, provides more choice for media companies to decide on the vertical integration of their mobile media engagements. Yet, in the **design of potential mobile media innovation commons**, intellectual property rights become the most essential lever for media companies. Patenting and licensing policies in the upstream mobile media value chain and DRM policies in the downstream mobile media value chain are key to further mobile media development. Flexible use of mobile media may become beneficial for media companies when they consider customer profitability across different media. Media companies will face new opportunities for cross-media audience flows and cross-media revenue flows when they take advantage of network externalities from their customers' social networks and allow for multi-device use and sharing of media content by **loosening mobile SIM lock measures and mobile DRM requirements**. Also if mobile communications' main function within an integrated cross-media approach refers to micro-coordination, an open and flexible approach to mobile intellectual property rights will be in the interest of media companies.

In the search of answers about the design of cross-media strategies and innovation policy for leveraging mobile media there are even **more questions that are emerging**. For instance:

Cross-media profitability: Mobile media offers will only stay (or become) an interesting strategic option when they lead to an increase in profitability. The suggested cross-media integration demands to start assessing cross-media profitability rather than a separate view about the profitability of one media channel only. This may pose organizational challenges to media companies, for example when profit centers in their management structure are organized according to specific media channels.

Parallel media usage behaviour: Mobile media can be used in parallel to watching television or surfing online media content. Next to this time budget dimension, parallel media use can refer to using multiple parts of a media brand meta-narrative, i.e. using a TV programs SMS chat while watching the program. Parallel use of mass media as well as parallel use of mass media and interpersonal communications is an interesting field of media use that still needs some basic research.

Cross-network service models: The idea of seamless media delivery possibilities using complementary strengths of fixed and wireless networks is compelling. Yet, many open questions remain such as who may become a cross-network ISP; payment contracts in the case of delivery failures across networks; DRM system design and content usage rights across networks; privacy issues in the case of personal automated agents; and intended media breaks as potential security components.

IPR and privacy policies: Media companies' quest to secure control over their mobile content raise a number of public policy concerns including the design of mobile DRM systems. Particularly in the case of mobile media there are a variety of opportunities to monitor users, via the data generated by mobile operators, e.g. information on location and on purchased mobile content items, or via the DRM system. Thus, the question emerges about how media companies should deal with these concerns in the light of their interest to broker this information to advertisers. The design of appropriate privacy policy issues is an important issue in the long run since mobile users may boycott or abandon mobile content services when they lead to nuisance and privacy intrusion.

Many more questions regarding mobile media provision arise concerning technological issues such as **battery power as a new bottleneck** of mobile devices, or challenges of voice-based navigation; economic issues such as the need for more research on **mobile information economics** and their characteristics and specific traits in relation to other digital media; social issues such as mobile media use by **users who actively choose not to use the Internet**; policy issues such as **licensing policies** of upstream industry development that affect media companies business models; or questions on sector-specific versus convergence regulation and the design of institutions for mobile media regulation.

This book has suggested in various chapters that the mobile phone will evolve into a **remote control and steering device for media consumption** in cross-media offers and that mobile media design should focus the social appropriation of mobile phones into everyday life. This approach implies that assumptions about mobile users browsing the Internet or watching videos via mobile phones are common misconceptions by mobile operators. Yet, mobile users in the next decade may in fact do similar things but in different ways than anticipated. In Germany, one potential analogy to UMTS development may be the rise, development, and decay of BTX. Introduced in 1977 at the IFA Berlin and commercially launched in 1980 some economic historians characterize the technology that combined telephone and TV sets as the 'dress rehearsal' for online shopping, tele-banking, chat, and e-mail. If nothing else it suggests that it will be worthwhile to follow the developments of hybrid mobile media services.

2
Outlook

Changes in the media are reflected by changes in society when the frontiers of the media are shifted and vice versa.[1] The greater context of the development of the media under the influence of mobile communications, thus, has to ask for the interrelationships between changes in media and society (S-2.1). It also has to consider what the discussed media economic, media managerial, and media political arguments on the provision of mobile media may imply for the direction of future research agendas (S-2.2).

2.1
Mobile media and its discontents: towards a nomadic society?

Arguments on the implications of mobile media on our changing society are controversial. Some scholars argue that we have become nomads again. SLOTER-DIJK (2001) emphasizes that a **neo-nomadic society** is not about the commute between summer and winter pastures, but about access options. Thinking in categories of portfolios and stock is migrating to a new thinking in categories of options.[2] GROEBEL (2005) also envisions the emergence of an **option society** under the influence of mobile communications and mobile media.[3] HORX (2001) depicts a nomadic society in which people increasingly spend time in transitory buildings and spaces such as airport lounges, train stations, or means of transportation.[4] LÉVY (1997), on the other hand, postulates that nomadism today is characterized by the changes of scientific, technological, economic, and mental landscapes that arouse movement even when people are not moving; in his understanding of nomadism, the space of today's nomads is not geographic territory but the **space of knowledge, skills, and thoughts,** they are not following herds but the evolution of mankind, and they reinvent themselves as collective. [5] Regardless of this variety of visions on societal development and the notion of a nomadic society one potential analogy to nomads may become essential for the provision of mobile media: nomads are leaving traces of their movements:

1   See Silverstone (1999), p. 146; McQuail (2000), pp. 4.
2   See Sloterdijk (2001), pp. 199.
3   See Groebel (2005).
4   See Horx (2001), p. 105.
5   See Lévy (1997), pp. 10.

animal traces of herds that are moving from water hole to water hole, from one fertile area to the next.[6] Wireless nomads are leaving **digital traces of their movements** as well, in cyberspace but increasingly also in the real world. Privacy and data protection concerns become increasingly evident as wireless nomads do not have a choice to blur their traces. The influence of mobile media on the evolution of society does not indicate revolutionary changes, but can be seen in the general evolution of the information society; yet, a more profound analysis of societies' potential discontents is needed that abstracts from simple analogies to nomadism.

2.2
Future research agenda

The analysis of the development of mobile media may pave the way for a **broader discussion of digital media economics and the political economy of digital media**. The economics of digital media delivery can differ substantially for different fixed and wireless networks and affect media design, creation, and production, media bundling and pricing, and media distribution from a supply-side perspective and media selection, adoption, and consumption from a demand-side perspective.

Emerging fertile research areas for media economics lie in a stronger integration of New Institutional Economics (NIE), industrial dynamics, and political economy. Under the assumption of asymmetric information distribution **NIE** analyses transaction costs, principle agent relationships, and the design of contracts.[7] For media economics, these aspects are relevant for further analysis of media firm's hierarchical design under the influence of digitisation as well as market transaction processes in the media industry that is dynamically shaped by digitisation and network economics.[8] Media industry evolution can be assessed using new research frameworks from **industrial dynamics** such as the systems of innovation framework. In the research tradition of evolutionary economics this framework strives to overcoming initial discussions on converging industries and offers the analysis of organizations and institutions instead.[9] Emerging policy developments in media as well as telecommunication policy can benefit from the contributions of **political economics**. This research area deals, among other things, with questions on the extent and type of public good provision, the size and form of redistributive programs, or comparative politics in democratic institutions.[10] For the analysis of digital media economics the focus shift to the political economy offers a fresh look on the tension between the provision of private and public media goods; financing media productions and

---

6   See Lévy (1997), p. 176
7   See for example Picot, Reichwald, and Wigand (2003).
8   See for example Zerdick et al. (2004).
9   See for example Edquist (2003b); Malerba (2004).
10 See for example Persson and Tabellini (2002). Kiefer also suggests to further integrate insights from political economy into media economic research frameworks, see Kiefer (2001), pp. 38.

allocating rights to access and usage; and the role of the media in a democratic society.

Whereas competitive strategy has found repercussions in the evolving media economics and media management literature[11] and contributes to sharpen the outlines of this academic field, the aforementioned areas of economic research still offer many opportunities for media economics to find greater acceptance and they can contribute to **leveraging media economics** as an essential discipline in both media communications as well as economics and business management. The analysis of mobile media in this book at the intersection of media economics, media management, and media and telecommunication policy may offer a modest approach in aligning some elements of these academic fields. Yet, the related research space is wide open and offers a broad, interesting, and challenging array of research questions on the development of the media.

11 See for example Sjurts (1996); Goldhammer and Zerdick (1999); Meckel (1999); Schumann and Hess (1999b); Karmasin and Winter (2000b); Wolf and Sands (2000); Siegert (2001); Hass (2002); Zerdick et al. (2000); Mueller-Kalthoff (2002b); Picard (2002); Zerdick et al. (2004).

Figures

Tables

Abbreviations

2G	Second Generation Mobile Network or Service
2.5G	Second Generation Enhanced Mobile Network or Service
3G	Third Generation Mobile Network or Service
3GPP	Third Generation Partnership Project
ACA	Australian Communications Authority
ARPU	Average Revenue Per User
ASP	Applications Service Provider
BTX	Bildschirmtext
CDMA	Code Division Multiple Access
CLI	Calling Line Identification
CPP	Calling Party Pays
CRS	Customer Reservation System
DRM	Digital Rights Management
DVB-H	Digital Video Broadcasting-Handheld
DVB-T	Digital Video Broadcasting-Terrestrial
EPG	Electronic Program Guide
ETSI	European Telecommunications Standards Institute
EDGE	Enhanced Data Rates for GSM Evolution
FCC	Federal Communication Commission
FOMA	Freedom of Multimedia Access
GDP	Gross Domestic Product
GPRS	General Packet Radio Service
GPS	Global Positioning System
GSM	Global System for Mobile Communications
GRX	GPRS Roaming Exchange
HLR	Home Location Register

HSCSD	High Speed Circuit Switched Data
HTML	Hypertext Markup Language
ICT	Information and Communication Technology
IEEE	Institute of Electrical and Electronics Engineers
IM	Instant Messaging
IMEI	International Mobile Equipment Identity
IMT-2000	International Mobile Telecommnications, Third Generation of Standards Approved by ITU
IP	Internet Protocol
IPR	Intellectual Property Rights
IPv6	Internet Protocol Version 6
ISP	Internet Service Provider
ITU	International Telecommunication Union
IWF	InterWorking Function
LAN	Local Area Network
MCF	Mobile Content Forum
MMS	Multimedia Messaging Service
MPHPT	Ministry of Public Management, Home Affairs, Posts and Telecommunications (Japan)
MNO	Mobile Network Operator
MPEG	Moving Pictures Experts Group
MVNO	Mobile Virtual Network Operator
NAT	Network Address Translator
NIE	New Institutional Economics
ODTR	Irish Office of the Director of Telecommunications Regulation
OFTEL	Office of Telecommunications (UK)
PAN	Personal Area Network
PDA	Personal Digital Assistant
PKI	Public Key Infrastructure
QoS	Quality of Service
RegTP	Regulatory Authority for Telecommunication and Posts, Germany
RPP	Receiving Party Pays
SIM	Subscriber Identity Module
SMP	Significant Market Power
SMS	Short Message Service

TLD	Top Level Domain
TV	Television
UMTS	Universal Mobile Telecommunications System
VJ	Video Jockey
VoIP	Voice over IP
WAN	Wide Area Network
WAP	Wireless Application Protocol
WiFi	Wireless Fidelity
WHO	World Health Organization
WIM	WAP Identity Module
WIPO	World Intellectual Property Organization
WTO	World Trade Organization

References

Aaker, David A., and Kevin Lane Keller (1990): Consumer evaluations of brand extensions. Journal of Marketing 54:27-41.

Aaker, Jennifer L. (1997): The malleable self: the role of self-expression in persuasion. Journal of Marketing Research 36 (February):45-57.

ACA (2002): Options for numbering of short message services (SMS) in Australia. Available from http://www.aca.gov.au/telcomm/telephone_numbering/8_digit_numbering/newnumb/discussion.rtf.

ACA (2003): Options for numbering of short message services (SMS) in Australia - following feedback received on an ACA SMS public discussion paper. Available from http://www.aca.gov.au/telcomm/telephone_numbering/new_numbers/optionspaper.rtf.

Adams, William James, and Janet L. Yellen (1976): Commodity bundling and the burden of monopoly. Quarterly Journal of Economics 90 (3):475-498.

Adar, Eytan, and Bernardo Huberman (2000): Free riding on Gnutella. First Monday 5 (10):1-9. Available from http://www.firstmonday.dk/issues/issue5_10/adar/.

Adner, Ron (2002): When are technologies disruptive? A demand-based view of the emergence of competition. Strategic Management Journal 23:667-688.

Adner, Ron, and Daniel Levinthal (2001): Demand heterogeneity and technology evolution: implications for product and process innovation. Management Science 47 (5):611-628.

Advani, Rajiv, and Khaled Choudhury (2001): Making the most of B2C wireless. Business Strategy Review 12 (2):39-49.

Ahy, Reza (2001): Developing areas of wireless. In The wireless industry, edited by Inside The Minds. Bedford, MA: Aspatore, 95-108.

Albarran, Alan, and Sylvia M. Chan-Olmsted (1998): Global media economics. Commercialization, concentration and integration of world media markets. Ames, Iowa: Iowa State University Press.

Alexander, Alison, James Owers, and Rod Carveth (1998): Media economics. Theory and practice. Mahwah, NJ: Lawrence Erlbaum Associates.

Alleman, James (2005): Mobile communications United States business model. In Mobile media. Content and services for wireless communications, edited by J. Groebel, E. M. Noam and V. Feldmann. Mahwah, NJ: Lawrence Erlbaum Associates (forthcoming).

Alline, Jean-Baptiste (2002): Administrating print and digital operations - the case of the Financial Times. Paper presented at 5th World Media Economics Conference, at Turku, Finland.

Altmeppen, Klaus-Dieter (1996): Oekonomie der Medien und des Mediensystems. Opladen: Westdeutscher Verlag.

Alven, David, Resmi Arjunanpillai, Reza Farhang, Sachin Kansal, Nauman Khan, and Ulrika Leufven (2001): WLAN hotspots - connect the dots for a wireless future Royal Institute of Technology, Stanford University, May 2001. Available from http://www.dsv.su.se/~mab/Alven.pdf.

Anand, Bharat, and Ron Shachar (2001): Multiproduct firms, information, and loyalty. Available from http://www.people.hbs.edu/banand/asbrandswp.pdf.

Anderson, Jamie, and Chris Voss (2001): Captive networks and elevator telematics. Business Strategy Review 12 (1):51-59.

Ansoff, H. Igor (1966): Management Strategie. Muenchen.

Antonelli, Christano (1997): A regulatory regime for innovation in the communciations industries. Telecommunication Policy 21 (1):35-45.

Apple (February 12, 2002): Apple, Ericsson and Sun team to create standards-based, wireless content delivery solution. Available from http://www.apple.com/pr/library/2002/feb/12wireless.html.

Aronson, Sidney H. (1981): Bell's electrical toy: What's the use? The sociology of early telephone usage. In The social impact of the telephone, edited by I. de Sola Pool. Boston, MA: MIT Press, 15-39.

Arrese, Angel, and Mercedes Medina (2002): Competition between new and old media in economic and financial news markets. In Media firms: structures, operations and performance, edited by R. Picard. New Jersey: Lawrence Erlbaum Associates, 59-75.

ART (2002): WiFi: ART adopts the texts allowing the use of wireless LANs. Available from http://www.art-telecom.fr/communiques/pressrelease/2002/13-11-2002.htm.

Bailey, Kenneth D. (1994): Typologies and taxonomies: an introduction to classification techniques. Thousand Oaks, CA: Sage.

Bakos, Yannis, and Erik Brynjolfsson (2000): Bundling and competition on the Internet: aggregation strategies for information goods. Marketing Science 19 (1):63-82.

Baldwin, Robert, and Martin Cave (1999): Understanding regulation: theory, strategy, and practice. Oxford: Oxford University Press.

Bar, Francois, Stephen Cohen, Peter Cowhey, Brad DeLong, Michael Kleeman, and John Zysman (2000): Access and innovation policy for the third-generation internet. Telecommunication Policy 24:489-518.

Barnett, H.G. (1953): Innovation: the basis of cultural change. New York.

Barney, J.B. (1991): Firm resources and sustained competitive advantage. Journal of Management 17:99-120.

BAT (2002): BAT Medienanalyse 2002: Wer will die neuen Alleskoenner? Freizeit aktuell,April 9, 2002.

Baudrillard, Jean (1995): Simulacra and simulation. Translated by S. Glaser. Ann Arbor: University of Michigan Press.

Bauer, Johannes M. (2002): A comparative analysis of spectrum management regimes. Paper presented at TPRC 2002. Available from http://intel.si.umich.edu/tprc/papers/2002/85/SpectrumManagement.pdf.

Baumgarten, Franziska (1989): Psychologie des Telefonierens (1931). In Telefon und Gesellschaft: Beitraege zu einer Soziologie der Telekommunikation, edited by Forschungsgruppe Telekommunikation. Berlin: Spiess, 187-196.

Baumgarten, Uwe (2002): Technische Infrastruktur fuer das mobile business. In Mobile Kommunikation. Wertschoepfung, Technologien, neue Dienste, edited by R. Reichwald. Wiesbaden: Gabler, 101-112.

Bechar-Israeli, Haya (1995): Nicknames, play, and identity on Internet relay chat. Journal of Computer-Mediated Communication 1 (2). Available from http://www.ascusc.org/jcmc/vol1/issue2/bechar.html.

Bechtold, Stefan (2004): From copyright to information law - implications of digital rights management. Available from http://www.jura.uni-tuebingen.de/-s-bes1.

Bechtold, Stefan (2004): Digital Rights Management zwischen Urheber- und Innovationsschutz. In E-merging media. Kommunikation und Medienwirtschaft der Zukunft, edited by A. Zerdick, A. Picot, K. Schrape, J. C. Burgelman, R. Silverstone, V. Feldmann, D. Heger, K. and C. Wolff. Heidelberg: Springer, 333-432.

Beck, Klaus (1989): Telefongeschichte als Sozialgeschichte: die soziale und kulturelle Aneignung des Telefons im Alltag. In Telefon und Gesellschaft: Beitraege zu einer Soziologie der Telekommunikation, edited by Forschungsgruppe Telekommunikation. Berlin: Spiess, 45-75.

Bekkers, Rudi, Bert Verspagen, and Jan Smits (2002): Intellectual property rights and standardization: the case of GSM. Telecommunication Policy 26:171-188.

Benkler, Yochai (1998): Communications infrastructure regulation and the distribution of control over content. Telecommunication Policy 22 (3):183-196.

Benkler, Yochai (2002): Some economics of wireless communications. Paper presented at TPRC, at Alexandria, VA. Available from http://intel.si.umich.edu/tprc/papers/2002/134/owlecon.pdf.

Benkler, Yochai (2005): Exclusive rights in information and mobile wireless mass media. In Mobile media. Content and services for wireless communications, edited by J. Groebel, E. M. Noam and V. Feldmann. Mahwah, NJ: Lawrence Erlbaum Associates (forthcoming).

Bennett, Colin, David J. Phillips, and PriscillaM. Regan (2002): Technology, geography, economics, and regulation: factors affecting surveillance and privacy in the implementation of wireless 911. Paper presented at TPRC, at Alexandria, VA. Available from http://intel.si.umich.edu/tprc/papers/2002/129/TPRC2002BennettPhillipsRegan.pdf.

Benninghoff, Arnd (2003): Von UMTS bis WLAN - Mobile Medienstrategien der Tomorrow Focus AG. Paper presented at Ringvorlesung Mobile Medien, at Freie Universitaet Berlin, May 26, 2003.

Bentele, Guenter (1992): Zeitstrukturen in den aktuellen Informationsmedien. In Zeit, Raum, Kommunikation, edited by W. Hoemberg and M. Schmolke. Muenchen: Oelschlaeger, 159-176.

Berg, Klaus, and Marie Luise Kiefer (2002): Massenkommunikation VI. Eine Langzeitstudie zur Mediennutzung und Medienbewertung 1964-2000, Schriftenreihe Media Perspektiven, Band 16. Baden-Baden: Nomos.

Bessen, James (2003): Patent thickets: strategic patenting of complex technologies. Available from http://www.researchoninnovation.org/thicket.pdf.

Bisenius, Jean-Claude, and Wolf Siegert (2002): Multi media mobile. Mobile services in digital broadcasting and telecommunications networks. Edited by Medienanstalt BerlinBrandenburg, Schriftenreihe der mbb. Berlin: Vistas.

Blumenthal, Marjory, and David Clark (2001): Rethinking the design of the Internet: end to end arguments vs. the brave new world. In Communications policy in transition: the Internet and beyond, edited by B. M. Compaine and S. Greenstein. Cambridge, MA: MIT Press, 91-140.

Blumler, Jay G., and Elihu Katz, (Eds.) (1974): The uses of mass communications: current perspectives on gratification research. Beverly Hills, CA: Sage.

Boell, Karin (1996): Merchandising: eine neue Dimension der Verflechtung zwischen Medien und Industrie. 2nd ed. Muenchen: Fischer. Originally published zugl. Univ. Diss. 1995.

Bourreau, Marc, and Pinar Dogan (2001): Regulation and innovation in the telecommunications industry. Telecommunication Policy 25:167-184.

Brand, Alexander, and Matthias Bonjer (2002): Mobiles Marketing im Kommunikations-Mix innovativer Kampagnenplanung. In Mobile Kommunikation. Wertschoepfung, Technologien, neue Dienste, edited by R. Reichwald. Wiesbaden: Gabler, 289-300.

Brecht, Bertolt (1992): Der Rundfunk als Kommunikationsapparat. Rede ueber die Funktion des Rundfunks. In Werke, Berliner und Frankfurter Ausgabe, edited by B. Brecht. Berlin/ Frankfurt a.M.: Aufbau/ Suhrkamp.

Breiter, Andreas, Hardy Dreier, Axel Zerdick, and Peter Zoche (1997): Workshop Summary. German-Japanese Cooperation Council for High-Tech and Environmental Technology (GJCC): Joint Japanese-German Workshop on "Youth and Multimedia", March 5 and 6, 1997 in Tokyo Freie Universitaet.

Breunig, Christian (2003): Internet: auf dem Weg zu einem kommerziellen Medium? Media Perspektiven (8):385-393.

Briggs, Asa (1981): The pleasure telephone: a chapter in the prehistory of the media. In The social impact of the telephone, edited by I. de Sola Pool. Boston, MA: MIT Press, 40-65.

Brint, Steven G. (2001): Gemeinschaft revisited: A critique and reconstruction of the community concept. Sociological Theory 19 (1):1-23.

Brown, Eric S. (2001): Wireless LAN go public. Technology Review (June). Available from http://www.technologyreview.com/articles/print_version/brown/061801.asp.

Brown, Timothy X. (2005): How can anyone afford mobile wireless mass media content? In Mobile media. Content and services for wireless communications, edited by J. Groebel, E. M. Noam and V. Feldmann. Mahwah, NJ: Lawrence Erlbaum Associates (forthcoming).

Brynjolfsson, Erik, and Michael Smith (2000): The great equalizer? Consumer choice behavior at Internet shopbots. Available from http://ebusiness.mit.edu/erik/TGE%202000-08-12.pdf.

Bughin, Jaques R., Stephen J. Hasker, Elizabeth S.H. Segel, and Michael P. Zeisser (2001): Reversing the digital slide. The McKinsey Quarterly (4):58-69.

Buhse, Willms (2002): The role of digital rights management as a solution for market uncertainties for mobile music. JMM - The International Journal on Media Management Volume 4 (Issue 3):172-179. Available from http://www.mediajournal.org/netacademy/publications.nsf/all_pk/1878.

Carey, James W. (1992): Communication as culture. Essays on media and society. 2nd ed. New York: Routledge.

Carey, John (2005): Contents and services for next generation wireless networks. In Mobile media. Content and services for wireless communications, edited by J. Groebel, E. M. Noam and V. Feldmann. Mahwah, NJ: Lawrence Erlbaum Associates (forthcoming).

Carter, Kenneth R. (2005): 3G or not 3G: the WiFi walled garden. In Mobile media. Content and services for wireless communications, edited by J. Groebel, E. M. Noam and V. Feldmann. Mahwah, NJ: Lawrence Erlbaum Associates (forthcoming).

Caspar, Mirko (2002a): Cross-Channel-Medienmarken. Strategische Optionen, Ausgestaltungsmoeglichkeiten und nachfragerseitige Bewertung. Frankfurt a.M.: Peter Lang.

Caspar, Mirko (2002b): Markenausdehnungsstrategien. In Markenmanagement. Grundfragen der identitaetsorientierten Markenfuehrung, edited by H. Meffert, C. Burmann and M. Koers. Wiesbaden: Gabler, 233-262.

Cassirer, Henry R. (1959): Audience participation, new style. Public Opinion Quarterly 23 (4):529-536.

Castells, Manuel (1997): The power of identity. Vol. II, The information age: economy, society and culture. Massachusetts: Blackwell Publishers.

Castells, Manuel (2000): The rise of the network society. 2nd ed. Vol. I, The information age: economy, society and culture. Oxford: Blackwell Publishers.

Castells, Manuel (2001): Informationalism and the network society. In The hacker ethic: a radical approach to the philosophy of business, edited by P. Himanen. New York: Random House, 155-178.

CDD (2001): TV that watches you: the prying eye of interactive television Center for Digital Democracy, June 2001.

Chaffee, Steven H., and Miriam J. Metzger (2001): The end of mass communications? Mass Communication & Society 4 (4):365-379.

Chaillee, Patrick (2003): Mobile Marketing - Die Erweiterung der klassischen Kommunikation. Paper presented at Ringvorlesung Mobile Medien, at Freie Universitaet Berlin, June 2, 2003.

Chan-Olmsted, Sylvia M., and Byeng-Hee Chang (2005): Mobile wireless strategy of media firms: examining the wireless diversification patterns of leading global media conglomerates. In Mobile media. Content and services for wireless communications, edited by J. Groebel, E. M. Noam and V. Feldmann. Mahwah, NJ: Lawrence Erlbaum Associates (forthcoming).

Chan-Olmsted, Sylvia M., and Yungwook Kim (2001): Perceptions of branding among television station managers: an exploratory analysis. Journal of Broadcasting & Electronic Media (Winter 2001):75-91.

Chan-Olmsted, Sylvia M., and Jung Suk Park (2000): From on-air to online world: examining the content and structures of broadcast TV stations' web sites. Journalism & Mass Communication Quarterly 77 (2):321-339.

Chaudhuri, Arjun, and Morris B. Holbrook (2001): The chain of effects from brand trust and brand affect to brand performance: the role of brand loyalty. Journal of Marketing 65 (April 2001):81-93.

Chesbrough, Henry (2003): Open innovation. The new imperative for creating and profiting from technology. Boston, MA: Harvard Business School Press.

Christensen, Clayton (1997): The innovator's dilemma: when new technologies cause great firms to fail. Boston, MA: Harvard Business School Press.

Chuang, John Chung-I, and Marvin A. Sirbu (1999): Optimal bundling strategy for digital information goods: network delivery of articles and subscriptions. Information Economics and Policy 11:147-176.

Chyi, Iris Hsuang (2004): Niemand wuerde dafuer zahlen? Internetinhalte als inferiore Gueter. In E-merging media. Kommunikation und Medienwirtschaft der Zukunft, edited by A. Zerdick, A. Picot, K. Schrape, J. C. Burgelman, R. Silverstone, V. Feldmann, D. Heger, K. and C. Wolff. Heidelberg: Springer, 45-46.

Clark, David D. (1997): A taxonomy of Internet telephony applications. Paper presented at TPRC, at Alexandria, VA, September 27-29. Available from http://itc.mit.edu/itel/pubs/ddc.tprc97.pdf.

Clark, David D., and John Wroclawski (2001): The personal router whitepaper. In MIT Laboratory for Computer Science. Boston.

Clark, Thomas (October 10, 2003): Plattenfirmen machen Millionen mit Klingeltoenen. Financial Times Deutschland. Available from http://www.ftd.de/tm/me/1065243037150.htm.

Clarke, Irvine (2001): Emerging value propositions for m-commerce. Journal of Business Strategies (Fall):133-148.

Cohen, Julie E. (2003): DRM and privacy.

Cohen, Kris, and Nina Wakeford (2003): The making of mobility, the making of self INCITE, University of Surrey in collaboration with Sapient. Available from http://www.soc.surrey.ac.uk/incite/AESOP%20Phase3.htm.

Cole, Jeffrey (2004): Multitasking bei der Internetnutzung. In E-merging media. Kommunikation und Medienwirtschaft der Zukunft, edited by A. Zerdick, A. Picot, K. Schrape, J. C. Burgelman, R. Silverstone, V. Feldmann, D. Heger, K. and C. Wolff. Heidelberg: Springer, 82-83.

Cole, Jeffrey, and John P. Robinson (2002): Internet use, mass media and other activity in the UCLA data. IT & Society 1 (2):121-133.

Compaine, Benjamin M. (2000a): Distinguishing between concentration and competition. In Who owns the media? Competition and concentration in the mass media industry, edited by B. M. Compaine and D. Gomery. Mahwah, NJ: Lawrence Erlbaum Associates, 537-581.

Compaine, Benjamin M. (2000b): The online information industry. In Who owns the media? Competition and concentration in the mass media industry, edited by B. M. Compaine and D. Gomery. Mahwah, NJ: Lawrence Erlbaum Associates, 437-480.

Compaine, Benjamin M. (2005): Are there content models for the wireless world? In Mobile media. Content and services for wireless communications, edited by J. Groebel, E. M. Noam and V. Feldmann. Mahwah, NJ: Lawrence Erlbaum Associates (forthcoming).

Compaine, Benjamin M., and Douglas Gomery, (Eds.) (2000): Who owns the media? Competition and concentration in the mass media industry. 3 ed. Mahwah, NJ: Lawrence Erlbaum Associates.

Cooper, Martin (2001): The real potential for wireless. In The wireless industry, edited by Inside The Minds. Bedford, MA: Aspatore, 109-136.

Dahan, Ely, and John R. Hauser (2001): The virtual customer: communication, conceptualization, and computation. Available from http://ebusiness.mit.edu/research/papers/104%20EDahan,%20JHauser%20Virtual%20Customer.pdf.

Dans, Enrique (2000): Internet newspapers: are some more equal than others? JMM - The International Journal on Media Management 2 (1):4-12.

David, Paul A. (2003): Koyaanisqatsi in cyberspace. The economics of an 'out-of-balance' regime of private property rights in digital data and information Stanford Institute for Economic Policy Research. Available from http://siepr.stanford.edu/papers/pdf/02_29.pdf.

Day, George S., and Christophe Van den Bulte (2002): Superiority in customer relationship management: consequences for competitive advantage and performance Marketing@Wharton Research Paper. Available from http://www-marketing.wharton.upenn.edu/ ideas/pdf/ van%20den%20bulte/sueriority%20in%20customer%20relationship%20manegement.pdf.

de Sola Pool, Ithiel (1990): Technologies without boundaries. On telecommunications in a global age. Edited by Eli M. Noam. Edited by E. M. Noam. Cambridge, Massachusetts: Harvard University Press.

de Sola Pool, Ithiel, Craig Decker, Stephen Dizard, Kay Israel, Pamela Rubin, and Barry Weinstein (1981): Foresight and hindsight: the case of the telephone. In The social impact of the telephone, edited by I. de Sola Pool. Boston, MA: MIT Press, 127-157.

Dean, David R. (2002): Wie man den "M-Commerce"-Kunden gewinnt. In Mobile Kommunikation. Wertschoepfung, Technologien, neue Dienste, edited by R. Reichwald. Wiesbaden: Gabler, 247-261.

Denison, D.C., and Ross Kerber (2002): Mobile weblogs (December 30, 2002) Boston Globe Online. Available from http://www.boston.com/dailyglobe2/364/business/mobile_weblogsP.shtml.

Dennis, Everette E., and James Ash (2001): Toward a taxonomy of New Media - management views of an evolving industry. JMM - The International Journal on Media Management, 07/2001 Volume 3 (Issue 1- Spring 2001):26-32. Available from http://www.mediajournal.org/netacademy/publications.nsf/all_pk/1878.

Dey, Anind K. (2001): Understanding and using context. Personal and Ubiquitous Computing 5 (1):4-7.

Dimmick, John, Susan Kline, and Laura Stafford (2000): The gratification niches of personal e-mail and the telephone. Communication Research 27 (No. 2, April 2000):227-248.

Doering, Nicola (2002): 1x Brot, Wurst, 5Sack ıpfel I.L.D. Zeitschrift für Medienpsychologie 14 (3):118-128.

Doeven, Jan (2003): A road map for broadcast technology. EBU Technical Review (April):1-10.

Domke, Uwe, and Christoph Wild (2002): Fernsehen braucht Radio. Media Perspektiven (7):294-307.

Dordick, Herbert S. (1989): The social uses of the telephone - an US perspective. In Telefon und Gesellschaft: Beitraege zu einer Soziologie der Telekommunikation, edited by Forschungsgruppe Telekommunikation. Berlin: Spiess, 221-238.

Dornan, Andy (March 4, 2002): Fast forward to 4G? Network Magazine. Available from http://www.networkmagazine.com/article/NMG20020304S0010.

Doty, Harold D., and William H. Glick (1994): Typologies as a unique form of theory building: toward improved understanding and modeling. Academy of Management Review 19 (2):230-251.

Doyle, Gillian (2002): Understanding media economics. London: Sage Publications.

Dreier, Hardy (2002): Vielfalt oder Vervielfaeltigung? - Medienangebote und ihre Nutzung im digitalen Zeitalter. In Cross-media Management: Content Strategien erfolgreich umsetzen, edited by B. Mueller-Kalthoff. Berlin: Springer, 41-60.

Dreier, Hardy (2004): Multimedial und multidimensional - Auswertungskonzepte im "digitalen Zeitalter". In E-merging media. Kommunikation und Medienwirtschaft der Zukunft, edited by A. Zerdick, A. Picot, K. Schrape, J. C. Burgelman, R. Silverstone, V. Feldmann, D. Heger, K. and C. Wolff. Heidelberg: Springer, 79-102.

Ducatel, K., M. Bogdanowicz, F. Scapolo, J. Leijten, and Jean Claude Burgelman (2004): Dafuer sind Freunde da - Ambient Intelligence (AmI) und die Informationsgesellschaft im Jahre 2010. In E-merging media. Kommunikation und Medienwirtschaft der Zukunft, edited by A. Zerdick, A. Picot, K. Schrape, J. C. Burgelman, R. Silverstone, V. Feldmann, D. Heger, K. and C. Wolff. Heidelberg: Springer, 195-218.

Duerscheid, Christa (2002): E-mail und SMS - ein Vergleich. In Kommunikationsform E-mail, edited by A. Ziegler and D. Christa. Tuebingen: Stauffenburg. Available from http://deuserv.uni-muenster.de/IfdSuLuiD/Lehrende/Duerscheid/duerscheid.pdf.

Dutta, Soumitra, and Arie Segev (2001): Business transformation on the Internet. In E-commerce and v-business: business models for global success, edited by S. Barnes and B. Hunt. Oxford: Butterworth Heinemann, 5-22.

EBU (2000): Comments on the framework directive: Proposal for a Directive on a common regulatory framework for electronic communications networks and services (COM(2000)393). Available from http://www.ebu.ch/departments/legal/pdf/leg_pp_communications_231000.pdf.

Edquist, Charles (2003a): The fixed Internet and mobile telecommunications sectoral system of innovation: equipment, access and content. In The Internet and mobile telecommunications system of innovation. Developments in equipment, access and content, edited by C. Edquist. Cheltenham: Edward Elgar, 1-39.

Edquist, Charles, (Ed.) (2003b): The Internet and mobile telecommunications system of innovation. Developments in equipment, access and content. Cheltenham: Edward Elgar.

Ehmer, Marco (2002): Mobile Dienste im Auto - die Perspektive fuer Automobilhersteller? In Mobile Kommunikation. Wertschoepfung, Technologien, neue Dienste, edited by R. Reichwald. Wiesbaden: Gabler, 459-472.

Eisner Gillett, Sharon, William Lehr, John Wroclawski, and David D. Clark (2000): A taxonomy of Internet appliances. Paper presented at TPRC, at Alexandria, VA. Available from http://itel.mit.edu/itel/docs/jun00/GLWC_appliances_nofigs.pdf.

Elliott, Philip (1974): Uses and gratifications research: a critique and a sociological alternative. In The uses of mass communications, current perspectives on gratification research, edited by J. G. Blumler and E. Katz. London, 249-269.

Elliott, Stuart (2002): Stephen King's New Book Is on the Beam, Literally. The New York Times, March 19, 2002. Available from http://www.nytimes.com/2002/03/19/business/media/19ADCO.html.

Englert, Marcus (2002): Cross-Media Branding - die mediale Markenfamilie fuehren. In Cross-media Management: Content Strategien erfolgreich umsetzen, edited by B. Mueller-Kalthoff. Berlin: Springer, 203-224.

Enzensberger, Hans Magnus (1997): Baukasten zu einer Theorie der Medien (1970). In Kursbuch 20, edited by P. Glotz. Muenchen: Fischer, 97-132.

Erdem, Tülin (1998): An empirical analysis of umbrella branding. Journal of Marketing Research 35 (August):339-351.

Ericsson (2001): IPv6 in 3G wireless networks. In White paper. Available from http://www.ipv6tf.org/PublicDocuments/WhitePaperonIPv6in3GWirelessNetworks-Ericsson.PDF.

ETSI (2002): Universal Mobile Telecommunications System (UMTS); Multimedia Broadcast/Multicast Service (MBMS); Stage 1 ETSI & 3GPP.

EURESCOM (2002): Always on - device unified services, February 2002. Available from http://www.eurescom.de/~pub/deliverables/documents/P1100-series/P1101/D1/p1101-d1.pdf.

European Commission (2000): Commission clears Vizzavi Internet portal venture between Vodafone, Vivendi and Canal+ subject to conditions. Available from http://europa.eu.int/rapid/start/cgi/guesten.ksh?p_action.gettxt=gt&doc=IP/00/821|0|RAPID&lg=EN.

European Commission (2002): Directive (2002/19/EC) on access and interconnection. Available from http://europa.eu.int/information_society/topics/telecoms/regulatory/new_rf/documents/I_10820020424en00070020.df.

Evans, Philip, and Thomas S. Wurster (2000): Blown to bits: how the new economics of information transforms strategy. Boston, Massachusetts: Harvard Business School Press.

Faratin, P., John Wroclawski, G. Lee, and S. Parsons (2002): The personal router: an agent for wireless access. Available from http://itc.mit.edu/itel/docs/2002/Peyman_Faratin.pdf.

Farquhar, Peter H., Y. Han Julia, Paul M. Herr, and Yuji Ijiri (1992): Strategies for leveraging master brands. Marketing Research 4 (3):32-43.

Farrell, Nick (2002): Spam off the menu in Japan (July 3, 2002) vnunet.com. Available from http://www.vnunet.com/news/1133197.

Faulhaber, Gerald R. (2002): Network effects and merger analysis: instant messaging and the AOL-Time Warner case. Telecommunication Policy 26 (5-6):311-333.

Faulhaber, Gerald R., and David J. Farber (2002): Spectrum management: property rights, markets, and the commons AEI Brookings Joint Center Working Paper. Available from http://aei-brookings.org/admin/pdffiles/php84.pdf.

Federman, Josef (2003): Cellphone entertainment industry may face threat from freebies. The Wall Street Journal Online, June 12, 2003. Available from http://online.wsj.com/article/e_mail/0,,SB105526605176634700,00.html.

Feldmann, Valerie (2001a): Markenstrategien von TV-Sendern - dargestellt an ausgewaehlten Beispielen. Berlin: Verlag fuer Wirtschaftskommunikation.

Feldmann, Valerie (2001b): Towards a context-driven approach of m-commerce. Paper presented at ICEC, at Vienna, November 3, 2001.

Feldmann, Valerie (2002a): Aggregation and pricing strategies for innovative wireless telecommunication data services. Paper presented at International Telecommunication Society 14th Biennial Conference, at Seoul, Korea, August 19, 2002.

Feldmann, Valerie (2002b): Competitive strategy for media companies in the mobile Internet. Schmalenbach Business Review 54 (October):351-371.

Feldmann, Valerie (2005a): Business models for mobile media content in the United States. In Mobile media. Content and services for wireless communications, edited by J. Groebel, E. M. Noam and V. Feldmann. Mahwah, NJ: Lawrence Erlbaum Associates (forthcoming).

Feldmann, Valerie (2005b): Mobile peer-to-peer content and community models. In Mobile media. Content and services for wireless communications, edited by J. Groebel, E. M. Noam and V. Feldmann. Mahwah, NJ: Lawrence Erlbaum Associates (forthcoming).

Feldmann, Valerie, and Axel Zerdick (2004): E-merging media. Die Zukunft der Kommunikation. In E-merging media. Kommunikation und Medienwirtschaft der Zukunft, edited by A. Zerdick, A. Picot, K. Schrape, J. C. Burgelman, R. Silverstone, V. Feldmann, D. Heger, K. and C. Wolff. Heidelberg: Springer, 19-30.

Ferguson, Douglas A., and Elizabeth M. Perse (2000): The World Wide Web as a functional alternative to television. Journal of Broadcasting & Electronic Media 44 (2):155-174.

Fetscherin, Marc (2002): Present state and emerging scenarios of digital rights management systems. JMM - The International Journal on Media Management Volume 4 (Issue 3):164-171. Available from http://www.mediajournal.org/netacademy/publications.nsf/all_pk/1878.

Fey, Antje (2001): Das Buch fuers Ohr wird populaer. Media Perspektiven (5):231-237.

Fischer, C. (1992): America calling: a social history of the telephone to 1940: University of CA Press.

Fisher, William (2002): Theories of intellectual property. Available from http://www.law.harvard.edu/Academic_Affairs/coursepages/tfisher/iptheory.html.

Flusser, Vilem (2000): Kommunikologie. 2nd ed. Frankfurt a.M.: Fischer.

Fosfuri, Andrea (2003): The licensing dilemma Paper presented at the Annual Meeting of the Academy of Management in Seattle, 2003. Available from http://www.uni-bocconi.it/doc_mime_view.php?doc=id18771&doc_seg_id=1.

Fox, Mark (2002): Technological and social drivers of change in the online music industry. First Monday 7 (2):1-14. Available from http://www.firstmonday.dk/issues/issue7_2/fox/.

Fox, Mark, and Bruce Wrenn (2001): A broadcasting model for the music industry. JMM - The International Journal on Media Management, 07/2001 Volume 3 (Issue 2 - Summer 2001). Available from http://www.mediajournal.org/netacademy/publications.nsf/all_pk/1947.

France, Emma, Karina Tracey, Georg Neureiter, Riccardo Pascotto, Miguel Serrano, Seppo Parkkila, and Juha Pirinen (2001): Where are the other mobile buddies around town? Available from http://www.eurescom.de/~ftproot/web-deliverables/public/P1000-series/P1045/IST-Mobile-Summit2001.pdf.

Franke, Nikolaus, and Sonali Shah (2002): How communities support innovative activities: an exploration of assistance and sharing among end-users. Research Policy 1380:1-22.

Freund, Natascha, and Olav Ruhle (2002): Regulatory concepts for fixed-to-fixed and fixed-to-mobile interconnection rates in the European Union. Available from http://userpage.fu-berlin.de/~jmueller/its/madrid/program/papers/Freund.pdf.

Frey, Siegfried (1999): Die Macht des Bildes: der Einfluss der nonverbalen Kommunikation auf Kultur und Politik. Bern: Hans Huber.

Freystaetter, Werner (2002): Mobile security - a European perspective. In Mobile Kommunikation. Wertschoepfung, Technologien, neue Dienste, edited by R. Reichwald. Wiesbaden: Gabler, 439-458.

Freytag, C., and L. Neumann (1999): Resource adaptive WWW access for mobile applications. Computers and Graphics 23:841-848.

Frueh, Werner, and Klaus Schoenbach (1982): Der dynamisch-transaktionale Ansatz. Ein neues Paradigma der Medienwirkungen. Publizistik 27 (1-2):74-88.

Funk, Jeffrey Lee (2001a): The mobile Internet and the new economics of information. Available from http://www.rieb.kobe-u.ac.jp/~funk/.

Funk, Jeffrey Lee (2001b): The mobile Internet: how Japan dialed up and the West disconnected. Kent: ISI Publications.

Funk, Jeffrey Lee (2002a): Global competition between and within standards: the case of the mobile phone. New York: Palgrave.

Funk, Jeffrey Lee (2002b): Japanese mobile Internet navigation services: competition between train information, map, and destination information providers. Available from http://www.rieb.kobe-u.ac.jp/~funk/navigation.pdf.

Funk, Jeffrey Lee (2004): Neue Technologien, neue Kunden und die "disruptive technology" des mobilen Internet: Erfahrungen aus dem japanischen Markt. In E-merging media. Kommunikation und Medienwirtschaft der Zukunft, edited by A. Zerdick, A. Picot, K. Schrape, J. C. Burgelman, R. Silverstone, V. Feldmann, D. Heger, K. and C. Wolff. Heidelberg: Springer, 103-124.

Funk, Jeffrey Lee (2005): The potential evolution of and opportunities for existing media in the mobile Internet: data from Japan's mobile Internet. In Mobile media. Content and services for wireless communications, edited by J. Groebel, E. M. Noam and V. Feldmann. Mahwah, NJ: Lawrence Erlbaum Associates (forthcoming).

Gaida, Klemens (2001): Mobile media: digital TV@Internet. Bonn: mitp-Verlag.

Gasser, Urs (2002): Rechtliche Aspekte des M-Commerce. Schweizerische Zeitschrift fuer Wirtschaftsrecht (1):13-29.

Geisselbrecht, Wolfgang, and Christiane Fotschki (2002): Transaktionsprozesse und strategische Positionierung im mobile commerce. In Mobile Kommunikation. Wertschoepfung, Technologien, neue Dienste, edited by R. Reichwald. Wiesbaden: Gabler, 231-245.

Gerhards, Maria, and Walter Klingler (2003): Mediennutzung der Zukunft. Media Perspektiven (3):115-130.

Geroski, Paul (2003): The early evolution of new markets. Oxford: Oxford University Press.

Geser, Hans (2002): Towards a sociological theory of the mobile phone. Available from http://socio.ch/mobile/t_geser1.htm.

Giddens, Anthony (1991): Modernity and self-identity: self and society in the late modern age. Cambridge: Polity Press.

Gleick, James (2001): Inescapably connected: life in the wireless age. The New York Times.

Glotz, Peter (2001): Klassische Medien in Konkurrenzsituation zum Internet. Available from http://www.gfk-ooe.at/projects/cp/politics/glotz/vortrag1.pdf.

Godin, Seth (1999): Permission marketing. New York: Simon and Schuster.

Goertz, Lutz (1995): Wie interaktiv sind Medien? Auf dem Weg zu einer Definition von Interaktivitaet. Rundfunk und Fernsehen 43:477-493.

Goffman, Erwing (1959): The presentation of self in everyday life. Garden City, NY: Doubleday.

Goldhammer, Klaus (2005): On the myth of convergence. In Mobile media. Content and services for wireless communications, edited by J. Groebel, E. M. Noam and V. Feldmann. Mahwah, NJ: Lawrence Erlbaum Associates (forthcoming).

Goldhammer, Klaus, and Axel Zerdick (1999): Rundfunk online. Entwicklungen und Perspektiven des Internet fuer Hoerfunk- und Fernsehanbieter. Berlin: Vistas.

Goltzsch, Patrick (June 30, 2003): Abkommen mit Vodafone staerkt Real Networks im Handy-Markt. FTD.

Gongolsky, Mario (May 20, 2003): Stimmen aus dem Web. Der Spiegel. Available from http://www.spiegel.de/netzwelt/technologie/0,1518,249330,00.html.

Graef, Peter (1992): Wandel von Kommunikationsraeumen durch neue Informations- und Kommunikationstechnologien. In Zeit, Raum, Kommunikation, edited by W. Hoemberg and M. Schmolke. Muenchen: Oelschlaeger, 371-386.

Grant, R. M. (1991): The resource-based theory of competitive advantage: implications for strategy formulation. California Management Review 33:114-135.

Greenstein, Shane (2001): Copyright in the age of distributed applications. In Communications Policy in transition: the Internet and beyond, edited by B. M. Compaine and S. Greenstein. Cambridge, MA: MIT Press, 369-396.

Groebel, Jo (2005): Mobile mass media: a new age for consumer, business, and society? In Mobile media. Content and services for wireless communications, edited by J. Groebel, E. M. Noam and V. Feldmann. Mahwah, NJ: Lawrence Erlbaum Associates (forthcoming).

Grossklaus, Goetz (1997): Medien-Zeit, Medien-Raum: zum Wandel der raumzeitlichen Wahrnehmung der Moderne. 2nd ed. Frankfurt a.M.: Suhrkamp.

Gruber, Harald, and F. Verboven (2000): The evolution of markets under entry and standards regulation - the case of global mobile telecommunications Centre for Economic Policy Research.

Gumpert, Gary (1989): The psychology of the telephone - revisited. In Telefon und Gesellschaft: Beitraege zu einer Soziologie der Telekommunikation, edited by Forschungsgruppe Telekommunikation. Berlin: Spiess, 239-254.

Habermas, Juergen (1995): Theorie des kommunikativen Handelns, Band 1: Handlungsrationalitaet und gesellschaftliche Rationalisierung. Frankfurt a.M.: Suhrkamp.

Hampe, Felix, and Gerhard Schwabe (2002a): Enhancing mobile commerce: instant music purchasing over the air. Paper presented at E-Business: Multidisciplinary Research and Practice, at Copenhagen, Denmark, June 9-11. Available from http://apache.iwi.uni-koblenz.de:8080/iwi/bks/publikationen/music.pdf.

Hampe, Felix, and Gerhard Schwabe (2002b): Mobiles Customer Relationship Management. In Mobile Kommunikation. Wertschoepfung, Technologien, neue Dienste, edited by R. Reichwald. Wiesbaden: Gabler, 301-316.

Hardin, Garrett (1968): The tragedy of the commons. Science 162:1243-1248.

Harhoff, Dietmar, Joachim Henkel, and Eric von Hippel (2002): Profiting from voluntary information spillovers: how users benefit by freely revealing their innovations. Available from http://web.mit.edu/evhippel/www/FreeRevealWP.pdf.

Harrigan, Kathryn Rudie (1983): Strategies for vertical integration: D.C. Heath and Company.

Hartmann, Peter H., and Ulrich Neuwoehner (1999): Lebensstilforschung und Publikumssegmentierung. Media Perspektiven (10):531-539.

Hass, Berthold (2002): Geschaeftsmodelle von Medienunternehmen: oekonomische Grundlagen und Veraenderungen durch neue Informations- und Kommunikationstechnik. Wiesbaden: Deutscher Universitaets-Verlag.

Hass, Berthold (2004): Desintegration und Reintegration im Mediensektor: wie sich Geschaeftsmodelle durch Digitalisierung veraendern. In E-merging media. Kommunikation und Medienwirtschaft der Zukunft, edited by A. Zerdick, A. Picot, K. Schrape, J. C. Burgelman, R. Silverstone, V. Feldmann, D. Heger, K. and C. Wolff. Heidelberg: Springer, 33-58.

Hätty, Holger (1989): Der Markentransfer. Heidelberg: Physica-Verlag.

Haucap, Justus (2003): Wettbewerb und Regulierung im Mobilfunk aus Sicht der oekonomischen Theorie.

Hauschildt, Juergen (1997): Innovationsmanagement. 2nd ed. Muenchen: Vahlen.

Hawkins, Robert P., Suzanne Pingree, Jaqueline Bush Hitchon, Eileen Gilligan, Leeman Kahlor, Bradley W. Gorham, Barry Radler, Prathana Kannaovakun, Toni Schmidt, Gudbjorg

Kolbeins, Chin-I Wang, and Ronald C. Serlin (2002): What holds attention to television? Strategic inertia of looks at content boundaries. Communication Research 29 (1):3-30.

Hess, Thomas (2004): Medienunternehmen im Spannungsfeld von Mehrfachverwertung und Individualisierung - eine Analyse fuer statische Inhalte. In E-merging media. Kommunikation und Medienwirtschaft der Zukunft, edited by A. Zerdick, A. Picot, K. Schrape, J. C. Burgelman, R. Silverstone, V. Feldmann, D. Heger, K. and C. Wolff. Heidelberg: Springer, 59-78.

Hess-Luettich, Ernst W.B. (1990): Das Telefonat als Mediengespraechstyp. In Telefon und Gesellschaft Band 2: Internationaler Vergleich - Sprache und Telefon - Seelsorge und Beratungsdienste - Telefoninterviews, edited by Forschungsgruppe Telekommunikation. Berlin: Volker Spiess, 281-299.

Hirakawa, Shuji (2002): Mobile multimedia broadcasting. Available from http://www.itu.int/itudoc/itu-t/workshop/converge/s5pm2-p2.pdf.

Hirsh, Lou (2002): Why consumers are not buying m-commerce (February 25, 2002) Wireless News Factor. Available from http://www.wirelessnewsfactor.com/perl/story/16484.html.

Hoeflich, Joachim (1989): Telefon und interpersonale Kommunikation - vermittelte Kommunikation aus einer regelorientierten Kommunikationsperspektive. In Telefon und Gesellschaft: Beitraege zu einer Soziologie der Telekommunikation, edited by Forschungsgruppe Telekommunikation. Berlin: Spiess, 197-220.

Hoeflich, Joachim (1996): Technisch vermittelte interpersonale Kommunikation. Grundlagen, organisatorische Medienverwendung, Konstitution "elektronischer Gemeinschaften". Opladen: Westdeutscher Verlag.

Hoeflich, Joachim (1999): Der Mythos vom umfassenden Medium: Anmerkungen zur Konvergenz aus einer Nutzerperspektive. In Die Zukunft der Kommunikation: Phaenomene und Trends in der Informationsgesellschaft, edited by M. Latzer, U. Maier-Rabler, G. Siegert and T. Steinmaurer. Innsbruck; Vienna: Studienverlag, 43-60.

Hoeflich, Joachim (2001): Das Handy als 'persoenliches Medium'. Zur Aneignung des Short Message Service (SMS) durch Jugendliche kommunikation@gesellschaft, Jg. 2, Beitrag 1. Available from http://www.uni-frankfurt.de/fb03/K.G/B1_2001_Hoeflich.pdf.

Hoeflich, Joachim R. (1995): Vom dispersen Publikum zu "elektronischen Gemeinschaften". Rundfunk und Fernsehen:518-537.

Hoeflich, Joachim, Stefanie Steuber, and Patrick Roessler (2000): Forschungsprojekt 'Jugendliche und SMS - Gebrauchsweisen und Motive'. Zusammenfassung der ersten Ergebnisse. Available from http://www.uni-erfurt.de/kw/forschung/smsreport.doc.

Hoemberg, Walter (1992): Punkt, Kreis, Linie: Die Temporalstrukturen der Massenmedien und die Entdeckung der Zeit in der fruehen Zeitungskunde. In Zeit, Raum, Kommunikation, edited by W. Hoemberg and M. Schmolke. Muenchen: Oelschlaeger, 89-102.

Holbrook, Morris B., and Elizabeth C. Hirschmann (1982): The experiential aspects of consumption: consumer fantasies, feelings, and fun. Journal of Consumer Research 9:132-140.

Hollander, Ed (2000): Online communities as community media. A theoretical and analytical framework for the study of digital community networks. Communications (25):371-386.

Hommen, Leif (2003): The Universal Mobile Telecommunications System (UMTS): Third generation. In The Internet and mobile telecommunications system of innovation. Developments in equipment, access and content, edited by C. Edquist. Cheltenham: Edward Elgar, 129-161.

Honma, Jun (June 2, 2003): Mobile content providers oppose MPEG-4 licensing policy. Nikkei Electronics Asia.

Horx, Matthias (2001): Arbeit, Freizeit und Leben in der mobilen Kommunikationsgesellschaft des 21. Jahrhunderts. In Zukunft mobile Kommunikation. Wirklichkeit und Vision einer technischen Revolution, edited by R. Lamprecht. Frankfurt a.M.: FAZ, 101-151.

Hummel, Johannes, and Ulrike Lechner (2001): The community model of content management - a case study of the music industry. JMM - The International Journal on Media Management, 07/2001 Volume 3 (Issue 1- Spring 2001):4-14. Available from http://www.mediajournal.org/netacademy/publications.nsf/all_pk/1875.

Hung, Kineta (2001): Framing meaning perceptions with music: the case of teaser ads. Journal of Advertising Research 30 (3):39-49.

Imhof, Kurt, and Peter Schulz, (Eds.) (1998): Die Veroeffentlichung des Privaten - die Privatisierung des Oeffentlichen. Opladen: Westdeutscher Verlag.

INTUG (2002a): Anti-competitive conduct and competition policy in telecommunications. Available from http://www.intug.net/talks/es_2002_11_geneva_text.html.

INTUG (2002b): Data protection issues - next generation roaming. Available from http://www.intug.net/views/europe/issues_next_gen_roaming.html.

INTUG (2002c): The regulation of mobile telecommunications. Available from http://www.intug.net/talks/es_2002_06_stockholm_text.html.

Intven, Hank, (Ed.) (2000): Telecommunications regulation handbook. Washington, DC: The World Bank.

Ito, Mizuko, and Okabe Daisuke (2001): Mobile phones, Japanese youth, and the re-placement of social contact. Available from http://www.itofisher.com/PEOPLE/mito/mobileyouth.pdf.

ITU (1999): Mobile cellular. World Telecommunication Development Report International Telecommunication Union.

ITU (2001a): Licensing of third generation 3G mobile. In ITU New Initiatives Programme. Geneva: International Telecommunication Union.

ITU (2001b): Recommendation ITU-R F.1399-1: Vocabulary of terms for wireless access.

ITU (2002a): Asia-Pacific Telecommunication Indicators 2002 International Telecommunication Union.

ITU (2002b): Internet for a mobile generation International Telecommunication Union.

ITU (2003a): Competition policy in telecommunications. Edited by Valerie Feldmann. In ITU New Initiatives Programme. Geneva: International Telecommunication Union.

ITU (2003b): Mobile overtakes fixed: implications for policy and regulation Authored by Valerie Feldmann. Available from http://www.itu.int/osg/spu/ni/mobileovertakes/resources/mobileovertakes_paper.pdf.

Iyengar, Deepali (2002): Understanding ultra wideband technology: advantages, applications, and regulatory policy. Available from http://itc.mit.edu/itel/students/papers/iyengar.pdf.

Jaeckel, Michael (1999): Medienwirkungsforschung. Ein Studienbuch zur Einfuehrung. Opladen: Westdeutscher Verlag.

Jenkins, Henry (2001): Convergence? I diverge. Technology Review (June 2001):93.

Jobson, Robert (2003): Ringtones to outsell singles Evening standard, August 12, 2003. Available from http://www.thisislondon.com/news/articles/6181007?source=Evening.

Johnstone, Bob (2001): A bright future for displays. Technology Review (June):81-85.

Jones, Steve (2004): Spielen im Internet. In E-merging media. Kommunikation und Medienwirtschaft der Zukunft, edited by A. Zerdick, A. Picot, K. Schrape, J. C. Burgelman, R. Silverstone, V. Feldmann, D. Heger, K. and C. Wolff. Heidelberg: Springer, 89-91.

Kaeding, Nadja (2002): Mobile Business und Datenschutz. In Mobile Kommunikation. Wertschoepfung, Technologien, neue Dienste, edited by R. Reichwald. Wiesbaden: Gabler, 193-206.

Kahn, Herman, and Anthony J. Wiener (1967): The year 2000: a framework for speculation on the next thirty-three years. New York: Macmillan.

Kannan, P.K., Ai-Mei Chang, and Andrew B. Whinston (2001): E-business and the intermediary role of virtual communities. In E-commerce and v-business: business models for global success, edited by S. Barnes and B. Hunt. Oxford: Butterworth Heinemann, 67-82.

Kapferer, Jean-Noel (1994): Strategic brand management: new approaches to creating and evaluating brand equity. New York: Free Press.

Karmasin, Matthias, and Carsten Winter (2000a): Einleitung: Kontexte und Aufgabenfelder von Medienmanagement. In Grundlagen des Medienmanagements, edited by M. Karmasin and C. Winter. Muenchen: Fink, 15-39.

Karmasin, Matthias, and Carsten Winter (2000b): Grundlagen des Medienmanagements. Muenchen: Fink.

Katz, Michael L., and Carl Shapiro (1985): Network externalities, competition, and compatibility. American Economic Review 75 (3):424-440.

Katz, Michael L., and Carl Shapiro (1986): Technology adoption in the presence of network externalities. Journal of Political Economy 94 (4):822-884.

Keegan, Victor (April 25, 2002): Heard it thru' the mobile. The Guardian. Available from http://media.guardian.co.uk/newmedia/story/0,7496,690414,00.html.

Keller, Kevin Lane (1998): Strategic brand management: building, measuring, and managing brand equity. Upper Saddle River, NJ: Prentice Hall.

Kelly, John (2005): Design strategies for future wireless content. In Mobile media. Content and services for wireless communications, edited by J. Groebel, E. M. Noam and V. Feldmann. Mahwah, NJ: Lawrence Erlbaum Associates (forthcoming).

Kiefer, Marie Luise (2001): Medienoekonomik: Einfuehrung in eine oekonomische Theorie der Medien. Muechen: Oldenbourg Verlag.

Killius, Nelson, and Jens Mueller-Oerlinghausen (1999): Innovative Geschaeftsmodelle in digitalen Medien. In Medienunternehmen im digitalen Zeitalter: neue Technologien - neue Maerkte - neue Geschaeftsansaetze, edited by M. Schumann and T. Hess. Wiesbaden: Gabler, 139-153.

Knoche, Manfred, and Gabriele Siegert, (Eds.) (1999): Stukturwandel der Medienwirtschaft im Zeitalter digitaler Kommunikation. Muenchen: Verlag Reinhard Fischer.

Knorr, Eric (2001): Mobile web vs. reality. Technology Review (June 2001):56-61.

Kortuem, Gerd (2002): Proem: a peer-to-peer computing platform for mobile ad-hoc networks. Available from http://www.cs.arizona.edu/mmc/10%20Kortuem.pdf.

Kortuem, Gerd, Jay Schneider, Dustin Preuitt, Thaddeus G.C. Thompson, Stephen Fickas, and Zary Segall (2001): When peer-to-peer comes face-to-face: collaborative peer-to-peer computing in mobile ad hoc networks. Available from http://www.cs.uoregon.edu/research/wearables/Papers/p2p2001.pdf.

Krafft, Manfred, and Thorsten Litfin (2002): Adoption innovativer Telekommunikationsdienste. zfbf 54 (February 2002):64-83.

Krempl, Stefan (2003): IFA special. heise online,August 28, 2003. Available from http://www.heise.de/newsticker/data/vza-28.08.03-001/.

Kroeber-Riehl, Werner, and Peter Weinberg (1999): Konsumentenverhalten. 7th ed. Muenchen: Vahlen. Originally published 1975.

Krotz, Friedrich (1995): Elektronisch mediatisierte Kommunikation. Rundfunk und Fernsehen 43:445-462.

Krotz, Friedrich (1999): Individualisierungsthese und Internet. In Die Zukunft der Kommunikation: Phaenomene und Trends in der Informationsgesellschaft, edited by M. Latzer, U. Maier-Rabler, G. Siegert and T. Steinmaurer. Innsbruck; Wien: Studienverlag, 347-365.

Ku, Raymond Shih Ray (2003): Consumer copying and creative destruction: a critique of fair use as market failure. Available from https://www.law.berkeley.edu/institutes/bclt/drm/papers/ku-consumercopying-btlj2003.pdf.

Kueng, Lucy (2002): How to ensure that ugly ducklings grow into swans. BBC News Online and the challenge of incumbent response to disruptive technology. Paper presented at 5th World Media Economics Conference, at Turku, Finland.

Kuhlmann, Stefan (2001): Future governance of innovation policy in Europe - three scenarios. Research Policy 30:953-976.

Kuhn, Thomas S. (1996): The structure of scientific revolutions. Third ed. Chicago: The University of Chicago Press. Originally published 1962.

Kunii, Irene M. (March 3, 2003): Wireless surprise. Business Week.

Kurth, Matthias (2001): Mobile virtual network operators - regulatory perspectives in Germany. Available from http://www.regtp.de/aktuelles/reden/02263/index.html.

Kurth, Matthias (2002a): Mobilfunk - Festnetz: Partnerschaft oder angespannte Konkurrenz? Available from http://www.regtp.de/aktuelles/reden/02666/index.html.

Kurth, Matthias (2002b): The vision of a mobile Europe. Available from http://www.regtp.de/aktuelles/reden/02664/.

Laats, Alex (2001): VoiceXML. In The wireless industry, edited by Inside The Minds. Bedford, MA: Aspatore, 161-183.

Laffont, Jean-Jaques, and David Martimort (2002): The theory of incentives: the principal-agent model. Princeton: Princeton University Press.

Laffont, Jean-Jaques, and Jean Tirole (2000): Competition in telecommunications. Edited by H.-W. Sinn, Munich Lectures in Economics. Cambridge, MA: MIT Press.

Lange, Ulrich T. (1989a): Telefon und Gesellschaft - eine Einfuehrung in die Soziologie der Telekommunikation. In Telefon und Gesellschaft: Beitraege zu einer Soziologie der Telekommunikation, edited by Forschungsgruppe Telekommunikation. Berlin: Spiess, 9-44.

Lange, Ulrich T. (1989b): Von der ortsgebundenen "Unmittelbarkeit" zur raum-zeitlichen Direktheit - technischer und sozialer Wandel und die Zukunft der Telefonkommunikation. In Telefon und Gesellschaft: Beitraege zu einer Soziologie der Telekommunikation, edited by Forschungsgruppe Telekommunikation. Berlin: Spiess, 167-185.

Latzer, Michael (1997): Mediamatik - die Konvergenz von Telekommunikation, Computer und Rundfunk. Opladen: Westdeutscher Verlag.

Lauff, Werner (2002): Schoener, schneller, breiter: die ungeahnten Moeglichkeiten von Kabel, DSL, Satellit und UMTS. Frankfurt/Wien: Ueberreuter.

Lawrence, Jonathan (2005): Automotive telematics: is it time for a renaissance or an obituary? In Mobile media. Content and services for wireless communications, edited by J. Groebel, E. M. Noam and V. Feldmann. Mahwah, NJ: Lawrence Erlbaum Associates (forthcoming).

Leclerc, France, and John D.C. Little (1997): Can advertising copy make FSI coupons more effective? Journal of Marketing 34.

Lehner, Franz (2001): Mobile Business und mobile Datendienste - eine Positionsbestimmung. Available from http://www-mobile.uni-regensburg.de/freiedokumente/berichte/mobile businessmobileservices.pdf.

Lehner, Franz (2003): Mobile und drahtlose Informationssysteme. Technologien, Anwendungen und Maerkte. Berlin: Springer.

Lehr, William, and Lee McKnight (2002): Wireless Internet access: 3G vs. WiFi?

Lehr, William, and Lee McKnight (2004): Drahtloser Internet-Zugang: 3G oder WiFi? In E-merging media. Kommunikation und Medienwirtschaft der Zukunft, edited by A. Zerdick, A. Picot, K. Schrape, J. C. Burgelman, R. Silverstone, V. Feldmann, D. Heger, K. and C. Wolff. Heidelberg: Springer, 175-194.

Lehr, William, Fuencisla Merino, and Sharon Gillett (2002): Software radio: implications for wireless services, industry structure, and public policy. Available from http://itc.mit.edu/itel/docs/2002/Software_Radio_Lehr_Fuencis.pdf.

Lessig, Lawrence (1999): Code and other laws of cyberspace. New York: Basic Books.

Lessig, Lawrence (2001): The future of ideas: the fate of the commons in a connected world. New York: Random House.

Leung, Louis (1998): Lifestyles and the use of new media technology in urban China. Telecommunication Policy 22 (9):781-790.

Leung, Louis, and Ran Wei (1998): The gratifications of pager use: sociability, information seeking, entertainment, utility, and fashion and status. Telematics and Informatics 15:253-264.

Leung, Louis, and Ran Wei (2000): More than just talk on the move: uses and gratifications of the cellular phone. Journalism & Mass Communication Quarterly 77 (2):308-320.

Lévy, Pierre (1997): Die kollektive Intelligenz. Eine Anthropologie des Cyberspace. Mannheim: Bollmann.

Liebowitz, Stan (2002): Re-thinking the network economy. True forces that drive the digital marketplace. New York: AMACOM.

Lin, Carolyn A. (2002): Perceived gratifications of online media service use among potential users. Telematics and Informatics 19:3-19.

Lin, Carolyn A., and Leo W. Jeffres (2001): Comparing distinctions and similarities across websites of newspapers, radio stations, and television stations. Journalism & Mass Communication Quarterly 78 (3):555-573.

Ling, Richard (1997): One can talk about common manners!: the youth of mobile telephony in inappropriate situations. In Themes in mobile telephony. Final report of the COST 248 Home and Work Group, edited by L. Haddon: Telia.

Ling, Richard (2002): The social juxtaposition of mobile telephone conversations and public spaces. Paper presented at 'The social consequences of mobile telephones', at Chunchon, Korea, July 2002. Available from http://www.telenor.no/fou/program/nomadiske/articles/rich/(2001)Mobile.pdf.

Ling, Richard, and Leslie Haddon (2001): Mobile telephony, mobility and the coordination of everyday life. Paper presented at 'Machines That Become Us' Conference, at Rutgers University, New Jersey, April 18-19. Available from http://www.telenor.no/fou/program/nomadiske/articles/rich/(2001)Mobile.pdf.

Loew, Martina (2001): Raumsoziologie. Frankfurt a.M.: Suhrkamp.

Loken, Barbara, and Deborah Roedder John (1993): Diluting brand beliefs: when do brand extensions have a negative impact? Journal of Marketing 57:71 - 84.

Longino, Carlo (July 17, 2003): Dead on arrival? The Feature.
Available from http://www.thefeature.com/articel?articleid=44768.

Ludwig, Johannes (1998): Zur Oekonomie der Medien: zwischen Marktversagen und Querfinanzierung. Opladen: Westdeutscher Verlag.

Mahler, Alwin, and Everett M. Rogers (1999): The diffusion of interactive communication innovations and the critical mass: the adoption of telecommunciations services by German Banks. Telecommunication Policy 23:719-740.

Maier-Rabler, Ursula (1992): In sense of space: Ueberlegungen zur Operationalisierung des Raumbegriffs fuer die Kommunikationswissenschaft. In Zeit, Raum, Kommunikation, edited by W. Hoemberg and M. Schmolke. Muenchen: Oelschlaeger, 357-370.

Maitland, Carleen F. (2005): Mobile commerce business models and network formation. In Mobile media. Content and services for wireless communications, edited by J. Groebel, E. M. Noam and V. Feldmann. Mahwah, NJ: Lawrence Erlbaum Associates (forthcoming).

Maitland, Carleen F., Johannes M. Bauer, and Rudi Westerveld (2002): The European market for mobile data: evolving value chains and industry structures. Telecommunication Policy (26):485-504.

Malerba, Franco (2004): Sectoral systems of innovation: concepts, issues and anlyses of six major sectors in Europe. Cambridge: Cambridge University Press.

Mansell, Robin, and Roger Silverstone, (Eds.) (1996a): Communication by design: the politics of information and communication technologies. Oxford: Oxford University Press.

Mansell, Robin, and Roger Silverstone (1996b): Introduction. In Communication by design: the politics of information and communication technologies, edited by R. Mansell and R. Silverstone. Oxford: Oxford University Press, 1-14.

Mansell, Robin, and W. Edward Steinmueller (2002): Mobilizing the information society. Strategies for growth and opportunity. Oxford: Oxford University Press.

Mariano, Gwendolyn (January 28, 2002): BMG to offer tunes on the go. CNet News.com. Available from http://news.com.com/2100-1023-824668.html.

Markoff, John (June 30, 2003): Global partnership puts RealNetworks's media player on Vodafone handsets. The New York Times.

Markoff, John (March 4, 2002): The corner Internet network vs. the cellular giants. The New York Times.

Martinez, J. Antonio Diaz (2000): Social trends of the information and communication technologies in Spain. Futures 32:669-678.

Marvin, Carolyn (1988): When old technologies were new: thinking about electric communication in the late nineteenth century. New York: Oxford University Press.

Mason-Schrock, Douglas (1996): Transsexuals' narrative construction of the 'true self'. Social Psychology Quarterly 59 (3):176-192.

Mateos-Garcia, Juan, and W. Edward Steinmueller (2003): The Open Source way of working: a new paradigm for the division of labour in software development? INK Open Source Re-

search Working Paper No. 1. Available from
http://www.uni-bocconi.it/ doc_mime_view.php?doc=id18767&doc_seg_id=1.

Mattern, Friedemann (2004): Ubiquitous computing: Szenarien einer informatisierten Welt. In E-merging media. Kommunikation und Medienwirtschaft der Zukunft, edited by A. Zerdick, A. Picot, K. Schrape, J. C. Burgelman, R. Silverstone, V. Feldmann, D. Heger, K. and C. Wolff. Heidelberg: Springer, 155-174.

McAfee, R.P., J. McMillan, and M.D. Whinston (1989): Multiproduct monopoly, commodity bundling, and correlation of values. Quarterly Journal of Economics 114 (May):371-384.

McDonough, Dan (August 22, 2001): MTV walks on wireless side with Music Award ads Wireless NewsFactor. Available from http://www.wirelessnewsfactor.com/perl/story/ 13009.html.

McDonough, Dan (May 24, 2002): Prepaid entertainment content coming to mobile phones Wireless NewsFactor. Available from http://www.wirelessnewsfactor.com/perl/story /17903.html.

McInnes, Ian, Janusz Moneta, Julio Caraballo, and Dominic Sarni (2002): Business models for mobile content: the case of m-games. Electronic Markets 12 (4). Available from http://www.electronicmarkets.org/modules/pub/view.php/electronicmarkets-420.

McKelvey, B. (1982): Organizational systematics: taxonomy, evolution, classification. Berkeley: University of California Press.

McKenna, Regis (1997): Real time: preparing for the age of the never satisfied customer. Boston: Harvard Business School Press.

McKie-Mason, J., S. Shenker, and Hal R. Varian (1996): Service architecture and content provision: the network provider as editor.

McKnight, Lee, Diana Anius, and Ozlem Uzuner (2002): Virtual markets in wireless grids: peering policy obstacles. Available from http://www.ai.mit.edu/~ozlem/tprc-wirelessGrid-uzuner.PDF.

McKnight, Lee, Raymond Linsenmayer, and William Lehr (2002): Best effort versus spectrum markets: wideband and Wi-Fi versus 3G MVNO? Available from http://itc.mit.edu/ itel/docs/2002/best_effort_v_spectrum.pdf.

McLuhan, Marshall (2001): Understanding media. The extensions of man. 9th ed. Cambridge, MA: MIT Press. Originally published 1964.

McMahon, Tamsin (May 30, 2002): European parliament accepts privacy law Europemedia.net. Available from http://www.europemedia.net/shownews.asp?ArticleID=10749&Print=true.

McQuail, Denis (1990): Telephone as an object of communication and social research. In Telefon und Gesellschaft Band 2: Internationaler Vergleich - Sprache und Telefon - Seelsorge und Beratungsdienste - Telefoninterviews, edited by Forschungsgruppe Telekommunikation. Berlin: Volker Spiess, 132-143.

McQuail, Denis (1999): The future of communication theory. In Die Zukunft der Kommunikation: Phaenomene und Trends in der Informationsgesellschaft, edited by M. Latzer, U. Maier-Rabler, G. Siegert and T. Steinmaurer. Innsbruck; Vienna: Studienverlag, 11-24.

McQuail, Denis (2000): McQuail's mass communication theory. Fourth ed. London: Sage Publications.

McQuail, Denis (2001): Looking to the future. In Media policy. Convergence, concentration and commerce, edited by D. McQuail and K. Siune. London: Sage Publications, 218-224.

Mead, George Herbert (1934): Mind, self and society: from the standpoint of a social behaviorist. Chicago: University of Chicago Press.

Meckel, Miriam (1999): Redaktionsmanagement. Ansaetze aus Theorie und Praxis. Opladen: Westdeutscher Verlag.

Meckel, Miriam (2005): Always on demand - the digital future of communication. In Mobile media. Content and services for wireless communications, edited by J. Groebel, E. M. Noam and V. Feldmann. Mahwah, NJ: Lawrence Erlbaum Associates (forthcoming).

Meffert, Heribert (1999): Wandel in der Markenfuehrung - vom instrumentellen zum identitaetsorientierten Markenverstaendnis. In Strategien zur Profilierung von Marken, edited by H. Meffert. Wiesbaden: Gabler, 287-312.

Meffert, Heribert, Andreas Bierwirth, and Christoph Burmann (2002): Gestaltung der Markenarchitektur als markenstrategische Basisentscheidung. In Markenmanagement. Grundfragen der identitaetsorientierten Markenfuehrung, edited by H. Meffert, C. Burmann and M. Koers. Wiesbaden: Gabler, 167-180.

Meffert, Heribert, and Christoph Burmann (2002): Theoretisches Grundkonzept der identitaetsorientierten Markenfuehrung. In Markenmanagement. Grundfragen der identitaetsorientierten Markenfuehrung, edited by H. Meffert, C. Burmann and M. Koers. Wiesbaden: Gabler, 35-72.

Meffert, Heribert, and Gerrit Heinemann (1990): Operationalisierung des Imagetransfers: Begrenzung des Transferrisikos durch ıhnlichkeitsmessungen. Marketing ZFP (1):5-10.

Meffert, Heribert, and Jesko Perrey (2002): Mehrmarkenstrategien - identitaetsorientierte Fuehrung von Markenportfolios. In Markenmanagement. Grundfragen der identitaetsorientierten Markenfuehrung, edited by H. Meffert, C. Burmann and M. Koers. Wiesbaden: Gabler, 167-180.

Mills, Casey (November 4, 2002): Vote 4 me 2day. Red Herring. Available from http:// www. redherring.com/insider/2002/11/sms_voting110402.html.

Motorola (March 12, 2003): MTV and Motorola rock the mobile world with three-year $75 million alliance. Available from http://www.motorola.com/mediacenter/news/detail/ 0,1958,2489_2027_23,00.html.

Mueller, Christian D., Peter Aschmoneit, and Hans-Dieter Zimmermann (2002): Der Einfluss von "Mobile" auf das Management von Kundenbeziehungen und Personalisierung von Produkten und Dienstleistungen. In Mobile Kommunikation. Wertschoepfung, Technologien, neue Dienste, edited by R. Reichwald. Wiesbaden: Gabler, 353-377.

Mueller-Kalthoff, Bjoern (2002a): Cross-media als integrierte Management-Aufgabe. In Cross-media Management: Content Strategien erfolgreich umsetzen, edited by B. Mueller-Kalthoff. Berlin: Springer, 19-40.

Mueller-Kalthoff, Bjoern, (Ed.) (2002b): Cross-media Management: Content Strategien erfolgreich umsetzen. Berlin: Springer.

Muniz, Albert M. Jr., and Thomas C. O'Guinn (2001): Brand community. Journal of Consumer Research Vol. 27 (March 2001):412-432.

Murray, Janet (1995): The pedagogy of cyberfiction: teaching a course on reading and writing interactive narrative. In Contextual media. Multimedia and interpretation, edited by E. Barret and M. Redmond. Cambridge, MA: The MIT Press.

Murray, Janet, and Henry Jenkins (1999): Before the holodeck: tracing Star Trek through digital media. In On a silver platter: CD-Roms and the promises of a new technology, edited by G. Smith. New York: New York University Press.

Myerson, George (2001): Heidegger, Habermas and the mobile phone. Cambridge: Icon Books.

N.N. (2001a): "Everyone is wrong." A conversation with Martin Cooper. Technology Review (June):83-86.

N.N. (2001b): Teletext - das unterschaetzte Medium. Media Perspektiven (2):54-64.

N.N. (2001c): Why mobile is different. The Economist,October 11, 2001.

N.N. (2002): Disney bringt Inhalte auf's Handy. w&v online. Available from http://www. wuv.de/news/article/2002/09/00713/index.html.

N.N. (2003a): Gaming's new frontier. The Economist,October 4-10, 65.

N.N. (2003b): Mobile research: user patterns in downloading ringing tones. Japan Mobile Marketing Magazine, September 10, 2003. Available from http://www.d2c.co.jp/english/ magazine_e/issue/1.html#5.

N.N. (2003c): Warner Bros. vergibt mobile Exklusivlizenz fuer Looney Tunes an Buongiorno. w&v online.

N.N. (April 4, 2002): 4G - beyond 2.5G and 3G wireless networks Mobile Info. Available from http://www.mobileinfo.com/3G/4GVision%26Technologies.htm.

N.N. (April 12, 2002): 3D for 3G 3G.co.uk. Available from http://www.3g.co.uk/PR/April2002/ 3148.htm.

N.N. (April 19, 2002): 3G digital content costs cut 3G.co.uk. Available from http://www.3g.co.uk/PR/April2002/3203.htm.

N.N. (April 25, 2003): Video streaming service for 3G FOMA phones www.3G.co.uk. Available from http://www.3g.co.uk/PR/April2003/5281.htm.

N.N. (August 9, 2002): Handy-Klingeltoene duerfen nicht mehr als drei Euro kosten. w&v online.

N.N. (August 15, 2002): O2 launch wireless Men in Black2 game 3G.co.uk. Available from http://www.3g.co.uk/PR/August2002/3912.htm.

N.N. (August 16, 2002): MTV und Reuters sind die wertvollsten Medienmarken. w&v online.

N.N. (August 18, 2000): Web music copyright wrangle is going mobile. Ananova. Available from http://www.ftd.de/tm/in/FTDVIOE33GC.html.

N.N. (August 20, 2003): Lara Croft goes wireless 3G.co.uk.
Available from http://www.3g.co.uk/PR/August2003/5743.htm.

N.N. (February 19, 2003): Ericsson und Sony starten mobile Download-Plattform. <e>Market. Available from http://www.wuv.de/static/news/84854.html.

N.N. (February 20, 2003): Operators to deliver 3GPP formats, RealAudio and RealVideo www.3G.co.uk. Available from http://www.3g.co.uk/PR/Feb2003/4928.htm.

N.N. (February 25, 2003): 3G mobiles in UK get ITN video news www.3G.co.uk. Available from http://www.3g.co.uk/PR/Feb2003/4948.htm.

N.N. (January 8, 2003): Sprint, Warner partner on cell ring tones Reuters. Available from http://lists/fiercemarkets.com/ct.html?s=69l,1jed,8mg,ebpr,7fch,d6on,lf4g.

N.N. (January 16, 2003): J-PHONE Sha-mail wireless handsets top 8 million www.3G.co.uk. Available from http://www.3g.co.uk/PR/Jan2003/4725.htm.

N.N. (January 29, 2003): Reuters to feed 3G mobiles www.3G.co.uk.
Available from http://www.3g.co.uk/PR/Jan2003/4796.htm.

N.N. (July 2, 2002): Popstar takes wireless to a new level 3G.co.uk.
Available from http://www.3g.co.uk/PR/July2002/3684.htm.

N.N. (July 7, 2003a): MTV und Motorola starten crossmediale Show. <e>Market.
Available from http://www.wuv.de/static/news/84854.html.

N.N. (July 7, 2003b): T-Mobile lines up video news www.3G.co.uk.
Available from http://www.3g.co.uk/PR/July2003/5587.htm.

N.N. (July 10, 2002): Barcode transactions in a flash with camera-enabled wireless handsets 3G.co.uk. Available from http://www.3g.co.uk/PR/July2002/3721.htm.

N.N. (July 15, 2002): Dashed digital dreams. Business Week.
Available from http://www.wuv.de/news/article/2002/09/00713/index.html.

N.N. (July 16, 2002): Classic video games come to wireless phones 3G.co.uk. Available from http://www.3g.co.uk/PR/July2002/3738.htm.

N.N. (July 21, 2003): World's first mobile phone for terrestrial digital TV 3G.co.uk. Available from http://www.3g.co.uk/PR/July2003/5647.htm.

N.N. (July 25, 2002): Scooby dooby do goes wireless 3G.co.uk.
Available from http://www.3g.co.uk/PR/July2002/3789.htm.

N.N. (July 28, 2003): Disney in talks with wireless firms Reuters.
Available from http://stacks.msnbc.com/news/944962.asp?cp1=1.

N.N. (June 13, 2002): NBC beams new shows on handhelds Reuters.

N.N. (June 21, 2002): Brand's the thing for new mobile service Internetnews.com. Available from http://www.internetnews.com/IAR/article.php/1369541.

N.N. (June 23, 2003): T-Mobile vermarktet '3 Engel fuer Charlie'. <e>Market. Available from http://www.wuv.de/static/news/84854.html.

N.N. (March 3, 2003a): 3G movie previews kick off in UK www.3G.co.uk. Available from http://www.3g.co.uk/PR/March2003/4979.htm.

N.N. (March 3, 2003b): Vodafone live! more wireless games www.3G.co.uk. Available from http://www.3g.co.uk/PR/March2003/4975.htm.

N.N. (March 7, 2003): T-Mobile announces partnership with Universal Music www.3G.co.uk. Available from http://www.3g.co.uk/PR/March2003/5006.htm.

N.N. (March 14, 2003): 2.5G wireless music trial in UK www.3G.co.uk. Available from http://www.3g.co.uk/PR/March2003/5051.htm.

N.N. (May 1, 2003): South Park goes wireless www.3G.co.uk. Available from http://www.3g.co.uk/PR/April2003/5302.htm.

N.N. (May 2, 2002): Celebrity images on your wireless phone 3G.co.uk. Available from http://www.3g.co.uk/PR/May2002/3300.htm.

N.N. (May 7, 2002): World's first folding dual-displayed wireless phone with FM radio 3G.co.uk. Available from http://www.3g.co.uk/PR/May2002/3322.htm.

N.N. (May 15, 2002): DoCoMo to introduce online bar code for paying phone bill Dow Jones Newswires. Available from http://sg.biz.yahoo.com/020515/15/2pjnu.html.

N.N. (May 23, 2002): Men in Black II comes to wireless 3G.co.uk. Available from http://www.3g.co.uk/PR/May2002/3430.htm.

N.N. (May 30, 2003): Sina, Bandai to launch mobile cartoons in China. Available from http://www.pmn.co.uk/20030530sina.shtml.

N.N. (November 18, 2002): James Bond on your mobile - in wireless colour, pictures and sound 3G.co.uk. Available from http://www.3g.co.uk/PR/November2002/4429.htm.

N.N. (November 23, 2002): Nokia v Microsoft: the fight for digital dominance. The Economist, 67-69.

N.N. (November 28, 2000): Bertelsmann will Produkte ueber UMTS-Netz verkaufen. Financial Times Deutschland. Available from http://www.ftd.de/tm/in/FTDVIOE33GC.html.

N.N. (October 9, 2002): Single licence for Internet music 'simulcast' EUbusiness.com. Available from http://www.eubusiness.com/cgi-bin/item.cgi?id=92856&cu=7c4eD51&km=4244.

N.N. (October 28, 2002): James Bond takes Sony Ericsson wireless phones 3G.co.uk. Available from http://www.3g.co.uk/PR/October2002/4312.htm.

N.N. (September 9, 2003): CNN for i-mode wireless 3G.co.uk. Available from http://www.3g.co.uk/PR/Sept2003/5810.htm.

N.N. (September 23, 2003): 3G Jackass 3G.co.uk.
Available from http://www. 3g.co.uk/PR/Sept2003/5867.htm.

N.N. (September 25, 2002): Finland launches mobile phone movie service Reuters.

Nalebuff, Barry J., and Adam M. Brandenburger (1997): Co-opetition. London: HarperCollinsBusiness.

Nausner, Peter (2000): Medienmanagement als Entwicklungs- und Innovationsmanagement. In Grundlagen des Medienmanagements, edited by M. Karmasin and C. Winter. Muenchen: Fink, 115-148.

Negroponte, Nicholas (1995): Being digital. New York: Alfred A. Knopf.

Neuberger, Christoph (2000): Massenmedien im Internet 1999. Media Perspektiven (3):102-109.

NFO Infratest, and IIE (2003): Monitoring information economics im Auftrag des Bundesministerium fuer Wirtschaft und Arbeit. Available from http://www.bmwa.bund.de/redaktion/inhalte/downloads/6-faktenbericht-vollversion,property=pdf.pdf.

Nichols, Michelle (January 9, 2002): Networks hit back at mobile phone crime report. Available from http://www.thescotsman.co.uk/uk.cfm?id=28242002.

Nie, Norman H., and Lutz Erbring (2002): Internet and mass media: a preliminary report. IT & Society 1 (2):134-141.

Noam, Eli M. (1998): Spectrum auctions: yesterday's heresy, today's orthodoxy, tomorrow's anachronism. Taking the next step to open spctrum access. Journal of Law and Economics 56 (2):765-790.

Noam, Eli M. (2000): Meeting on the organization of the 'Transatlantic Dialogue 2001/02', personal communication with V. Feldmann, New York, December 16, 2000.

Noam, Eli M. (2001): Interconnecting the networks of networks. Cambridge, Massachusetts: MIT Press.

Noam, Eli M. (2005): Access of content to mobile wireless: opening the "walled airwave". In Mobile media. Content and services for wireless communications, edited by J. Groebel, E. M. Noam and V. Feldmann. Mahwah, NJ: Lawrence Erlbaum Associates (forthcoming).

Nobe, Grant (1989): Towards a 'uses and gratifications' of the domestic telephone. In Telefon und Gesellschaft: Beitraege zu einer Soziologie der Telekommunikation, edited by Forschungsgruppe Telekommunikation. Berlin: Spiess, 298-307.

Noesekabel, Holger, and Franz Lehner (2002): Integration von web- und mobilbasierten Diensten. In Mobile Kommunikation. Wertschoepfung, Technologien, neue Dienste, edited by R. Reichwald. Wiesbaden: Gabler, 127-144.

Nokia (2001): Digital rights management and superdistribution of mobile content White Paper. Available from http://www.uow.edu.au/~quong/papers/mobile_drm_whitepaper.pdf.

North, D.C. (1990): Institutions, institutional change and economic performance. Cambridge: Cambridge University Press.

Novak, Thomas P., Donna L. Hoffman, and Yiu-Fai Yung (2000): Measuring the customer experience in online environments: a structural modeling approach. Marketing Science 19 (1):22-44.

Obstfeld, Mark (September 25, 2002): SMS TV market brings in the revenue but faces challenges Europemedia.net. Available from http://www.europemedia.net/showfeature.asp?ArticleID=12767.

Odlyzko, Andrew (2001a): Internet pricing and the history of communications. In Internet Services, edited by L. McKnight and J. Wroclawski. Cambridge, MA: MIT Press. Available from http://www.dtc.umn.edu/~odlyzko/doc/history.communications1b.pdf, last seen 03/27/02.

Odlyzko, Andrew (2001b): Talk, talk, talk: so who needs streaming video on a phone? The killer app for 3G may turn out to be--surprise--voice calls.

ODTR (2002): A framework for value-added text messaging services. Available from http://www.odtr.ie/docs/odtr0214.doc.

Oehmichen, Ekkehardt, and Christian Schroeter (2002): Zur Habitualisierung der Onlinenutzung. Media Perspektiven (8):376-388.

Oehmichen, Ekkehardt, and Christian Schroeter (2003): Funktionswandel der Massenmedien durch das Internet? Media Perspektiven (8):374-384.

Ofta (2002): Inter-operator SMS - the regulator's perspective. Available from http://www.ofta.gov.hk/speech-presentation/ddg_2002_1_15.pdf.

OFTEL (2002): An evaluation of the proposition that regulation of call termination charges would weaken competition in the retail mobile market (August 30, 2002).

Oh, Christopher Jungsuk, and Suk-Gwon Chang (2000): Incentives for strategic vertical alliances in online information product markets. Information Economics and Policy (12):155-180.

Olderog, Torsten, and Bernd Skiera (2000): The benefits of bundling strategies. Schmalenbach Business Review 52 (April 2000):137-159.

Olsen, Stephanie, and Evan Hansen (April 7, 2003): Disney preps wireless video service. CNet News.com. Available from http://new.com.com/2100-1031-995846.html.

Ott, Klaus (September 14, 2002): Rundfunkgebuehr fuer UMTS-Handys. Sueddeutsche Zeitung.

Owen, Bruce M., and Steven S. Wildman (1992): Video economics. Cambridge, Massachusetts: Harvard Business Press.

Palen, Leysia, Marilyn Salzman, and Ed Youngs (2000): Going wireless: behavior and practice of new mobile phone users. Available from http://www.cs.colorado.edu/%7Epalen/Papers/cscwPalen.pdf.

Palmer, Jonathan W., and Lars Eriksen (1999): Digital news - paper, broadcast and more convergence on the Internet. JMM - The International Journal on Media Management 1 (1):31-34.

Palmgreen, Philip (1985): An expectancy-value approach to media gratifications. In Media gratification research: current perspectives, edited by K. E. Rosengren, L. A. Wenner and P. Palmgreen. Beverly Hills, CA: Sage, 61-72.

Papadopouli, Maria, and Henning Schulzrinne (2001): Performance of data dissemination among mobile devices. Available from http://www1.cs.columbia.edu/~library/TR-repository/reports/reports-2001/cucs-005-01.pdf.

Pavlik, John V., and Shawn McIntosh (2005): Mobile news design and delivery. In Mobile media. Content and services for wireless communications, edited by J. Groebel, E. M. Noam and V. Feldmann. Mahwah, NJ: Lawrence Erlbaum Associates (forthcoming).

Pease, Edward C., and Everette E. Dennis (1994): Radio - the forgotten medium. New Brunswick: Transaction Publishers.

Pedersen, P.E., and H. Nysveen (2003): Usefulness and self-expressiveness: extending TAM to explain the adoption of a mobile parking service. Paper presented at 16th Electronic Commerce Conference, at Bled, Slovenia, June 9-11.

Pedersen, P.E., H. Nysveen, and H. Thorbjørnsen (2003): Identity expression in the adoption of mobile services: The case of multimedia messaging services SNF Working Paper No. 26/03. Foundation for Research in Economics and Business Administration.

Peha, Jon M., and Sooksan Panichpapiboon (2003): Real-time secondary markets for spectrum. Paper presented at TPRC, at Alexandria, VA. Available from http://intel.si.umich.edu/tprc/papers/2003/208/realtimesecondarymkt.pdf.

Pérez Saiz, Hector, Juan Miguel De Sande Caldera, and Luis Castejón Martín (2002): MVNO regulation: weak or strong? Lessons from experience. Paper presented at ITS Europe. Available from http://userpage.fu-berlin.de/~jmueller/its/madrid/program/papers/PerezSaiz.pdf.

Persson, Torsten, and Guido Tabellini (2002): Political economics. Explaining economic policy. Cambridge, MA: The MIT Press.

Pflug, Volkmar, and Felix Meyer (2002): Ortsbezogene mobile Dienste - Wertschoepfung und praktische Beispiele. In Mobile Kommunikation. Wertschoepfung, Technologien, neue Dienste, edited by R. Reichwald. Wiesbaden: Gabler, 399-415.

Phillips, Leigh (June 2, 2003): MTV becomes latest Swedish operator Europemedia.net. Available from http://www.europemedia.net/shownews.asp?ArticleID=16530.

Picard, Robert (1989): Media economics: concepts and issues. Newbury Park, CA: Sage.

Picard, Robert (2000): Changing business models of online content services. JMM - The International Journal on Media Management 2 (2):60-68.

Picard, Robert, (Ed.) (2002): Media firms: structures, operations and performance. Mahwah, New Jersey: Lawrence Erlbaum Associates.

Picot, Arnold, and Dominik Heger, K. (2004): Braucht das Internet eine neue Wettbewerbspolitik? - Ein globales Problem aus deutscher Perspektive. In E-merging media. Kommunikation und Medienwirtschaft der Zukunft, edited by A. Zerdick, A. Picot, K. Schrape, J. C. Burgelman, R. Silverstone, V. Feldmann, D. Heger, K. and C. Wolff. Heidelberg: Springer, 343-360.

Picot, Arnold, and Rahild Neuburger (2002): Mobile Business - Erfolgsfaktoren und Voraussetzungen. In Mobile Kommunikation. Wertschoepfung, Technologien, neue Dienste, edited by R. Reichwald. Wiesbaden: Gabler, 55-70.

Picot, Arnold, Ralf Reichwald, and R. Wigand (2003): Die grenzenlose Unternehmung - Information, Organisation und Management: Lehrbuch zur Unternehmensfuehrung im Informationszeitalter. Wiesbaden: Gabler.

Pierce, John R. (1977): The telephone and society in the past 100 years. In The social impact of the telephone, edited by I. de Sola Pool. Boston, MA: MIT Press.

Pine, Joseph B. II (1993): Mass customization: the new frontier in business competition. Boston: Harvard Business School Press.

Plant, Sadie (2000): On the mobile - the effects of mobile telephones on social and individual life. Available from http://www.motorola.com/mot/documents/0,1028,296,00.pdf.

Poblocki, Kacper (2001): The Napster Music Community. First Monday Volume 6 (Number 11 (November 2001)). Available from http://firstmonday.org/issues/issue6_11/poblocki/index.html.

Pogue, David (February 27, 2003): Keeping an eye on things, by cellphone. The New York Times.

Popper, Karl R. (2000a): Prognose und Prophetie in den Sozialwissenschaften. In Vermutungen und Widerlegungen: das Wachstum der wissenschaftlichen Erkenntnis, edited by K. R. Popper. Tuebingen: Mohr Siebeck, 487-503.

Popper, Karl R. (2000b): Vermutungen und Widerlegungen: das Wachstum der wissenschaftlichen Erkenntnis. Tuebingen: Mohr Siebeck.

Porter, Michael E. (1980): Competitive strategy. New York: Free Press.

Porter, Michael E. (1985): Competitive advantage. New York: Free Press.

Powell, Michael (2002): Broadband migration III: New directions in wireless policy Speech delivered at the University of Colorado at Boulder, October 30, 2002. Available from http://ftp.fcc.gov/Speeches/Powell/2002/spmkp212.html.

Raff, Fritz (2002): Online heute aus der Sicht der ARD. Media Perspektiven (3):117-120.

Raja, Siddhartha, and Francois Bar (2003): Transition paths in a spectrum commons regime. Paper presented at TPRC, at Alexandria, VA. Available from http://intel.si.umich.edu/tprc/papers/2003/235/raja-bar-tprc2003.pdf.

Rangaswamy, Arvind, and Sunil Gupta (1998): Innovation adoption and diffusion in the digital environment: some research opportunities. Available from http://www.ebrc.psu.edu/publications/papers/pdf/1999_02.pdf.

Rawolle, Joachim, and Thomas Hess (2000): New digital media and devices. An analysis for the media industry. JMM - The International Journal on Media Management 2 (2):89-98.

Rawolle, Joachim, Stefan Kirchfeld, and Thomas Hess (2002): Zur Integration mobiler und stationaerer Online-Dienste der Medienindustrie. In Mobile Kommunikation. Wertschoepfung, Technologien, neue Dienste, edited by R. Reichwald. Wiesbaden: Gabler, 335-352.

Reed II, Americus (2002): Social identity as a useful perspective for self-concept-based consumer research. Psychology & Marketing 19 (3):235-266.

RegTP (2003): RegTP News Nr. 1/03. Available from http://www.regtp.de/imperia/md/content/aktuelles/regtpnews/regtpnews200301.pdf.

Reichwald, Ralf, Natalie Fremuth, and Michael Ney (2002): Mobile communities - Erweiterung von Virtuellen Communities mit mobilen Diensten. In Mobile Kommunikation. Wertschoepfung, Technologien, neue Dienste, edited by R. Reichwald. Wiesbaden: Gabler, 521-538.

Reichwald, Ralf, and Roland Meier (2002): Generierung von Kundenwert mit mobilen Diensten. In Mobile Kommunikation. Wertschoepfung, Technologien, neue Dienste, edited by R. Reichwald. Wiesbaden: Gabler, 207-230.

Reichwald, Ralf, Roland Meier, and Natalie Fremuth (2002): Die mobile Oekonomie - Definition und Spezifika. In Mobile Kommunikation. Wertschoepfung, Technologien, neue Dienste, edited by R. Reichwald. Wiesbaden: Gabler, 3-18.

Reichwald, Ralf, Michael Ney, and Michael Wagner (2002): Kundenintegrierte Entwicklung mobiler Dienste. In Mobile Kommunikation. Wertschoepfung, Technologien, neue Dienste, edited by R. Reichwald. Wiesbaden: Gabler, 301-316.

Reichwald, Ralf, and Christian Schaller (2002): M-Loyalty - Kundenbindung durch personalisierte mobile Dienste. In Mobile Kommunikation. Wertschoepfung, Technologien, neue Dienste, edited by R. Reichwald. Wiesbaden: Gabler, 263-288.

Reimers, Ulrich (2002): Online: Was ist technisch moeglich? Media Perspektiven (3):132-134.

Reinartz, Werner J., and V. Kumar (2000): On the profitability of long-life customers in a noncontractual setting: an empirical investigation and implications for marketing. Journal of Marketing (October):17-35.

Reitze, Helmut (2002): Online morgen aus der Sicht des ZDF. Media Perspektiven (3):135-139.

Rheingold, Howard (2002): Smart mobs - the next social revolution. Cambridge: Perseus.

Ridder, Christa-Maria (2002): Onlinenutzung in Deutschland. Media Perspektiven (3):121-131.

Riedel, Hergen H., and Andreas Schoo (2002): Cross-Media Management im Medienverbund von Print und Online: das Beispiel TV Movie. In Cross-media Management: Content Strategien erfolgreich umsetzen, edited by B. Mueller-Kalthoff. Berlin: Springer, 139-165.

Roberts, E.B. (1987): Managing technological innovation - a search for generalizations. In Generating technological innovations, edited by E. B. Roberts. New York/Oxford, 3-21.

Rogers, Everett M. (1995): Diffusion of innovations. 4 ed. New York: The Free Press.

Rohlfs, Jeffrey (2002): Efficient pricing with cross-elasticities, network externalities and a budget constraint with application to termination charges of mobile telecommunication operators. Available from http://userpage.fu-berlin.de/~jmueller/its/madrid/program/papers/Rohlfs.pdf.

Rook, Dennis W. (1987): The buying impulse. Journal of Consumer Research Vol. 14 (September):189-199.

Rosengren, Karl Erik (1974): Uses and Gratifications: A paradigm outlined. In The uses of mass communications: current perspectives on gratifications research, edited by J. G. Blumler and E. Katz. Beverly Hills, CA: Sage, 269-286.

Rosengren, Karl Erik, L.A. Wenner, and Philip Palmgreen, (Eds.) (1985): Media gratification research: current perspectives. Beverly Hills, CA: Sage.

Rubin, Alan M., and Charles R. Bantz (1989): Uses and gratifications of videocassette recorders. In Media use in the information age: emerging patterns of adoption and consumer use, edited by J. L. Salvaggio and J. Bryant. Hillsdale, NJ: Lawrence Erlbaum Associates, 181-195.

Rueter, Klaus (2002): Medienrechtliche und -politische Aspekte von Rundfunk online. Media Perspektiven (3):144-147.

Rust, Roland T., and Mark I. Alpert (1984): An audience flow model of television viewing choice. Marketing Science 3 (2):113-124.

Sabat, Hemant Kumar (2002): The evolving mobile wireless value chain and market structures. Telecommunication Policy (26):505-535.

Sadeh, Norman (2002): M-commerce. Technologies, services, and business models. New York: Wiley.

Saltzer, J.H., D.P. Reed, and D.D. Clark (1984): End-to-end arguments in system design. ACM Transactions in Computer Systems 2 (4):277-288.

Samsioe, Joergen, and Anette Samsioe (2002): Introduction to location based services - markets and technologies. In Mobile Kommunikation. Wertschoepfung, Technologien, neue Dienste, edited by R. Reichwald. Wiesbaden: Gabler, 417-438.

Samuelson, Pamela (2003): Intellectual property and the digital economy: why the anti-circumvention regulations need to be revised. Available from http://www.sims.berkeley.edu/~pam/papers/dmcapaper.pdf.

Samuelson, Pamela, and Hal R. Varian (2001): The 'new economy' and information technology policy.

Sandvig, Christian (2002): Communication infrastructure and innovation: the Internet as end-to-end network that isn't. Paper presented at Symposium for the next generation of leaders in science and technology policy, at Washington D.C.

Sandvig, Christian (2003): Assessing cooperative action in 802.11 networks. Paper presented at TPRC, at Alexandria, VA. Available from http://intel.si.umich.edu/tprc/papers/2003/229/AssessCoopAction.pdf.

Sassen, Saskia, (Ed.) (2002): Global networks, linked cities. New York: Routledge.Sarkar, Mitra Barun, Brian Butler, and Charles Steinfield (1996): Intermediaries and cybermediaries: a continuing role for mediating players in the electronic marketplace. Journal of Computer Mediated Communication 1 (3).

Sawhney, Harmeet (2003): WiFi networks and the reorganization of wireline-wireless relationship. Paper presented at TPRC, at Alexandria, VA. Available from http://intel.si.umich.edu/tprc/papers/2003/189/JayakarandSawhney.pdf.

Sawhney, Nitin (1998): Contextual awareness, messaging and communication in nomadic audio environments, Program in Media Arts and Sciences, School of Architecture and Planing, Massachusetts Institute of Technology, Boston. Available from http://www.media.mit.edu/~nitin/msthesis/www/thesis.html.

Sawhney, Nitin, and Chris Schmandt (2000): Nomadic radio: speech and audio interaction for contextual messaging in nomadic environments. ACM Transactions on Computer-Human Interaction 7 (3):353-383.

Schenk, Michael, and Joachim Donnerstag, (Eds.) (1989): Medienoekonomie. Einfuehrung in die Oekonomie der Informations- und Mediensysteme. Muenchen.

Schilcher, Mathaeus, and Ingo Deking (2002): Geoinformationen als Basisbausteine fuer mobile Services. In Mobile Kommunikation. Wertschoepfung, Technologien, neue Dienste, edited by R. Reichwald. Wiesbaden: Gabler, 381-398.

Schlobinski, Peter, Nadine Fortmann, Olivia Gross, Florian Hogg, Frauke Horstmann, and Rena Theel (2001): Simsen. Eine Pilotstudie zu sprachlichen und kommunikativen Aspekten in der SMS-Kommunikation. Available from http://www.mediensprache.net/networx/networx-22.pdf.

Schmalensee, Richard (1984): Gaussian demand and commodity bundling. Journal of Business 57 (January):211-230.

Schmid, Beat F., and Katarina Stanoevska-Slabeva (2002): Towards successful m-commerce applications. St. Gallen.

Schneider, Irmela (1997): Medienwandel und Wandel durch Medien. Einige Anmerkungen. In Qualitative Perspektiven des Medienwandels, edited by H. Schanze and P. Ludes. Opladen: Westdeutscher Verlag, 95-105.

Schrape, Klaus (2004): Evolutionaere Perspektiven. In E-merging media. Kommunikation und Medienwirtschaft der Zukunft, edited by A. Zerdick, A. Picot, K. Schrape, J. C. Burgelman, R. Silverstone, V. Feldmann, D. Heger, K. and C. Wolff. Heidelberg: Springer, 219-230.

Schrape, Klaus, and Josef Trappel (2000): Evolution statt Revolution. Message (1):16-23.

Schumann, Matthias, and Thomas Hess (1999a): Content-Management fuer Online-Informationsangebote. In Medienunternehmen im digitalen Zeitalter: neue Technologien - neue Maerkte - neue Geschaeftsansaetze, edited by M. Schumann and T. Hess. Wiesbaden: Gabler, 69-87.

Schumann, Matthias, and Thomas Hess (1999b): Medienunternehmen im digitalen Zeitalter: neue Technologien - neue Maerkte - neue Geschaeftsansaetze. Wiesbaden: Gabler.

Schumann, Matthias, and Thomas Hess (2000): Grundfragen der Medienwirtschaft. Berlin: Springer.

Schumpeter, Joseph A. (1975): Capitalism, socialism and democracy. New York: Harper and Brothers. Originally published 1942.

Seiffert, Helmut (1996a): Einfuehrung in die Wissenschaftstheorie 1: Sprachanalyse - Deduktion - Induktion in Natur- und Sozialwissenschaften. 10th ed. Muenchen: C. H. Beck.

Seiffert, Helmut (1996b): Einfuehrung in die Wissenschaftstheorie 2: Geisteswissenscahftliche Methoden: Phaenomenologie - Hermeneutik und historische Methode - Dialektik. 10th ed. Muenchen: C. H. Beck.

Senge, Peter M., and Goran Carstedt (2001): Innovating our way to the next industrial revolution. MIT Sloan Management Review (Winter 2001):24-37.

Sewczyk, Juergen (2002): Online aus der Sicht eines kommerziellen Anbieters. Media Perspektiven (3):115-116.

Shapiro, Carl (1999): Competition policy in the information economy. Available from http://faculty.haas.berkeley.edu/shapiro/comppolicy.pdf.

Shapiro, Carl (2001): Navigating the patent thicket: cross licenses, patent pools, and standard-setting. In Innovation policy and the economy, edited by A. Jaffe, J. Lerner and S. Stern. Cambridge, MA: The MIT Press. Available from http://faculty.haas.berkeley.edu/shapiro/thicket.pdf.

Shapiro, Carl, and Hal R. Varian (1999): Information rules: a strategic guide to the network economy. Boston, MA: Harvard Business School Press.

Sherman, Erik (2001): Big little screen. Technology Review (June):65-69.

Siegert, Gabriele (2000): Medienmanagement als Marketingmanagement. In Grundlagen des Medienmanagements, edited by M. Karmasin and C. Winter. Muenchen: Fink, 173-198.

Siegert, Gabriele (2001): Medien Marken Management: Relevanz, Spezifika und Implikationen einer medienoekonomischen Profilierungsstrategie. Muenchen: Reinhard Fischer.

Siegrist, Hannes (2004): Geschichte und aktuelle Probleme des geistigen Eigentums (1600-2000). In E-merging media. Kommunikation und Medienwirtschaft der Zukunft, edited by A. Zerdick, A. Picot, K. Schrape, J. C. Burgelman, R. Silverstone, V. Feldmann, D. Heger, K. and C. Wolff. Heidelberg: Springer, 313-323.

Sigurdson, Jon (2001): WAP OFF - Origin, Failure and Future. Available from www.hhs.se/eijs/eastp.

Silberer, Guenter, Jens Wohlfahrt, and Thorsten H. Wilhelm (2001): Beziehungsmanagement im mobile commerce. In eCRM - Electronic Customer Relationship Management: Management der Kundenbeziehungen im Internet-Zeitalter, edited by A. Eggert. Stuttgart: Schaeffer-Poeschel, 212-227.

Silverstone, Roger (1999): Why study the media? London: Sage.

Silverstone, Roger (2004): Regulierung, Medienkompetenz und Medienbildung. In E-merging media. Kommunikation und Medienwirtschaft der Zukunft, edited by A. Zerdick, A. Picot, K. Schrape, J. C. Burgelman, R. Silverstone, V. Feldmann, D. Heger, K. and C. Wolff. Heidelberg: Springer, 373-388.

Silverstone, Roger, and Leslie Haddon (1998): Design and the domestication of information and communication technologies: technical change and everyday life. In Communication by design: the politics of communication and information technologies, edited by R. Mansell and R. Silverstone, 44-74.

Simonin, Bernhard L., and Julie A. Ruth (1998): Is a company known by the company it keeps? Assessing the spillover effects of brand alliances on consumer brand attitudes. Journal of Marketing Research 35 (February):30-42.

Sinn, Wolfgang (2002): Drahtlose Uebertragungswege und Zugangsmedien. In Mobile Kommunikation. Wertschoepfung, Technologien, neue Dienste, edited by R. Reichwald. Wiesbaden: Gabler, 113-126.

Sjurts, Insa (1996): Die deutsche Medienbranche. Eine unternehmensstrategische Analyse. Wiesbaden: Gabler.

Sjurts, Insa (2002a): Cross-media Strategien in der deutschen Medienbranche: eine oekonomische Analyse zu Varianten und Erfolgsaussichten. In Cross-media Management: Content Strategien erfolgreich umsetzen, edited by B. Mueller-Kalthoff. Berlin: Springer, 3-18.

Sjurts, Insa (2002b): Similarity despite variety: an economic explanation of the tendency towards standardization in the media markets, using Germany as an example. Paper presented at 5th World Media Economics Conference, at Turku, Finland.

Sloterdijk, Peter (2001): Welt-Ortsgespraeche. Anmerkungen zum Kultursinn von Mobilitaets- und Kommunikationstechnologien. In Zukunft mobile Kommunikation. Wirklichkeit und Vision einer technischen Revolution, edited by R. Lamprecht. Frankfurt a.M.: FAZ, 193-244.

Smith, Michael D., Joseph Bailey, and Erik Brynjolfsson (2000): Understanding digital markets: review and assessment. In Understanding the digital economy: data, tools, and research, edited by E. Brynjolfsson and B. Kahin. Cambridge, MA: MIT Press.

Smith, Tony (April 24, 2003): London's Soho to get blanket 802.11 cover for voice, data. The Register. Available from http://www.theregister.co.uk/content/59/30404.html.

Smits, Ruud (2002): Innovation studies in the 21st century: questions from a user's perspective. Technological Forecasting & Social Change 69:861-883.

Spitulnik, Debra (1993): Anthropology and mass media. Annual Review of Anthropology 22 (1993):293-315.

Stamer, Soeren (2002): Technologien als Enabler fuer effizientes cross-media publishing. In Cross-media Management: Content Strategien erfolgreich umsetzen, edited by B. Mueller-Kalthoff. Berlin: Springer, 89-121.

Standage, Tom (1998): The Victorian Internet: the remarkable story of the telegraph and the nineteenth century's on-line pioneers. New York: Berkley Books.

Standage, Tom (2003): Beyond the bubble. The Economist, October 11-17, 2003, 3-7.

Steemers, Jeanette (2001): Onlineaktivitaeten der BBC. Media Perspektiven (3):126-132.

Steinbock, Dan (2000): Building dynamic capabilities. The Wall Street Journal Interactive Edition: a successful online subscription model. JMM - The International Journal on Media Management 2 (III/ IV):178-194.

Steinbock, Dan (2001): The Nokia Revolution: the story of an extraordinary company that transformed an industry. New York: AMACOM.

Steiner, Florian (2002): M-Business - Chancenpotenziale eines Mobilfunkbetreibers. In Mobile Kommunikation. Wertschoepfung, Technologien, neue Dienste, edited by R. Reichwald. Wiesbaden: Gabler, 71-84.

Steinfield, Charles, and Junghyun Kim (2002): Providing location and context aware services for mobile commerce: technological approaches, applications, and policy issues. Paper presented at ITS 14th Biennial Conference, at Seoul, Korea. Available from http://www.its2002.or.kr/pdffiles/papers/174-Steinfield.pdf.

Stempel III, Guido H., and Robert K. Stewart (2000): The Internet provides both opportunities and challenges for mass communications research. Journalism & Mass Communication Quarterly 77 (3):541-548.

Stengel, Daniel (2004): Intellectual property in philosophy. Archiv fuer Rechts- und Sozialphilosophie 90 (1).

Stern, Hawkins (1962): The significance of impulse buying today. Journal of Marketing (April 1962):59-62.

Stipp, Horst (2000): Nutzung alter und neuer Medien in den USA. Media Perspektiven (3):127-134.

Stumpf, Ulrich, and Lorenz Nett (2003): Institutional arrangements for frequency trading WIK Consult. Available from http://www.wik.org/content/in_institut_arrangem_freque_trading.pdf.

Sutherland, Ewan (2001): International roaming charges: overcharging and competition law. Telecommunication Policy 25 (1/2):5-20.

Swartz, J. (2001): E-commerce and megamachines: identification, connectivity, and inference engines. Technology in Society 23:159-175.

Takenaka, Kyoshi (June 3, 2002): DoCoMo cameraphone to use Sony's Memory Stick. Reuters. Available from http://www.reuters.com/news_article?type=search&storyID=1040646.

Tanenbaum, Andrew S. (2002): Computer networks. 4th ed. Upper Saddle River, NJ: Prentice Hall PTR.

Tannenbaum, Percy H. (1956): Initial attitude toward source and concept as factors in attitude change through communication. Public Opinion Quarterly 20 (2):413-425.

Tannenbaum, Percy H. (1990): The individual in social and technical networks. In Telefon und Gesellschaft Band 2: Internationaler Vergleich - Sprache und Telefon - Seelsorge und Beratungsdienste - Telefoninterviews, edited by Forschungsgruppe Telekommunikation. Berlin: Volker Spiess, 124-131.

Taylor, A. S., and R. Harper (2001): Talking 'activity': young people and mobile phones. Paper presented at CHI 2001 Workshop, Mobile communications: understanding users, adoption and design, at Boulder, Colorado, April 1-2. Available from http://www.cs.colorado.edu/~palen/chi_workshop/papers/taylorharper.pdf.

Taylor, A. S., and R. Harper (2003): The gift of the gab: a design oriented sociology of young people's use of mobiles. Journal of Computer Supported Cooperative Work 12 (3):267-296. Available from http://www.surrey.ac.uk/~hus1at/Files/Gift_of_the_gab.pdf.

Thorngren, Bertil (2001): Why 'seamless' is important right now. Available from http://www.dsv.su.se/~mab/ThorngrenTone.html.

Thorngren, Bertil (2005): Profitable at any speed? In Mobile media. Content and services for wireless communications, edited by J. Groebel, E. M. Noam and V. Feldmann. Mahwah, NJ: Lawrence Erlbaum Associates (forthcoming).

Timmers, Paul (1998): Business models for electronic markets. Electronic Markets 8 (2):3-8.

Townsend, Anthony (2000): Life in the real-time city: mobile telephones and urban metabolism. Journal of Urban Technology 7 (2):85-104.

Townsend, Anthony (2001): The science of location: why the wireless development community needs geography, urban planning, and architecture. Paper presented at CHI 2001 Wireless Workshop, at University of Colorado, Boulder, April 1-2. Available from
http://www.cs.colorado.edu/~palen/chi_workshop/papers/townshend.pdf.

Towse, Ruth (2002): Copyright and creativity in the cultural industries. Paper presented at 5th
World Media Economics Conference, at Turku, Finland. Available from http://www.
tukkk.fi/mediagroup/5WMEC%20papers/towse.pdf.

Trepte, Sabine, Eva Baumann, and Kai Borges (2000): 'Big Brother': Unterschiedliche Nut-
zungsmotive des Fernseh- und Webangebots? Media Perspektiven (12):550-561.

Tschoepe, Sven (2001): Jurisdictional and choice-of-law-apects of mobile commerce and mobile services (part 1). RTkom 53 (4/01):208-216.

Tuomi, Ilkka (2002): Networks of innovation: change and meaning in the age of the Internet.
New York: Oxford University Press.

Tuomi, Ilkka (2004): Virtuelle Gemeinschaften, Raum und Mobilitaet. In E-merging media.
Kommunikation und Medienwirtschaft der Zukunft, edited by A. Zerdick, A. Picot, K.
Schrape, J. C. Burgelman, R. Silverstone, V. Feldmann, D. Heger, K. and C. Wolff. Heidel-
berg: Springer, 233-254.

Turkle, Sherry (1998): Leben im Netz: Identitaet in Zeiten des Internet. Reinbek: Rowohlt.

Ulset, Svein (2002): Mobile virtual network operators: a strategic transaction cost analysis of
preliminary experiences. Telecommunication Policy 26:537-549.

UMTS Forum (2002a): Benefits and drawbacks of introducing a dedicated Top Level Domain
within the UMTS environment UMTS Forum.

UMTS Forum (2002b): Support of third generation services using UMTS in a converged network environment UMTS Forum.

Utterback, J., and W. Abernathy (1975): A dynamic model of process and product innovation.
Omega 3 (6):639-656.

Valletti, Tommaso M. (1999): A model of competition in mobile communications. Information Economics and Policy 11:61-72.

Valletti, Tommaso M. (2002): Is mobile telephony a natural oligopoly? Available from
http://www.ms.ic.ac.uk/tommaso/natural.pdf.

van Eimeren, Birgit, Heinz Gerhard, and Beate Frees (2003): Internetverbreitung in Deutschland: unerwartet hoher Zuwachs. Media Perspektiven (8):338-358.

Varian, Hal R. (2000a): Intermediate microeconomics: a modern approach. 5 ed. New York:
W.W. Norton & Company.

Varian, Hal R. (2000b): Market structure in the network age. In Understanding the digital
economy: data, tools, and research, edited by E. Brynjolfsson and B. Kahin. Cambridge,
MA: MIT Press.

Visiongain (2002): SMS TV. Forecasts 2002-2007. Available from http://www.ewirelessnews.com/
pdfs/SMS-TV.pdf.

Voeth, Markus (2002): Nachfragerbuendelung. zfbf 54 (Maerz 2002):113-127.

Vogel, Andreas (2001): Onlinestrategien der Pressewirtschaft. Media Perspektiven (12):590-
601.

von Hippel, Eric (1986): Lead users: an important source of novel product concepts. Management Science 32 (7):791-805.

von Hippel, Eric (1988): The sources of innovation. New York: Oxford University Press.

von Hippel, Eric (1998): Economics of product development by users: the impact of 'sticky' local information. Management Science 44 (5):629-644.

von Hippel, Eric (2002): Open source software projects as user innovation networks. Available
from   http://www.idei.asso.fr/Commun/Conferences/Internet/OSS2002/Papiers/Von
Hippel.pdf.

von Hippel, Eric, and Ralph Katz (2002): Shifting innovation to users via toolkits. Available
from http://web.mit.edu/evhippel/www/Toolkitsfinal.pdf.

von Hippel, Eric, and Georg von Krogh (2003): Open source software and the private-collec-
tive innovation model: issues for organization science. Organization Science.

268 References

Wathieu, Luc (1997): Habits and anomalies in intertemporal choice. Management Science 43 (11):1552-1563.

Wathieu, Luc, and Michael Zoglio (2001): Empowering consumers. In Working Paper Harvard Business School.

Watzlawick, Paul, Janet Beavin Bavelas, and Don D. Jackson (1967): Pragmatics of human communication. A study of interactional patterns, pathologies, and paradoxes. New York: Norton & Company.

Wee, Thomas Tan Tsu (1999): An exploration of a global teenage lifestyle in Asian societies. Journal of Consumer Marketing 16 (4):365-375.

Weiber, Rolf, and Markus Weber (2001): Das Management von Kundenwerten im Electronic Business: Ansaetze zur Kundenwertsteigerung in der Marketing-Mix-Gestaltung. In Kundenwert: Grundlagen - innovative Konzepte - praktische Umsetzungen, edited by B. Guenter and S. Helm. Wiesbaden, 693-721.

Weilenmann, Alexandra, and Viktoria Larsson (2000): Collaborative use of mobile telephones: a field study of Swedish teenagers. Available from http://www.comlab.hut.fi/opetus/040/weilenmann.pdf.

Weiss, Ralph, and Jo Groebel, (Eds.) (2002): Privatheit im oeffentlichen Raum. Medienhandeln zwischen Individualisierung und Entgrenzung. Opladen: Leske und Budrich.

Wellman, Barry (2002): Designing the Internet for a networked society: little boxes, glocalization, and networked individualism. Communications of the ACM 45 (5):91-96. Available from http://www.chass.utoronto.ca/~wellman/publications/designinginternet/cacm2b-all.PDF.

Wellman, Barry, Jeffrey Boase, and Wenhong Chen (2002): The networked nature of community: online and offline. IT & Society 1 (1):151-165. Available from http://www.stanford.edu/group/siqss/itandsociety/vol01-1/Vol01-1-A10-Wellman-Boase-Chen.pdf.

Wellman, Barry, Anabel Quan-Haase, Jeffrey Boase, and Wenhong Chen (2002): Examining the Internet in everyday life. Available from http://www.chass.utoronto.ca/~wellman/publications/euricom/Examinig-Euricom.PDF.

Wellman, Barry, Janet Salaff, Dimitrina Dimitrova, Laura Garton, Milena Gulia, and Caroline Haythornthwaite (1996): Computer networks as social networks: collaborative work, telework, and virtual community. Annual Review of Sociology 22:213-238.

Werbach, Kevin (1997): Digital tornado: the Internet and telecommunication policy FCC OPP Working Paper No. 29, March 1997. Available from http://www.newamerica.net/Download_Docs/pdfs/Pub_File_1001_1.PDF.

Werbach, Kevin (2000): Location-based computing: wherever you go, there you are Release 1.0, June 28, 2000.

Werbach, Kevin (2002): Open spectrum: the new wireless paradigm New America Foundation. Available from http://www.newamerica.net/Download_Docs/pdfs/Pub_File_1001_1.PDF.

Werbach, Kevin (March 5, 2002): Monster mesh: decentralized wireless broadband The Feature. Available from http://www.thefeature.com/index.jsp?url=article.jsp?pageid=13890.

Werle, Raymund (2001): Standards in the international telecommunications regime (Discussion Paper 157) Hamburgisches Welt-Wirtschafts-Archiv. Available from http://www.hwwa.de/Publikationen/Discussion_Paper/2001/157.pdf.

Wernerfelt, Birger (1984): A resource-based view of strategy. Strategic Management Journal 5:171-180.

Wersig, Gernot (2000): Informations- und Kommunikationstechnologien: eine Einfuehrung in Geschichte, Grundlagen und Zusammenhaenge. Konstanz: UVK Medien.

Wilke, Juergen (1992): Mediennutzung und Zeitgefuehl. In Zeit, Raum, Kommunikation, edited by W. Hoemberg and M. Schmolke. Muenchen: Oelschlaeger, 257-276.

Williams, Martyn (February 25, 2003): Samsung starts testing next 'Matrix' phone Info World. Available from http://www.infoworld.com/article/03/02/25/HNmatrix_1.html?wireless.

Winer, Russell S. (2001): A framework for customer relationship management. California Management Review 43:89-105. Available from http://groups.haas.berkeley.edu/fcsuit/pdf-papers/crm%20paper.pdf.

Wirtz, Bernd W (1999): Stand und Entwicklungsperspektiven der empirischen Beziehungs-marketingforschung. Available from http://notesweb.uni-wh.de/wg/wiwi/wgwiwi.nsf/1084c7f3cb4b7f4ac1256b6f005851c5/1c6e41a93869cdc1c1256c5d004c5d2e/$FILE/jav9904.pdf.

Wirtz, Bernd W (2000): Rekonfigurationsstrategien und multiple Kundenbindung in multimedialen Informations- und Kommunikationsmaerkten. zfbf 52 (Mai 2000):290-306.

Wirtz, Bernd W, and Alexander Mathieu (2001): DBW Stichwort: Mobile Commerce. Die Betriebswirtschaft (5).

Wolf, Michael J. (1999): The entertainment economy: how mega-media forces are transforming our lives. New York: Random House.

Wolf, Michael J., and Geoffrey Sands (2000): Nachrichten vom Laptop. Message (1):10-15.

WTO (1996): Reference Paper for the WTO's Agreement on Basic Telecommunications. Available from http://www.wto.org/english/tratop_e/serv_e/telecom_e/tel23_e.htm.

Wu, Shin-yi, Pei-yu Chen, and G. Anandalingam (2002): Optimal pricing scheme for information services Center for Electronic Markets and Enterprises. Available from http://www.rhsmith.umd.edu/ceme/research/service%20pricing.pdf.

Yen, Benjamin P.-C., and Kenny Y.M. Ng (2001): Electronic catalog for personalized mobile phones and its impact. Paper presented at International Conference on Electronic Commerce (ICEC), at Vienna, October 31-November 4.

Yen, David C., and David C. Chou (2001): Wireless communication: the next wave of Internet technology. Technology in Society 23:217-226.

Yoffie, David B. (1997): Introduction: CHESS and computing in the age of digital convergence. In Competing in the age of digital convergence, edited by D. B. Yoffie. Boston, MA: Harvard Business School Press, 1-35.

Yoon, Sung-Joon, and Joo-Ho Kim (2001): Is the Internet more effective than traditional media? Factors affecting the choice of media. Journal of Advertising Research (November/December 2001):53-60.

Zeglis, John (2001): Make it simple. In The wireless industry, edited by Inside The Minds. Bedford, MA: Aspatore, 11-32.

Zerdick, Axel (1990): Die Zukunft des Telefons - zum Wechselverhaeltnis sozialpsychologischer und oekonomischer Faktoren. In Telefon und Gesellschaft Band 2: Internationaler Vergleich - Sprache und Telefon - Seelsorge und Beratungsdienste - Telefoninterviews, edited by Forschungsgruppe Telekommunikation. Berlin: Volker Spiess, 9-23.

Zerdick, Axel (2002): Book discussion 'Mobile Media', personal communication with V. Feldmann, Berlin, August 31, 2002.

Zerdick, Axel, Arnold Picot, Klaus Schrape, Alexander Artope, Klaus Goldhammer, Ulrich T. Lange, Eckart Vierkant, Esteban Lopez-Escobar, and Roger Silverstone (2000): E-conomics. Strategies for the digital marketplace, European Communication Council Report. Berlin: Springer.

Zerdick, Axel, Arnold Picot, Klaus Schrape, Jean Claude Burgelman, Roger Silverstone, Valerie Feldmann, Dominik Heger, K., and Carolin Wolff, (Eds.) (2004): E-merging media. Kommunikation und Medienwirtschaft der Zukunft, European Communication Council Report. Heidelberg: Springer.

Printing and Binding: Strauss GmbH, Mörlenbach